The Three-Personed God

Batter my heart, Three-Personed God

—John Donne

Affairs are now soul size.
The enterprise
Is exploration into God.

—Christopher Fry:
A Sleep of Prisoners

William J. Hill

The Three-Personed God

THE TRINITY
AS A MYSTERY OF
SALVATION

THE CATHOLIC UNIVERSITY
OF AMERICA PRESS
Washington, D.C.

LIBRARY OF CONGRESS CATALOGING
IN PUBLICATION DATA
Hill, William J., 1924–
    The three-personed God.

    Bibliography: p.
    Includes index.
    1. Trinity.   I. Title.
BT111.2.H54   231'.044   81-18012
ISBN 0-8132-0560-3   AACR2
0-8132-0676-6 (pbk.)

CONTENTS

PREFACE

"Rester fidèle à ce qu'on fut, tout reprendre par le début."[1] This observation of Maurice Merleau-Ponty, to the effect that one must at once remain faithful to what one has been and at the same time take up everything all over again from the beginning, is applicable to the theological enterprise. Among the doctrines and symbols of Christianity perhaps none has been as subject to theological neglect as that of the Trinity. Seemingly, it should occupy a central place in Christian thought because it is at once a doctrine concerning God in his own being and identity and a doctrine concerning God's saving activity in history. Nonetheless, Karl Rahner is undoubtedly correct in his judgment that "Christians are, in their practical life, almost mere 'monotheists'," and were the doctrine to be eliminated as false, "the major part of religious literature could well remain virtually unchanged."[2] At the very least, the prevailing attitude has been one of indifference (apart from a purely formal and verbal confession), dismissing the Trinity as a "mystery," in the sense of a mystification. Recently, however, there have been stirrings in the theological world seeking to remedy this neglect—from Rahner and Heribert Mühlen as Catholic voices, and from Eberhard Jüngel and Jürgen Moltmann on the Protestant side.[3] The present volume is intended as one contribution to that theological discussion beginning anew concerning the triunity of God. Obviously, it represents but one point of view, and no denial of the relativity of that angle of vision is intended here. But it is suggested that the stance adopted remains a viable one for contemporary believers, and so is deserving of a hearing.

One characteristic of the theology at work here is that of making room for the historical dimension on the grounds that present

---

[1] Maurice Merleau-Ponty, *Signes* (Paris: Gallimard, 1960), p. 12.

[2] Karl Rahner, *The Trinity*, transl. by Joseph Donceel (New York: Herder & Herder, 1970), pp. 10–11.

[3] Rahner, op. cit.; Heribert Mühlen, *Der heilige Geist als Person. In der Trinität bei der Inkarnation und im Gnadenbund: Ich, du, wir*, 2nd ed. (Münster: Verlag Aschendorf, 1967); Eberhard Jüngel, *The Doctrine of the Trinity* (Grand Rapids, Michigan: William B. Eerdmans, 1976); Jürgen Moltmann, *The Crucified God*, transl. by R.A. Wilson and John Bowden (New York: Harper and Row, 1974); *The Trinity and the Kingdom*, transl. by Margaret Kohl (New York: Harper and Row, 1981).

understanding is forged out of the past even as it brings to light in
the present aspects of truth that are genuinely new. Theology
cannot rest content with being a mere repetition of the past—not
as long as its wellspring remains divine revelation as God's self-
unveiling *(alētheia)* which continues as an occurrence within consciousness, and thereby always brings to theology the marks of con-
temporaneity. Another way of saying this is to acknowledge that
though the theologian works with accepted texts and the already
formulated doctrines and symbols of a tradition, he does so by way
of entering into a living dialogue with his subject matter itself, which
is ultimately God himself mediating himself to mankind. At the same
time, since this dialogue with the subject matter occurs in history,
it cannot be entered upon apart from the New Testament in which
Christian experience gained a first and normative articulation into
language, nor from the shaping of the tradition by such as Tertullian, Origen, Athanasius and others in the Patristic era, nor apart
from the attempt at scientific systematization in medieval Scholasticism, nor from such sea-changes as were effected during periods
such as the Reformation and the Enlightenment. In short, the past
must be mined, in its achievements and its failures, for such a past
is determinative, to a degree, of the present. But even here—or
especially here—it is obvious that no claim of completeness is being
made, lest an already lengthy volume get out of hand. Most notable
among the omissions is that concerning the dispute between the
Western and Eastern Churches that focuses on the *filioque* question.
That is a topic which demands attention in its own right, but the
long and tortuous history attending the question renders it a distinct
task beyond the scope of this study.

Another characteristic of the theology that gives rise to this volume derives from the conviction that there still remains something
to be said for a view of theology as affording insights into the mystery of God's own being and identity. The doctrine of the Trinity
will thus, at the very least, enable us to know God not as some self-
enclosed Absolute but rather as a self-communicating God of salvation, a God of men who live in history. This can be maintained
and pursued without calling into question (even surreptitiously) the
radical incomprehensibility of God. Indeed, this latter must remain
operative in theological consciousness to prevent any collapse into
ideology that is both irrelevant and alienating. Part of the burden
in maintaining this tension—between an incomprehensible God and
a theology that is emboldened to speak of God as he is in himself—
lies in the unique way that religious language functions. Such lan-

guage is always relational, and signifies by indirection; thus, it is always the language of myth, symbol, or analogy—whether operative in narrative form, or in the structuring of models and paradigms.

Some of the burden, however, resides in the anthropological element that is indigenous to all theological statements. If it be an exaggeration to say that theology *is* anthropology, it is at least true that every strictly theological statement (i.e., every statement about God) is at the same time a statement about the being of man. One consequence of this is that the sole approach to the Trinity is by way of Christology. It cannot be the other way around at the very beginning of theological exploration, for then there is no way of grounding knowledge of the Trinity in human experience. For the same reason, the Christology with which one begins must be an "ascending" Christology rather than a "descending" one. But, useful as that distinction might be for the Christologist, there is always the danger of overstating it precisely because an "ascending" Christology, if it be true to itself, must eventually rejoin a "descending" Christology, from which it is only artificially separated in the first place. For faith in Jesus as the Christ of God is operative in this so-called Christology "from below" all along. This is only to say that, from the very beginning, our intense concern with this man, Jesus of Nazareth, is explained by the fact that we already acknowledge him as the one who has been raised by God and whose earthly claim to proffer salvation to men from God within the parameters of our history has been vindicated by God. This is true even in the early phases of Christology where the emphasis falls more markedly on the search for the grounds of believing than on the content of what is believed, precisely because even this search is carried on in the ambiance of faith. Similarly, man first encounters the Trinity within the economy of salvation, but is spontaneously brought to where he is enabled to speak, however haltingly, of the "immanent" Trinity, of that triunity as it is constitutive of God's very being. Ultimately, then, theology is about God in himself even though that question cannot be separated from the question concerning God's meaning for us.

The contribution intended by this volume, then, is a very modest one: to understand one direction that reflection on the mystery of the Trinity can be seen as taking, a direction that is rooted in Christian tradition even if it is not explicitly developed therein, on the conviction that this is not only a true development but an illuminating and enriching one—and then to reappropriate and further such a development in contemporary perspectives, on the conviction that, when so inculturated, it remains a true and so still viable vision of the mystery. This view offers itself as an alternative to two prevalent views in contemporary theology. The first understands the Trinity as arising out of the creative symbolizing power of the human spirit, as itself a religious symbol that is a vehicle of truth, but a truth that is lost if one seeks to grasp it in any literal sense. The other understands the Trinity economically or modalistically (whether in ancient or modern form) as formally constituting the process of God's mediation of himself to the world. The sole remaining alternative is tritheism, a position that, significantly, has never gained a serious hold on Christian faith and imagination.

What is offered here can only be a very small part of a greater whole. But hopefully it can contribute to the larger discussion by clarifying one understanding of the trinitarian mystery, an understanding that comes eventually to both a dogmatic and a systematic expression, because it is both a confession of faith and a search for meaning on the most demanding critical grounds. As presuppositions to this, dogma cannot be dismissed as merely coercive, nor can system be viewed as ultimately only a seducer of critical thought.

In the end, what is intended is to enhance, not retard, the larger discussion which can be conducted only as unhindered dialogue. Moltmann is right: "Only truth can be the soul of a free community of men and women."[4]

---

[4]Jürgen Moltmann, *The Trinity and the Kingdom,* p. xiii.

ACKNOWLEDGMENTS

Writing a book means accumulating debts of gratitude to many others along the way. I would be remiss if I were not to thank Thomas C. O'Brien for his editorial assistance, Robert F. Conway, O.P., and Frank Hunt for their careful copy editing and proofreading, and Sara Kerr for typing the final draft. Special gratitude is due also to Kathleen Cannon, O.P., for compiling the bibliography from notes and for preparing the indices as well.

Grateful acknowledgment is likewise made to the University of Chicago Press for permission to quote from *Systematic Theology*, Vol. I, by Paul Tillich; Copyright 1951 by The University of Chicago.

W.J.H.

PART ONE

BACKGROUND
Theology Listening to the Past

[1]

RELIGIOUS EXPERIENCE
New Testament Matrix of the Trinity

Christian thought and practice has consistently appropriated divinity in the three symbols of Father, Son, and Holy Spirit. Moreover, such a confession lies at the very origins of Christianity, resonating in the language of the New Testament itself—where the symbols first appear, however, as God, Christ, and Spirit. Whatever development the later *doctrine* of the Trinity represents, there would appear to be little ground for dismissing it as a mere arbitrary development that nowise forms part of the objective deposit of revelation and so is extraneous to faith. Nineteenth-century Liberal Protestantism did just that in allowing that the doctrine was perhaps of value to Christianity but was not crucial to the question of God and every other specifically Christian question.[1] On the other hand, it is not possible to discern in the New Testament texts themselves anything amounting to an explicit revelation of a Trinity immanent in the Godhead. What can be asserted is that the New Testament, as the literary articulation of a people's experience of God at work in their midst, offers solid grounds for recognizing an inherent threefoldness in God's dealings with men. It can be argued that such threefoldness is ingredient in God's activity precisely as self-revelation (Karl Barth), or it is possible to go further and urge that all divine activity betrays this triadic character, but in either case one is clearly engaged in theologizing upon the Scriptural data. What cannot be gainsaid, however, is that the New Testament did inaugurate a way of thinking about God that employed a threefold religious symbolization, and that eventually gave rise in history to the trinitarian doctrine.

---

[1]This, of course, is the view of the Trinity introduced into theology by Friedrich Schleiermacher, one that has been elaborated today by theological writers such as Paul Tillich and Cyril Richardson; see Chapter Four.

3

OLD TESTAMENT AMBIANCE

The notion of God in the Old Testament possesses, in its remote origins, many of the characteristics of the pagan gods of Canaan. But there are marked differences that cannot be dismissed merely as the end-products of an evolutionary process, and these gradually become more and more explicit. Henotheism (worship of one of a group of gods) is eventually transformed into genuine monotheism (one sole God). If God first appears as a personification of the forces of nature, in time he is recognized less as a cosmic God than as a God present and acting in history. By the time of Moses he is a God who has assumed a strong and explicit personal character. In later Judaism, that personal character manifests itself in terms of an all-holy God of righteousness and love, morally immutable towards the people of his Covenant.

Yahweh as Father of the Elect

Eventually such a God came to be represented as Father, though more frequently in equivalent than in literal terms (e.g., *Exodus* 4:22; *Isaiah* 63:16; *Wisdom* 2:16; *Psalms* 2:7, 89:26; *II Kings* 7:8). The designation differs, however, both qualitatively and intensively, from that which the term will assume in the New Testament. Its basis is God's creative act, but even more decisively, his election of and Covenant with Israel. In the Old Testament, God is Father not vis-à-vis a divine Son within his own being but rather towards his chosen people. It is Israel the nation that is God's Son, on the basis of God's own election of it, and for this reason that it is understood as destined to fulfill the role of Messiah (*Daniel; I & II Maccabees; Tobit; Wisdom; Judith;* and *Sirach*). Later on the title of Messiah will be transferred to a representative of the Nation, to a descendant of David (*Isaiah* 9:6) or to a prototype of the people (e.g., the mysteriously preexistent "Son of Man" in *Daniel* 7:13). As Messiah, however, such a one will readily receive designation as God's chosen Son and will make manifest God's exercise of Fatherhood towards his people. At any rate, there is no expectation of a Messiah who is divine, and no ontic connotation to the phrase "Son of God." The emphasis falls rather on Yahweh himself, who is to inaugurate the Messianic Kingdom: "God himself will come and save us" (*Isaiah* 35:4); "Make straight the paths of the Lord, behold the Lord will come in strength" (*Isaiah* 40:3).

Dabar and Ruah Yahweh

The notion that underlies Yahweh's fatherly concern for the people of the Covenant is two-faceted. It involves on the one hand awesome power *(El)* which disposes all things, is itself inaccessible and nowise at man's disposal and, on the other hand, a freely chosen relationship of concern and care. The Father is at once far away and near at hand; the transcendence implied, while primitive, is profound. It would appear to allow for a certain ambivalence: God is at such an ontic remove from all that his *fiat* summons into being that his initiatives appear to be implemented by way of intermediaries, yet paradoxically those agents are themselves divine, and in the final analysis none other than the one God himself acting in the world. The Semitic mind preserves the tension in speaking of the Word *(Dabar)* and the Breath or Spirit *(Ruah)* of Yahweh; Yahweh is the One who saves, but through his Word and his Spirit. Yet in the end such utterance and creative force is God himself acting. The "firstborn before all creatures" *(Sirach* 1:4) and "worker of all things" *(Wisdom* 7:21) is an effluence from God, or the energy stemming from God, that in the final analysis is itself divine. The personification is a literary device, not meant to imply another than Yahweh. The same is true of the Breath of God that "inspires," "guides," "instructs," comes down upon kings and prophets, etc. What is at issue is God's relationality to men and the Old Testament presentation is suggestive of a trinary structure in this relationship.

To discern in this anything suggestive of the Christian Trinity is, of course, to move beyond what can be attained exegetically from the Old Testament texts by themselves. The Old Testament offers no obvious teaching of real and personal distinctions in God. Such, at any rate, is not part of the public revelation made to Israel and, granted the strong and constant emphasis upon monotheism, this is hardly surprising. Only when read in light of the New Testament is it possible to discern the underlying trinary structure in the earlier Testament. It is a matter, then, of an *eisēgēsis* rather than exegesis— but a quite legitimate one as long as there is no distortion of the meanings that the Old Testament materials have in their own proper context. The earlier Scriptures lend themselves to the type of hermeneutical act in which later questions can be brought to bear upon them, and through what the text does say one is enabled to hear what it does not say. Read dogmatically rather than exegetically, that is to say in light of both the New Testament and later doctrinal development, the Jewish Scriptures betray a revelatory climate that lends itself to what is to come.

NEW TESTAMENT SYMBOLS IMPLYING A SECOND IN GOD

Son of God

The Old Testament ambiance of Yahweh regarding the Elect as His Son supplies the context which comes eventually to predominate as the one in which the New Testament writers seek to locate Jesus of Nazareth. He is the "Son of God" (*Mk.* 1:1; *Rom.* 5:10; *Gal.* 4:4; *Col.* 1:13), and represented as claiming such Sonship for himself (*Mt.* 11:27; *Lk.* 10:22). He is "the Christ, the Son of the living God" (*Mt.* 15:13); the Father's "own Son" (*Rom.* 8:3); who calls God "my heavenly Father" (*Mt.* 15:13); and addresses him with the child's sound *"Abba"* (*Mk.* 14:36). Furthermore, this sonship of which the New Testament speaks is distinctive in kind: Jesus is the "Only-Begotten of the Father" (*Jn.* 1:14; 3:16; *I Jn.* 4:9), so that "no one knows the Father except the Son" (*Mt.* 11:27; *Lk.* 10:22). Walter Kasper notes that the exclusive way the phrase "my Father" is employed by Jesus "implies a nontransferable, unique relationship between Jesus and God."[2]

The meaning originally intended is that available from Judaism: he is Son in the sense of being elected by God to function in a messianic role. This is the basis for an initial adoptionist Christology—though not in the later heretical sense of the term, because here it intends to say nothing of Jesus' nature. Paul writes of Jesus "proclaimed the Son of God in all his power through his resurrection from the dead" (*Rom.* 1:4), and the early chapters of *Acts* (2:32–36; 5:31) suggest that the preaching of the primitive community rested on a similar understanding. In this, Paul appears to defer the sonship until the Resurrection, but the term "proclaimed" may mean to convey "manifestation to others" of what Jesus already is by right, and the "in all his power" suggests less a beginning of sonship itself than of its full exercise after the Resurrection vis-à-vis men. *Acts* 2:36 does betray an adoptionist tone, but the titles given here are *Kyrios* and Christ, not Son; moreover, it is improbable that *Kyrios* as yet carries the connotation of divinity it will later acquire.

But this adoptionist Christology rather quickly proves to be an inadequate expression of the disciples' post-Easter experiences. This

---

[2]Walter Kasper, *Jesus the Christ,* transl. V. Green (New York: Paulist Press, 1976), p. 109.

comes to light in recognizing that Jesus' present lordship is at once the vindication and the consummation of his death and indeed of his entire life as the "suffering servant." Thus other texts move his election back to the transfiguration (*Mk.* 9:7), or to the moment of his baptism when the Father claims him as Son (*Mk.* 1:11), or to his birth (the infancy narratives). John Knox has observed that at this point only two alternatives to adoptionist Christology are available: the docetist or the kenotic.[3] The first would deny the genuineness of Christ's humanity and is resisted by the writers of the New Testament; the latter is adopted and finds richest expression in *Philippians* 2:6. But it carries into the New Testament the whole question of preexistence. The use of the *kenōsis* myth, moreover, is later confirmed by recourse to the image of a "descent" from on high. If Jesus has ascended to the right hand of the Father, it is reasonable to suppose that he descended therefrom in the first place (*Jn.* 3:13). This is rooted in the confession, nourished in a Eucharistic context, of a presently exercised Messiahship. Jesus is the Son of God in his exercise of lordship *(Kyrios)* from the "right hand of God" (see *Mk.* 12:35, *Lk.* 20:41–45—citing *Psalm* 110). What the Christian liturgy celebrates is the very presentiality of the risen Jesus to the believing community. This experience of a postearthly existence quite logically at least poses the question of preexistence. This is not to imply that the idea of preexistence originates solely from the disciples' experience of Christ as living after death; the concept is ready at hand not only in Hellenic and Gnostic religions but in the Old Testament itself, suggested by the Primal Man of Daniel's vision and even by the use of *Sophia* in the *Book of Wisdom*. Fred Craddock cites eleven New Testament texts explicitly referring to Christ as preexistent: *Jn.* 1:1; 8:58; 17:5; *I Cor.* 8:6; 10:4; *II Cor.* 8:9; *Phil.* 2:6; *Col.* 1:15; *Heb.* 1:2; 11:26; *Rev.* 22:13.[4]

All-important, however, is what the primitive community means to convey by the preexistence texts. What sort of original reinterpretation of their own, for example, do they give to the *kenōsis* myths that are already available from other sources? There is no question as yet of using preexistence as a metaphysical notion with the conceptual precision it will later acquire; at this point its use remains

---

[3] John Knox, *The Humanity and Divinity of Christ* (Cambridge: At the University Press, 1967), p. 96.

[4] Fred B. Craddock, *The Pre-existence of Christ in the New Testament* (Nashville, Abingdon Press, 1968).

a symbolic one. Yet the symbol is already purified of certain mythic connotations not congenial to Christian purposes—for example, the polytheistic connotations of paganism, the dualistic from Gnosticism, the pantheistic from Stoic forms of Hellenism. The New Testament usage is weighted heavily towards the historical order in which salvation has been encountered: God's "sending" his Son into the world is meant to be a way of calling attention to a dimension of the events of Jesus' historical life and death—that dimension which means that God himself is active in and through those events. The reference, then, is not to some primal time before creation or before Christ's birth, nor to some primordial event in God's inner life. In Eduard Schweizer's words, "The affirmation concerning the sending of the Son, who had lived with God from all eternity, was not intended to make any claims about the time between creation and the birth of Jesus or the time before creation, nor even about his coming from the Father at his birth; it was intended to outline the 'dimension' in which one must perceive what took place on the cross."[5] Reginald Fuller couches a similar conclusion in different terms in speaking of two dimensions in the historical transaction that constitutes Jesus' historical life.[6] The first is a temporal transaction with his disciples; the second is an eternal transaction with his Father, inseparable from the former and logically prior to it.

Nonetheless, this New Testament meaning of preexistence is no contradiction of what later theology will mean in referring to the eternal utterance of the Word, or the eternal generation of the Son, as something immanent in God's being, quite apart from any consideration of creation and salvation. Contrary to what Schweizer says, such a confession by the later Church is not a denial of the genuineness of the humanity assumed by God in time. When the virtualities of metaphysics come to be employed instrumentally in the act of theological explanation, there will be a resistance to all mythological images of primordial time and place prior to creation—quite as the New Testament writers use such preexistence imagery to carry a meaning that is uniquely Christian. The concept of eternity, eventually elaborated within various metaphysical systems, does not refer to some mode of duration prior to the origin

---

[5] Eduard Schweizer, *Jesus*, transl. D. E. Green (Atlanta: John Knox Press, 1971), pp. 84–85.

[6] Reginald H. Fuller, "On Demythologizing the Trinity," *Anglican Theological Review* 43, no. 2 (April 1961), p. 123.

of the cosmos, a sort of primordial time proper to God, but to an ontic situation transcending the conditions of temporality. Eternity is timelessness, not in an abstract and negative sense (as one might speak of a number as timeless), but in the actual and positive sense of transcending time in such wise as to include causally all time and all duration (analogous to the way the infinite includes and explains all instances of finitude). Just as the New Testament writers do not intend this sense, neither do they intend to preclude it.

But even granting this, the New Testament does present the sonship of Jesus as, first and foremost, a *functional* one. He is Son in virtue of his messianic, soteriological work; as one upon whom God has descended—a usage allied to that of Old Testament and pagan religion. Even Cullmann understands all titles implying preexistence as purely functional, i.e., serving only a soteriological purpose and lacking ontological meaning. Still, it is difficult to disallow another level of meaning beneath the surface that later on will be explicated as the ontological sense. The full impact of functional sonship demands ontic roots. Thus Fuller can write:

> The functional affirmations of the earliest Jewish Christology inevitably lead to the ontic affirmations of the gentile mission . . . [so that] . . . it should be clearly recognized that the latest stratum does go on precisely to make ontic affirmation statements which raise ontological questions.[7]

The New Testament use of the symbol "Son," then, would seem to have evolved from employing it in a Semitic sense to designate sonship in a functional sense to using it in a distinct sense based upon the importation of mythological materials which are selected and reinterpreted in such wise as at least to raise questions of sonship in a fully entitative and ontological sense.

This identification of Jesus as the Son of God is, of course, a Church construction born of the faith-experience that follows the events of Easter and Pentecost. The title itself arises in the cultural ambiance of the Hellenic communities outside Palestine and on the occasion of preaching to the Gentiles. Still, there is no reason for doubting that the texts represent the genuine faith-experience of Christians; if Jesus does not call himself Son of God, his believing disciples do. Whether he is indeed the Son of God, and what that title means to convey, are difficult questions. What is not question-

---

[7]Fuller, *The Foundations of New Testament Christology* (New York: Charles Scribner's Sons, 1965), pp. 256–57, note 1.

able is that the writers of the New Testament say that he is, and believe what they say even to the point of martyrdom. And whatever may have been Jesus' grasp of his own identity, it is gratuitous to maintain that the Son-of-God title is an extraneous and arbitrary addition to that understanding. C. F. D. Moule, for one, is able to make a strong case for this title, along with others, deriving from equivalent ways in which Jesus may have referred to himself and to his mission.[8] If so, then the later titles come to light less by way of a heterogeneous evolution than by way of a development that, while not exactly homogeneous, at least bespeaks continuity. Moule's position can claim the support of Oscar Cullmann and Reginald Fuller, but even a position that prefers to emphasize a more radical break between Jesus' self-understanding and the Church's understanding of Jesus—for example, that represented by John Knox's "patterns of development"—need not suggest that the later titles implying divinity are arbitrary inventions, or that they arise otherwise than out of faith in Jesus Christ.[9] It is a different matter entirely to acknowledge that the New Testament does call Jesus the Son of God, and then dismiss this as simply a Gnostic notion on grounds of a lack of evidence that the title originates with Jesus himself, either directly or indirectly.[10] Walter Kasper notes that even if Jesus does not refer to himself as Son of God, he does call God "*my* Father" (*Jn.* 20:17), and may well have used the more neutral title "Son" in the context of his mission from the Father (*Mt.* 11:27; *Lk.* 10:22). If so, it becomes to all practical purposes equivalent to Son of God, and the latter may be no more than a reworking by the inspired writers of a way in which Jesus did refer to himself.[11]

Logos

The *Logos* of John's Prologue is explicitly said to be God: "In the beginning, the Word was with God, and the Word was God" (*Jn.*

---

[8]C.F.D. Moule, *The Origin of Christology* (Cambridge: At the University Press, 1977); significantly Moule's book is entitled *The Origin* not *The Origins*.

[9]See Oscar Cullmann, *The Christology of the New Testament,* transl. S. C. Guthrie and C. A. M. Hall (Philadelphia: Westminster Press, 1959); Fuller, *Foundations;* Knox, *Humanity and Divinity of Christ.*

[10]This at least would appear to be what is done by the authors of *The Myth of God Incarnate,* ed. John Hick (London: SCM, 1977).

[11]Kasper, pp. 109ff.

1:1). This is one of three New Testament texts in which Raymond Brown allows that it is exegetically certain that Jesus is clearly and unequivocally called "God"—the other two being *Hebrews* 1:8: "To his Son he says: God, your throne shall last for ever and ever," and *John* 20:28: "Thomas replied, 'My Lord and my God.' "[12] The *Logos* here is no mere creature, since "through him all things come to be" (*Jn.* 1:3); and something more than moral unanimity is voiced in the claim "I and the Father are one" (*Jn.* 10:30). The connotation of preexistence is patently clear in John's use of *Logos;* moreover, by it he intends to convey the notion of a divine being rather than of an intelligible principle of all reality. In this sense, the language of *Logos* is more mythological than philosophical.

The designation of Jesus in this way comes from Alexandria; there the tradition had grown among Greek-speaking Jews of personifying the wisdom of God referred to in such Old Testament texts as *Baruch* 3:29; *Proverbs* 8:22ff.; *Wisdom* 9:1-2, etc. This is the divine wisdom and divine word through which God makes everything. Philo's doctrine of the *Logos* undoubtedly owes something to this practice, except that he concedes too much to the Hellenistic influence. His understanding of *Logos* is really that of the Stoics, which he transposes, however, into the schema of Middle Platonism.[13] There it becomes both a Platonic Idea (thought immanent to God) and a Jewish version of the world-soul (God's uttered Word). The latter betrays the influence of *Timaeus* 32B, and presents the *Logos* as in the guise of the demiurge who is agent both of creation and of the mind's apprehension of God. At any rate, the mainstream of Alexandrian Judaism resisted such extreme Hellenization.

Paul, drawing rather from Palestinian practice, prefers to present Christ as in the line of David who is chosen as the Son of Yahweh-God himself, but even so describes that Son as "preexistent" in terms that parallel what is said of God's wisdom and God's word by Jews of the Diaspora. But John opts for the quite distinct practice of early Christians in Alexandria, who, under the influence of Hellenic Judaism, spontaneously confess the preexistent *Logos* of God in an early Christian creation hymn. He reproduces this hymn in the first

---

[12] Raymond E. Brown, *Jesus: God and Man* (Milwaukee: Bruce, 1967), pp. 23ff.

[13] See Jean Daniélou, *Gospel Message and Hellenistic Culture,* transl. and ed. J. A. Baker (London: Darton, Longman, and Todd; Philadelphia: Westminster Press, 1973), p. 364.

five verses of his Prologue, but then goes on to identify Jesus as identical with that *Logos*. Once that identity is made, John's meaning becomes clear: in encountering Jesus we encounter the very One who was present as God's word at creation. In John, as in Paul, preexistence conveys a depth dimension to what transpires in the history of Jesus, namely, that in the events of his life it is God who acts. The focus is the historical figure of the Gospels, but to him has been transferred what was said of the *Logos* who was with God before time. This means to say that that very *Logos* has become flesh in Jesus. And thus, even more explicitly than "heavenly Son of God," the *Logos*-title bespeaks a divine being who is with God before time, and indeed is God. Undoubtedly, there were mythological uses of *Logos* too, but the symbol has been already largely demythologized in its use by Alexandrian Jews, as well as in the Christian hymn John borrows as his source.

Son of Man

What would appear on the surface to be Jesus' own preferred designation for himself—Son of Man—suggests at first a creaturely as opposed to a divine identity. Upon reflection, however, even this symbolic title bespeaks existence mysteriously transcending the limits of time and space. This is a title the Evangelists put on the lips of Jesus between seventy or eighty times (dependent upon variant readings), whereas they do not use it as their own name for Jesus— with the one exception of *Acts* 7:56 where it occurs on the lips of Stephen at his stoning. (Fuller sees two other exceptions, *Hebrews* 2:5-7 and *Revelation* 1:13.)[14] The constancy of this designation in the Synoptic Writers suggests that it might be a genuine *logion* of Jesus, testifying to their remembrance that it was the name he appropriated to convey his own sense of personal identity. A resolution of the question, however, demands distinguishing between three different strata of such sayings: those referring to a present Son of Man, a Son of Man about to enter upon suffering, and a Son of Man to come in the future. The last mentioned comes closest to representing what may have been Jesus' own claims. Eduard Schweizer concedes that these usages are from the oldest strata in the tradition and yet denies that they go back to Jesus himself; Cullmann is inclined to trace them back to Jesus and to allow that

---

[14]R. Fuller, *Foundations*, p. 120.

the Church puts them into the context of one who is to suffer on behalf of the people; Fuller finds the evidence for this "inconclusive."[15] Strangely, Paul does not use the name at all, though this might be explained by his preference for Hellenic thought-forms; *Barnasha* is a pronounced Semitism. More important, however, is what the name means. It certainly appeals to the vision in the *Book of Daniel* (7:13) of primordial and/or consummated man, of man taken protologically or eschatologically. This is a Semitism meaning the quintessence of something; there are equivalent expressions elsewhere in the Bible, e.g., "son of wrath," "son of wealth," etc. The sense is not that of Aristotle's abstract essence existing only in the mind, but is markedly existential. It carries the overtone of origins beyond history with God, of timeless existence. Whatever it means in *Daniel,* it is reshaped in the New Testament to mean heavenly man, transcending time. Moreover, the notion is restricted there to Christ; men by contrast exist within the parameters of time and history.[16] This is not a direct implication of divinity, but only of preworldly and postworldly existence. But it tends to strengthen the claim to divinity explicit in the title Son of God. It is more probable, however, that the name is put on the lips of Jesus as singularly apt to express the prophetic and eschatological character of his preaching. The term itself has a flexible range of meanings that fits it for this use. Jesus (in this interpretation) uses it in the third person to refer to an anonymous representative of the Kingdom he preaches. So employed it calls attention to the existential immediacy of that Kingdom ("the Kingdom of God is at hand"), and in mythical terms mediates the call to decision. The figure of "man" in the expression may well symbolize something characteristic of the New Israel to come; Craddock, for example, pictures it as "a symbol for the community of faithful Israel as over against the nations (pictured as beasts)."[17] The symbolism is even richer, however, when located in the tension between suffering and exaltation: the Kingdom of God (of which the Son of Man is the eschatological representative) is mediated through the suffering of Christ, and will be the vindication of mankind in its very humiliation. Thus, even if Jesus speaks in the third person, and uses mythological language, he may intend an

---

[15]E. Schweizer, *Jesus,* pp. 54ff.; O. Cullmann, *Christology,* pp. 137ff.; R. Fuller, *Foundations,* p. 120.
[16]See Craddock, p. 84.
[17]Ibid., p. 45.

oblique reference to himself. In the final analysis, it must be said
that the trinitarian implications of the Son of Man sayings are
remote, if existent at all. The most that can be said is that they
portray Jesus as one who exercises the authority of God in a unique
way; he is presented, if not as God, as one acting divinely. And, if
from other sources he be acknowledged as the divine Son of God,
all that this title makes clear is that it is the Son in God who is the
representative of saved mankind, and not he who is the Father of
the Son.

Kyrios

The name *Kyrios,* unlike Son of Man, does carry unambiguous
connotations of divinity. It is taken from the Septuagint, where it
is a translation of *Adonai,* the latter being a name for God. Paul uses
the title repeatedly in this context, not only of Jesus after the Resurrection but during his earthly life: "The Lord on the night he was
betrayed . . ." (*I Cor.* 11:23). The lordship here owes much to the
concept of kingship, especially that realized in David. But what is
implied is the exercise of a sovereignty that belongs by right to God
alone. This could still mean only that Jesus, who has been made
now both Messiah *(Christos)* and Lord *(Kyrios),* is commissioned by
God to an exercise of the authority proper to God. But, all taken
together, the texts seem to bear a deeper intentionality. For Paul,
Christ is confessed as one who is active contemporaneously, and that
action is precisely *saving* action. "Jesus is the Lord" means "Jesus
saves"; yet salvation is God's act alone. It is not only that God has
acted in Jesus and continues to act; more than this, it is that Jesus
is the agent of that salvation—more than its proclaimer, more than
its instrument. A passage from G. W. H. Lampe illumines this with
considerable clarity:

> "Jesus is Lord" affirms that the present Lord, that is, God as he is
> encountered in what Paul speaks of as our life as sons of God . . . is in
> some mysterious way identical with Jesus the Galilean teacher.[18]

Apart from the restricted but real sense in which the above four
symbols suggest Jesus' eternal origin, there are other ways in which
the New Testament at least suggests a Second in God. One is the

---

[18]G. W. H. Lampe, *God and Spirit,* The Bampton Lectures, 1976 (Oxford:
Clarendon Press, 1977), p. 2.

indirect argument for Christ's divinity that permeates the New Testament as a whole. There is the latent claim to divinity in his conduct: he forgives sins in his own name; begins his teaching not like the prophets of old with "Yahweh says" but with "Amen, Amen, I say unto you"; violates the Sabbath; eats with sinners; refuses to sanction divorce; etc.—in short, he dares to act in God's stead.[19] ≈ *Prophets*

Paul's reservation of *ho Theos* (*the* God, with the definite article) intends not to deny divinity to Christ, who was "in the form of God" (*Phil.* 2:6), and of whom it is said "all things were created through him" (*Col.* 1:13), but to keep in focus the distinctness between Father and Son. Besides, in *Romans* 9:5 Paul may very well be applying *Theos* without the definite article to Christ; something that may be true of *II Peter* 1:1 as well. Stephen, knowing that God alone forgives sin, prays in this name, "Lord, lay not this sin to their charge" (*Acts* 7:59).

This ascription to Christ of the prerogatives of divinity is not such as to call into question the genuineness of his humanity, in spite of a Jewish-inspired "angel-Christology" in some quarters, and the "*Logos*-Christology" hinted at in *Colossians* that is later to predominate. He is never thought of as God in exactly the same sense in which Yahweh is said to be God, who is alone *ho Theos* (*the* God). But the implications of this are quickly drawn: if Jesus is Son of *the* God, then God comes to new identity as Father. The name Father—as a correlate of Son—undergoes a metamorphosis, designating now not the benign relationship of the Godhead to all creatures but a unique relationship of God to Jesus. He is the Only Begotten Son, and other men are sons in a new way but only in virtue of discipleship to Jesus. John commonly calls God "Father" in this sense—all told at least fifteen times—whereas he does not ordinarily refer to God as the Father of men; one exception being *Jn.* 20:17, "I am ascending to my Father and your Father," but even here he does not say to "our" Father. In the Lord's Prayer, Jesus does say "*Our* Father . . ." but he is saying to his disciples "this is how *you* should pray"; he does not imply that God is Father to himself and other men in exactly the same way. Paul uses "Father" of God some forty times, and tends to interchange the two names "God" and "Father."

---

[19]The import of this argument is developed in James M. Robinson, *A New Quest of the Historical Jesus* (London: SCM, 1959), pp. 14–15, following up on suggestions of Ernst Fuchs.

Some Subordinationist Texts

One mark of the refusal to rationalize the humanity away are the so-called subordinationist texts. Jesus himself says, ". . . the Father is greater than I" (*Jn.* 14:28). He refuses to claim knowledge proper to God: "But as for that day or hour, nobody knows it, neither the angels of heaven, nor the Son; no one but the Father" (*Mk.* 13:32); or a goodness equal to God's: "Why do you call me good, God alone is good" (*Mk.* 10:18). The difficulties such texts present can be obviated if it is allowed that Jesus is speaking here of his endowments *as man*. Reginald Fuller makes a case of "Son" (in *Mk.* 13:32) as shorthand for "Son of Man."[20] This ties in, at any rate, with the tendency of Mark's Christology to throw emphasis upon the mission of Jesus insofar as it is accomplished in the flesh. Obviously it does not enter Mark's purview to think in terms of anything approaching the much later categories of Chalcedon. Still and all, the *Logos* (and not just the humanity) is "subordinate" to the Father *in the economy.*

Throughout the New Testament, Christological concerns are subordinate to soteriological ones; even more remote is anything that might be considered of properly trinitarian interest. Not to be discounted either is the influence of *Psalm* 118; against such a background Mark can state simply that the Father knows the Day of Judgment and the Son does not. But it would be a gratuitous leap to conclude that Mark is implicitly denying that Jesus' Sonship gives him divine status and ontic equality with the Father. He is simply choosing a perspective different from that of Matthew (11:27) and Luke (10:22), who for apologetic purposes choose a context that will enable them to speak of Jesus' knowledge as omniscience.

The subordinationist texts in St. Paul are more revealing, e.g., *I Cor.* 15: 28: "And when everything is subjected to him then the Son himself will be subject in his turn to the One who subjected all things to him, so that God may be all in all"; and *Phil.* 2:6: "His state was divine, yet he did not cling to his equality with God but emptied himself to assume the condition of a slave." Beyond question, both these passages subordinate the Son to the Father. While that can readily be interpreted as a subordination within the economy, it is nonetheless the Son or the preexistent *Logos* who is subordinate to his Father—even if he is such precisely as incarnate, as "in the form of a slave" and as bringing mankind under the final reign of God.

---

[20] R. Fuller, *Foundations*, pp. 114, 165.

But something more is hinted at, if not explicitly said—namely, that these roles within the economy are themselves grounded in an ontic situation that prevails within God's own inner being. The implication remains that the functional structure is grounded in a structure indigenous to divinity itself, one that can only be surmised, however paradoxically, as a pure order without subordination. Paul is striving to say that function is grounded in being, that the distinction between Father and Son that appears in the economy mirrors a real distinction in God quite apart from his saving activity. God's reve- lation is a self-communication; he reveals himself in a triune way because he is himself a Trinity. In this sense, at least, the economic Trinity is the immanent Trinity. The very ineffability of this, as well as the limits of finite language, force him to have recourse to terminology that in ordinary usage conveys inferiority. It led the Greek Fathers to describe the relationships between the persons with the Greek term for cause, with the implication that the Son and Spirit were effects and so creatures; it is an inadequacy inherent in Platonic language of participation. But the overall context of Paul's writings purges this implication from his thought. He does not allow the "subordination" of Son to Father to be eroded into that of the otherness of creature from God. He conveys, in effect, that the Son is God as is the Father; the two are on the same level—yet the Son is always from the Father. More philosophical precisions, involving "origin" and "relation," are outside Paul's religious motivation. The sort of subordination Paul has in mind is not, paradoxically, inimical to equality; it constitutes in fact the mystery. Only much later will it be conceptualized as a pure order that precludes all subordination, whether of time or being.

Paul seeks, as do the Evangelists, an understanding of salvation. The God of Absolute Mystery, inaccessible to man, saves us only in virtue of his own sovereign initiatives, that is to say, in virtue of uttering his Word, which Word is not God *tout court,* but the Son of God. Subordinationism is to have a long and tortuous history in the Church Catholic, largely in tension against a Modalism that risks collapsing Christianity into Unitarianism. The New Testament knows nothing of such a dichotomy, and so does not lend itself to either solution.

NEW TESTAMENT SYMBOLS IMPLYING A THIRD IN GOD

In the Synoptics, Jesus proclaims a coming Kingdom of the universal Fatherhood of God, one wherein God is already the Father, in a unique and exclusive sense, of Jesus who announces and makes imminent that Kingdom. Thus, he promises some extension to men of God's fatherly love and concern, whereby they too become "sons of God." John's Gospel prefers to reserve the designation "Son" *(huios)* for Christ, and to use the term "children" *(tekna)* for other men who are "begotten of God" *(Jn.* 1:12–13).[21] Paul uses the phrase *huios thesia (Gal.* 4:5), which bears the technical sense of legal adoption. But there is a strong note of futurity; what Christ says is, to a large extent, offer and promise. The sonship is one that will be imparted to the Elect in a definitive age of salvation to come. Thus the phrase "sons of God" nearly always bears an eschatological force. Still, the reference is not to a kingdom that has not yet begun and is not presently real, nor one whose consummation will mark radical discontinuity with present life before God. John's "rebirth" and Paul's "new creation" and "adoption" have already occurred in present history, though consummation awaits us. The point, however, is God's continuing realization in men of what is already accomplished in Christ.

Pneuma

This constitution of men as "sons of God" is, of course, properly the work of God, but the New Testament puts the character of this work into sharp relief when it designates God as so acting by the name "Spirit." What was *Ruah Yahweh* in the Old Testament now appears as *Pneuma,* the latter term occurring three hundred and seventy-five times in the New Testament, with a variety of meanings. The original meaning of "breath" or "wind" has largely disappeared (a notable exception being the Descent at Pentecost), but the neuter grammatical form tends to convey the notion of an intangible force, frequently impersonal in kind. Still, that force is a life-principle that transforms those upon whom it falls into "sons of God," so that it is itself the "spirit of sons" and makes us cry out "Abba, Father" *(Rom.* 8:14–17, *Gal.* 4:6). This leads Paul in the very next verse of *Romans* to personify it: "The Spirit himself and our spirit bear united witness that we are children of God." At this point, Paul clearly teaches the Spirit to be nothing less than God, and God acting as person. Once again in the forefront is the soteriological,

---

[21]See Cyril C. Richardson, *The Doctrine of the Trinity* (Nashville: Abingdon Press, 1958), p. 41.

the functional interest; what is conveyed is a saving dynamism whose ⚹
source is nothing less than God, yet God presenting himself differently from the way in which he did relate to mankind during Jesus'
earthly existence, and even somewhat differently from the way he
now relates through the glorified humanity of the *Kyrios*. The New
Testament rarely speaks of the Spirit other than in terms of the
saving economy wherein his identity is contrasted to that of the
historical Christ. This is in spite of not always clearly distinguishing
the *Logos* from the *Pneuma,* and (in Paul at least) the Risen Christ
from the *Pneuma*. The Spirit continues what Christ has begun, but
in a different mode—invisibly rather than visibly, by way of inwardness rather than of accessibility in symbolic reality (bodiliness).

Moreover, Christ himself in his own earthly life is what he is
through a full and lasting possession of this self-same Spirit "without
measure" (*Jn.* 3:34). The Spirit descends on him like a dove at his
Baptism (*Mt.* 1:10, *Lk.* 3:22); leads him into the wilderness (*Mt.* 4:1,
Lk. 4:1) and sustains him during the temptations there; and leads
him back to Galilee (*Lk.* 4:14). The term here appears to designate
an agency that comes into the depths of human consciousness from
without, that is itself divine, and that thus bespeaks divine presence.
St. Paul views it as coming to full realization in Christ at the Resurrection, with the clear implication that the spirit (neuter) we have
received is that of the Risen Christ (*Rom.* 8:9). Seemingly, he means
that the power that lies at the root of Jesus' bodily transformation
touches us and orients us towards the same transformation without
exhibiting as yet the bodily manifestations. The Spirit dwells in us
by way of reproducing in believers those attitudes and dispositions
which characterize Christ now "at the right hand of the Father."

But Paul does not regard the Glorified Christ and the Holy Spirit
as simply interchangeable. At the very least, the humanity which
Christ possesses and the Spirit lacks prevents this. This gives rise to
the far more difficult question of whether Paul offers grounds for
a real distinction within God between the *Pneuma* and the Son as
preexistent and nonincarnate. Sometimes the Spirit appears as simply the saving power of God at work within men; at other times he
assumes an identity in contrast to the Father (cf. *Rom.* 8:26ff. where
God is said to understand what the Spirit expresses within us). The
basis for this appears to be the distinct mediating role which the
character of the Spirit enables him to assume. But then in what
sense is this Spirit other than the *Kyrios*—i.e., apart from differing
roles in the economy where the functional distinction is quite clear?
Cyril Richardson observes that Paul's "in Christ" is synonymous with

his "in the Spirit" and suggests that this may explain such characteristic Pauline teachings as that of the indwelling Christ and the exalted Christ interceding for us quite as does the Spirit (*Rom.* 8:34).[22] The Christians at Ephesus, asked if they have received the Spirit, confess that they have never heard of the Spirit (*Acts* 19:2, reflecting Pauline theology); this suggests an absence of any early teaching on the Spirit as other than the power of the Risen Christ. Paul at least allows us to think of the Spirit as the divine element in Christ, brought to its fullest exercise in the Resurrection, and now operative somewhat differently in and through the disciples. The preexistent *Kyrios* and the *Pneuma* are God acting in a mediatory way; they are differentiated by Paul from the Father (*ho Theos*) who is the Jewish God of utter transcendence, but it is less certain that Paul distinguishes them from each other in more than a functional way within the economy. The ontological consideration is far from Paul's intent, but it begins to urge itself as a question in the Pauline writings. What Paul's thought refuses is any facile rationalizing of a mystery whose elements he prefers to hold in dialectical tension: God saves us through sending his Son *and* his Spirit.

In St. John the contrast is somewhat more sharply drawn between the Spirit and the man Jesus: the Spirit takes the place of the risen and now absent Christ to whom he bears witness (*Jn.* 15:26); it is Christ who sends the Spirit (ibid.), and precisely in virtue of his establishment in glory: "As yet the Spirit was not given, *because* Christ was not yet glorified" (*Jn.* 7:39). There is no basis here for thinking of Christ as a unitary "Spirit-Man," because John seeks out categories for distinguishing the Spirit from the eternal Son. The latter is *Logos* and never *Pneuma.*

Paraclete

More significant is John's eventual substitution of the name Paraclete for *Pneuma.* The substitution is made in five passages from John's Gospel, all during the discourse in the upper room (14:16; 14:26; 15:26; 16:7; and with less certainty, 16:13), and more strongly suggests the distinct personhood of the Spirit (especially 14:16; 15:26; and 16:7). For one thing, Paraclete is a masculine name and so more suggestive of personhood than the neuter term *Pneuma.* (The equivalent for *Pneuma* in some Syriac versions of the

---

[22]Richardson, p. 51.

Gospel is feminine, as is the Hebrew *Ruah;* also the Greek version of John's Gospel refers to the *Pneuma* by way of a masculine pronoun.) Also, in *Revelation* (2:7, 3:6, 14:13) the Spirit addresses the community as a person. This is something more than personifying divine action that would otherwise be anonymous, for John identifies in a specific way the one who acts on the basis of the distinctive character of his action: He is *Paraklētos,* one who is summoned to our side, who pleads for us. He is contrasted with what is symbolized rather as uttered Word or as Truth, and with one of John's recurrent motifs, Light (*Jn.* 8:12, 9:5, 12:35). The Paraclete is not himself Truth but one who witnesses to the truth. He has no doctrine of his own: "He will not be speaking as from himself but will say only what he has learnt" (*Jn.* 17:13).

In identifying the Holy Spirit as Paraclete, John stretches the latter symbol to the point that it begins to approximate what is conveyed by the use of proper names. That this is so gains confirmation from the precise function his Gospel assigns to the Paraclete. He comes as "the spirit of truth . . . who . . . will be my witness" (15:26) and who "will accuse the world about sin . . . and about judgment" (16:8). This judgment is one of condemnation of the world that refuses the light, that refuses to believe. The Paraclete, then, is not only advocate for the disciples but adversary against the world. But in the literature of late Judaism (e.g., the Qumran *Testament of Judah*) this role is assigned to an angel expressly called the "spirit of truth" whose mission is "to testify and accuse." George Montague makes the point that this angelology motif lies behind John's use of Paraclete.[23] The monotheism inherited from Judaism explains a disinclination on his part (shared by the other New Testament authors) to refer to the Spirit in explicitly personal terms. But John has no hesitancy in obliquely suggesting the latter's personhood in transferring an angelic function to the Holy Spirit. Moreover, Montague believes the author of the Fourth Gospel is aware of an Old Testament precedent for what he is doing. This is *Isaiah* 63:11, where the Lord is said to send his "holy spirit" in the midst of the people and where "holy spirit" is really Isaiah's reworking of the angel figure in chapter 33 of *Exodus.* Yet the texts of John's Gospel certainly do not mean to say that the Paraclete is in truth an angel; the angelology motif is simply an effective Semitic literary device. But

---

[23]George T. Montague, *The Holy Spirit: Growth of a Biblical Tradition* (New York, Paramus, N.J., Toronto: Paulist Press, 1976), pp. 357–59.

the Old Testament also supplies warrant for what John does intend
because the angel figure in *Exodus* is shown to be in reality Yahweh
himself (the Lord first promises an angel but then accedes to Moses'
insistence that the Lord himself, "face to face," accompany them).
Accordingly, Montague can write:

> ... John not only knew of the Is 63 tradition and its Christian inter-
> pretation (witnessed by Heb 13:20) but ... in identifying the Paraclete
> as the Holy Spirit he did with the militant angelology of late Judaism
> exactly what the author of Is 63 did with the exodus angel tradition. ...
> The term *paraclete* emphasizes the personhood and the militant activity
> of the Holy Spirit inadequately conveyed by previous images. (Pp.
> 358–59)

From this it can be concluded that the Paraclete is taking on the
characteristics of what is traditionally conveyed by "person," and
explaining thereby the presence of the Father and Son as also a
personal one. What is not clear, once again, is whether and how the
Spirit might differ personally from the other two who are said to
be God.

At the very least, however, John's Gospel does afford some
grounds for the making of subsequent theological distinctions—
granting that such distinctions can only be artificially imposed on
John's own texts. Even if the actual terms of the Gospel—*Pneuma*
and Paraclete—retain a meaning that is symbolic, and so function
as symbols rather than as proper names, as Edmund Dobbin has
persuasively argued,[24] they nonetheless remain *symbols given to
thought*. Thus, even in John's own context, his symbols are laden
with meanings on which (in Ricoeur's phrase) they invite thought.
This gains added clarity in light of Ricoeur's contention that thought
is not presuppositionless but rather begins from within the midst of
speech.[25] One of the more significant of these reflections distinguishes the Spirit as the agent or motivating principle of belief from
the Word as the content or object (personal) of belief. If Christ too
can be called Paraclete (*Jn.* 16:7), since he likewise is solicitous for
us, John makes clear that by Holy Spirit he means "another Para-

[24]Edmund J. Dobbin, "Towards a Theology of the Holy Spirit," *Heythrop
Journal* 17, nos. 1 and 2 (January and April 1976), Part I, pp. 5–19; Part
II, pp. 129–49.
[25]Paul Ricoeur, "The Hermeneutics of Symbols and Philosophical Reflection," transl. D. Savage, *International Philosophical Quarterly* 2, no. 2 (May
1962), pp. 191–218.

clete" (*Jn.* 14:16, *I Jn.* 2:1). In John, the Spirit, with all the prerogatives of divinity, has gained a mysterious autonomy vis-à-vis the Father and the Son. It is he who instructs the disciples (14:26); bears witness to Jesus (15:26); represents Christ to the disciples (7:39); convinces the world of sin (16:8); and in general is active in the interim period of the Church (14:16).

A COVERT SYMBOL FOR A THIRD IN GOD: *SHEKINAH YAHWEH*

If St. John comes closest to a definitive affirmation of the Spirit's distinct personhood, other New Testament authors are open to a similar interpretation in a less formally exegetical way. Forming the backdrop to the whole biblical revelation is a pronounced sense of God, which to the Semitic mind means an invisible God dwelling with his people in some domain of visibility. This complements the activity of God expressed by *Dabar* and *Ruah*. In the *Targumim* this was thematized in the image of the *Shekinah Yahweh*, the "dwelling place" of God in some perceptible manner. The expression itself does not occur literally in the Bible, but what it means is conveyed there by equivalent phrases expressing God's presence and activity under various guises. The Old Testament is replete with such figures: the pillar of fire leading the Israelites in the desert, the cloud at the Red Sea and at Sinai, the Ark of the Covenant, the angelic theophanies, etc. The *Shekinah* concept is applicable whenever visible, earthly realities are involved, behind which or in which God comes to appearance, so that he can be said to dwell therein.

The New Testament confession of Jesus as of divine status meant a deepened understanding of this. The humanity was not simply a creaturely mediation of God, as were the earthly realities appropriated by God in the Old Testament; rather God had *become* man. "The Word became flesh and dwelt among us" (*Jn.* 1:14) did not mean that God was appearing in the guise of a man, but that in his very humanity Jesus was the Son of God. The body of Jesus, then, is the new *Shekinah Yahweh*, the locus of God's dwelling with his people. But the death of Christ marks his disappearance beyond the horizon of historical and visible existence with men. It is not to be wondered at that Christians gradually came to an awareness of a new mode of God's being with those who continued to believe in Christ. This was experienced as an abiding presence, not now in the mode of the natural visibility of a man, but in the mode of an interior animating principle of the community of love—the Spirit in us as the Spirit of Jesus, the Advocate who "unless I go will not come to you" (*Jn.* 16:7). The disciples of Jesus, the newly formed community of believers, now become the visible dwelling place of God. The Church becomes the New Israel; the body which is the Church becomes the surrogate, as it were, for the natural body of Christ. This invisible dwelling gains a surrogate visibility in the symbols and rites of the community of belief. Here are the faint beginnings of prayerful thinking about the Holy Spirit as other than the Father, other than the absent Word Incarnate. In the liturgy, the Spirit begins to assume a distinct identity; he is the One sent by the Father through the risen Christ to form Christ in us, making us to be adoptive sons of the same Father. The community of believers is the new dwelling place of God, but God present now preeminently as the Spirit who inaugurates and sustains what is gradually coming to be seen (with the delay of the Parousia) as Christian history, i.e., the creative advance into a future that is not yet closed. Such history, while not arbitrary because it retains as its horizon God's definitive act in the dying and rising of Christ, begins to appear as a project whose consummation lies in the future.

Josephine Massyngberde Ford has indicated how this theme is worked out differently in the Gospel of Luke and in the Letters of Paul, especially *First Corinthians*.[26] Her endeavor moves beyond mere textual criticism and attempts to discern an underlying structural theme at work in both of these New Testament writers. In both instances, a contrast is drawn between the body of Jesus and the "body" of believers—as each can be considered the *Shekinah Yahweh*. The difference is that in the first case God dwells on earth as *Logos*-Son, in the second as *Pneuma*-Paraclete. Luke works from the implicit theme of the Mary-Church parallel: the Church is viewed as a type of Mary, the Mother of Jesus, who is the "new daughter of Sion," i.e., the new representative of God's chosen people after they have turned to sin. As God was "in the midst of Israel" so does he become present in the womb of Mary. Schillebeeckx has drawn attention to the long-recognized affinity here between Luke and the prophet Zephaniah:[27]

---

[26]Josephine Massyngberde Ford, "Holy Spirit in the New Testament," *Commonweal*, November 8, 1968, pp. 173–79.

[27]Edward Schillebeeckx, *Mary, Mother of the Redemption*, transl. by N. D. Smith (New York: Sheed and Ward, 1964), p. 8.

Zephaniah (3:14ff.)	*Luke* (1:28ff.)
"Shout for joy, daughter of Zion, Israel, shout aloud! Rejoice, exult with all your heart, daughter of Jerusalem! . . . Yahweh, the king of Israel is in your midst."	"Rejoice so highly favored! The Lord is with you . . . . Mary, do not be afraid; you have won God's favor. Listen! You are to conceive and bear a son . . ."

And as God was in the world in the womb of Mary so now is he in the bosom of the Church. The parallelism is that of the conception of Christ at the visitation of the archangel Gabriel to the conception of the Church at Pentecost (cf. *Luke* 24:49). Just as God dwells in the world in the womb of Mary at the conception, so does he come differently to dwell in the "womb" of believers at the conception of the Church (Pentecost). As the *Logos* is conceived in Mary's womb, the Spirit is "conceived" at the heart of the assembly that Mary prefigures. If, in Luke, the Spirit is the spirit of Jesus, not yet differentiated from the risen Christ, this marks the beginning of a development to come.

Paul prefers to feature the messianic mission of Christ in contrast with the mission entrusted to the Church. At his baptism, there comes to the forefront of Jesus' consciousness an awareness of the messianic mission to which he is summoned by his Father, a mission for which he is fitted by his receiving of the Spirit, in the tradition of the prophets of old upon whom the *Ruah Yahweh* descended. At Pentecost (which can be metaphorically seen as the Church's baptism), the same Spirit descends now upon the Apostles and disciples entrusting them with the continuation of Christ's mission in the world. They are charged with a ministry that is an extension of Jesus' own, and have poured out upon them the Gifts of the Spirit that will enable them to enter upon that ministry (cf. *I Cor.* 12:4; *Acts* 4:13, for the Gifts of the Spirit; *Gal.* 5:22, on the Fruits of the Spirit). For Paul too, the Spirit is at times either the impersonal empowering of God, or the presence in a spiritual mode of the risen *Kyrios* at work within believers. But the attempt to live out the mission of Jesus by preaching and witnessing in historically changing circumstances points gradually to the Spirit's own distinctive personhood. The new life experienced through faith in the risen Lord brings an awareness of Christ as the sender from his Father of "another Counselor."

But what is understood in the development of this theme in both Luke and Paul is a presence of nothing less than the invisible God himself who comes to dwell within the visible body of believers, thereby achieving visibility in the symbols of faith. Yet this is sub-

sequent to, dependent upon, and different in mode from the way
God is understood as present in the womb of Mary and in the
Galilean ministry of Christ. It is this that brings to the consciousness
of the early community the name and symbol of "Spirit." Only with
the passage of time, as Christians experience the activity of the
Spirit—who teaches, counsels, accuses, calls to mind the teaching of
Christ, and in *Revelation* (2:7, 3:6, 14:13) addresses the community
as a person—do they come gradually to grasp the distinct personhood of the Spirit over against that of the Father and *Logos*-Son-
Kyrios. The distinct mode of presence is not arbitrary but is radicated
in a distinctiveness within God himself that is grasped religiously in
terms of what answers to common and universal experience of "personhood." A sense of the absolute oneness of God precludes any
suggestion in this of three consciousnesses; that is a modern problem, legitimate in itself but not one that confronts primitive Christian faith-experience. As this experience of God at work within them
unfolds and to some degree at least is reflected upon, the distinct
"personal" or "hypostatic" (both terms are of later provenance) character of the *Pneuma* comes to be recognized. Thus, what is called
the "Spirit of the Risen *Kyrios*" (in Paul) is later called "Another
Paraclete" (in John).

RETROSPECT: AN EMERGING TRINITARIANISM IN
FUNCTION OF DEVELOPING CHRISTOLOGIES

In retrospect, Father, Son, and Spirit are not so much proper
names in the New Testament, with immediate connotations of personhood, as they are symbols of God arising spontaneously out of
religious experience that in its tripartite character is indigenously
Christian. God is grasped by those who "follow after Jesus" as utterly
transcendent (but lovingly and trustingly so in the mode of a caring
father), as mediated and available to us in the reality of a human
life (i.e., as saving us through the humanity of Jesus), and as immanent in the world (i.e., as a force working invisibly in the depths of
human consciousnesses forming the believing community). The
focus is entirely on Jesus of Nazareth, whose own unique experience
of God as his Father (his *Abba* experience) issues in the confession
of Jesus as the Son of God. The New Testament itself does not
make the explicit transfer from "Son of God" to "God the Son." But
it does provide the matrix for the later Church's doing so—in the
sense that an implicit trinitarianism is gradually coming to light in
the New Testament itself in function of some of its developing
Christologies. Even today it is Christology that provides the way to

a confession of the Trinity, and not the other way around. Thus the New Testament itself is far from any *doctrine* of the Trinity or of a Triune God who is three co-equal Persons of One Nature. There is no question in the New Testament of later contrasting categories of *physis, ousia, natura, essentia,* or *substantia,* on one hand—and *prosōpa, hypostaseis, subsistentiae,* or *personae,* on the other. Nonetheless the tripartite formulas do emerge in the New Testament as a whole, witnessing to an acceptance early on in the Church. These are echoed in the *Didachē* (vii:1–4) and in Justin Martyr's *Apology* (i:61). Matthew—whose emphasis upon the presence of Jesus through his word and disciples leads him to neglect the role of the Spirit—offers the one explicit text: "Go, therefore, make disciples of all the nations; baptize them in the name of the Father and of the Son and of the Holy Spirit" (28:19). This text, however, does not occur in the other Gospels, and Peter in *Acts* mentions Baptism only "in the name of Jesus Christ" (2:38), though even here one receives as a consequence "the gift of the Holy Spirit." But even if the text is not a genuine saying of Jesus, it is commonly accepted as an authentic part of Matthew's *Gospel.* Still, it says nothing of the equality of the three, nor of the nature of their distinction. But the more general indexes are perhaps stronger; for example, the very literary structure, as well as the content, of *Romans* and *Galatians,* and somewhat less clearly *First Corinthians,* is markedly trinitarian.[28]

Without addressing itself explicitly to the metaphysical question—involving categories alien to the Semitic religious mind that could only be anachronistic in the New Testament—the ontic meaning is nonetheless there, unsaid and unthematized. By this is meant that the symbols *Logos*-Son and *Pneuma*-Paraclete, even in their proper context within the New Testament, constitute a matrix from which can be brought forth the meaning of essential divinity and personality. The primary concern is soteriological, only secondarily Christological, and even more remotely trinitarian. To the extent a trinitarian dimension appears at all, it does so in function of the other two concerns. Thus when Jesus is understood to be Son, God then comes to be called "Father" in a new sense; and when Jesus disappears from earthly view, the continued inward working of God leads

---

[28] A. W. Wainwright, *The Trinity in the New Testament* (London: S.P.C.K., 1926), pp. 257ff; Wainwright's thought is reproduced by R. G. Crawford, "Is the Doctrine of the Trinity Scriptural?" *Scottish Journal of Theology* 20 (1967), p. 290.

to recognition of the Spirit. But everything points to an awareness, however underdeveloped, of ultimate foundations for this threeness in the depths of divine being. The least that can be said then is that the New Testament provides the data or the raw materials from which the doctrine of the Trinity was developed with some continuity. Oscar Cullmann offers a guarded version of this thesis in allowing that the trinitarian forms of the New Testament are a later evolutionary development, from liturgical sources, of Christological confessions that are originally binitarian.[29] But this appears minimal and arbitrarily restrictive. A developing understanding of salvation in Christ is taking place within the New Testament itself, and this has trinitarian overtones. St. Paul in a very suggestive way and St. John, less richly but more clearly, come gradually to articulate the *Kerygma* in terms closer to what might be termed an "elemental trinitarianism." It is elemental in supposing that trinitarian forms are indigenous to the New Testament, present from the very beginning alongside the Christological ones—though in an entirely implicit way. It represents an alternative to the position of Cullmann, and finds endorsement in the work of J. N. D. Kelly.[30] The precise question of equality among the Persons does not arise, and indeed distinctness of identity among the Three is not pursued apart from their roles in the economy. But still triadic thinking continues to prevail, and there is no collapsing of trinitarian language into unitarian or binitarian speech. One reason for the reluctance to trace the distinct identities back into the Godhead is an awareness of the impropriety of thinking of plurality in God in numerical terms—the culture at this time was as yet without linguistic categories with which to express transcendental plurality.

God remains Incomprehensible Mystery, but there is something new that takes the New Testament writers beyond the Old Testament notion of Yahweh-God. The threeness which characterizes God as he acts in the saving of man is rooted within divinity itself. Because God's loving initiatives towards men are both self-revealing and self-communicating, faith, in however obscure a way, attains to the inner reality of God as he is himself—in confessing a divine Father who saves through his Son and in the Spirit.

---

[29]Cullmann, *Christology*, p. 1; see also his *The Earliest Christian Confessions*, transl. J.K.S. Reid (London: Lutterworth Press, 1949).

[30]J.N.D. Kelly, *Early Christian Creeds* (London: Longmans, Green and Co., 1950), pp. 23, 94.

[2]
HELLENIZATION
The Trinity in the Greek Fathers

On balance, the New Testament offers a primitive kerygma in the Synoptics and a theology developed therefrom in John and Paul. The kerygma is soteriological, with foundations for a Christology; to the extent that the trinitarian dimension appears at all, it does so in function of the latent Christology, and so as a third level of understanding. The preexistent *Kyrios* of Paul and the *Logos* of John represent an explicit Christology (the soteriological concern is now markedly Christological, i.e., salvation is seen not in moral terms but within a religion of redemption); but the Christology introduces only the specifically trinitarian *question*. Early Christian confessions were triadic—but they were confessions of God, Christ, and the Spirit rather than Father, Son, and Spirit. Yet, the later trinitarian question does derive legitimately from understanding Jesus as *Kyrios* and *Logos*. Moreover, it is a question rooted in worship and confession, and so cannot be dismissed as the mere search for an explanatory construction. There is no *doctrine* of the Trinity in the New Testament in the sense of an understanding of triunity. But the triadic formulas used to express God's action in the world, as a self-manifestation and a self-communication, raise of themselves the further question concerning God's own ineffable being. This is but to say that actions reveal the natures of those who act; such understanding is "not just a quirk of the Greek mind, but a universal apperception."[1] As the Church proclaims the Gospel (which it cannot be content merely to repeat), questions are posed in terms that lead to the doctrines of the Incarnation and the Trinity. This occasions an immense shift in language and meaning that raises a general problem of interpretation; reflection on that, however, will be deferred until it can be viewed in retrospect at the conclusion of this chapter.

---

[1] Fuller, *Foundations*, p. 248.

ECONOMIC TRINITARIANISM: JUSTIN MARTYR

Early attempts to bypass the theologizing of John and Paul in a return to the Synoptic kerygma tend to eliminate trinitarian overtones in the New Testament. Theodotus is cited by Eusebius as an example of those who view Jesus as a pure man elevated to divine status at his Baptism, a process that is consummated at the Resurrection.[2] "Spirit" is then used as a synonym for "God." But adherents of this position (as Eusebius himself notes) were forcing the scriptural data to yield to rationalistic explanation. The mainstream of Christian reflection went by another route entirely in the period immediately subsequent to the New Testament. The determinant in this would appear to be the prevalence of confessions of faith (differing from Church to Church) that were used at baptism. These initial creeds—the so-called Apostles' Creed, reproduced in early form in the *Didachē* (dated as early as 60 A.D. by J. P. Audet) and by both Justin Martyr's (+ 165) *Apology* and his *Dialogue with Trypho the Jew*—are attempts to render the kerygma in summary form and clearly show dependence on *Mt.* 28:19. They are triadic in structure and content, and are thus resistant to the rationalizing of the kerygma by such as Theodotus. Not until Theophilus of Antioch (+ c. 180) will God himself be called a "Triad," but the triadic formulas are used constantly in confessing God. Justin Martyr reflects an established liturgical use of "to the Father, through the Son, and through the Spirit," employing such triadic language three times in the *Apology*, in references to worship in general, to baptism, and to the Eucharist. Ignatius of Antioch (+ c. 110) gives ample evidence that these early confessions included Christ as God[3] and *I Clement* (written before 101) extends this to God, Christ, and Spirit. But precisely at this point, this inherited religious understanding of the kerygma is supplemented by an appropriation of the *Logos* doctrine of John's Gospel. The motive is apologetic and on two counts: first, the Christian community no longer lives in the shadow of the Synagogue but feels the impact of the thought-forms of Graeco-Roman philosophy, and secondly, Gnostic religions have begun to make inroads into Christian beliefs, interpreting them in eclectic ways and forcing a clearer statement of what Christians genuinely intended

---

[2] Eusebius, *Hist. eccl.*, V, 28 (Migne: *PG* 30. 513).
[3] See *Magn.*, xi (Migne: *PG* 5. 672); also *Trall.*, ix (Migne: *PG* 5. 681); *Smyrn.*, i (Migne: *PG* 5. 708).

in their confessions. Justin Martyr begins the dialogue with Hellenic culture; Irenaeus is perhaps most representative of the anti-Gnostic reaction.

Justin's own background was pagan rather than Jewish, and he acknowledges influences prior to his conversion to Christianity from various current philosophies: Stoic, Peripatetic, Pythagorean, and (eventually predominant) Middle Platonism. All these had become in the first century A.D. religious philosophies; in Platonism the emphasis fell upon a doctrine of the *Logos* as a mediating principle between God and man. Whereas Paul and the author of *Hebrews* prefer the designations *Kyrios* and "Son of God," John explicitly presents Christ as the *Logos* of God.[4] All three titles are intended to convey preexistence and incarnation (the *Kyrios* title in virtue of its borrowing in the Septuagint as the translation of *Adonai*). Ignatius of Antioch, at any rate, picks up the Johannine term and Justin Martyr develops it into an integral *Logos*-Christology. For Justin, the term *Logos* resonates with both Platonic and Stoic undertones. Platonic use makes it an agent in creation; Stoic use views it as divine in the sense of being the intelligible structure immanent in nature. Justin adds to this the Christian element, noting that the *Logos* has these functions in virtue of its origin in God as the rational principle within deity. The *Logos* thus comes forth first as agent and underlying structure in creation and then appears finally and fully in Christ. One of the gains of this line of thinking is that it promotes the view of Christianity as a universal religion. Plato and the prophets of the Old Testament are instructed by the *Logos,* and so their teachings point implicitly to his coming incarnation in the man Jesus.

Hellenistic thought, like Gnosticism in its dualistic doctrine, put considerable emphasis on the total transcendence of God, thus the appeal of a system which mediated God to world as *Logos.* For Justin, God is "nameless" and "unmoved";[5] and in the Apologists generally there is a tendency to shy away from the anthropomorphic language in which the Old Testament represents God at work in the world— such expressions they interpret allegorically. The alien, and dangerously new, element here is the suggestion that the *Logos* arises solely in function of this mediation to a world. The *Logos* is always

---

[4]Concerning the sources for the use of *Logos* in John's Gospel, see Fuller, *Foundations,* pp. 222–23. Fuller agrees with Bultmann's dismissal of *Dabar, Memra, Torah,* and the *Logos* of the Stoics and Heraclitus, but is not inclined to dismiss so readily the *Sophia* of Hellenistic Judaism.

[5]*Dialog.,* 127 (Migne: *PG* 6. 540).

radically within God, as Athenagoras makes clear, but not seemingly as any distinctive feature of his being apart from creation and incarnation. Prior to these divine acts, the *Logos* is like the Wisdom of God mentioned in *Proverbs* 8:22. Another Apologist, Theophilus of Antioch, promotes this way of thinking when he borrows from Stoicism the distinction between the *Logos* as immanent within God (λόγος ἐνδιάθετος) and as uttered by God (λόγος προφορικός).

Though the *Logos* is not "divided" from God the Father, still he comes forth somewhat after the fashion in which fire derives from fire and, moreover, as an act of the Father's will.[6] Thus Justin leaves us with the impression that the *Logos* somehow emanates from the Father. He makes the *Logos* of St. John approximate the quite distinct *Logos* of Philo, which latter if at times a power or energy emanating from God is also at other times a second, intermediary God. Justin is not doing philosophy but only using philosophical categories instrumentally in working out an understanding of religious realities. But what does occur is an instance of Hellenization, at least in form. While not Hellenizing to the extent Philo does, his use of the categories of Greek rational thought is not flexible enough to do justice to the Gospel.

At times, in Tatian for example, the Hellenizing would seem to be such also in content. The latter views the Triad as if it were a chain of being. It would be anachronistic to interpret the Apologists too demandingly. They represent less the origins of speculative interest than a desire to locate their soteriological concern in a universal perspective. They mean to say: Jesus teaches men *as God* because he is the self-same Word originally uttered by God in the act of creating, now newly spoken. Some confirmation of this appears in their almost total neglect of the Spirit; the latter is clearly of divine status, but the term is used sometimes as a synonym for God, sometimes as another name for the *Logos*. Occasionally he does appear as a Third in addition to the other Two, as in Theophilus,[7] but this is due to a sense of reverence for the traditional triadic formula. How the Spirit might be distinguished from Father and Son is never broached, though sometimes this is attempted by referring to the Third in God as "Wisdom."[8]

---

[6]Justin Martyr, *Dialog.*, 128 (Migne: *PG* 6. 540).

[7]Theophilus, *Ad Autolycum,* I, 7 (Migne: *PG* 6. 1036) and II, 15 (Migne: *PG* 6. 1077).

[8]Theophilus, ibid.

Irenaeus (+ c. 202), whose theology, remarkable for its vast synthetic vision, differs markedly from that of the earlier Apologists, represents in his own way this Economic Trinitarianism. The danger ⊁ in the enterprise of the Apologists who preceded him was the tendency to allow a philosophical doctrine of universal reason to incorporate within itself the Christian *Logos* of St. John. The deepest theological instincts of Irenaeus, by contrast, harken back to the thought of Ignatius of Antioch where primacy is given to the *oikonomia,* to God's saving dispensation. The Word and the Spirit are simply the two hands of God in this work.[9] God, whose absolute oneness Irenaeus takes for granted, relates to the world in the form of Word and Wisdom—the latter his name for the Spirit.[10] On this basis, God's oneness includes an underlying threeness but solely in the sense that he lives eternally with his Thought and his Wisdom. The distinctness of the Three is suppressed and emerges only in terms of roles within the economy. Needless to say, there is not the slightest suggestion in this of three co-equal "persons."

For Irenaeus the focus is on the revelation of God's plan, basically on the recapitulation of his original design in creating. The chosen ⊁ economy knows two moments: creation and incarnation. The former is achieved through the divine *Logos,* also called Son; the latter is the reappropriation after sin of this original intent of God through Christ who is this very *Logos* now incarnate as the "Second Adam." The tendency is to present Father and Son in terms of God as invisible and as visible, so that the Son is always with the Father but as the medium of his manifestation.[11] Thus it is the *Logos* who appears in the Old Testament theophanies and finally in Christ. But though the *Logos* is undeniably in the humanity, Irenaeus suggests a certain autonomy from the manhood, which thus is given its own individuality.[12] This implicit adoptionist Christology is merely the sign of an undeveloped trinitarianism. It confirms the conclusion that Irenaeus has no clear understanding of the Son as distinct from the Father in anything approaching what later will be termed personhood. The suggestion of a Second (and Third) *in* God, found in the early Apologists such as Justin and Tatian, is really not explicit

---

[9]*Adversus haereses,* IV, Praef. (Migne: *PG* 7. 975).

[10]Irenaeus thus tends to differentiate these two names, whereas Justin uses them interchangeably.

[11]*Adv. haereses,* IV, 6, 6 (Migne: *PG* 7. 989) and II, 30, 9 (Migne: *PG* 7. 822).

[12]Ibid., III, 19, 3 (Migne: *PG* 7. 941).

in Irenaeus. Though he goes beyond the mere use of triadic formulas (characteristic of the Apostolic Fathers), his trinitarianism is purely economic and lacks the connotation of genuine triunity.

MONARCHIAL TRINITARIANISM: TERTULLIAN

By the time of Tertullian (+ c. 220) a major implication of Economic Trinitarianism begins to surface, namely, the suspicion that God is three solely in function of the economy. This marks a retrogression to Old Testament understanding of divine transcendence. Where the New Testament is concerned, interest at this point centers upon the primitive kerygma in preference to the more developed Johannine-Pauline theology. The *Logos* doctrine recedes somewhat, and at least in one instance—that of Theodotus, at the very end of the second century—is repudiated.[13] This a-trinitarianism receives an extreme statement from Sabellius (who appears in Rome about 217): God remaining One appears to men under different aspects. Father, Son, and Spirit are successive manifestations of God; ultimately the difference is of name only. This is Modalism in its purest form. Tertullian, inveighing against its advocacy by Praxeas, expresses alarm at its popularity among ordinary believers. And Pope Callistus, though excommunicating Sabellius, offers himself what is a modified version of it: God in uniting himself to the flesh of Jesus acquires visibility and is called Son, but he remains Father in his invisibility—so that Father and Son are one *prosōpon*. Athanasius explains that the Sabellians mean that God is at one time Father and at another Son; thus they call God "Son-Father."[14]

What really is at work in all of this, however, is Monarchianism— the strict and somewhat conservative monotheism that held tenaciously to an understanding of God's utter transcendence as *Monarchia*. The term conceives God as "the sole ruling power" and is used polemically against both polytheism and dualism. It is Tertullian, more than others, who sees the deeper dimension of understanding that is being neglected. He rescues trinitarianism (i.e., a specifically Christian notion of God) by insisting that God is three *in Himself*. Remaining the *Monarchia*, he "economizes" himself in a trine way, in relating to the world. Thus God is found to be three-

---

[13]See Eusebius, *Hist. eccl.*, V, 28 (Migne: *PG* 20. 513).
[14]*Or. contra Arianos*, III, 4 (Migne: *PG* 26. 328); see also *Expos. fidei*, I (Migne: *PG* 25. 204).

fold within the dispensation, but there he makes *himself* to be three. It is not merely a matter of names or of temporary forms of appearance. There is still no breaking out of the economic perspective: apart from his chosen relationship to the world, Tertullian's God is One, the *Monarchia*. Prior to creation God contains Reason but not yet expressed as Word *(Sermo)*.[15] But it is the inner nature of that *Monarchia* to assume intrinsically such triplicity, to disperse itself as it were in a threefold manner. Hence the descriptive phrase for Tertullian's theology, "Monarchial Trinitarianism," does do service. He embraces Monarchianism wholeheartedly; he refuses adamantly any Modalist rationalization. His coining of the Latin term *trinitas* indicates his awareness of three who are one. At this point, his background in Stoic philosophy plays him false.[16] What is "economized" into three is God's own substance, i.e., that which remains to undergird or ground the threeness (that which is *sub-stans*). But Tertullian views this idiosyncratically, as something akin to rarefied (spiritual) matter. God "stretches himself out," one might almost say, into Father, Son, and Holy Spirit. Tertullian's own examples are those of root, stem, and fruit, or source, river, and stream.[17] Obviously, Tertullian understands this divine economizing into trinity as willed by the Father—first in creation (as Word) and in incarnation (as Son), then secondly, after Christ's exaltation, as Spirit. As the Word was originally indistinct within God, so the Spirit is indistinct in the Incarnate Word until the moment of his pouring forth (here Tertullian's Montanist sympathies may well be at work).

Tertullian, of course, also introduces the technical Latin term *persona,* and uses it with marked consistency: Father, Son, and Spirit are three *personae* of the one substance *(unius substantiae); they* are *unum* but not *unus.*[18] Similarly, Christ is the one *persona* who is the *Logos* and Son, now incarnate. With this, he is approaching an understanding of distinction within the Godhead, beyond any of his predecessors. One has to be careful of reading too much into this term; later controversy will give to the word intelligibilities it lacks for Tertullian. He appears to employ it as intending what Hippol-

---

[15]*Adv. Praxeam,* 5 (Migne: *PL* 2. 160).
[16]This is contrary to A. von Harnack's view that Tertullian's terminology is rather forensic in kind, derived from Roman Law. In support of this, see the introduction by E. Evans to his *Tertullian's Treatise against Praxeas* (London: S.P.C.K., 1948).
[17]*Adv. Praxeam,* 8 (Migne: *PL* 2. 163).
[18]Ibid., 3, 7, 11, 25 (Migne: *PL* 2. 157–58, 161–62, 166–67, 188).

ytus (whose *Contra Noetum* antedates Tertullian's *Adversus Praxeam*
by about ten years) means by *prosōpon*. From originally meaning a
mask, and thence an actor's role played by someone, it assumes the
sense of a concrete manifestation or an individual presentation of
something. Tertullian contrasts *persona* with *substantia,* and *persona-
liter* with *substantialiter,* but *substantia* is also contrasted with *forma* and
species.[19] Thus it is reasonable to assume that Tertullian views the
person-substance relationship as analogous to the form-matter distinction. Substance means (at least in the *Adversus Praxeam*) matter
abstracting from all form; its use is abstract, as for example in saying
"stone" rather than "a stone." *Persona* is then the concrete appearance or presentation of such substance. But, as Harnack notes, this
enabled Tertullian to safeguard pluralism in God against the unitarianism of the Monarchians.[20]

All this makes clear what is at first a startling truth in Tertullian,
namely that by "economy" he does not mean the order of creation
or redemption, but the order within God's own being; he means the
Trinity as a dispensation within God that allows for a sort of organic
unity. While he uses *oikonomia* to mean a dispensation within God
in function of the creation and redemption, he understands this as
foundationally a distribution in the immanent being of the Godhead.
The appearances of God in the world (as Son and Spirit) are traced
back into the depths of God's own being where they find their
explanation. G. L. Prestige and R. A. Markus can thus refer to this
distribution as eternal.[21] However, this immanent and eternal distribution within God does not exactly correspond to the Trinity that

---

[19]See *Adv. Praxeam,* 12, 6 (Migne: *PL* 2. 168); *Adv. Val.,* 7, 9 (Migne: *PL*
2. 550–51); and *Adv. Praxeam,* 2, 1 (Migne: *PL* 2, 157); xiii, 10 (Migne: *PL*
2. 170). On the meaning of Tertullian's vocabulary, see G. C. Stead, "Divine
Substance in Tertullian," *Journal of Theological Studies,* n.s., 14 (1963), pp.
46–66, who disputes the claim of Ernest Evans that *substantia* has for Tertullian a meaning akin to Aristotle's *ousia.*

[20]A. von Harnack argues that Tertullian is using forensic language, one
that has a technical sense implying many subjects of legal rights. G. C. Stead,
p. 58, cites both C. Andresen in *Zeitschrift für die Neutestamentliche Wissenschaft*
52 (1961), pp. 1–39 and C. C. J. Webb, *God and Personality* (1918), p. 66 as
suggesting that Tertullian's development of the word *persona* is the result
of his explorations in the domain of biblical exegesis.

[21]This is the interpretation convincingly argued for by G. L. Prestige, *God
in Patristic Thought* (London: S.P.C.K., 1952), p. 111, and R. A. Markus,
"Trinitarian Theology and the Economy," *Journal of Theological Studies,* n.s.,
9 (1958), pp. 89–102.

comes into the world for man's redemption. Indeed, the third chapter of Tertullian's *Adversus Hermogenem* suggests, on two counts, that this latter Trinity is a temporal one: first, in maintaining that the Word immanent in the Godhead is the Son of God and a person only from the moment of creation onward, and secondly, in writing that "there was a time when there was . . . no Son to make God a Father." Integrally considered, then, Tertullian is not free of the spirit of Economic Trinitarianism.

What Tertullian has done, along with his contemporaries, Hippolytus and Novatian, is to show that the plurality manifested in the temporal economy reaches back into the immanent life of the Godhead. God is multiple from the beginning (substance is never without form); he has so economized himself eternally. This explains why he can appear in creation and redemption as Son and Spirit. Still, the personalist idiom is entirely muted when he talks about the eternal moment in God. And when he does use personalist language of the Trinity, in the temporal sphere of salvation history, there is no note of subjectivity or existential relationality; the most that is conveyed is a sense of concrete presentation or appearance, of something approximating individuality.

SUBORDINATIONISM: ORIGEN

Clement of Alexandria (+ c. 216), a contemporary of Tertullian's, manifests a similar proximity to the work of the Apologists. He appropriates their *Logos* doctrine in his polemic against the Gnostics, but in a way peculiar to himself: the *Logos* reveals the inaccessible God in a manner that leads beyond common faith into a Christian *gnōsis*. This opens the way for his disciple Origen (+ 254) who furthers Clement's esoteric thought by giving expression to it in the language of Middle Platonism. The original suggestion of doing this is probably to be laid to Ammonius Saccas; this is plausible on the grounds of Eusebius's observation that Origen was for a time a student of Ammonius.[22] Middle Platonism was a decidedly religious philosophy which sought to rescue Platonism from the enervating skepticism to which the Academy had succumbed. It attempted this by replacing the Good (which Plato had placed at the apex of reality as the supreme Form) with the Divine Mind (Aristotle's thought [*Nous*] thinking thought?) in which the Forms existed as divine ideas.

[22]*Hist. eccl.*, VI, 19 (Migne: *PG* 20. 564ff.).

During Origen's own lifetime Plotinus, a Greek-speaking Egyptian, will alter this latter-day Platonism into yet another thought system, eventually to be known as Neo-Platonism. This powerful system of religious philosophy turns on the emanation of everything from the One: first comes forth the *Nous* containing the ideas of all that can be; then from *Nous* the Demiurge or World-Soul; ultimately from the latter come souls, bodies, and last and least of all, matter.

Origen, however, makes very clear at the beginning of his *De Principiis*[23] that his procedure is entirely under the norm of the rule of faith—though he seems to mean by this not any Creed or set of specific doctrines as much as his own personal summary of the Church's developed understanding of the New Testament. Still, following Clement's lead, he adheres to the *Logos* doctrine, with a strong insistence that the *Logos* is also the *generated* Son. This transition is crucial for Origen because it enables him to explain that "Son" unlike "Word" bears the connotation of separate being and of possessing its own essence.[24] For the first time it is made crystal clear that the Second in God is eternally distinct. Origen accomplishes this by borrowing a Hellenistic thought-form and employing it in a systematic interpretation of the Gospel.

In the background of Origen's thinking is an understanding of God—common to Hellenistic rationalism and to Gnosticism, and now finding Neo-Platonic expression—as Absolute Spirit for whom contact with the visible and material world, the world of darkness and mutability, is repugnant. It is really the *Logos* (the Son and Christ; Origen uses the names interchangeably) who directly creates the world and is active within it, but at the will of the Father. Twice, in Origen's *Commentary on John*, Christ is called "demiurge"; he is himself "divine," but mediates between rational creatures and God.[25] Origen calls him "God" (θεός) but never "the God" (ὁ θεός), and he reserves for the Father the name "God Himself" (αὐτόθεος).[26] When

---

[23]The *De Principiis* is no longer extant in the original Greek text but only in a Latin translation by the monk Rufinus (+ 410), who readily acknowledges altering it so as to minimize any implications of Arianism. Athanasius in his *De Decretis* cites only passages that are free of Arianist implications, while Justinian writing in the mid sixth century cites passages from Origen's Greek text that are clearly intended to foster an Arianist reading of the Alexandrian.

[24]*Comm. in Joann.*, I, 24 (Migne: *PG* 14. 61–64).

[25]Ibid., I, 17 (Migne *PG* 14. 53); *Contra Celsum*, III, 39 (Migne: *PG* 11. 969–72).

[26]Ibid., II, 2 (Migne: *PG* 14. 108).

Origen refers to the *Logos* as "another" from the Father in *ousia*, *hypostasis*, and *hypokeimenon*,[27] one can only conclude that he looks upon the *Logos* as numerically distinct. Most frequently, the Second in God is said to be numerically distinct as a *hypostasis*, but Origen interchanges this word with *ousia;* Cicero had translated the latter term as essence *(essentia)*, but Origen uses it more in the sense of "concrete existing entity." This second *hypostasis*, however, is eternally begotten, born before all creatures; thus, "there never was when he was not."[28] Origen could not be clearer on this. It is true that he also calls the *Logos* a "creature" *(ktisma)*, but this literal inconsistency is explained by the fact that he takes *Proverbs* 8:22 to refer to the Son. His intentions are entirely on the side of an eternal ✗ ⍥ generation as opposed to a temporal production. The Son is divine even if a "secondary God."[29]

Still, eternal generation does not of itself give divine status because Origen views all spiritual beings, both what he calls *theoi* and human souls, as eternal. Only with the fall of souls into material bodies by way of punishment, from which the *human* soul of Christ alone is excepted, is there a beginning to time. This raises the question as to why the *Logos* is divine and other emanating spirits are not. There is no hesitancy or incertitude at all in Origen's conclusion that such is the case. The sources for this are such scriptural sayings as: "The Father and I are one" *(Jn.* 10:30); "The Father is in me and I am in the Father" *(Jn.* 10:38); "Whoever sees me sees the one who sent me" *(Jn.* 12:45), etc. But Origen can find no explanation beyond the immediacy of the emanation and the Father's willing of the unity between them.[30] Only the second reason holds in the case of the Holy Spirit, to whom Origen also gives divine rank. Triadic language forms a universal rule of faith, and Origen draws a sharp line of demarcation between the Three who alone are divine and all lesser eternal spirits who are not. But in such an explanation the true unity of God is imperiled. Origen's system plays him false in that it can find no way to explain a unity that is other than moral

---

[27]*Contra Celsum*, VIII, 12 (Migne: *PG* 11. 1334).
[28]*De Principiis*, I, 2, 9 (Migne: *PG* 11. 138) and IV, 28 (Migne: *PG* 11.403).
[29]*Contra Celsum*, V, 39 (Migne: *PG* 11. 1243).
[30]Though Origen understands that lesser spirits also emanate eternally, they do so mediately and in a descending order of greater and greater remove from the Father as the αὐτόθεος; this explains their involvement in evil and so confirms their nondivine status.

in kind, although his *Against Celsus* makes the case that Christians
do not worship two Gods. What is at work here is an implication of
Monarchianism, namely, that the unity of *Logos* and *Pneuma* with
the Father is petitioned in terms of their origin from him as the *fons
divinitatis*. The unity is hierarchical in kind rather than essential and
unavoidably suggests that the Son and the Spirit enjoy a diminished
divinity. Origen views the Father as ἑνάς, the one and only God; he
is the *archē* from which the Son and Spirit derive their divinity, a
view that John Damascene will share a bit later.[31] Novatian had
earlier thought along similar lines: "... Christ Jesus, by abiding in
him, ... has succinctly proved that his Father is the one and only
true God."[32] Origen's own language at this point is well known: the
Son is "secondary in rank" and the Spirit is God "of the third rank."
The translation in Justinian's fragment of the *De Principiis*, at any
rate, is subordinationist in the extreme: "One of these things is the
Son, who is less than the Father and whose influence reaches to
rational beings only, for He is second from the Father. Still inferior
is the Holy Spirit, who penetrates only the saints; so that in this way
the power of the Father is greater than that of the Son, but that of
the Son is more than that of the Holy Spirit."[33] Justinian's rendering
is, of course, unsympathetic, but even the less pejorative accounts
of Rufinus and Athanasius (which absolve Origen of blame for the
subsequent heresy of Arius) only succeed in muting somewhat the
subordinationist overtones.

A few lines later in the passage just cited Justinian expressly
charges Origen with reducing the Son to the rank of a creature, in
the latter's use of the term κτίσμα. Even if this be discounted,
Origen's *Commentary on John* states flatly that "of all things made
through the *Logos*, the Holy Spirit is more honorable than all others
and ranks above all other things made by the Father through
Christ."[34] Rufinus's translation of the *De Principiis*, on the other

---

[31] For John Damascene's opinion, see *Expositio fidei*, 7 (Migne: *PG* 94.
804ff.).

[32] Novatian, *Treatise on the Trinity*, 31, Eng. transl. Russell J. DeSimone,
The Fathers of the Church, vol. 67 (Washington, D.C.: The Catholic University
of America Press, 1972), p. 111 (Migne: *PL* 3. 952).

[33] Justinian citing Origen in his *Letter to Menna against Origen* (Migne: *PG*
86[1]. 982); the translation here given is that of R. S. Franks in *The Doctrine
of the Trinity* (London: G. Duckworth, 1953), pp. 93–94, from the Rede-
penning edition of the *De Principiis*.

[34] *Comm. in Joann.*, II, 6 (Migne: *PG* 14. 128–29).

hand, refutes these implications, stating that "there was nothing that was not made except the nature of the Father and the Son and the Holy Spirit."[35] There are two possible explanations of this discrepancy: either (a) Rufinus has altered Origen's text to preclude an Arian interpretation, or (b) there is no clear distinguishing at this time between to be generated or born and to be made or created. Whatever be the case, Origen makes clear that only the Father is *agenētos* (a term Newman translates as "unoriginate" and which only later will be given the distinct connotation of "unbegotten," *agennētos*). Moreover, Origen dismisses Tertullian's word *prolatio* as explanatory of how the *Logos* emanates from the Father, apparently because he cannot share the understanding that Tertullian has of unity of substance. In short, Origen's three *hypostaseis* or *ousiai* are not coequal and identical in essence, but constitute a graded hierarchy. *Homoousios,* the pivotal term from Nicaea on, is attributed to Origen only in a translation of Pamphilus by Rufinus, the former citing in his *Apology* from a lost fragment of Origen's *Commentary on Hebrews.*[36] The term, however, runs counter to the prevailing thrust of Origen's thought. If he did in fact use the word, it could hardly have been in the sense only later given to it by Athanasius, i.e., the sense of identity. In all likelihood, Origen would have meant no more than that the Son's *ousia* is not separate or divergent from the Father's, but rather some sort of Platonic sharing in the latter. At any rate, it can hardly be denied that with Origen subordinationism has become explicit in Greek theology of the Trinity.

BEGINNINGS OF TRIUNITY: ATHANASIUS

If Origen is a "Nicene before Nicaea" (A. von Harnack), he also can be seen as a forerunner of Arius. The latter simply draws out the rational implications of Origen's subordinationism, concluding

---

[35]*De Principiis,* IV, 35 (Migne: *PG* 11. 409).

[36]Nevertheless, von Harnack accepts the text as genuine (as do McGiffert and Bethune-Baker) and views Origen as "a Nicene before Nicaea," implicitly advocating the *homoousion.* Still, it is the subordinationist strain that is uppermost, and seemingly the most Origen could be implying is some sort of generic, or better, hierarchical oneness rather than identity. Another puzzling phrase—"nothing in the Trinity can be called greater or less," *De Principiis,* I, 3, 7 (Migne: *PG* 11. 153)—is either an alteration of Rufinus again or, if genuine, has to be viewed as an eccentric expression in light of the overall direction of Origen's thought.

that the *Logos* is γεννητός ("originated," in the sense not only of "begotten" but of "created"), and κτίσμα (a creature); he is not eternal since "there was when he was not" (an expression Tertullian had used earlier). Whereas Origen holds to the Apostolic rule of faith, to which however he is not always able to do theological justice, Arius and his followers allow a rationalistic interpretation to distort it, to dispel elements of mystery held in dialectical tension. What is immediately surmised by the Christian populace is the soteriological implications of Arius's preaching: if the *Logos* is not God then the humanity he has assumed is not by that very fact redeemed and saved; mankind is still in its sin. The Council of Nicaea (325) responds with the famous *homoousios*. The term—suggested by Ossius, who was chaplain to the Emperor Constantine, as a compromise word—was already commonplace in Gnostic religion. It is used at Nicaea, however, in a quite singular sense to convey that the *Logos* is God in the very sense that the Father is; he is not God only in some secondary and diminished sense. It is an attempt, pure and simple, to safeguard the kerygma which Arius had thrown into jeopardy; only in later discussions is it to gain any technical precision of meaning. But it is a nonbiblical expression and gave rise to bitter controversy. Paul of Samosata had earlier used the term, but in what was an attempt to revive the sort of Modalism begun by Theodotus and Artemon, who believed *Logos* signified simply the *power* of God descended upon the man Jesus. Paul uses *homoousios* then to suggest that *Logos* is simply another name for God as He is "in conjunction with" (συνάφεια) Jesus the man. So used, the word fosters an Adoptionist Christology and is decidedly antitrinitarian. This is Adoptionism in a sense that goes beyond the purely functional adoptionism of New Testament Palestinian Christianity. It fully intends to say something about Christ's nature, and for it Paul was condemned in 268. At Nicaea the word was resorted to for anti-Arian motives, but there is subsequent resistance to it on the grounds that it compromises the pluralistic strain stemming from the Apologists and from Origen. This explains the popular support for the substitute term *homoiousios* (ὁμοιούσιος), "of like substance" rather than "of the same substance." This expression formulated by Basil of Ancyra was favored by Cyril of Jerusalem and at first by the Cappadocian Fathers.[37] By contrast, the term *homoios* (ὅμοιος), meaning merely

---

[37]Epiphanius records the adoption of the term at the Synod of Ancyra under Basil's leadership in 358; see *Haer.*, 73, 3–11 (Migne: *PG* 42. 408ff.).

"like," gained little support since it was rightly seen as nothing more than a subtle attempt to circumvent the unacceptable shibboleth of the pure Arians, *anomoios* (ἀνόμοιος), meaning "unlike."[38] Arius then has brought the ontological question center stage. Impatient with the dialectical tensions in the thought of the early Apologists and in Tertullian and Origen (relying respectively on Stoic and Platonic categories), he has recourse to the simple Judaeo-Christian categories: God is unoriginate *(agenētos)* and all else is originated *(genētos)*. Since Christians confess the Son to be generated and begotten, he falls into the latter category. Arius has here identified *gennētos*, meaning "begotten," with the distinct Greek term *genētos*, meaning "created." He has preserved the absoluteness of the *Monarchia* by extruding therefrom the *Logos,* leaving the latter as perfect creature. The resolution is rationalistic in doing away with apparent contradictions. It is an instance of Hellenization for which the followers of Arius are then able to find explicit scriptural grounds in such texts as *Romans* 8:29, "the firstborn among many brethren," and *John* 17:3, "that they may know thee the only true God, and him whom you did send, Jesus Christ." But the question Arius has urged is: What do the Scriptures *mean?* Does the confession "Jesus is the Lord" mean to ascribe divinity in a genuinely ontic sense to Jesus? Or is it merely a matter of metaphorical language? Does the kerygma mean to speak of Jesus in himself or only of his significance for us? The answer which becomes explicit in the reaction against Arius is that the Christ *for us* in the functional Christology of the New Testament rests upon who or what Christ is in himself. Thus the emerging categories of *homoousios-homoiousios* are responses to a question that is, in John Courtney Murray's words, "new, inevitable, legitimate, and exigent of an answer that would have to be an answer of faith."[39]

Another interpretation entirely of Arius is possible, one that views him as not rationalizing the kerygma at all, thereby making Christ as begotten Son into a pure creature, but pursuing the profound insight that the divine dimension in Christ is not to be sought outside of what constitutes him human.[40] Such a benign interpretation

---

[38]Formulas using the ὅμοιος appear in the Creeds of Nicé (359) and of Constantinople (360) at the instigation of Acacius; see J. N. D. Kelly, *Early Christian Doctrines,* 5th ed. (London: Adam and Charles Black, 1977), p. 251.

[39]*The Problem of God* (New Haven: Yale University Press, 1964), p. 40.

[40]See the illuminating study by R. Gregg and D. Groh, *Early Arianism— A View of Salvation* (Philadelphia: Fortress Press, 1981).

would have Arius seeking to say that God truly appears not only *in* Jesus but *as* Jesus of Nazareth. But, if so, the theological language equal to such a task was lacking (and indeed one can ask how adequately it has been supplied even today). The orthodox Church Fathers, at any rate, chose to read early Arianism as calling the divinity of Christ into question. What the choice at Nicaea amounted to, perhaps, was a decision to accept the question Arius had raised, less in his own terms than in those of the more prevalent Platonic thought according to which the appearances of things tended to obscure rather than to reveal their true essence and so to defend Christ's divinity as lying behind (so to speak) his humanity. The greater danger was seen to lie in following Arius's line of thought which tended to conceive of the *Logos* as a sort of "divine" creature (created, but before time). The caution to be exercised here, then, is that the Nicene dogma coming down clearly on one side of the question must not be interpreted so one-sidedly as to obscure the revelation itself historically made in the Jesus-event. Nicaea affirmed the Son's consubstantiality with the Father; Chalcedon later (451) balanced this by insisting upon Jesus' consubstantiality with mankind. What Arius *may* have surmised, however unsuccessful he was in securing it, was an insight that simply could not find expression in terms of a two-nature theory. On the other hand, this may be no more than the importation of contemporary Christological, and so trinitarian, concerns into ancient thought. Whatever the case, the choice of the Church at Nicaea closed off the Arian route as the Fathers there read its direction; it need not close off serious reflection upon what may be seen today as the grain of truth in Arius's view.

It is in the discussion precipitated by Arius that the contribution of Athanasius (+ 373) looms large. His own concerns from the very beginning were, and ever remained, soteriological and it is precisely here that he ranges himself against Arianism. He is an adherent of *theōpoiēsis:* "The *Logos* became man in order that we might become God."[41] He champions the cause of Nicaea because he understands that only an Incarnate God can destroy sin and deify. The *Logos* of Arius cannot because, being God only by participation, he is himself a subject of deification and not its source.[42] The difference is clearer

---

[41]*De Incar.*, 54: "Αὐτὸς γὰρ ἐνηνθρώπησεν ἵνα ἡμεῖς θεωποιηθῶμεν" (Migne: *PG* 25. 192).

[42]Athanasius, *Or.* I, 6 (Migne: *PG* 26. 324); *De Synodis*, 51 (Migne: *PG* 26. 784–85).

in understanding that Athanasius begins with a biblical distinction within God (Father–Son), whereas Arius works from what is also a philosophical distinction (Creator–creature). Also, not entirely beside the point is the emphasis on bodily redemption in Athanasius in contrast to Origen's notion of spiritual redemption. But in the aftermath of Nicaea and its repudiation of Arius, a reaction set in. This arises out of a strong, if undeveloped, trinitarianism, interpreted by way of an Origenist background which Athanasius shares, one pledged to the "three hypostases" of Origen. Fearing anything that erodes distinctness within God, this attitude detects a covert Sabellianism in Nicaea's *homoousion*. Paul of Samosata had been condemned earlier at Antioch for using this term to make the *Logos* a mere attribute of God at work in Christ. But Marcellus, bishop of Ancyra, had interpreted the word rather in a modalistic sense, in a treatise written about ten years after Nicaea, and this is the understanding against which the Synod of Ancyra reacts under the influence of Basil of Ancyra in 358. Rallying around Eusebius of Caesarea, this group, making its influence felt in the East, finds itself more comfortable with the term *homoiousios*. Athanasius finds himself caught in the middle; his deepest instincts are defensive towards *homoousios*, but his Origenist background and his own religious understanding gives him insight into what it is that the Homoiousians are striving to safeguard.

At this point, Athanasius initiates a major advance in discerning that the distinctions in God (to which the Homoiousians rightly cling) must be seen not in light of a unity that is generic, or mere homogeneity, but against the background of what, on another conceptual level, is rather identity. His debates with the Eusebians had led him to see that the distinctions in God must not be understood as inimical to substantial unity in this full sense. The prevailing objection against *homoousios* viewed it as Sabellianistic, as collapsing all real distinction in God. But Athanasius is led to see the truth implicit in what was explicitly stated at Nicaea. *Homoousios* does not mean the one *ousia* that makes the Father to be Father, it means the one *ousia* which makes the Father to be God, the *ousia* of the Godhead. In the former way of thinking, the Son loses his distinct identity, in the latter he can retain it—but such distinction is nowise a distinction on the level of divinity. In his *De Synodis* Athanasius explains that the Son is everything that the Father is except what makes him Father; thus in Chapter 20 he writes, "The Son is not just similar to the Father, but is the same thing in similitude out of the Father." This represents the developed understanding of Athanasius and not that of the Fathers at Nicaea themselves. Their concern was religious: the belief that the *Logos* was God as was the Father and not as some sort of lesser intermediary. Earlier thinking of the Father as Absolute and the Son as Mediator tended to suggest a diminished divinity for the latter. Both a return to biblical understanding and a reaction against Arianism led to the point being made at Nicaea. For this the ordinary third-century understanding of *homoousios* — meaning a generic similarity, a homogeneity — was adequate. This is the meaning the word bears in the Gnostic religion of the time, and it is the most that the word can imply in Origen's system. But said of God, the truth is more than this — and Athanasius comes to see it. The Godhead, absolute and without beginning *(agenētos)*, is numerically one in concrete being or essence *(homoousios)*, or, as Tertullian said, "of one substance" *(unius substantiae)*, though the latter understands by this some sort of rarefied materiality. With this, Athanasius has closed off the way to conceiving the unity in Monarchian terms (i.e., as grounded in the Father alone) and so to Subordinationism. It enables him to go one step further: either the Holy Spirit is God as is Father and Son, or he is a mere creature. His anti-Arianism will not allow locating the Spirit on the side of the creature, not if the latter is a true agent of sanctification, as the rule of faith has always insisted. Thus Athanasius readily applies the *homoousion* to the Holy Spirit.[43]

Father, Son, and Spirit, then, are inseparably one God. But how are the three in fact distinct? Here the thought of Athanasius fails to explain what he asserts. It does not occur to him to distinguish *ousia* and *hypostasis* at the point where such a distinction might be most helpful.[44] Nicaea, in its anathemas, had used the terms interchangeably, and — though later, in 381, the Council of Constantinople I will confess a oneness only of *ousia* — Athanasius conforms to the prior practice. His attempt to surmount the dispute between Homoousians and Homoiousians goes only halfway towards reconciliation. One can say either One Hypostasis or Three Hypostases as long as one means "God" in the first phrase and "Father, Son, and Spirit" in the second.[45] Everything will now turn on what intel-

---

[43]Athanasius first makes this clear in a Council held at Alexandria in 362; he later makes it more explicit against Macedonius, who was denying the divinity of the Spirit; see *Tomus ad Antiochenos*, 3 (Migne: *PG* 26. 800).

[44]See *Ep. ad Afr.,* 4 (Migne: *PG* 26. 1036); *De Synodis,* 41 (Migne: *PG* 26. 765); and *De Decretis,* 27 (Migne: *PG* 25. 465).

[45]*Tomus ad Antiochenos,* 5, 6 (Migne: *PG* 26. 801).

ligibility can be given to *hypostasis* when said of the members of the
Trinity. Athanasius offers no help here; but he has secured the
homoousion and dispelled the misgivings of the Homoiousians about
the term. In this, he has set the terms within which the question of
what *hypostasis* means will be answered. The way to genuine Trinity has been opened.

ORTHODOX TRINITARIANISM: THE CAPPADOCIAN SETTLEMENT

The Cappadocian Fathers—Basil (+379), Gregory of Nazianzus
(+390), and Gregory of Nyssa (+394)—are more markedly Origenist in spirit than Athanasius. The latter's advocacy of the *homoousion*
meant that *logically* his thought tended towards a dissolution of the
three into the divine unity—in spite of his verbal refusal to allow
it to do so. The deepest instincts of the Cappadocians are with the
homoiousion formula, with its corresponding emphasis upon plurality
within the Godhead; their *point de départ* is the three *hypostaseis*. But
the influence of Athanasius (especially his sympathetic understanding of what the *homoiousios* supporters really intend) has precluded
once and for all any tendency to think in subordinationist terms.
The Cappadocians continue to teach, it is true, that the *Logos* and
Spirit are God in virtue of their origin from the Father as the *fons
divinitatis*. But this sort of thinking no longer presents itself as a
residue of Monarchial Trinitarianism. Since Athanasius, it is
acknowledged that Son and Spirit are divine not in virtue of a
hierarchical order to the Father but by a numerical identity of
essence *(ousia)*. How the three are distinguished is clarified by making explicit a distinction that Athanasius neglected and Origen only
hinted at, namely that between *hypostasis* and *ousia*. Once surmised,
the distinction prevents using the terms interchangeably. There are
three in God, numerically distinct as *hypostaseis*, but undistinguished
in essence or substance *(ousia)*.
    However, Basil sows further difficulty by understanding the distinction in terms of the relationship of an individual (τὸ καθ'
'ἕκαστον, 'ἴδιον) to a universal (κοινόν).[46] Gregory of Nazianzus further compounds the difficulty, in offering as illustration or analogy
for this the instance of Adam, Eve, and Seth as three individuals of

---

[46] Basil, *Ep*. 38, 2 (Migne: *PG* 32. 325–28); 214, 4 (Migne: *PG* 32. 789).

one human nature.[47] This reduces the divine unity to essence taken abstractly, dependent upon an act of the mind. Once again, conceptual tools are inadequate. But the difference now is that the Cappadocians are fully aware of the limits of their language. The particular-universal distinction is balanced dialectically with statements that compromise and correct it: each divine hypostasis is the *ousia* of God by an "identity of nature" ($\tau\hat{\eta}\varsigma\ \phi\acute{\upsilon}\sigma\epsilon\omega\varsigma\ \tau\alpha\upsilon\tau\acute{o}\tau\eta\tau\alpha$);[48] the Three in God differ numerically but not according to substance ($o\mathring{\upsilon}\sigma\acute{\iota}\alpha$).[49] Gregory of Nyssa, in his *On Not Three Gods*, makes clear what is intended, namely that the divine oneness is not abstract and notional, but real and concrete.[50] The latter especially makes clear that unity in operation ($\mathring{\epsilon}\nu\acute{\epsilon}\rho\gamma\epsilon\iota\alpha$) makes manifest an underlying unity in concrete being.[51] To maintain real distinction within this concrete oneness of being, then, demands a conceptual clarification of the term *hypostaseis*. This now comes to mean "objective presentations" of the Godhead or its simultaneous "modes of being" ($\tau\rho\acute{o}\pi\sigma\iota\ \mathring{\upsilon}\pi\acute{\alpha}\rho\xi\epsilon\omega\varsigma$).[52] These express distinct characteristics or properties ($\mathring{\iota}\delta\iota\acute{o}\tau\eta\tau\alpha$)[53] which are explained in terms of the distinct relations that the hypostases bear towards one another on the basis of the origins of Son and Spirit from the unoriginate Father. On this basis, the Three are named, respectively: Unbegotten, Begotten, and Proceeding. Gregory of Nyssa gives the most detailed explanation: the Father is "cause," the *Logos* and Spirit are "caused," but the former directly and the latter through the Word.[54]

---

[47]Gregory of Nazianzus, *Oratio* 31, 11 (Migne: *PG* 36. 143–46); Gregory of Nyssa offers the very different illustration of Mind, Word spoken therefrom, and Breath in which it is spoken; see *Orat. catechetica magna*, I and II (Migne: *PG* 45. 13–16, 17).

[48]Didymus the Blind, reflecting the doctrine of the Cappadocians, in *De Trinitate*, I, 16 (Migne: *PG* 39. 336).

[49]Gregory of Nazianzus, *Oratio* 29, 2 (Migne: *PG* 36. 75–76).

[50]In defense of this thesis, Gregory of Nyssa wrote his *Quod non sint tres Dii* (Migne: *PG* 45. 115–36).

[51]Gregory of Nyssa's teaching can be found in Basil's *Ep.* 189, 6 (Migne: *PG* 32. 691–94); a similar approach appears in the *Fourth Book against Eunomius* of Pseudo-Basil (Migne: *PG* 29. 676). It is on such grounds that the Cappadocians defend the divinity of the Holy Spirit; the activity of sanctification ascribed to him can only be an instance of the one activity of God.

[52]The phrase occurs in a fragment of Amphilochius of Iconium, an associate of Basil, entitled *Sententiae et Excerpta* (Migne: *PG* 39. 112).

[53]Gregory of Nazianzus, *Oratio* 31, 9 (Migne: *PG* 36. 144).

[54]See *Quod non sint*, ad fin. (Migne: *PG* 45. 115–36).

The recovery of the concept of eternal origin leads to the discovery of a new category (to be more fully exploited later), that of mutual "relations" (σχέσεις).[55] At this point, a ground for really distinguishing the three hypostases has been found, one which leaves uncompromised the ontological simplicity of the divine essence: God is "undivided in Three who are distinct" (ἀμέριστος ἐν μεμερισμένοις).[56] What this means is deepened somewhat with the doctrine that each hypostasis "inheres" in the other two[57]—the doctrine called by the Greeks *perichorēsis* and by the Latins *circumin-sessio* or *circumincessio*. In the end, the Cappadocians, without sacrificing the truth-claim of *homoiousion*, have come to terms with the complementary truth of Athanasius's *homoousion*. With this, subordinationism, the most marked characteristic of Greek speculative thought on the Trinity before Athanasius, comes to its definitive end. The unity of the Three is no longer hierarchical in kind, i.e., petitioned in virtue of a reduction of Son and Spirit back to their Source (the Father), but is a matter of ontological identity on the level of *ousia*. The advance has consisted in giving precision to the word that has long been accorded preeminence, namely, *hypostasis*. Its intelligibility is that of "objective presentation" or "mode of concrete being"; each presentation or mode admits of real but merely relational differentiation from the others. *Prosōpon*, used earlier, lacks the connotation of an eternal, ontological state of affairs, suggesting more an appearance for the sake of the *oikonomia*. Tertullian's *persona* (possibly a Latin rendering of the Greek *prosōpon* by way of the Etruscan language) is a slight improvement on *prosōpon* in that it traces the distinctions back into the Godhead, but the unity is ultimately monarchial in kind (residing in God identified as Father) and is preserved in the case of the *Logos* and the Spirit only with the categories of Stoic materialism. The element of subjectivity, radicated in consciousness, has not yet been broached.

The entire historical development unquestionably exhibits a process of Hellenizing the kerygma, but a kerygma already enriched by

[55]The term occurs in Gregory of Nazianzus, *Oratio* 29, 16 (Migne: *PG* 36. 96) and 31, 9 (Migne: *PG* 36. 144). TeSelle, *Augustine the Theologian* (New York: Herder and Herder, 1970), p. 295, cites Chavalier, who traces the term also to the *De Spiritu Sancto* of Didymus the Blind.

[56]Gregory of Nazianzus, *Oratio* 31, 14 (Migne: *PG* 36. 149).

[57]Basil, *Ep.* 38, 8 (Migne: *PG* 32. 340); J. N. D. Kelly, *Early Christian Doctrines*, p. 264, note 1, observes that though attributed to Basil, the true author may be Gregory of Nyssa.

the inspired theologizing of John and Paul. Most noteworthy, however, is the controlling and corrective process continually at work—
so that in the end it is a faith-confession that appropriates for itself
Hellenistic categories and in the process transforms them. The Cappadocian Settlement so-called is but a theological explanation of the
Nicene-Constantinopolitan Creed of Constantinople I in 381. Further clarifications will come after the Christological problem receives
an initial resolution at Chalcedon in 451. And a final synthesis of
Greek trinitarianism will appear with John Damascene's *De fide ortho-
doxa* in the eighth century. But already *"Trinitas"* (coined by Tertullian) is understood to mean "Tri-unity" and is the hallmark of
orthodoxy.

RETROSPECT: THE EMERGENCE OF DOGMA

In retrospect, one cannot fail to acknowledge a major shift that
has occurred from the articulation of religious experience in the
language of the New Testament to the often acrimonious delibera-
tions that issued in the categories of the Fathers and ultimately of
Nicaea. Succinctly put, the Gospel message came to be rendered into
dogma. The transition was from truth expressed in narrative form,
in multiple, spontaneous symbolic expressions and images, to the
one concept of Nicaea that the *Logos* (and by implication the *Pneuma*)
is consubstantial with the Father. Bernard Lonergan has put this
baldly by stating that Nicaea synthesized the content of the New
Testament into the one question for judgment: Is Christ God or
not?—to which the answer could only be "yes" or "no"; it is true or
it is not true.[58] The Council concluded that everything true of the
Father is true of the Son, except that the Son is not the Father.
Lonergan views this as a development from an undifferentiated
religious consciousness to a differentiated one. The move can be
characterized as that from symbolic expression to conceptual expression, from the existential to the essential, from the phenomenological to the ontological, from things as they concern us to things as
they are in themselves, from the historical, the particular, and the

---

[58]Bernard Lonergan, *The Way to Nicea*, transl. C. O'Donovan of *De Deo
Trino*, Part I (Philadelphia: Westminster Press, 1976); for a sharp criticism
of Lonergan's theory of development see J. S. O'Leary, "The Hermeneutics
of Dogmatism," *Irish Theological Quarterly* 47, no. 2 (1980), pp. 96–118.

relative to the metaphysical, the universal, and the formally unconditioned.

Looking back on this brief historical survey, it is exceedingly difficult to deny that what did happen historically does in fact illustrate
a general progression from *mythos* to *logos.* Moreover, this seems
native to man's structure as the kind of body-spirit, self-conscious
being he is. Thus, in a first sense, revelation grounds dogmas in
that the latter are only correct judgments on the meaning and truth
of what has been revealed; it remains true then that Scripture alone
is the *norma non normata* to which the Church is always subject. In
this sense, it is the mythic language of John's Prologue: "In the
beginning was the Word, and the Word was with God, and the
Word was God" that grounds the more rational judgment of Nicaea
that the Son is consubstantial with the Father. But in quite another
sense, in their very formulation, dogmas assume the function of
grounding revelation. They do this because to believe is spontaneously to seek both understanding of what is revealed and foundations for so believing. The latter can be sought only in the domain
of reason, not pure reason but reason illumined by faith. Such reason, moreover, is not only metaphysical but historical as well—and
it must needs remain aware of the analogical character of its functioning. But the move to dogma does manifest itself as a tethering
down of mythic and symbolic speech in dogmatic speech that evidences more of the conceptual and the rational. The sole alternative
to this would be to allow that revelation is in fact groundless, simply
there to be confessed in authentic decision (the faith of Neo-Orthodoxy) or to be responded to without critical explanation after the
fashion of aesthetic response to a work of art.

But it is precisely at this point that a reservation needs to be
registered. The emergence of dogma, and its function, should not
suggest an end to dialogue, a failure to perceive the discontinuities
and irreducible pluralism that remains. In short, dogmas, for all
their greater dimension of rationality, are themselves historically and
culturally conditioned. Too narrow a focus on the rational component can obscure the nonrational elements that are operative, e.g.,
the historical, the imaginative, the affective, etc. This is only to suggest that one can read the developments of the second, third, and
fourth centuries in such wise that the dogmas are made to obscure
revelation itself. A valuable antidote to this is Heidegger's notion of
truth as *alētheia,* as the unconcealment of things to human consciousness by the varied manner in which they "presence" themselves—
which need not exclude a theory of truth as *also* conformity of mind

in judgment and proposition to reality. What needs to be said of the process charted here, issuing in the Creed of Nicaea, and leading eventually to the orthodox trinitarian formula, is that to a notable degree play was allowed to these arational elements. For example, Athanasius in his loyalty to *homoousios* was clearly motivated by his own faith confession of Jesus' divinity, something not subject to logical analysis. Moreover, his subsequent interpretation of Nicaea is not free of historical factors, nor without imaginative and creative elements of its own. In fine, openness to the Spirit prevails over strictly logical procedures.

[3]

MEDIEVAL SCIENCE
The Trinity of the Theologians

CRYPTOMODALISM IN THE WEST: AUGUSTINE AND THE CONCEPT OF RELATION

The account by St. Augustine (+430) in the *Confessions* of his religious conversion in the year 386 relates how from "thinking only of my Lord Christ as of a man of excellent wisdom" he came to confess him as "that Mediator between God and man, the man Christ Jesus, who is over all God blessed forever."[1] On grounds such as these, the thought of earlier Christian Fathers representing the *Logos* as a divine mediator became central in Augustine's thinking also. This view was enhanced by his intellectual conversion, concurrent with his religious conversion, to Neo-Platonism with its doctrine of the *Nous* which emanates from the One in the Christian form it enjoyed in certain quarters in Italy.[2] From the very beginning, at any rate, which is to say long before the *De Trinitate*, Augustine's thought is markedly trinitarian, although he is content simply to

---

[1]*Confessions*, VII, 19, no. 25, and 18, no. 24 (Migne: *PL* 32. 745–46). The account of the conversionary experience proper occurs in VIII, 12, nos. 28–30.

[2]Details of Augustine's initial contact with the Christian Neo-Platonists at Milan, and the central influence of the Socratic figure of Simplicianus, who appears to have introduced Augustine to the *Enneads* of Plotinus, can be found in Eugene TeSelle's introduction to his *Augustine the Theologian* (New York: Herder and Herder, 1970); also in John J. O'Meara, *The Young Augustine* (New York: Longmans, Green, 1954), and Peter Brown, *St. Augustine of Hippo* (Berkeley: University of California Press, 1967). TeSelle suggests that Augustine read the *Enneads* most probably in the translation of Marius Victorinus, who had himself become a Christian under the influence of Simplicianus, whereas Willy Theilor (*Porphyrios und Augustin*, Schriften des Königberger gelehrten Gesellschaft, geistwissenschaftliche Klasse, X, I [Halle: Niemeyer, 1933]) prefers to see Augustine's Neo-Platonism mediated in Porphyry's version since on important points, e.g., the soul-body union, Augustine mirrors the view of Porphyry rather than Plotinus.

confess the mystery on the basis of the *regula fidei*, which for him
is the living tradition of the Catholic Church. Olivier du Roy has
noted three successive phases in Augustine's reflective thought on
the Trinity: the ontological, the analogical, and the anagogical.[3] The
first seeks a trace of the Trinity in the structure of finite being; the
second within the psyche of man; and the third suggests the movement from the trinity in man to the Trinity which is God. These
serve well as three systematic moments in Augustine's trinitarianism
as long as they are not too artificially employed.

The Ontological Trinity

At first, Augustine has no inclinations to explore the immanent
Trinity in itself, his earliest interest being rather to seek some reflection of this inaccessible mystery in finite reality. The participationist
doctrine of the Neo-Platonists, once Christianized to the point where
the One becomes God contemplating the Ideas as the eternal pro-
totypes of temporal realities, means that the world must manifest in
its own structure the secret being of God. Augustine's eye is taken
by the tripartite "measure, number, and weight" of the *Book of Num-
bers* (11:21), which he transposes into the Neo-Platonic categories of
"mode, species, and order."[4] Operative here is a dynamic conception

---

TeSelle also calls attention to the fact that some scholars have professed
to see Augustine's conversion as primarily to Neo-Platonism and only secondarily to Christianity, e.g., Prosper Alfaric, *L'Evolution intellectuelle de S.
Augustin*, 2 vols. (Paris: E. Mourry, 1918). This position gains some plausi-
bility in light of the religious character of Neo-Platonism at this time and
of Augustine's odyssey through such systems as the Academy (represented
by Cicero) and Manichaeism, as well as by the fact that he was a Christian
from birth even if unbaptized. But this is not Augustine's own account of
the matter, even granting that the passages in the *Confessions* are a much
later interpretation of the affair by him. Moreover, it runs counter to the
subsequent course of his life: his immediate baptism, retirement to the sol-
itude of Cassiciacum, profession of celibacy, etc. TeSelle would seem to be
close to the mark in writing: "But to Augustine it now appeared that the
life of philosophy could be pursued only along the path marked out by the
gospel" (p. 40).

[3]*L'Intelligence de la foi en la Trinité selon saint Augustin: Genèse de sa théologie
trinitaire jusqu'en 391* (Paris: Etudes Augustiniennes, 1966), cited by TeSelle,
p. 117, note 25. See also the article by du Roy in *New Catholic Encyclopedia*,
s.v. "Augustine."

[4]*De nat. boni*, 3 (Migne: *PL* 42. 533).

of being reflecting the emanation of everything from the Divine One and the recoil of things to that Source. There is little at any rate of the Aristotelian notion of substance and accidents.[5] He merely means to explain that, once having accepted the revelation of the Trinity, one can discern within temporal reality the formalities of (i) "being" (in its modes determined by God), (ii) "form or structure," and (iii) "inner dynamism or élan." At this point, Augustine makes no attempt to question what the Trinity might be in itself.

The Analogical Trinity

In a subsequent period, after his return to Africa and his ordination in 391 up until about 412 (a period that thus extends into the first stage of his drafting the *De Trinitate*), Augustine re-presents his thought now in the categories of interiority, of conscious psychological experience. It is the mark of Augustine that he subjects everything to the test of experience; if God is to be confessed as threefold this truth must be reflected somewhere within Christian consciousness.[6] He is still seeking traces of the Trinity in the created world, but now within the psyche of man as "made in the image of God."

With this, Augustine introduces his famous development of psychological analogies to the Trinity.[7] Karl Rahner has called Augustine to task precisely here, that is, in beginning not with the divine Trinity revealed within the economy of salvation but with a search for created analogues to the uncreated Trinity. This leads, he maintains, to "an almost mathematically formalized theology of the Trinity by means of what Augustine had developed as a 'psychological' theology of the Trinity."[8] Edmund Hill, however, has rightly taken

---

[5] Aristotle's influence on Augustine is slight; he mentions in the *Confessions* (IV, 16 and 28) only having read the *Categories* at age 20. For that matter, his firsthand acquaintance with Plato was probably limited to the *Timaeus* and the *Meno*.

[6] "Augustinian Christianity furnishes a symbolic language for expressing human experience. . . . It expressed, not any mere theory, but human life itself . . . [thus] in our Western tradition no other thinker can touch the power of the thought of St. Augustine." John Herman Randall, Jr., *Hellenistic Ways of Deliverance and the Making of the Christian Synthesis* (New York: Columbia University Press, 1970), pp. 191 and 189.

[7] *De Trin.*, IX–XI, XIV (Migne: *PL* 42.959ff.).

[8] *Theological Investigations*, vol. 4 (Baltimore: Helicon Press, 1966), p. 85, note 12; *The Trinity*, transl. J. Donceel (New York: Herder and Herder, 1970), p. 18, note 13.

exception to the overly facile and somewhat arbitrary character of this dismissal, noting (i) that the early books of the *De Trinitate* are developed entirely from the New Testament; (ii) that there is a persistence throughout the whole work of the doctrine of the temporal missions; and (iii) that the doctrine of "appropriation" is far more subtle than Rahner allows.[9]

Augustine is now reflecting seriously on what has become universally accepted in East and West as the Nicene doctrine: "three persons of one substance." The role he has assumed, with some reluctance, as a bishop in Africa helps to explain this ecclesial and somewhat conservative approach. His concern at any rate is to explain how it is reasonable to believe that the Three are one. Already in the *Confessions* he had advanced the illustration of being, knowing, and willing.[10] This becomes in the *De Trinitate*: the mind (*mens*), its knowing, and its love; but this quickly gives way in turn to the preferred: memory, knowledge, and love of self (*memoria sui, intelligentia sui, voluntas sui*).[11] Memory here does not mean at all the sense faculty of recall but something closer to self-consciousness or continued presence to self.[12] This is further perfected in a final ascending step into: memory, knowledge, and love *of God*.[13] The insight he is now in possession of is that each of these activities is identical with the one self which is acting and yet relationally distinct from the other two activities. The concept that is given the explanatory role now is that of "relation," something that can account for distinction within an essence without compromising the numerical unity of the latter. The concept had already been subjected to analysis in Books V and VII of the *De Trinitate*. Irénée Chavalier has argued persuasively that Augustine discovered the trinitarian role of "relation" sometime around 413 in reading the Cappadocians,

---

[9] "Karl Rahner's 'Remarks on the Dogmatic Treatise *De Trinitate*' and St. Augustine," *Augustinian Studies*, vol. 2 (Villanova University, 1971), pp. 67–80.

[10] *Confessions*, XIII, 11, no. 12 (Migne: *PL* 32. 849).

[11] *De Trin.*, IX, 4, no. 4 (Migne: *PL* 42. 963).

[12] Augustine would appear to be suggesting here an underlying structure and dynamism of the soul that is conscious but preconceptual; see *De Trin.*, IV, 7. Not to be overlooked here is Augustine's opening the way at this point to conceiving the Holy Spirit in terms of love, not explicitly done before him.

[13] *De Trin.*, XIV, 12, no. 5 (Migne: *PL* 42. 1048) and XV, 20, no. 39 (Migne: *PL* 42. 1088).

most likely Gregory of Nazianzus, and possibly Didymus the Blind.[14] Augustine adopts at this point a procedure of Gregory himself in his polemical writing against the Neo-Arianism of Eunomius. He drops once and for all the misleading categories of "substance," versus "relation" as a mere accident thereof, and casts his thought henceforward in terms of an intrinsic "relationality" as the inner structure of an "essence" that remains one. The Cappadocians, of course, were attempting to explain the divine Trinity, whereas Augustine is still exploring its created analogues. But he is on the verge of saying something more; one intermediate step remains to be taken.

The Anagogical Trinity

The triadic structure discerned at the interior of human consciousness is a facsimile of the divine Trinity, which in typical Augustinian fashion calls for the presence of that Trinity within the soul. From here Augustine moves easily to describe the psychological process of ascending through mystical prayer to contemplative union with the divine Three. He explains this in his own words: "After the inferior image has responded as it were to our interrogation in language, with which our human nature itself is more familiar, we may be able to direct a better-trained mental vision from the illuminated creature to the unchangeable light."[15] Still this ascent of the spirit needs to be freed now from the exclusively intellectualist character it has in Neo-Platonic thought. It is not the upward ascent of the mind alone from a world of appearances to the realm of the subsisting Forms. Its motivating force is not logic but love. Love is the distinguishing mark of the Christian, for "God

---

[14]*Saint Augustin et la pensée grecque: Les relations trinitaires* (Fribourg en Suisse: Collectanea Friburgensia, 1940), pp. 141ff. TeSelle, pp. 294–95, cites this discovery of Chavalier and its confirmation by Berthold Altaner. For the pertinent passage from Gregory of Nazianzus, see *Oratio* 29, 16 (Migne: *PG* 36. 95–96); from Didymus the Blind, see *De Trinitate*, I, 16 (Migne: *PG* 39. 336). Chavalier's thesis would mean a recasting of the *De Trinitate* after 413 in light of Augustine's discovery; thus Books V–VII are of late composition and the analogies in the later books were probably redone. John J. O'Meara has the work finished in a first draft by 406, first released to friends in 416, and appearing in final form in 419; see his *An Augustine Reader* (Garden City, N. Y.: Doubleday Image Books, 1973), p. 252.

[15]*De Trin.*, IX, 12, no. 17 (Migne: *PL* 42. 970).

is love, and he that dwells in love, dwells in God."[16] Such love is capable of bringing the Christian into intimate union with the Three who are God.

Augustine's explanation of how this comes about is ingenious. He tells us that the Christian is enabled to experience within his consciousness this very loving activity itself as a refraction in the soul of God's love for it. The *De Trinitate* distinguishes "love itself" from "he that loves" and from "that which is loved."[17] This amounts to an awareness of the presence of God as the enabling and animating principle of the soul's own loving of God. Characteristically, Augustine's *crede ut intelligas* (not to be confused with Anselm's later *fides quaerens intellectum*) is at work here. Conversion, in the sense of a surrender to the truth already suffused in the soul by God in some primal and undifferentiated way, renders possible an explicit and experiential understanding of the content of such truth. The truth in this case is that taught by the apostle John (*I Jn.* 4:16) that God *is* love: "*Deus caritas est.*" Augustine means to say in effect that the Christian experiences love as the pure gift of God—as grace, thus as a sharing in that love which is proper to God. But to this he now adds his own expanded understanding (not explicit in any Father before Augustine) that such love in God is the Holy Spirit: "We presuppose, however, that the truth itself has persuaded us that, as no Christian doubts, the Son is the Word of God, so the Holy Spirit is love."[18] He has accomplished this by making the created trinity in man of "lover, beloved, and the love that binds them together"[19] function anagogically. To experience our love as divine gift is to experience it as the love that binds together Father and Son. It is in fact to experience, in a mediated way and within the darkness of faith, the Spirit as love in God—not however as essential love, which fails to be distinctive of the persons, but as personal love.[20] Thus,

---

[16]*De Trin.*, VIII, 8, no. 12 (Migne: *PL* 42. 958); Augustine is here citing *I John* 4:16.

[17]*De Trin.*, VIII, 10, no. 12 (Migne: *PL* 42. 960).

[18]*De Trin.*, IX, 12, no. 17 (Migne: *PL* 42. 970); Augustine is here ascribing love to the Holy Spirit by the law of "appropriation"; such love as constituting the very essence of God is equally the prerogative of all three Persons, but the grounds for "appropriating" it to the Spirit lie in the unique relationality of the latter to the Father and the Son, neither of whom are called love in this personal sense. For a clear statement of how "appropriation" functions, see Thomas Aquinas, *Summa theologiae*, I, q. 39, aa. 7 and 8.

[19]*De Trin.*, VII, 10, no. 14 (Migne: *PL* 42. 960).

[20]*De Trin.*, XV, 19, no. 37 (Migne: *PL* 42. 1086).

this uncreated Spirit animates our love, a love that finds cognitive direction in its focus upon the Word become flesh. And finally, since the Spirit already lovingly binds the Son to the Father, he bears us through that Word to loving union with the Source whence that Word is uttered.

Augustine is here anticipating a dominant theme in much of contemporary theology, namely, that God is the implicit and unthematic horizon of human, conscious striving. His earlier development of the theory of divine illuminism serves as an epistemological counterpart to this preunderstanding. He explicitly extends this to our understanding of God in his triunity. Our Christian loving experienced as a unitive force is a faint reflection of the unity of Father and Son in their Spirit. The rectitude and salvific power of such love comes from its object, whose implicit horizon is the Word, giving it the "form" of righteousness. This affords Augustine grounds for inaugurating a transition to the divine Trinity which has "taken up its abode" within the soul, and it introduces his teaching on the temporal "missions." The Father sends the *Logos,* and together they send the Spirit, into the hearts of just men. The Incarnation is merely one very special instance of the first mission made necessary by the sinful alienation of men blinding them to the invisible presence of God and calling for its external manifestation in flesh. The purpose of the invisible missions is the knowing (through the *Logos)* and the loving (through the Spirit) of God, and so the initiation of men into sharing divine life. "For a Divine Person to be sent is to be known and loved,"[21] thus some created human activity of knowing and loving is essential for this new presence, or new mode of being with God. The knowing and loving is "appropriated," respectively, to the Word and the Spirit, but through such activity there is achieved real union with the divine Persons in their personal distinctness, including the Father as the sender of Son and Spirit. On the temporal missions, Augustine is a realist, and the one source on which this conviction rests is God's activity in the history of salvation. The "psychological" doctrine intends to be an analogous explanation of this real Trinity.

The Inner-Divine Trinity

Augustine is now in possession of categories that will enable him to speak not only of the Trinity in the economy of salvation but of

---

[21]*De Trin.,* IV, 20, no. 28 (Migne: *PL* 42. 907).

the Trinity immanent in and identical with the Godhead. He inaugurates then a movement from the Trinity reflected in man's soul
to the Trinity as it is in itself; that is to say, from the uncreated
Trinity as mediated to man's soul through created realities, to the
Trinity in its pure immediacy of uncreated existence.[22] Nevertheless,
his concern remains language about God and not any metaphysics
of divine Being. He has come to understand that the real distinctions
of Father, Son, and Spirit are entirely relational in kind; this involves
understanding that such relationality said of God is without any
connotation of accidentality. Quite simply, God is conceived of as
self-related substance. However, the category of "substance," implying as it does a changeless substratum underlying "accidents," proves
to be less than suitable. Augustine wants to explain that the relationality is not something "within" God but is rather itself constitutive of Divinity. For this, he has recourse to the Latin term *essentia*
which he uses as equivalent to the Greek *ousia*, denoting a principle
of intelligibility or that which answers to the definition of something.
The scriptural names used to designate the Three in God convey
this sense of inner relationality and without any explicit reference
to a sole substance. This is quite clear in the Father-Son formulas;
and though less clear in the case of the Third in God, it does gain
some clarity in speaking of Lover, Beloved, and Love Itself.

At this point it has become clearer to Augustine how one can
speak of plurality within the one God, of Three who are the Divinity. But three what? This is Augustine's own question to himself and
marks the limit to which his own thinking has come. If we ask,
"Three what?" human speech is at a loss, and "if we say three Persons, it is not so much to affirm something as to avoid saying nothing"[23] when the question is put. The explanation for using the category of "person" is simply that the formula of faith in the West,
to which Augustine is loyal, reads "*tres personae unius substantiae.*"
Because Christians profess "three persons" Augustine personifies
the triadic relationality in God. In consequence, he goes on to
describe the Three as subjects, as distinct sources of a single agency.
But the move is dictated by fidelity to the rule of faith and Augustine supplies us with no logical warrant for it in his own theology.
And in fact he makes clear his own mental unease in introducing

---

[22]*De Trin.*, IX, 12, no. 17 (Migne: *PL* 42. 970).
[23]"Dictum est tamen tres personae, non ut illud diceretur, sed ne tace-
retur." *De Trin.*, V, 9, no. 10 (Migne: *PL* 42. 918) and VII, 4, no. 7 and no. 8
(Migne: *PL* 42. 939–41).

personalist categories which raise for him, a Westerner, the specter of Arianism. To forestall any such untoward implications, he hedges by an extensive reliance upon the doctrine of appropriation. The primary emphasis falls on the unity: there is only one divine agency, even while it is true to say there are Three who so act as one. What Augustine's thought means to say is that God is really one subject, one self, who however is self-referencing in his being and acting. This is the basis of Harnack's facile dismissal of Augustine as a modalist. Karl Rahner would also appear to treat Augustine in a somewhat similar cavalier fashion in arbitrarily maintaining that the overriding theme of the *De Trinitate* is a Greek concept of divine unity artificially imposed upon the New Testament data and preventing Augustine, in contrast to the Greek tradition before him, from appreciating the distinctions in God. As Edmund Hill has pointed out, this ignores the almost exclusive reliance upon New Testament texts that characterizes the early books of the *De Trinitate* and the sustained recourse throughout to Augustine's understanding of the temporal missions, as well as the subtlety of his use of appropriation.[24]

Still, it is true that the fullest implications of Augustine's thought are that God is *one* "Person," within whose divine consciousness there is a threefold self-relatedness. He has already grasped that the trinitarian use of the term *personae* conveys relationship, but—proceeding introspectively and using human consciousness as an analogue of divine conscious reality—he understands this as a relationality internal to individual consciousness.[25] What he has not been able to anticipate is how the relationship of one individual consciousness to another or to others might offer an analogue, from the finite human realm, that would more richly illumine the mystery of the Trinity. It is fairly obvious that Augustine would have viewed any thinking in this fashion as tritheistic. And, clearly, the concept of human person—as an individual substance existing accidentally in social relationship with others—cannot be projected onto divinity. Augustine felt no temptation towards such anthropomorphism. But the concept of person is tractable to further refinement, freeing it from these strictures of finitude and endowing it with a flexibility that will allow for the free play of analogical usage. Once achieved,

---

[24]See notes 8 and 9.
[25]For similar suggestions along this line, see A. C. Lloyd, "On Augustine's Concept of a Person," in *Augustine: A Collection of Critical Essays*, ed. R. A. Markus (Garden City, N.Y.: Doubleday Anchor, 1972), pp. 191–205.

such an enriched understanding of person will be able to serve as a corrective model to the cryptomodalism latent (logically, though nonintentionally) in Augustine's trinitarianism.

METAPHYSICS OF NOTIONAL ACT: AQUINAS

The theological work of Thomas Aquinas, marked as it is with the rigorous methodology of the medieval Scholastics, has given rise to some serious misunderstanding concerning the spirit in which he enters upon that enterprise; nowhere is this more patent than in his treatments of the Trinity. This calls for brief explanations of at least three points, by way of supplying a key to the spirit of Aquinas's thought.

Three Methodological Considerations

First of all, his definitive handling of the problem of the Trinity in the *Summa theologiae* is entirely subsequent to a prior consideration of God in the unity of his nature. This has led to the charge that the first *tractatus* constitutes a "natural theology," which prejudices all subsequent reflection upon the Trinity.[26] All recourse to revelation, in the latter endeavor, is evacuated of its genuine illuminative power because the meaning of God's work in history is fitted to the "procrustean bed" of reason. Actually, Aquinas's first attempt to deal with the Trinity implicitly acknowledged this difficulty. In the commentary on the *Sentences* of Peter Lombard, there is no differentiation at all between considering God as One and as Three.[27] Later, in a second attempt in the *Summa contra gentiles,* he opted for a radical separation of the two tracts, treating God as One in Book I and leaving God as Three for Book IV.[28] In both cases, extrinsic factors were determinative: the order already chosen by the Lombard in the *Sentences,* and the audience addressed in the *Contra gentiles,* i.e., nonbelievers. But when free to follow the exigencies of his own notion of the theological task, in the *Summa theologiae,* the result is two sets of questions which, while distinguished, are not separated from one another but coalesce to form one theologically integral

---

[26]See, for example, Karl Rahner, *The Trinity,* p. 16.
[27]*Scriptum super libros Sententiarum,* I, dist. 1–48; written 1252–56.
[28]*Summa contra gentiles,* I, cc. 10–102 and IV, cc. 2–26; written 1259–64.

treatise on God.[29] The order between the two is clear and represents a *démarche* from God under the concept of nature to God under the concept of person(s). But revelation is at work in the earlier treatise as much as it is in the later.[30] The entire work is unified as a summa *of theology*, to which discipline its opening inquiries (on the nature of the theological task and the reality of God) belong; its intelligibility is such (deceptively perhaps) that no one part can be insulated from the whole. What Aquinas seeks out at the very beginning of the work (q. 2) are "ways" (*viae*, not "proofs," "arguments," or "demonstrations") by which the human spirit, in its powers of transcendence, might ascend to an affirmation of God—and in actual fact, that God who has already addressed his Word to man. The move from *essential* unity (qq. 3–26) to *interpersonal* unity (qq. 27–43) acknowledges that the mind grasps the kind of thing something is (its nature) more readily than it does the mysterious subject uniquely existing as an actual instance of that kind of thing (the existent, the person). The former is tractable to the mind's indigenous tendency to grasp in a thematic or conceptual way, whereas the latter seeks the personal encounter which does not yield to conceptual grasp at all because it lies in the existential realm beyond the essential.

Also, this heuristic perspective—that of the continual questing of finite spirit for the *viae* to a God whose reality lies beyond the parameters of the empirical—is not abandoned in turning to the scriptural categories in which God's triunity is brought to language. Rather they are able to be handled critically precisely because some resolution has been reached previously on the problem of how language about the transcendent can in fact signify. Thus Question Thirteen on the Divine Names is worked out in light of revelatory language—about Christ, for example—and offers the foundations

---

[29]*Summa theologiae*, I, qq. 2–26 and qq. 27–43; written 1266–73. The *Quaestio disputata De potentia*, addressing itself in ten questions to an academic disputation on God's power, treats of that power as at once creative and generative; written 1265–66.

[30]*Ipsum esse subsistens* is not a name for God arrived at purely philosophically; it is God's revealed identity coming from Sacred Scripture. Etienne Gilson puts its thus: ". . . le Dieu de la Révélation s'est lui-même offert à la fois sous le nom le plus haut qu'ait jamais osé revendiquer le Dieu des philosophes. La raison le nomme l'être, lui-même enseigne qu'il se nomme qui est." "L'être et Dieu," *Revue Thomiste* 62 (1962), p. 410. One indication of this is Aquinas's ontological interpretation of *Exodus* 3:14; while not the meaning of the text arrived at exegetically, it is *a* meaning, and one consonant with what would have resounded in the Hebrew ear.

for appropriating such terms as "Father," *Logos, Pneuma,* etc. There the *via negativa* is given its due, but as a negating that proves ultimately to be an enrichment rather than an impoverishment because it leads inexorably to a *via affirmativa,* to the positive acknowledgement of God as a *Deus absconditus.*[31] It is not so much that God is unknown as that he is positively known to be unknown and unknowable, i.e., truly transcendent. Thus, decided limits are placed on trinitarian language, but in a preliminary question on God-language.

There is, however, an even more basic explanation for the order between the two treatises. An understanding of what it means to say that God is the Pure Act of Be-ing (the central theme of qq. 3–26) grounds, in a spontaneous move of intelligence, what it can mean to say that God is not a self-enclosed Absolute but a self-communicating tripersonal God (qq. 27–43). The full implications of this will inform a later attempt at a constructive theology of the Trinity (Chapter 9); for now it will suffice to call attention to the fact.

Previous to this is a second problem with St. Thomas's overall methodology, one resident in the genuinely metaphysical character of that theology. His response to the focal question of what "person" as said of God might possibly mean, for example, is profoundly metaphysical (unlike Augustine's, which, as we noted earlier, is left on the psychological level) and to that extent not congenial to contemporary understanding. By contrast, Aquinas himself stands in a tradition of several hundred years that did not conceive of doing theology in any other way. Only since Immanuel Kant have theologians thought it possible to ignore the historical past and build a theology on the immediacy of present experience alone. Quite apart

[31]See *Expositio super librum De causis,* I, lect. 6 (Vivès ed., vol. 26) where St. Thomas explicitly refers to God as *supra ens,* noting that "Dei quidditas est ipsum esse, unde est supra intellectum." W. J. Hoye, *Actualitas Omnium Actuum* (Verlag Anton Hain: Meisenheim am Glan, 1975) observes: "St. Thomas sincerely and literally meant that our ultimate and most perfect knowledge of God consists of knowing that He is completely unknowable ... [and] ... referred to our ignorance in regard to God's essence as itself positive knowledge, a 'learned ignorance'" (pp. 13–14). Similarly, D. Burrell, *Exercises in Religious Understanding* (Notre Dame, Ind.: University of Notre Dame Press, 1974) characterizes Aquinas's methodology as one "asserting what cannot be said of God, and then trying to show how this restrictive predication reveals not deficiency but transcendence" (p. 86). This does not imply that God is utterly unknowable to reason, otherwise man would lack all capacity for revealed knowledge; for the limits to such awareness, however, see *Summa theologiae,* I, q. 12, a. 12.

from this, Aquinas believed man, launched upon a quest for the full intelligibility of the real, to be indigenously metaphysical. So much so, that to fail to be such was to suffer a loss of nerve in the high human endeavor (there is peril in the doing of metaphysics) and to pay the price of shallowness of understanding.[32]

More pointedly, however, is the concern for theology as *real* assent of the intelligence to God. What is real for man is the domain of being, of what "is," and metaphysics was precisely understood as the science of being as such (*ens inquantum ens*). Only out of such thinking could the mind attain to the Creator God, a God of mystery. The metaphysical thought at work here, unlike much of contemporary metaphysics, is not concerned with a formal and conceptual grasp of being. This is exactly what it transcends as *Ta Meta ta Physika.* In its concern for being, it is necessarily existential; the intellectuality at work is not rationalism. A remark by Giles Hibbert, that "the transcendence involved depends upon rather than abstracts from its being rooted in objective reality," is right on the mark.[33] The abstractness of procedure must not be misconstrued: it is not a question of knowledge *of* the abstract, but of abstract (and so penetrating) knowledge of the actual and so the concretely real. Here is found the *point de départ* of that vector of the human spirit that carries it into the presence of the living God, which movement goes beyond concern with mere formal analysis.

What needs to be borne in mind, too, is the unusual employment of metaphysics at work here. What is at issue is not knowledge about the universe of the finitely real but *discourse* about what transcends that world so as to be nowise a part of it. Metaphysical theology (and the metaphysical is only one of the virtualities of theology) does not, as it were, lift the veil on the divinity. Rather, it clarifies the way in which language can be used of a God beyond our reach. But this is not to say that it can content itself with a mere analysis, formal in kind, of language and concept. The nerve of the process is, for Aquinas at any rate, analogy (Question Thirteen again), which allows that theological statements can be not only meaningful but also true. It enables one to maintain that human transcendence, in such utter-

---

[32]One index of this is the endeavor among a considerable segment of English-speaking Protestant theologians to employ a neoclassical metaphysical system, deriving from Whitehead, in the construction of a new theological synthesis.

[33]Giles Hibbert, "Mystery and Metaphysics in the Trinitarian Theology of St. Thomas," *Irish Theological Quarterly* 31 (1964), p. 194, note 20.

ances, is at once apophatic and kataphatic. The elimination of every creaturely mode of signifying (the *modus significandi*) coupled with the retention of the pure intelligibility (the *ratio significata*) as a real perspective onto the Transcendent means that positive affirmations can be made of God by way of a dialectic of negation.[34] An advantage of this is that it precludes any cessation to the cognitive striving of human spirit towards God. Everything that is being said is at the same time being negated, due to the perdurance of the human mode of signifying—without, however, ceasing to be true in its limited way.

If all of this involves recourse to categories of Greek thought, it should be noted that these are not being imposed upon the divine Reality but simply introduced into our talk about that Reality.[35] The borrowing, moreover, is never arbitrary but always under the control of biblical categories and images. And once again the formal content of the concept, its determinateness, is constantly being surpassed—in the dynamism of analogy as an élan of spirit towards the Unknown.

A third and final obstacle to understanding Aquinas's trinitarian theology in its medieval milieu lies in a presupposition native to it. This is the location of the truth-question in faith-confession prior to theological reflection. Theology is the study of God revealed in Jesus Christ. Such revelation is encounter with the Word of God become incarnate and historically mediated in the faith of the believing community. This living presence of God in his Church means that the theologian can work only from within that body which is the Church. Since what is mediated there is not any set of propositions, the theological task is not manipulation of concepts, but encounter with Christ—yet in a properly human way and from within an ongoing historical context. Thomas thus has delivered to him as starting points such expressions as "Father," "Son," "Only-Begotten," "Spirit," "mission," "procession," etc. In the *Contra gentiles,* due to its particular genre, there is a *dogmatic* procedure, i.e., that of appealing to the authority of Scripture and tradition to jus-

---

[34]See W. J. Hill, *Knowing the Unknown God* (New York: Philosophical Library, 1971), chap. 4. The most significant reference to Aquinas is *Summa theologiae,* I, q. 13, a. 3, with the application made in aa. 5 and 6.
[35]Hibbert, p. 201, explains that St. Thomas's treatment of the term "relation" in its trinitarian context "examines and clarifies *a human way of talking about reality* and affirms that, given the theological data, this is a suitable or even necessary way of talking about God."

tify the Church's teaching. But when free to pursue his own chosen methodology, as in the *Summa theologiae,* even this is eschewed, and he embarks directly onto the *systematic* task, that of seeking an understanding of the mysteries. There is no endeavor in any case to prove or demonstrate what can only be believed. It is obvious, for example, that the anthropological insights into finite spirit that illumine the entire trinitarian consideration are not philosophical starting points that establish the fact of immanent processions within God.

All of this is a theological option in marked contrast with a widespread contemporary bias. Schleiermacher's dictum that "the theses of faith must become the hypotheses of the theologian"[36] inaugurates a radically different view of theology. David Tracy has made it his own, certainly implying in *Blessed Rage for Order* that the Christian thinker, precisely as a theologian seeking the scientific foundations for faith, does not proceed on the grounds of his own belief—even though he is bound to consider the Christian texts.[37] On this view, the fundamental loyalty of the theologian is not to any confessional doctrines but to the community of scientific inquiry; secular "faith" is thus normative for religious faith.[38] Aquinas would surely insist that the scientific community is already beholden to the nature and method of its particular discipline, which in this case is a *sacra doctrina,* a holy teaching from God. There are public criteria, but these are to be found in the living Apostolic Tradition rather than in an autonomous natural or secular theology. Fundamental theology can be distinguished from confessional theology—examples of the former being the establishment that God "is," and that the coincidence of his essence with his existence places him beyond our understanding—but even in its fundamental task theology remains a discipline practiced by those enlisted in the ranks of believers. Theology functioning in this manner remains a theology that is something other than philosophy of religion. A reflection of this can be seen in recent tendencies to speak of foundational the-

---

[36]Quoted by David Tracy in *Blessed Rage for Order* (New York: Seabury Press, 1975), p. 45.

[37]Tracy, p. 44.

[38]For a detailed reservation on this basic thesis of Tracy's, see the review article on his book by Avery Dulles in *Theological Studies* 37, no. 2 (June 1976), pp. 304–16, as well as similar cautions by William Shea in another review article in *The Thomist* 40, no. 4 (October 1976), pp. 665–83.

ology (Lonergan's name most readily comes to mind) rather than fundamental theology.

A decided disadvantage with which the more traditional position has to live is that it does constrict the area of dialogue proper to the theologian. But the alternative demands that the Christian *Weltanschauung* give way to the world-view of secularity. Or, at least, it so stresses the continuity between the two views that Christianity offers only one answer, albeit a privileged one, to questions that arise from secular existence. Possibly the difference can be softened in acknowledging that God's address is ingredient in the very questions raised by human existence. At least, with Pannenberg, it can be asked: Does not man "always already stand in the experience of the reality about which he is concerned in his question?"[39] Thus, a genuine doctrine of God "discovers the religious answers which always precede philosophical reflection and which are the first to reveal to it a specifically new understanding of the question of existence."[40] For Aquinas, too, the beliefs which ground theological reflection locate the theologian in a domain of *truth* from the very beginning. This differs, to a degree, from Lonergan's notion of theology as a method rather than a discipline, in which one starts not with truths but with data whose truth has to be critically achieved in a judgment of virtual unconditionedness.[41] A point of convergence undoubtedly lies in Lonergan's acknowledgment that such judgments must use foundational categories achieved in an act of intellectual conversion rooted in a prior religious conversion.

Aquinas characterizes the methodology developed in his *Summa theologiae* as that of a *via doctrinae* in distinction from a *via inventionis*, a way of discovery. The *via doctrinae* is a "way" determined by the known rather than by the exigencies of the knower; such a way is not vitiated by the fact that the known can only be grasped in a manner consonant with the limitations of the knower. His procedure is not that of biblical theology, kerygmatic theology, salvation history, etc. It pursues not a historical order, nor the dogmatic order of magisterial pronouncements, nor an order of doctrinal development, but what is strictly an order of intelligibility within what it seeks to know. An order of intelligibility proceeds from what is most

---

[39]Wolfhart Pannenberg, *Basic Questions in Theology*, vol. 2 (Philadelphia: Fortress Press, 1971), p. 225.

[40]Ibid., p. 226.

[41]Bernard Lonergan, *Method in Theology* (New York: Herder and Herder, 1972).

intelligible in itself and in virtue of its relation to that throws light on all else. But the first intelligible is God insofar as he is the source of all other meaning. Theology thus concerns itself with God in his pure intelligibility, even as it consciously highlights the limited access to the divine afforded man in God's self-communication. True enough, God is only known to us in the *oikonomia,* and so after the temporal missions of the Son and Spirit. But from these temporal missions—the sending of the Son and the gift of the Spirit—Aquinas seeks to reach towards the eternal processions within the Godhead, for in these latter lie the beginning of an understanding, however faint, of the former. The motivation, once again, is not disinterested conceptual or linguistic analysis; it is rather "that we may have the right view of the salvation of mankind, accomplished by the Son who became flesh and by the gifts of the Holy Spirit."[42] Even the most cursory reading does indicate, it is true, an exacting concern for language. However, this is not a pure or formal logic, but one that spontaneously opens the way into ontology; it is an onto-logic. The process is one indigenous to the human mind, at least in Thomistic gnoseology; concepts are not themselves ultimate objects of contemplation but simply mediate contact with the realities they intend.

The import of all that has been said now needs to be shown in the specific instance of Aquinas's theology of the Trinity. The definitive treatment in the *Summa theologiae* brings to light an intelligible order represented by the tripartite move from "processions" (q. 27), to "relations" (q. 28), to "persons" (qq. 29–43). His own thinking, however, arrives at this order only at the end of a far less simple process.

Relation: Beyond Psychology to Ontology

From the tradition, Aquinas inherits the faith formula "Three Persons of One Substance," with the problem this sets of how plurality can be predicated of God (or, as it was more frequently put in the East, how identity can be said of the Three). Standing squarely in the Western tradition, he has already a clue from Augustine (derived in turn from Gregory of Nazianzus): the notion of "relation." But he construes this key to the problem—the notion of inner-relationality—differently; he envisages it on a metaphysical

---

[42]*Summa theologiae,* I, q. 32, aa. 1 and 3.

rather than a psychological plane, or (differently put) he thinks out
its implications on an ontological rather than merely logical level.
Augustine was simply seeking in man's psyche something that might
serve to illumine what was believed of God. What he finds is a
certain threeness (that of *mens, verbum,* and *amor*) that does not
violate an underlying unity; but as noted earlier this does not go
beyond a threefold self-referencing. While this gives a certain dynamism to Augustine's view of the Trinity, it leaves him with the very
real problem he ever remains at a loss to resolve. His analogies,
consequently, have an extrinsic character; their illuminative power
is akin to that of metaphor; what is true of the human psyche suggests in a creative and symbolic way something of what it means to
speak of God as triune. Aquinas deliberately attempts a transition
beyond the psychological processes of the soul to its very beingness.
The resultant relationality is an ontological one, grounded in being
itself as a dynamism and not merely a self-referencing achieved by
way of the soul's activity. The knowing and naming of God moves
in the same direction as it did for Augustine, namely, from revelation about God to the perceiving of analogies in the soul. But behind
the notion of God as Trinity lies the notion of God as the Pure Act
of Being, wherein "to be," "to know," and "to love" coincide in
absolute self-identity.[43] This opens up for Thomas the possibility
that the use of analogy can take upon itself an intrinsic character,
enabling it to serve as an instrument of speech in making assertions
about the intrinsic beingness of God himself.[44] At the same time,
such manner of "saying" retains its strictly analogical character
whereby, in the case of predication about the divine, it is no more
than a human naming of the Unknown. It remains a designating
from the perspective of a creaturely concept of what cannot be represented in the determinateness of any concept.

At this point the only thing clear is that relation helps in understanding how one might speak of plurality in God. For further penetration, Thomas looks to the analysis of that category by Aristotle.[45]
This delivers the insight that relation is not a *tertium quid* mediating

---

[43]Once again, this is not a retrogression to pure metaphysics, but a movement of intelligence seeking understanding under the light of faith; see
note 5.

[44]*Summa theologiae,* I, q. 13, a. 2.

[45]Ibid., q. 28, esp. a. 2; Aristotle's development of relation is found primarily in the *Categories,* with scattered references in the *Physics* and *Metaphysics.*

between two extremes, but an accidental modification within a substance. As an accident, it has no self-sustaining actuality but inheres within a substance as a modification of the being of that substance. Thus, it bespeaks a certain bilateral character: a relation of a subject to some term implies another relation within the term referring it back to the subject. But there is a second feature to relation—not its common feature as accident, but its proper feature as this distinct kind of accident—which consists in a pure ordering of the related subject *to some other* as a correlative. Its distinctive beingness is not some modification of the substance in reference to itself but a pure regarding of, or referencing towards, something else.[46] The concept inseparably involves the two aspects of *esse in* and *esse ad,* i.e., inexistence vis-à-vis some subject and pure order towards some term.

Relation as Constitutive of Person

The analogical projection of such a notion upon God means (i) on the one hand, an absolute identity of the relation with the divine substance since it is unthinkable that anything could accidentally accrue to divine being as an acquisition previously lacking, yet (ii) on the other hand, a pure reference of a relating subject to some other as term to which it is related. It is logically coherent then to speak of subsistent relations within the Godhead, for there is something interior to divine being that is at once *subsistent* (nowise distinct from divinity, save in thought) and *relative* (positing, therefore, another in real opposition). In brief, there is real distinction within God enabling one to speak in plural terms, yet a distinctness that is purely relative in kind (that is, operative only between the correlates) such that each instance of distinction and all of them together are indistinguishable from divinity.

But all of this has not yet broached the question of how these really and mutually distinct relationalities within God answer to the concept of "person"—which is how they are confessed in faith. Clearly, the confessional language cannot mean three consciousnesses, three autonomous instances of divine freedom. This could not be exonerated from the error of tritheism and would be a repudiation of what has just been established, namely, that as subsistent the relations are the self-identical God. It is necessary to avoid

---

[46]Boethius, cited frequently by St. Thomas on this point, designates relation as *ad aliquid,* a translation of Aristotle's πρὸς τί; see *De trinitate,* 4 (Migne: *PL* 64. 1252).

all anthropomorphism, yet there is no way of using "person" apart from some anchorage in the meaning it has as the distinct conscious and free unit within the human community. At the barest minimum this implies a subject of a distinct act of existing. Here, only Aquinas's Christianizing of metaphysics saves him from a covert anthropomorphism. His notion of being is a purely dynamic one; be-ing (hyphenated to emphasize the term's retention of its original participial form) is act; it is the exercise by an existent-subject of its "to be." From this, God's reality is best surmised as the Pure Act of Being, the act of sheer "isness" unreceived by any limiting form or essence. This enabled Aquinas to conceive of the relations, not simply as subsistent, but as subsisting in the mode of subjects exercising that act which is the pure regarding of the other.[47] Such act is identical with that which constitutes the very being of divinity (essential act), but is here grasped as "notifying," as making known, the Persons of the Trinity (thus designated as "notional act"). Clearly enough, it does not mean transitive activity or operation, as in creation when God posits something distinct from himself in being. On these grounds, relation not only *distinguishes* the Three in God, it also *constitutes* them as answering to the notion of subject that is intrinsic to the meaning of personhood.[48] Thinkers earlier than St.

---

[47]This relational distinctness within a common nature is also verified analogously on a radically inferior level, in the case of the distinct persons within one human nature, though here the distinctness is not purely relational but involves as well the individuation coming from quantified matter.

[48]Aquinas's teaching at this point is marked with great subtlety: ". . . paternitas divina est Deus Pater qui est persona divina. Persona igitur divina significat relationem ut subsistentem. Et hoc est significare relationem per modum substantiae quae est hypostasis subsistens in natura divina; licet subsistens in natura divina non sit aliud quam natura divina. Et secundum hoc verum est quod hoc nomen 'persona' significat relationem in recto et essentiam in obliquo; non tamen relationem inquantum est relatio, sed inquantum significatur per modum hypostasis. Similiter significat essentiam in recto et relationem in obliquo, inquantum essentia idem est quod hypostasis. Hypostasis autem significatur in divinis ut relatione distincta. Et similiter relatio per modum relationis significata cadit in ratione personae in obliquo." *Summa theologiae*, I, q. 29, a. 4.
To risk trying to put this simply: person said of God signifies relation (rather than anything absolute), which is a pure order to another (*esse ad*). But the formality of language at work here designates that relation less under the aspect of its actual relating than under the aspect of its subsisting within God (*esse in*). But since what subsists is in fact relation (and thus oppositional) it is simultaneously distinct within God and identical with the divine nature; in a word, it corresponds to what the Greeks tried to convey

Thomas had acknowledged that relation might explain the distinction of the Persons, but they sought the very constitution of such personhood elsewhere.[49] But this resulted in thinking of the Father as a distinct person prior to (in a logical sense) his eternal generation of the Son. Something of this is reflected in the contemporary work of Karl Rahner, who represents the First Person as conceptually identical with the Godhead in a way that Son and Spirit are not.[50] This calls for considerable subtlety if one is to avoid the pitfalls of a covert subordinationism.

It should be noted that Aquinas has, in effect, elevated relation (as identified with person) to the level of the transcendentals. That is to say, it is not used in a generic or specific sense since this would be to introduce determination into God. Rather it marks out the uniqueness characteristic of person, not on the basis of determinacy which would be in fact a limiting, but on the basis of oppositional relationship alone. It is this which enables Aquinas to understand that number said of God (either one or three) is not to be taken as predicamental number based on quantity but as number in a transcendental sense. The import of ontologizing relation should not be missed. It draws attention to the startling insight that at the very heart of being as such, of all being, there resides a mysterious *respectus ad alterum*. A certain inner-relationality is revealed in the depths of reality that is not merely incidental. And, what is more, the inner-relationality is not reducible to mere *essential* otherness.

Relation as Grounded in Knowing-Loving

Further illumination on the character of this "relating act" comes in the realization that God's being is simultaneously a knowing and a loving. But this must be grasped as a pure dynamism (it is act and not static essence); divine being prolongates itself, as it were, by

---

with the term *hypostasis*. One of the implications of this is that it makes it impossible to seek some fourth divine reality, absolute in kind rather than relative, "behind" the Trinity. If the three personal names necessarily connote the nature, we cannot speak of Father, Son, Spirit, *and Nature*. Karl Barth, from an entirely different theological perspective, has drawn attention to the impropriety of such an attempt; see *Die kirchliche Dogmatik*, I/1 (Zurich, 1932), p. 315.

[49]Aquinas had in mind here Richard of St. Victor in his *De Trinitate*, IV, 15 (Migne: *PL* 196. 939); see *Summa theologiae*, I, q. 40, a. 2 and *De potentia*, q. 8, a. 3, obj. 13.

[50]"The Bible and the Greeks would have us start from the one unoriginate God, who is already Father even when nothing is known as yet about generation and spiration." *The Trinity*, p. 17.

inner necessity into self-knowing and self-loving. The knowing is the very being precisely as it is self-expressive (in the case of man, for example, it is possible to conceive his unique mode of being as linguisticality). At its very core, this drive to noetic expression precipitates an "eruption," *un jaillissement,* in which a "word" expressive of all that is known breaks forth in the mysterious fecund power of being and is posited over and against (relative to) that other which is constituted as its "speaker." But this very dynamism itself releases a further *dynamis.* Once distinction is achieved, so that now there are two, being-knowing assumes the further formality of loving. There can be no love, strictly speaking, without the other, the beloved. Still, once there is awareness of some other, love cannot fail to arise on at least some level since it is impossible that the other entirely lack all goodness—otherwise it would be mere nonbeing. Thus, by metaphysical necessity knowledge breaks into love, but paradoxically love is at the same time antithetical to knowledge. The directionality of its dynamism is inverse to that of knowing. Love's élan is not expressive and so not a positing of the "utterance" over and against the one who utters; it is rather unitive in kind and so more a centripetal movement, a return. But the phenomenon of love, too, principles an "eruption" proper to itself in which the lovers bring forth within themselves, as the term of their loving activity, a reality (called by Aquinas the *res amoris*) in which the act of love intrinsically consummates itself.[51] This terminus is a reality insofar as it is a real transformation of spirit, a new and enduring quality of consciousness. It is the *state* of being in love which appears phenomenologically as the habitual affecting of the lover by the beloved, the abiding love-presence of the beloved in the lover. In the divine instance, since the love by which the Father loves the Son and the love by which the Son loves his Father is the same identical love— the "*res amoris*," that which their love spirates forth, is not two, but one. But it constitutes a Third in God, standing in a real relation of opposition to Father and Son. When that relation is grasped as

---

[51] By this he means a reality in the lover precisely as loving. His descriptions of it are varied: it is an *impression* of the beloved in the lover ("quaedam impressio, ita loquar, rei amatae in affectu amantis, secundum quam amatum dicitur esse in amante," *Summa theologiae,* I, q. 37, a. 1); an *inclination* towards the loved (ibid., q. 27, a. 4); an attraction exerted by the beloved on the lover ("perficitur in attractione amantis ad ipsum amatum," *Compendium theologiae,* c. 46); an intrinsic impulse of the lover ("amatum in voluntate existit ut inclinans, et quodammodo impellens intrinsecus amantem in ipsam rem amatam," IV *Summa contra gentiles,* c. 19).

an act of relating, attention is brought to a subject conceived as exercising it; it then appears as interpersonal act and as constituting a third *personal* reality within God.

An analysis of the phenomenon of love makes it clear that the good loved becomes present to the lover in an intentional way proper to love.[52] But if the love is personal (as in the case of the first two Divine Persons) rather than utilitarian in kind, the good of the beloved cannot be absorbed into, and function merely as an increment of, the being of the lover. Rather, the friend is loved precisely for his own sake; he is the other loved in his very otherness. Such love does not subordinate the friend to one's own concerns but "lets him be" in his distinctness from oneself; it even contributes to the constitution of the full personhood of the other. Inversely, the friend assumes the role of a second personality within oneself. This brings readily to mind Augustine's phrase: "Well did one say to his friend 'thou half of my soul.' " The implication of this is that the mutual love of Father and Son, far from being an absorption of each into the other, is the primordial ground of a mysterious creative productivity at the heart of love. Divine love is not a sterile symbiosis of lovers but an élan of perfect life wherein the love itself becomes a reality over and against the lovers with all the density of ontological personhood. This is what is meant in saying that the Holy Spirit is the mutual love of Father and Son, namely, that he is the personal issue of that love in its purely altruistic character.

The contemporary religious mind tends to be baffled by this unembarrassed "metaphysics of faith." Yet, it remains at bottom a *"fides quaerens intellectum."* The understanding is sought in a penetration into the structure of finite spirit and consciousness; the reality of what is to be understood is not found there, but presupposed in the encounter of faith. The twofold dynamism—that of knowing and that of loving—reveals itself as possessing a circular character. The circle closes itself, as it were, so that there is no further procession—and thus no fourth person in divinity. Also, it needs to be borne in mind that the origins of the divine persons are not by way of mere emanations, as if by a process of natural resultancy. What is at issue are true *actions* of God, his eternal acts of self-knowing

---

[52]The presence or union is the affective one proper to love, the moral or intentional dwelling within consciousness that inaugurates the drive towards physical or "real" union. In God, of course, no such real distinction between the intentional and the ontic prevails.

and self-loving. This is necessary in order that the origin of the persons be rooted in the transcendent freedom of God as pure spirit. The generation of the Son and the spiration of the Spirit cannot not be. But they "occur" out of that knowing and loving that constitutes the life of spirit, i.e., as the conscious acts of transcendent freedom. As transcendent, this is not to be confused with election or freedom of choice; it lies beyond all necessity, all contingency, and mere spontaneity. The distinction needs to be maintained, too, between conceiving of these as actions and as processions of the persons; it is the distinction between action in God as essential and as notional. There is no shadow of distinction (other than that due to the process of finite human analysis) between God's knowing and God's loving; both are identically God's being. Neither are real distinctions possible between God's knowing and his being known, his loving and being loved. But the mind's making of these precisions releases an intelligibility whereby being is revealed as possessing an eternal event-like character. Loving is understood as rooted in a *logically* prior knowing, and knowing is understood as rooted in a *logically* prior beingness.

A final illuminative power in this schema lies in its enabling us to understand that—due to the divine "productions," i.e., the origins of the Persons at the heart of the divine knowing and loving—God is not a self-enclosed Absolute but a self-communicating Freedom. The full implications of this come to the fore in realizing how it enables us to think first of creation and secondly of salvation. In the creative act, what St. Thomas has suggested as a circular dynamism *within* God opens itself as the principle of productions of an entirely different kind outside of God.[53] God the Father "prolongates" his utterance of his eternal Word so as to utter man as his finite, temporal, and non-divine "word." Then the Father's loving himself in both his divine Image and his human images is, in effect, a dynamism of reuniting them to himself (without any merging of their identity in his own) in the Holy Spirit. What issues into existence in this "opening of the circle"—which is entirely a matter of God's free election and so need not be at all—are even here principally personal beings, but created rather than uncreated persons. Still, the

---

[53]"Inside" and "outside" here are, of course, metaphors. Indeed, the deepest implication of St. Thomas's understanding of the reality of the finite order is that it exists only "in" God; in the creative act God empties himself out kenotically, as it were, making room "within" himself for the nondivine.

finite human person elicits a circular dynamism of its own in knowing and loving. But there is one major difference. The human person in knowing structures a world around itself, an intentional world arising from within consciousness. Thus, the completion of the circle is in the drive of love out to the realities themselves. Yet the circle does not close there as in the perfect interiority of God; it remains an open circle. The finite character of what is known and loved makes the circle a spiral one, one continually rising upward to God. In the mystery of salvation, granting the alienating consequences of sin, this *exitus* and *reditus* reoccurs on an entirely different plane. Here, the eternal Word and Spirit enter the world in their very uncreated personhoods. At this point, God is not simply the maker of man but becomes man himself; he is no longer simply the lord of history but assumes human history as his own.

In summary, reflection upon the revealed mystery moves, within the originating psychological process of St. Thomas's own thinking, from the concept of "persons" (received in faith), to that of "relations" (as explanatory of distinction), back to that of "persons" understood now as subsisting subjects of such relationary act, and lastly to a grasp of such notional act as "processions," grounded in the essential acts of knowing and loving proper to the Pure Act of Be-ing. But the construction of the *Summa theologiae*, informed by the *via doctrinae* as an order of intelligibility, inverses this previous order of discovery. There, a consideration of God's essential being (one that begins and remains under the light of faith) consummates itself in a logically subsequent consideration of God's interpersonal being. And within the latter investigation the order is: (i) processions, (ii) relations, and (iii) persons.

At bottom, Aquinas's trinitarianism is a variation on Augustine's focal concept of relational unity. Augustine's own thought suffered the limitation of emasculating "person" of any real import when said of God in the plural. The advance consists in Aquinas's explaining how "person" can be said of *mens*, *verbum*, and *amor*, not as a mere accommodation but as something bearing ontological density. However, this represents a deliberate option on the part of Thomas. In making it, he is rejecting the Dionysian schema whose *point de départ* is a notion of the First Person in God as *"fons divinitatis."* This allows Pseudo-Dionysius to view the Father as person in a way not readily extended to the *Logos* and *Pneuma*. The deepest instinct in such thought is Neo-Platonic; the Trinity is explained on the basis of emanations from the Father who is acknowledged to be God prior (conceptually) to his giving origin to Son and Spirit. Unity in God

is then explained by a "reduction" of the Second and Third Persons
to their Unoriginate Source. The unity is hierarchical rather than
purely relational—a mode of thinking betrayed in the very title of
the writings of Pseudo-Dionysius: *De Hierarchia*. This approach
enjoyed an ascendency in the Eastern tradition. It does rich service
to the salvational import of the mystery. Its limitations, as a theological explanation, lie in the direction of an "Economic Trinitarianism," or more consistently perhaps, a crypto-subordinationism.
The former tends to regard God as a Father holding out to the
world his Son and Spirit as the two "arms" of divinity; the latter
runs the risk of diminishing the full divinity of the *Logos* and
Pneuma. The contrast with Western theology—owing what it does
to Augustine and Aquinas—is perhaps most graphically seen in the
Filioque controversy, a doctrine integral to Western tradition but
fiercely resisted in the East.[54]

LOVE AS SOCIETAL: THE INFLUENCE OF RICHARD OF ST. VICTOR

What Aquinas's thought did have to contend with, nonetheless,
was the cryptomodalism latent in the earlier work of Augustine.
This did in fact bring him closer to the Dionysian tradition, but as
mediated by a Western and medieval thinker. The most significant
development, in the long period between Pseudo-Dionysius and
Augustine on the one hand and Aquinas on the other, was that
achieved by Richard of St. Victor. It is Bonaventure who will bring
Richard's vision to full intelligibility in the thirteenth century, but
his influence is felt by Aquinas also. Richard's *De Trinitate* begins
with God in the oneness of his nature, but stresses love as the most
distinctive and identifying trait of that nature.[55] Uppermost, almost

----

[54]The teaching that the Holy Spirit is from the Father alone and not
from the Son also is first made into a controversial issue by Photius in the
ninth century, after the unauthorized insertion of *filioque* into the Creed on
the part of the Western Church in Spain; it was definitively reintroduced
by Michael Cerularius in the eleventh century. Concord was reached in the
two so-called reunion councils—Lyons II in 1274 and Florence in 1439—
but the agreement was only theoretical in kind and never accepted in practice by the Orthodox Church. At Florence, St. Thomas's strong endorsement of the Greek formula "from the Father, through the Son" played a
considerable role in the theoretical resolution.
[55]*De Trinitate*, III, 1, 2, and 11 (Migne: *PL* 196. 915, 916, and 922).

surely, is the inspiration of St. John's "God is love." But, with some originality, Richard notes that love is a tending to the other; by its very nature it demands the other, and in God this can only be the infinitely lovable other, i.e., another within God. If love of desire (*amor concupiscentiae*) only demands another thing, love of friendship (*amor benevolentiae*) demands another person. Thus, there must be at least two who constitute the Godhead. But perfect love of friendship in fact involves a third. This is rooted in the altruistic character of pure love, which eliminates every trace of selfish satisfaction. The lover seeks a third to share the regard in which he beholds the beloved and to be regarded by the beloved as the beloved is regarded by him. Here lies unveiled the character of love as social. The Divine Society terminates at Three, since anything more would be superfluous. But this opens the way to further created societies.

The import of this remarkable thought is not lost on Aquinas. Its clearest reflection is found in his adoption of the Victorine principle that the Holy Spirit proceeds from the mutual love of Father and Son, a principle at odds with the more Dionysian tendency to view the love in question as essential rather than notional.[56] But Richard's theory fails to sustain itself; it reaches a point where its underlying Neo-Platonic character precipitates a collapse back into the trinitarianism of Pseudo-Dionysius. Love demands plurality as a precondition of its occurrence; it does not explain this societal beingness in the first place. But goodness does—because of its self-diffusive character. Here the Victorine has recourse to what functions as a first principle determining all else: *bonum diffusivum sui*. But this diffusiveness has as its primordial source the fecundity of the Father who is (once again) the *fons divinitatis*. If, for Richard, the divine persons are distinguished by their relations (of love), they are constituted rather by their origins. The Father's personal identity then lies precisely in his lack of origin, in his "*innascibilitas*."

From all that has been said, it is clear that Thomistic speculation on the Trinity did not follow this more basic movement in Victorine theology. Aquinas does accept the principle of *bonum diffusivum sui*, but this mysterious *jaillissement* surges up out of God's essential being and not out of that being as in a purely relative distinctness it constitutes a primal Divine Personhood. There was an enrichment coming from Richard of St. Victor, but what was borrowed was rethought in the perspective of a quite different theological wisdom.

---

[56]". . . the Father and the Son, by the Holy Spirit or Love proceeding, are said to love both each other and us." *Summa theologiae*, I, q. 37, a. 2.

PART TWO

FOREGROUND
Theology Speaking in the Present

[4]
THE TRINITY OF
RELIGIOUS SYMBOLISM
The God of Liberalism

The rupture between East and West in the Church during the Great Schism of the ninth and eleventh centuries, turning as it did on the *Filioque* controversy, underscored the unquestioned prominence given to the doctrine of the Trinity. The major theological differences of the Reformation during the sixteenth century are fully intelligible only if one acknowledges the common confession of the Trinity as a nonnegotiable stance above the disputes. A notable exception to this arose when the Reformational principle of *sola Scriptura* was carried to antitrinitarian extremes in the movements of Socinianism, Arminianism, Moravianism, and less explicitly, in Pietism generally. Still, these were precisely exceptions departing from a tradition common to Catholicism, Greek Orthodoxy, and the founders of the Evangelical and Reformed Churches. But all of this changed radically with the dawn of modernity, in the intellectual upheaval precipitated by the Enlightenment. Prior to this, the Trinity enjoyed a position of centrality in Christian theology, subordinate only to the doctrine of Christ—a significance it had acquired in the period immediately subsequent to that of the New Testament. The decline can be traced to the late Middle Ages when the mystery was eviscerated of all dogmatic import and relegated to the domain of piety and devotion. There were some attempts to appropriate the mystery for Christian thought, but these were lacking in creativity and tended to be "speculative" in the pejorative sense of the word, that is, characterized by an abstract and cerebral formalism that undercut the salvational import of the doctrine and so its *essential* relationship to faith. But it was the aftermath of the Enlightenment that saw the Trinity finally dislodged from its position of doctrinal centrality; thenceforward theology pursues it as either a postscript to Christian faith of merely historical or antiquarian interest, or as a mental construct that is not an essential ingredient of faith itself even if it serves a certain utilitarian purpose in giving expression to what is of faith.

THE SPECULATIVE TRINITY: FRIEDRICH SCHLEIERMACHER

The pivotal figure in the Romantic reaction against the impact of the *Aufklärung* upon Christian thought is Friedrich Schleiermacher (+1834). His contribution, where the doctrine of the Trinity is concerned, was radical indeed; in authoring an original system of dogmatics in *The Christian Faith*,[1] he simply excluded the Trinity altogether. He chose to deal with the mystery in a summary at the end of the book in the form of an appendix and not as something belonging properly to dogmatics itself.[2] No matter how elaborately worked out, "such a doctrine of the Trinity . . . could find no place in a Christian Dogmatic. . . . We should firmly maintain that as a doctrine it was different . . . [and] . . . of no sort of use in Christian doctrine."[3] Schleiermacher, skeptical of both authority and reason, attempted to reach behind the Christian texts (the New Testament, the Fathers, and the Councils) to their common experiential ground. This led him to view the Trinity as not itself one of the elements of that experience, but as a second-level construct that merely synthesized in a useful way the various components that did constitute the experience. It is thus an instance of speculation, and even of bad speculation insofar as it was an attempt to probe the inner being of God, his aseity. His inclusion of the doctrine in a summary is indication that Schleiermacher did not oppose speculation as such but only its confusion with dogmatics. In fact, his understanding of the theological enterprise pivots on the move from dogmatics viewed as a historical and orthodox study of the actual belief of the community to philosophical theology viewed as a speculative and hermeneutical task which aims at heterodoxy (in Schleiermacher's nonpejorative use of that term).

---

[1] *Der christliche Glaube*, first published in 1821; an English translation, *The Christian Faith*, of the second German edition by H. R. Mackintosh and J. S. Stewart appeared in 1928 (Edinburgh: T. & T. Clark; newly available, Philadelphia: Fortress Press, 1976); citations to follow are from the Harper Torchbook edition, 2 vols. (New York and Evanston, Ind.: Harper and Row, 1963).

[2] "But the assumption of an eternal distinction in the Supreme Being is not an utterance concerning the religious consciousness, for there it could never emerge. Who would venture to say that the impression made by the Divine in Christ obliges us to conceive such an eternal distinction as its basis?" *The Christian Faith,* vol. 2, no. 170, p. 739.

[3] Ibid., p. 741.

What Schleiermacher is least disposed to allow is that the Trinity could function as a point of departure for affirming the central truths of Christian experience. Albrecht Ritschl (+ 1889), whose *The Christian Doctrine of Justification and Reconciliation* came to supersede Schleiermacher's influence, opposes even the speculative interest in the Trinity shown by Schleiermacher. He offers only peripheral references to the doctrine, which plays no significant role at all in his system. Returning to a more markedly Kantian position and so a more pronounced agnosticism, he views the Trinity as an instance of a disinterested theoretical knowledge that stands at a remove from genuine religious knowledge. The latter is characterized by its involvement with value judgments, and locating the Trinity entirely outside that sphere means that it is no longer regarded as a mystery of salvation. Adolf von Harnack (+ 1930), after detailed investigations into the development of the Trinity in his influential *History of Dogma*, dismisses it as without foundation in the New Testament, declaring in *What Is Christianity?* that Jesus' message is only of God as a Father of all men and not of himself as the Son of God. Schleiermacher's thought, with its focus upon Christ's awareness of the Absolute present to his consciousness—and even more Ritschl's, with its emphasis upon ethical endeavor in the building of the Kingdom—understandably led to the quest for the historical Jesus. The New Christology called into question the Christology of Chalcedon and put into disuse the trinitarianism that had found expression in the Creeds. An attempt to recover the weightiness of credal trinitarian language would begin only with Karl Barth in the 1920s, after the rediscovery of the eschatological dimension in the New Testament by Johannes Weiss and Albert Schweitzer.

Schleiermacher's thinking was done in the shadow of Kant, whose two *Critiques*, curtailing as they did the power of reason, had actually signaled an end to the *Aufklärung*. But Kant's agnostic spirit did not so much check the excessive encroachment of reason into the domain of faith as banish reason from it entirely; in the end his thought served only to widen the chasm between Christian belief and what had now become the autonomous realms of nature and history. Schleiermacher saw his task as one of finding a common denominator for the two *Critiques*, of uniting again the domains of thought and action. Quite simply, he looked for a source of unity transcending the dualism of spirit and nature. Due to his commitment to a philosophy of consciousness, to a marked preference for the categories of subjectivity inherited from Kant, he finds this (in his *Dialektik*, published posthumously in 1839) not in God but in religion itself. Midway between the determinations of thought by its own a priori structures and practical reason's determination of its own world, there arises from within consciousness an instinct (*Gefühl*) of belonging to the whole in which these opposites are reconciled. Schleiermacher discovered God as the Ground of the world which discloses itself in terms of the tension between spirit and nature. But it is not the reality of God that takes his attention; it is the felt relationship to God of consciousness. This relationship he most frequently described as a primordial sense of dependence upon the Absolute which otherwise remains hidden.[4] It is something indigenous to finite consciousness, functioning as the precondition for both thought and willing. Simply put, it is "feeling," by which Schleiermacher means not psychological emotion but something closer to intuition, meaning an intuition of the Absolute that is indigenous to self-consciousness. Unlike knowing and willing, it is objectless, but in such wise as to call attention to the original unity from which all subject-object dichotomies emerge.

Behind Schleiermacher's thought lies a philosophy of dialectical identity, inherited from Hegel. It enables him to understand that, in feeling, self-consciousness is made aware of its oneness with all reality. Differently put, this means that through feeling self-consciousness is disclosed as grounded in God. This awareness of God is not by way of inference but is a direct awareness in which God is surmised as the Whence of things. This is not yet the later, fully objective grasp of God in concept or symbol, because as feeling it remains without any object in the sense of an objectification as "other." And, seemingly, this rescues Schleiermacher from the charge of pantheism that has been leveled at him, since God is not world but the Whence of the world. What Schleiermacher intends by "feeling" then is something strongly suggestive of the inner nameless compulsion that animated the Pietist movement, which could not have failed to influence him during his early Moravian education, and to which he refers much later in one of his letters, writing, "I have become a Moravian again, only of a higher order."

This "feeling" for the Absolute as ground of nature and spirit meant an understanding of God as working within time so that history could no longer be left as an autonomous realm (as the

---

[4]First expressed in *On Religion: Speeches to Its Cultured Despisers,* English translation by J. Oman (New York: Frederick Ungar, 1955). This is characterized in the introduction to *The Christian Faith* (vol. 1, no. 4) as a "feeling" (*Gefühl*) of absolute dependence, whose religious modification is "piety" or "God-consciousness."

Deists of Schleiermacher's time sought to do). Unlike his predecessor, Fichte, Schleiermacher refused to sublimate history into a metaphysical system. Rather, choosing Johann Herder over Kant in this matter, he understands history as the unfolding of the purposes of the Absolute in the world. Consciousness is thus historical consciousness; or put differently, history is the development of spirit, which at bottom is mankind's sense of the active presence of God. This consciousness of the active presence of God in and through history becomes manifest in a privileged way in Christ and in the Church. What the early Church understood as the divinity of Christ was thus his intense subjective awareness of the presence of God at work within him. Christian faith is the recognition and acknowledgment of the correspondence between the experience of Jesus and what we ourselves experience, though deficiently, in the depths of our consciousness. This revised Christology meant necessarily a revised trinitarian theology. Thus, Schleiermacher understands "Son of God" as only the believer's way of designating Jesus' own privileged awareness of the divinity present within his consciousness. To speak of his divine nature is "exceedingly inconvenient," for it is "the God-consciousness in Him [that]. . . must be regarded as a continual living presence, and withal a real existence of God in Him."[5] Correspondingly, he understands "Spirit" as a parallel way of designating a similar consciousness within the Christian community, one mediated in the prior manifestation of that consciousness by Christ. The Holy Spirit is "the common spirit of the new corporate life founded by Christ"; and other thought-forms "ought none of them to be taken as equivalent to New Testament statements, which as a matter of fact represent the Holy Spirit as always and only in believers."[6] The Trinity, then, is a Christian doctrine "not like the other doctrine" (that of Christ) in that it only summarizes on a secondary level the three confessions: about Christ, about Spirit, and about the Absolute.

Obviously, Schleiermacher is saying nothing about the inner being of God himself, a venture he views as presumptuous. Even the attributes traditionally ascribed to the divine nature cannot in fact be predicated of God, much less the trinitarian distinctions. We must content ourselves with knowing only that God is absolutely simple (though he offers no explanation for this one exception to Kantian

---

[5] Ibid., no. 96, 3, p. 397.
[6] Ibid., no. 121, 1, p. 560 and 2, p. 562.

agnosticism). But the trinitarian distinctions are even contradictory
to this assertion of divine simplicity:

> The ecclesiastical doctrine of the Trinity demands that we think of
> each of the Three Persons as equal to the Divine Essence, and vice
> versa, and each of the three Persons as equal to the others. Yet we
> cannot do either the one or the other, but can only represent the Per-
> sons in a gradation, and thus either represent the unity of the Essence
> as less real than the three Persons, or vice versa.[7]

This ceases to be a problem, however, as soon as one realizes that
these are symbols which refer neither to the divine reality nor to
our immediate knowing of what is actual for faith; they belong
rather to the sphere of speculation. Coming out of a philosophical
background that lends itself to Idealism, Schleiermacher means by
"speculation" the grounding by thought of what is actual (in this
instance, the God-consciousness given in our self-consciousness) in
terms of pure possibility. The Trinity, then, is a speculative construct
supporting what is actual for faith, namely, the dialectical relationship between finite consciousness and Infinite Consciousness. It is
not at all indispensable to faith and cannot at any rate be transposed
into a dogmatic formula. Schleiermacher, after all, cannot allow that
man can know God as an object, for then God would be finitized
and lose all character as absolute. In short, a way to God other than
that afforded by feeling would be available. Such objective knowledge is rather characteristic of beliefs, all of which are secondary to
and derivative from feeling. Dogmatic statements, then, are statements about states of soul, about our felt relationship to God, not
about God himself. Some doctrines are descriptive of our inner
experience and so arise in a more or less immediate way, such as
that concerning the God-consciousness of Christ. But Schleiermacher is not nearly so sanguine about other doctrines that he views
as at a further remove from the doctrine about Christ's person, for
example Christ's preexistence, his Resurrection, Ascension, and Parousia. At any rate, the Appendix to *The Christian Faith* explicitly tells
us that the Trinity is a doctrine of the second rank because it does
not form part of the belief that God was in Christ. Still, Schleiermacher's genuine meaning should not be lost here: the Trinity safeguards the truth that nothing less than God himself is in Christ and
Christians.[8] It is in this sense that he calls it the "coping stone" of

---

[7] Ibid., no. 171, p. 742.
[8] Ibid., no. 172, 1, pp. 747–48.

Christian doctrine and undoubtedly here his thought approximates that of primitive Christianity, justifying his citation of the Pauline "God was in Christ" and the Johannine "the Word became flesh."

But why at this point is Schleiermacher adamant in not allowing the doctrine of the Trinity to be extrapolated into a doctrine of the inner-divine Trinity? Seemingly, his governing principle of the divine-human relatedness suggests the reasonableness of such a move. Instead he wants to retain Christology as central to his system, but a Christology without a Trinity. The explanation would seem to lie in Schleiermacher's unqualified emphasis upon the absoluteness of God. The immanence of God to finite consciousness is no compromise of that absoluteness; the relatedness so operative elsewhere in his thought is never a relatedness in God himself. Far from being a coprinciple with the creature (as in contemporary process theology), God is the ground of a relationship which is actual on the side of the creaturely awareness. The anthropological shift has occurred significantly in Schleiermacher's theology, and the reason for it is the priority given the principle of God's total otherness and inaccessibility. Once God is conceived of as Ground already undergirding everything, it makes no sense to conceive of him as self-communicating. Thus, God as Absolute stands in opposition to God as Trinity; God as Ground is not processive or self-communicating and to that extent is a self-enclosed Absolute. At this juncture it becomes questionable if Schleiermacher does full justice to the personal character of God; Ritschl's theology at any rate appears to offer a corrective to this. Also, Schleiermacher's refusal to take exception to the term "pantheism," as long as it is used in its loftiest sense, now becomes a bit more understandable.

The import of this anthropological turn in Schleiermacher's theology is that finite spirit is viewed as subscending to its Ground in an attempt to overcome its opposition to nature. The knowing which issues from this thus takes upon itself the character of a continuous symbolizing of a fundamental sense of primordial identity that is at the base of religion.

These emerging symbols are first of all relegated to the periphery of faith by Schleiermacher. But then, especially in light of the principle that God unfolds his purposes in time, they are seen as subject to a process of continual reinterpretation. If God is already the Ground of all that is, the traditional understanding of the Parousia makes little sense; the Fall gains in meaning when understood as man's willful state of refusing the development of God-consciousness to which he is summoned; the Resurrection can become a symbolic way of appropriating Christ's own triumph and his enduring influence upon Christians.[9]

What delivers such conclusions to Schleiermacher is, at bottom, the methodological principle at work in his theology. Basing everything on present experience means dismissing any theory of verbal inspiration, and so of infallibility, where the New Testament is concerned. In short, what is decisive for Schleiermacher is a new concept of revelation, one that relativizes all language expression by way of image or concept, and opens the way to a modern understanding of hermeneutics. Aiding this was the tendency already underway at this time to discount the historicity of the Fourth Gospel; obviously this undercut much of the earlier basis for the trinitarian doctrine. Schleiermacher expressly refers with approval to the formula of Sabellius in which the symbol of the Trinity is seen as expressing three successive phases in the God-man relationship.[10] He suggests that it might "render us equal service" in comparison with the Athanasian hypothesis. But Schleiermacher alters it to mean not three phases of divinity itself (Sabellius's own intention) but three phases of God's coming to manifestation within our consciousness. It is difficult to see this as anything other than a trinity of finite knowing, granting nonetheless its basis in the revelatory action of God. In the final analysis, then, Schleiermacher's trinity is found, not in God, but within finite conscious knowing.

There is, however, another dimension of meaning intended by Schleiermacher in his essay on Sabellius and Athanasius that should not be overlooked here. If the trinitarian symbols are basically symbols of our felt relationship to God, they remain in an important sense symbols *of God himself*—not in the sense of bespeaking real distinctions within the Godhead, but in the sense of expressing a dialectical identity between the hidden God (*Deus in se*) and the revealed God (*Deus pro nobis*). This is the meaning Schleiermacher comes to give to the *homoousios* of Nicaea, namely, that God is one

---

[9]Ibid., no. 99, 1–2, pp. 417–24; on the Fall, vol. 1, no. 72, 1–6, pp. 291–304.

[10]Ibid., vol. 2, no. 172, 3, p. 750; also "On the Discrepancy between the Sabellian and Athanasian Method of Representing the Doctrine of the Trinity," *The Biblical Repository and Quarterly Observer* 5 (1835), pp. 265–353 and 6 (1835), pp. 1–116, translation by Moses Stuart of "Ueber den Gegensatz zwischen der Sabellianischen und der Athanasianischen Vorstellung von der Trinität," *Sämtliche Werke*, 31 vols. in 3 parts (Berlin: G. Reimer, 1835–64), 1.2.

(*homoousios*) with his revelation in Jesus and in the Christian community; in the Son and the Spirit we experience nothing less than the very presence of God.

Still, in the end, the Trinity represents less a divine reality confessed than a symbol of faith itself. Schleiermacher, of course, lacked any developed theory of symbol, but he prepared the way for what was to come. Paul Tillich is perhaps preeminent among modern theologians who have pursued that way.

THE TRINITY AS COGNITIVE SYMBOL: PAUL TILLICH

Schleiermacher's influence, as the father of Liberal Theology, upon succeeding thinkers would be well-nigh impossible to exaggerate. It has been so all-pervasive as to establish not a school at all but a movement. Karl Barth assigns him "the first place in a history of the theology of the most recent times," noting that Emil Brunner in 1914 was the first to depart from his premises.[11] In Catholic theology, to take a quite different illustration, Bernard Lonergan's increasing emphasis upon conversionary experience as the wellspring of authentic theological endeavor is intellectually cognate to it.[12] Claude Welch has noted the considerable number of those who have accepted and furthered the implications of Schleiermacher's reduction of the Trinity to a doctrine of the second rank.[13] Notable among these is Brunner, who in spite of repudiating Schleiermacher's methodology remains a true continuer of him in describing the Trinity as a "defensive doctrine," a mental construct at one remove from what faith essentially confesses and formulated not as expressive of any truth of its own but to give extrinsic rational support to the truth that God is in Christ. A.C. Knudson's *The Doctrine of God*, published in 1930, makes explicit what is a primary implication in Schleiermacher's own work when he (Knudson) writes that the Trinity is a "category of the finite mind," not at all essential to

---

[11]*Protestant Thought* (New York: Simon & Schuster, 1969), pp. 306ff. This is a translation by Brian Cozens of the first eleven chapters of *Die protestantische Theologie im neunzehnten Jahrhundert* (Zollikon-Zurich: Evangelischer Verlag, 1960).

[12] See his *Method in Theology.*

[13]*In This Name: The Doctrine of the Trinity in Contemporary Theology* (New York: Charles Scribner's Sons, 1952), esp. chap. II.

Christian faith; "a symbol constructed by human understanding as an attempt to express the nature of divine love," of practical value insofar as it "dramatizes the divine love," which it does by expressing the "Christlikeness of God."[14] But the spirit of Schleiermacher's trinitarianism comes to fullest flower in the theological work of Paul Tillich.

Paul Tillich's Dialectical Humanism is developed in the context of German Transcendentalism; its starting point being reason's move beyond the subject-object dichotomy to the ground of being and meaning, which reveals itself as what ultimately is mystery made manifest in the revelatory situation. This marked proclivity towards existential philosophy expresses itself especially in the pronounced distinction between essence and existence.[15] The former remains abstract and ideal and represents (somewhat as it does for Feuerbach) the realm of the possible; only in Jesus the Christ has that essence come to full realization. Existence, by contrast, represents concrete humanity in its actual condition of estrangement from the realization of its ideal essence. This polarity, experienced in all of human life, is intensified in the encounter with Christ. But prior to that it already characterizes man's posing of the very question of God.[16] This means simply that man experiences a tension between, on the one hand, thinking of God as abstract and one in essence, and on the other, as concrete and plural within the conditions of actual life. This tension is overcome by a synthesis which conceives

---

[14]Albert C. Knudson, *The Doctrine of God* (Nashville: Abingdon Press, 1930), quoted by Welch, pp. 54–56.

[15]Paul Tillich, *Systematic Theology*, 3 vols. (Chicago: University of Chicago Press, 1951–63); "True being is essential being and is present in the realm of eternal ideas, i.e., in essences. In order to reach essential being, man must rise above existence. He must return to the essential realm from which he fell into existence. In this way, man's existence, his standing out of potentiality, is judged as a fall from what he essentially is. The potential is the essential, and to exist, i.e., to stand out of potentiality, is the loss of true essentiality." *Systematic Theology*, 2:22.

[16]"The question of God is possible because an awareness of God is present in the question of God. This awareness precedes the question. . . . It shows that an awareness of the infinite is included in man's awareness of finitude. Man knows that he is finite, that he is excluded from an infinity which nevertheless belongs to him. He is aware of his potential infinity while being aware of his actual finitude. If he were what he essentially is, if his potentiality were identical with his actuality, the question of the infinite would not arise." Ibid., 1:206.

God as triune, and thus the doctrine of the Trinity is introduced.[17] The Trinity is not an immediate datum of faith but only expresses the precondition for faith, which admits of formulation in ways other than the trinitarian.

The origin of the trinitarian doctrine involves an ambivalent movement of understanding, one that runs simultaneously in opposite directions. As a confession of Christian faith it begins with the *Logos* doctrine.[18] Thus, once Jesus is called the *Logos*, Tillich allows that the Trinity becomes a matter of concern for human existence. Christ is the Word of God to us because he is the essence of manhood under the conditions of existence.[19] It is in this sense that he is divine; insofar as in his human essence he is dialectically one with the essence of God. Though he concretely exists, Christ does not belong to the sphere of existence at all, for he is nowise estranged from God. Human essence, bracketed from the alienating conditions of existence, is essentially one with the divine.[20] Christ's relationship with God is more a unity than a union, in the sense that the essential form of humanity is precisely identity with the *Logos* as the structural principle within divinity. This essential oneness with God is no absorption of the humanity by divinity but rather the giving to the former of its own true essence; moreover, it comes about only due to the gracious activity of God, bringing about the New Being. It is on such grounds as these that Tillich's Christology is frequently looked upon as approximating classical Nestorianism. This is somewhat misleading, however, because it means the imposition upon

---

[17]". . . the need for a balance between the concrete and the absolute drives him [man] toward trinitarian structures." Ibid., 1:221. "The trinitarian problem is the problem of the unity between ultimacy and concreteness in the living God." Ibid., 1:228.

[18]"Any discussion of the *Christian* doctrine of the Trinity must begin with the Christological assertion that Jesus is the Christ" (emphasis in the original). Ibid., 1:250.

[19]"The paradox of the Christian message is that in *one* personal life essential manhood has appeared under the conditions of existence without being conquered by them." Ibid., 2:94.

[20]Tillich repeatedly makes clear that the relationship between God and man is not that of an absolute distinction but of a correlation. Essential humanity includes the divine, so that the mystery in the Incarnation is not the *essential* unity of the divine and human (this is already given in the dialectic of infinite and finite) but its *historical* achievement; see Donald J. Keefe, *Thomism and the Ontological Theology of Paul Tillich* (Leiden: E.J. Brill, 1971), p. 258.

Tillich's thought of categories that are alien to it, an imposition that displaces the intelligibility he intends with his own categories. The intelligibility it does seek to express is nonetheless different from that intended by the Chalcedonian formula, particularly as it gained systematic expression in the thought of Thomas Aquinas. There, the human and the divine, retaining their essential differences, were united in the sphere of existence, in a union by way of *hypostasis*.[21] Here, in Tillich, existence denominates man's ontological state of alienation from his true essence, which already belongs to the sphere of the divine. The trinitarian formula is merely a way of stating this essential oneness of man's true nature with God, as already achieved in Christ under the conditions of temporal existence.

But simultaneous with this is a movement of understanding which is inverse in its direction, a shuttle of thought running from God to the Christ-experience. There is a presupposition to the *Logos* confession which is the awareness of God as Spirit,[22] an awareness that while readily made explicit within Christian belief is not in itself exclusively Christian. Man himself in his existentiality is the *question* about God. The answer to that question, by contrast, is not derivable from man's nature or his history, but is constituted by the response of God.[23] This is Tillich's principle of correlation, the basic operative principle in his theology. This revealing act of God's, available only to faith, is the unveiling to man of his own true essence. But God's response is dialectical in that it takes up both man's question and his projected answers, negating the latter in order to respond by way of a synthesis. God's revelation as synthesis is the revelation of himself as Spirit, that is to say, of himself as reconciling and uniting opposites. Spirit in God here takes to itself the character of love, albeit love in its human form as (Hegel-like) it strives for unity. This divine synthesis as the overcoming of the existential dichotomy of

---

[21]See *Summa theologiae*, III, q. 2, aa. 1–3.

[22]"The situation is different if we do not ask the question of the Christian doctrines, but rather the question of the *presuppositions* of those doctrines for an idea of God. Then we must speak about the trinitarian principles, and we must begin with the Spirit rather than with the Logos. God is Spirit, and any trinitarian statement must be derived from this basic assertion." *Systematic Theology*, 1:250.

[23]". . . man is continually a question because he is continually correlated to the answer . . . [but] . . . God, not man, is the source or ground of man's being, and therefore of the God-man correlation, which cannot be deduced from man." Keefe, p. 261.

God and man—that is to say, this revelation of God as Spirit—is
the basis for the doctrine of the Trinity and is something logically
prior to its specifically Christian confession in terms of *Logos*. If man
is the image of God, then he cannot think of God save as the correlate of his own ontological structure.[24] He thinks of God, then, as
reconciling the tension within himself of essence and existence, of
his own ambiguous tending at one and the same time towards what
is abstract and absolute and what is concrete and relative; in a word,
he conceives of God as synthesizing Spirit. Christ is the *Logos* of God
only on the presupposition that God is Spirit. The Trinity enables
the believer to say that his striving to achieve his own essence and
destiny is a striving for identity with the structural principle within
God (the *Logos* as divine form and meaning), which is at the very
same time an identity with God in his absoluteness and power (the
Father as divine Abyss). So to conceive God is to conceive him as
Spirit reconciling and uniting Being in its very depth as resistant to
nonbeing and so as assuming structure and meaning.

At this point, Tillich should be allowed to speak for himself. In
three lucid and revelatory paragraphs he advances an understanding of the Trinity as a human symbol of what is in God, respectively:
the element of abyss, the element of form, and the unity of the two.

> God's life as spirit, and the trinitarian principles are moments within
> the process of the divine life. Human intuition of the divine always has
> distinguished between the abyss of the divine (the element of power)
> and the fulness of its content (the element of meaning), between the
> divine depth and divine *Logos*. The first principle is the basis of God-
> head, that which makes God God. It is the root of his majesty, the
> unapproachable intensity of his being, the inexhaustible ground of
> being in which everything has its origin. It is the power of being infi-
> nitely resisting nonbeing, giving the power of being to everything that
> is. During the past centuries theological and philosophical rationalism
> have deprived the idea of God of this first principle, and by doing so
> they have robbed God of his divinity. He has become a hypostatized
> moral ideal or another name for the structural unity of reality. The
> power of the Godhead has disappeared.
>
> The classical term *Logos* is most adequate for the second principle,
> that of meaning and structure. It unites meaningful structure with cre-
> ativity. Long before the Christian Era—in a way already in Heraclitus—
> *Logos* received connotations of ultimacy as well as the meaning of being
> as being. According to Parmenides, being and the *Logos* of being cannot
> be separated. The *Logos* opens the divine ground, its infinity and its

---

[24]"Therefore, man symbolizes that which is his ultimate concern in terms
taken from his own being." *Systematic Theology*, 1:243.

darkness, and it makes its fulness distinguishable, definite, finite. The *Logos* has been called the mirror of the divine depth, the principle of God's self-objectification. In the *Logos* God speaks his "word," both in himself and beyond himself. Without the second principle the first principle would be chaos, burning fire, but it would not be the creative ground. Without the second principle God is demonic, is characterized by absolute seclusion, is the "naked absolute" (Luther).

As the actualization of the other two principles, the Spirit is the third principle. Both power and meaning are contained in it and united in it. It makes them creative. The third principle is in a way the whole (God is Spirit), and in a way it is a special principle (God has the Spirit as he has the *Logos*). It is the Spirit in whom God "goes out from" himself, the Spirit proceeds from the divine ground. He gives actuality to that which is potential in the divine ground and "outspoken" in the divine *Logos*. Through the Spirit the divine fulness is posited in the divine life as something definite, and at the same time it is reunited in the divine ground. The finite is posited as finite within the process of the divine life, but it is reunited with the infinite within the same process. It is distinguished from the infinite, but it is not separated from it. The divine life is infinite mystery, but it is not infinite emptiness. It is the ground of all abundance, and it is abundant itself.[25]

The tension between essence and existence, so central to Tillich's thought, is not anything operative within divinity itself. God is rather Being-Itself, the Creative Ground of all that is, and so, far from being dipolar in his own reality, he is the overcoming of all polarity.[26] That tension rather constitutes man's beingness, but so totally so that it determines all his cognitive striving vis-à-vis God. Man's knowledge of God is dipolar in that he thinks of God only on analogy with his own finite being. This is equivalent to saying that all distinctions which do come to the fore concerning God characterize not the Godhead itself but the dynamics of human conscious being as it seeks union with its ground. Such dynamism, it is true, would be impossible if man were not in ontological correlation with the divine. Thus, what Tillich really intends to clarify is man's relation to God. "Ultimate concern," then, is man's subjective disposition concerning the final meaning of life. The Ultimate about which he expresses concern is called "God," not in the sense of what is other

---

[25] Ibid., 1:251.

[26] "The polar character of the ontological elements is rooted in the divine life, but the divine life is not subject to this polarity. Within the divine life, every ontological element includes its polar element completely, without tension and without the threat of dissolution, for God is being itself." Ibid., 1:243.

than man as a Being, but in the sense of Being-Itself as the divine-human substratum to all of reality. When it is said by Tillich that *Logos* in God is the principle of divine "structure," "dynamics," and "meaning," this conveys only that nontemporal event in which God, out of his beingness as unfathomable Depth and primordial Power resistant to nonbeing, is understood as becoming the essence of humanity, or at least as explaining the ontological correlation of the divine and the human. What is truly ultimate is less any autonomous Deity than this characteristic of being as at bottom a divine-human correlation. But, then, this latter is the ideal and purely possible realm in which man's essence finds its precondition and its destiny. It is simply *posited* as the grounding principle of man as he actually is, as encountered under the conditions of life and existence. Tillich escapes the charge of making such positing entirely gratuitous by calling it a "belief-ful" act. Yet the implications for his thought are inescapable, suggesting less a theology than a humanism; a dialectical humanism that is not only religious and Christian in kind, but indeed a high instance of both. The point at issue is that this really reduces the trinitarian distinctions to categories of human conscious intentionality, simply traced back to the ground of such life-expression as a way of explaining the phenomenon.

Another way into this understanding of what lies at the base of Tillich's *Systematic Theology* is provided by his developed theory of symbol, which functions there as a basic methodological tool. All genuine religious utterances are by their nature symbolic in kind.[27] The well-known discrepancy in the *Systematic Theology* itself only serves in the end to show how universally Tillich intends this to be taken. In the earlier passage, all symbolic statements about God are controlled by the sole exception to this, namely, the nonsymbolic statement that God is Being-Itself.[28] If all such language were symbolic without exception, then the meaning assumed by the symbols would be entirely arbitrary, without any objective norm by which to tether it down. But this one literal expression is enough to open the way to some version of the classical theory of analogy which will

---

[27]This necessitates Tillich's deliteralizing and demythologizing of the conciliar pronouncements such as that of Chalcedon. His opposition to all literal meaning here rests upon an understanding of such meaning as limited to the order of empirically experienced phenomena, thus necessarily univocal in kind and closed off to all growth and expansion in meaning; see Keefe, pp. 249 and 254.

[28]*Systematic Theology*, 1:238–39.

allow that God is knowable in himself, even if in the most limited way. Thus, in the later passage, Tillich rescues his project by explaining that the one nonsymbolic utterance is not a predication about God at all, but actually is only a way of describing man's quest for God. ". . . If we make one nonsymbolic assertion about God, his ecstatic-transcendent character seems to be endangered . . . [so] . . . we must speak nonsymbolically about God, but in terms of a quest for him."[29] The referent of this literal expression, then, is not God as something transsubjective; it is our ultimate concern about our own being as it participates in infinity.

Symbols, unlike signs, participate in what they symbolize. But Tillich's meaning should not be misconstrued here. Symbols are existential realities, indigenous to finite consciousness insofar as the latter belongs to the ambiguous realm of existence. Thus, they emerge and disappear from the conscious horizon in a totally spontaneous way; they are not so much true or false as they are useful or not useful. They are by-products of existence searching for the true essence from which it is estranged, thus bespeaking an awareness of that essence as a possibility held out to it. This says a great deal about the dynamic of conscious life as self-transcendence; it says nothing about the Transcendent. The trinitarian symbols do not assert something about God; they rather mark achievements of finite spirit as it endlessly seeks its mysterious ground. There is no inner-divine Trinity, at least not one knowable to man. There is only a certain threefoldness to the symbols which express finite spirit's striving for its own divine-human primordial depth.

There is a second point on which Tillich's understanding of the Trinity represents a departure from the tradition first seriously questioned by Schleiermacher. This is signaled by the inability within his system to designate the distinctions within God as personal. Trinitarian language involves a threefold set of symbols within knowledge, three ways in which man cognitively appropriates God. True enough, that knowledge is knowledge of God, but even here it is a knowledge of God in terms of man's own ontological structure. What is at issue then, once again, is the divine-human correlation as constituting an eternal "God-Manhood" (earning from some of Tillich's critics the charge of a cryptopantheism).[30] The trinitarian

---

[29]*Systematic Theology*, 2, Introduction, p. 9.
[30]Preeminent among them, perhaps, is Kenneth Hamilton, *The System and the Gospel: A Critique of Paul Tillich* (London: SCM, 1963), pp. 85ff.

implications of this are: (i) that the Trinity signifies not God himself but the ontological relationship of God and man, and (ii) that such a Trinity is not at all a triunity of persons but of essential properties. The structural moments in man's knowing are participations in being, i.e., in the essential structure of the latter. At this point, the Platonist inspiration of Tillich's theology asserts itself, notably in the reduction of being to essence (even granting the fragmentation of the latter in existence). What is ultimately real is essence whose unity becomes disrupted in the concrete order of existence, much as Plato's pure forms lose their true reality in the shadow world of appearances. In this light, it is difficult to assign to Tillich's deity the prerogatives of personhood, much less a triunity of personhood. It is existential man who gives rise to what is meant by "person," which is thus reality that belongs to the realm of phenomena, available to empirical encounter. Thus, while the *Logos* in Christ is not of the order of person, Christ himself on an entirely other level does assume the prerogatives of person:

> The Messiah, the mediator between God and man, is identical with a personal human life, the name of which is Jesus of Nazareth.[31]

But what is obviously meant is something phenomenal in kind, Jesus' concrete individuality, achieved in the exercise of his freedom. Christ's finitude, in fact, constitutes a temptation to assert his personal autonomy over and against his essential unity with God, a temptation towards existential separation.[32] This is a repudiation of Chalcedon, for it asserts that in his person Christ is precisely *not* divine. It is on these grounds that Tillich feels immune to allegations that his position implies Monophysitism or Nestorianism: there simply is no autonomous humanity (that is, no distinct human nature in the Aristotelian-Thomistic sense) to be absorbed by the divine (Monophysitism) or adopted by it (Nestorianism). There is only the divine-human essence on the one hand and the conditions of existence on the other. Again, the categories of thought are asymmetrical here; those of one system cannot be imposed upon the alien system. At any rate, the trinitarian symbols of the *Systematic Theology* regard not God but the dialectic rooted in the ontological correlation of the divine and the human, which in the end is something redu-

---

[31]*Systematic Theology*, 1:229–30.
[32]See Keefe, p. 252.

cible to the realm of essence. The doctrine of the Trinity no longer
signifies a triunity of persons, or hypostases, or subsistences.

There is a third and final reaction to Tillich's trinitarianism that
deserves at least brief mention. He has defined faith, in existential
terms, as "being grasped by the transcendent unity of unambiguous
life." There are obvious strengths in this formula. One is the notion
of revelation operative in it as something that occurs at the interior
of consciousness and so is not a theory of verbal inspiration but one
of the coming to pass of meaning which assumes a structure analogous to man's own ontological makeup. Another is the emphasis
upon the receptive character of finite consciousness in the face of
the transforming power of ultimate reality. The first seeks to endow
revelation with a universality that protects it against a fideistic exclusivity. The second attempts to give revelation an objective character
that will enable it to appear as indeed God's word. But the impression persists that the way the former is achieved neutralizes the
latter. It is difficult to avoid the feeling that the symbols expressive
of the Trinity are only anthropologically derived, in the final analysis. They too readily appear as the products of an analysis of
human existence in the ambiguity of its actual finitude and its
potential infinity. This leads one to question whether Tillich's project in the end is anything more than a Christian reflection upon the
human prerequisites of revelation. His notion of faith tends to make
the content of faith as supplied by beliefs to be quite arbitrary in
kind. Though Tillich ascribes a uniqueness to the historical Jesus,
there is no reason in his thought why this should be so, no reason
why the Christian commitment to Christ could not be transferred
to some other historical personage with identical salvific consequences. If the *Logos* is not God Incarnate but the element of structure and meaning in the God-man relationship, then the Christ-
event is no longer the act of God on man worked out in the sphere
of history. Missing here is any indication that "God's word must
interpret itself" and in so doing reveal more than "what man has
thought out for himself about himself and about God, whether *a
priori* or *a posteriori*."[33] The freedom of God in historical revelation
seems to succumb to an ontological schema. The Spirit is no longer
the immanence of God as a personal "other" who "breathes where

---

[33]Hans Urs von Balthasar, *Glaubhaft ist nur Liebe* (Einsiedeln: Johannes
Verlag, 1963), p. 32.

he will," but only the symbol for a process of unification obedient to love viewed as a law of being and thought.[34]

In the end, the specific element in Tillich's trinitarianism is its dialectical character. But that opens itself to two differing interpretations. It can be viewed as a mere dialectic of finite human consciousness in its own process of self-transcendence. Then the charge of a crypto-atheism can seemingly be urged against it. But there is a second interpretation that appears to accord more readily with Tillich's own intentions. Here the dialectic is one proper to "spirit," but spirit manifesting itself as at once divine and human (in a dialectical sense, not a pantheistic one), as *Theos-anthropos*. The movement is from (i) man subordinate to God, to (ii) man in autonomy from God, culminating in (iii) man as God. It is a process from theism, through atheism, terminating in a religious humanism that can be called transtheistic. It is this that finds expression in the symbols of the Trinity.

THE TRINITARIAN SYMBOL AS PARADOX: CYRIL RICHARDSON AND OTHERS

Few modern theologians deal with the problem of the Trinity in the context of a system as coherent and ontologically dense as Tillich's. But many share his view of the Trinity as a construct which, while possessing values of its own, is itself inessential to Christian faith. Cyril Richardson's book *The Doctrine of The Trinity*[35] is an instance in point. The norm for his conclusion is the New Testament itself; we are simply confronted in the New Testament with three dominant symbols of God as a constant given. But the revelatory power of those symbols has been distorted by the manner in which they have been structured into the doctrine of "three Persons of one divine nature." Thus, "the major patterns of trinitarian thinking ... all involve arbitrary and unsatisfactory elements ... [so that finally] ... the solutions they propose do not commend themselves."[36] It is rather true, for Richardson, that the "three dominant

---

[34]This represents a Hegelian understanding of love as the fateful working out of an abstract principle rather than as underivable historical happening which might well be other than it is.

[35]Cyril C. Richardson, *The Doctrine of the Trinity* (Nashville: Abingdon Press, 1958).

[36]Ibid., p. 141. The patterns that Richardson explores reduce to the four Trinities of: (i) mediation, (ii) love, (iii) revelation, and (iv) God's activity.

ways in which the New Testament speaks to us about God," namely, as Father, Son, and Spirit, involve symbols which "do not form a precise Trinity [but] . . . point beyond themselves to basic theological issues."[37] All these issues reduce to the foundational one: the paradox of God as at once beyond the world yet related to it. The trinitarian names are not meant to suggest distinct persons in God; they draw attention to the necessity of distinguishing between God as Absolute and God as Relative, yet without being themselves the actual distinctions. Indeed, the three particular names all express God's relationship to men in revelation; even "Father," for example, bespeaks not the character of being unoriginate but the relationship of creation and providential love. But the coalescence of these into a doctrine of Trinity is an artificial construct attempting to convey that the God who so relates himself remains beyond such relationality. It is, moreover, a construct more productive of confusion than of illumination. Logically, Richardson maintains, God cannot be both One and Three, yet we must say both. Trinity is a symbolic way of conveying this antinomy. Immediately an apparent discrepancy regarding this use of the Trinity symbol is noticed. It speaks in categories of threeness about what in fact only manifests a duality; it seeks to clarify the dipolarity of God in terms of tripolarity. Richardson notes that this problem disappears once it is understood the two symbols "*Logos*" and "Spirit" are simply two ways of saying the same thing. Thus it follows that "no distinction between the divine in Jesus and God's Spirit is really cogent."[38] The name "Son" does not even raise a problem because its meaning is entirely intended in the context of the Incarnation, and cannot be read back into the Godhead itself.[39] But the name *Logos*, which does intend something within divinity, means nothing other than what is conveyed (with a differing emphasis only) by the name "Spirit." "A distinction between two kinds of God-in-Relation, one called 'Word'

---

[37] Ibid., p. 142.

[38] Ibid., p. 48.

[39] "In short, the terms Father and Son are inadequate symbols to describe the nature of God's being; and by retaining them we introduce a confusion into our thinking and pose for ourselves a variety of unnecessary and insoluble problems which stem directly from the unfitting nature of our original terms. Son is fitting, to be sure, when applied to the humanity of Christ. When we think of Jesus of Nazareth in his relation to his heavenly Father, we understand what sonship means. But this is very different from trying to apply the same category to a distinction in the Godhead." Ibid., p. 43.

and the other 'Spirit', was really untenable."[40] This is true of at least one of the two distinct meanings the latter term has in the writings of St. Paul. Its first meaning there is simply God in action; Spirit is the divine activity as creative of all reality (*Gen.* 1:2); of Jesus in the womb of Mary (*Mt.* 1:20, *Lk.* 1:35); of the Church and new life in the Christian (*Gal.* 5:22ff.); and by extension in the Old Testament of the Eschaton to come (*Joel* 2:28). *Logos* says the same thing, merely serving to draw attention to the quality of God's action as intelligent and as intelligible to men. Granting this identity, all talk of a procession of the *Pneuma* from the *Logos*, of a *Filioque* doctrine, becomes a matter of theological abuse. It is difficult to avoid the impression that Richardson at this point is trimming the texts to fit a preconceived thesis. Also, on purely exegetical grounds, Arthur Wainwright is at least one scholar who maintains to the contrary that later Pauline and Johannine thought clearly distinguishes between the *Logos* and *Pneuma*.[41] This is especially significant in the case of John, since he is the writer who introduces the *Logos* concept. But there is another sense to Spirit, one meaning something akin to self-consciousness, "not merely God's breath, but his self-awareness, his mind, his inner being,"[42] signifying two senses, one relative and one absolute. The same is true of "Father," which "means a relation of love and care and discipline, but it means also a transcendent mystery. The Father is the one that is above restraint. He comes and goes as he pleases. . . . Hence the symbol as applied to God refers both to transcendence and to relationship."[43] "Trinity" then is a way of saying that the names "Father," "Word," and "Spirit," while designating God in his relations with the world, are always used simultaneously in tension with the background idea of God as transcending all relationality. Thus, it is the aspect of paradox and antinomy that guarantees that God is the referent of the language. The retention of the paradoxical element forbids any collapse into Sabellianism, whether in its original form of successive phases in divinity or in the modern form it assumes in Schleiermacher and Tillich where it expresses a threefold character in the believer's experience of God. The paradoxical aspect, moreover,

---

[40] Ibid.
[41] See his *The Trinity in the New Testament* (London: Wm. Clowes & Sons, 1962).
[42] Richardson, p. 50.
[43] Ibid., p. 30.

stands over against any tendency to conceive God in interdependence upon the world, which latter is an alternative position adopted by contemporary process theology.

All of this is understood by Richardson in such wise that there is no possibility of assigning logical priorities between these polar aspects;[44] the relatedness of God cannot be derived from his absoluteness, nor is the inverse true; the eternal does not logically precede the temporal, nor vice versa. The trinitarian names, in effect, designate the activities towards the world of a God who does not thereby become related to it in any of the ordinary senses of that term. They do not designate any real distinctness in God himself, much less a personal distinctness; only in a grammatical sense can they be considered "personification." As incorporated within the construct "trinity," such names function as symbols pointing beyond themselves to a God of mystery, simultaneously affirming real relationality and negating it. One senses at this point in Richardson's thinking a failure to assume the speculative power of genuine theology, a taking of refuge in the ambiguity of religious experience recounted in the New Testament, and an avoidance of the hard questions by facile recourse to the language of paradox. At any rate, for him, the Trinity says nothing positive about God's inner life; it is reconstructed into a symbol conveying only that God's being always negates our finite categories. Tillich's dialectic between the tendency towards ultimacy and the tendency towards concreteness has been transformed by Richardson into an antinomy of the absolute and the relative. Neither is speaking of God, but of the dialectic within human consciousness.

Paul Lehmann, in an article entitled "The Tri-Unity of God,"[45] is somewhat less skeptical than Richardson regarding the Trinity of revelation, suggesting that "Trinity" in fact is *the* revealed name of God. It cannot, then, be arbitrarily jettisoned by the Christian in favor of terms which might alter the threeness into, for example, a

---

[44]Thus he explains that the "reason why the analogy of 'begetting' is misleading lies in the fact that it assumes the priority of God's beyondness. But we have no reason to suppose this. He is these two things, he exists in these two modes of being—but neither is prior to the other." Ibid., pp. 35–36.

[45]*Union Seminary Quarterly Review* 21, no. 1 (November 1965), pp. 35–39. Responses to Lehmann by Thomas J. J. Altizer, John Macquarrie, Christopher Mooney, and Cyril Richardson appeared in the subsequent issue of this journal, 21, no. 2, pt. 2 (January 1966).

duality or quaternity (as Richardson is quite content to allow). But the term for all its indispensability remains a mere symbol—"mere" in the sense that it cannot be given any literal, transsubjective meaning, as would be the case in treating it as a concept able to be predicated analogically. Lehmann insists that theology, as distinct from faith, must resist two temptations: that of saying too much and that of saying too little.[46] In the former, there is an unjustifiable tendency to project onto the very nature of God the distinctions expressed in the symbols. In the latter, *the* name for God is neglected in favor of the names available in the New Testament accounts, which latter are only instances of believers exercising their own naming function. "Trinity," then, is the revealed symbol for God, one pointing in all the ambiguity of finite knowing to a God who remains anonymous apart from the assertion of his triunity. The symbol says that God is not a monadic absolute on the one hand, nor is he limited on the other hand to what is conveyed by the names "Father," "Son," and "Spirit" with their personalist connotations.

A somewhat similar caution against making dogmatic statements about the inner life of God, against theology's "saying too much" in its use of trinitarian language, is manifest in the work of Maurice Wiles.[47] He acknowledges only three possible explanations of the origin of the trinitarian doctrine.[48] The first rests upon the assumption of a theory of propositional revelation; this he views as theologically discredited, but allows that were it the case it would be justifiable to interpret the doctrine as making assertions about God himself. The second possibility maintains that while revelation does not convey truth in propositional form, nevertheless it does communicate truth in such wise that every action of God is understood as manifesting a radical threefold character. This necessitates the conclusion, immediate from revelation itself, that God's very being is so triunely structured. Overtones of Karl Barth are clearly discernible here, but Wiles dismisses this as an ingenious reconstruction of the first explanation. It avoids the objections brought to bear upon the prior position, but remains in fact a search for a new foundation for the Trinity within revelation itself. The third possibility, toward which Wiles himself is disposed, follows through on

---

[46]Lehmann, p. 37.
[47]See "Some Reflections on the Origins of the Doctrine of the Trinity," *Journal of Theological Studies* 8, pt. 1 (April 1957), pp. 92–106.
[48]Ibid., p. 104.

the consequences of a radical break with any theory that sees the Trinity as directly revealed. Rather, it is, once again, a doctrine of the second rank, a nonnecessary analysis of the religious experience recounted in the New Testament, one not without values of its own but still inessential to faith. D.M. Edwards is sympathetic to this view and "cannot see any necessity of thought for fixing on the number three, neither less nor more," and avers that "no convincing reason can be given why, in view of the rich manifoldness of divine functions and activities, the number of the hypostases may not be increased indefinitely."[49] Wiles himself lays bare what lies at the heart of this stance: "The threeness of the completed orthodox doctrine of the Trinity can logically be known only on the basis of a propositional revelation about the inner mysteries of the Godhead or through some other kind of specific authoritative revelation."[50] Lacking this, the Trinity is not an ontic assertion about God, but a symbol of our experience of God. Here Schleiermacher remains, if not the father, at least the grandfather of modern theology.

SUMMARY

What the thrust of the thought of this present chapter comes down to, then, can be summarized in two conclusions: (i) the Trinity as a mystery of the inner life of God is not itself revealed but rather derived in a mediate way from what is immediately revealed, namely, that the human existence of Jesus conveys in some unique fashion the presence and action of God; and (ii) the Trinity as a doctrine is a mental construct expressing *symbolically* the self-transcending movement of religious (Christian) consciousness in the encounter with Christ. Succinctly put, this is to say the Trinity is a Christian symbol, not of God but of man's knowledge of God, useful but not indispensable to faith. The operative word is "symbol," and what it means is fairly clear from the use to which it is put in a trinitarian context by the authors considered. The symbol is a factor in that indigenously human phenomenon which is the occurrence of meaning. The latter is something which comes to pass within

---

[49]Cited by Wiles, ibid., p. 106, citing from D. M. Edwards, *Christianity and Philosophy* (Edinburgh: T. & T. Clark, 1932), pp. 339, 354, 355.
[50]Ibid.

consciousness, in which the symbol functions as both the yield of whatever meaning does occur and the catalyst for further meaning. It is thus at once the progeny and the creative origin of thought. Most importantly, the symbol needs to be differentiated from another quite distinct factor in thought, which is the concept. Symbols express meaning mediately, by way of indirection, that is, in a form other than the form that is proper to what is being known through them. Concepts, by contrast, register meaning by reproducing a meaning that is intentionally identical with what is meant. Conceptualization is a process whereby the intelligible form to be known gains a new mode of existence in the knower; the same form enjoying a natural existence in the reality to be known now achieves a new psychic existence in the knower, thanks to a process of abstraction. Unlike the symbol, then, the concept signifies literally rather than symbolically. "Literally" here, however, must not be understood as synonymous with "univocally," but includes in its scope analogy and some forms of "models" as instances of nonfigurative, nonsymbolic predication.

Other characteristics of symbols are less important to our purposes here. Some of the more significant might be briefly noted, however. For example, a symbol is more than a "sign," which bears no meaning of its own and merely functions as a cognitive pointer to something else; the symbol, by contrast, embodies the meaning it expresses, thereby participating in it. Again, symbols may be language-realities (e.g., metaphors) or nature-realities (e.g., what is usually meant by the term "image"). As linguistic in kind, symbols admit of multiple and varied modes; myth, for example, is simply a symbol in an extended narrative form. Further, it is characteristic of symbols that they arise and disappear from consciousness with a certain spontaneity. Thus, they operate with special power in evoking the unknown, but by the same token tend to be impermanent, undefined, tentative, and ever changing. Symbol systems are constitutive of communities, yet at the same time subject to continual transformation by the community.

From all this it is clear that any investigation of the role of symbolization in Christian life and thought uncovers a marked emphasis upon creativity. To this extent concern shifts from the discovery of truth under the direction of God's Word to a creative expression of the meaning of life precisely in its religious dimension, i.e., vis-à-vis God. There are two obvious gains in this modern rediscovery of the power of symbols: first, a sense of the religious dimension as essential to all human existence at a certain depth level (including secular existence in its very secularity);[51] and secondly, a corrective to the sterile dogmatism that historically did congeal into an alienating ideology, to the point that Christian language began to signify something far removed from its original intent. The Trinity, perhaps, came to illustrate this latter malaise more than any other doctrine.

These very gains, however, have occasioned a shift in the intellectual foundations of Christian thought, a shift from reason illumined by historical revelation to a historical perspectivism, more relative in kind and synonymous with the creativity of the self and society. Meaning assumes a subjective origin, obviously not arbitrary in kind but rooted in some sort of encounter with God, yet an encounter that loses any objectively verifiable character. The risk is that of religious meaning taking upon itself something of the evanescent quality of human existence in its radical contingency. The risk has its value, notably the rich one of fostering the religious instinct in its dynamics of self-transcendence. The spirit is emboldened in feeling the liberating power of the future upon it, a power capable of surmounting the dead weight of the past and the limitations of the present. But precisely here a question arises that cannot be refused. Does not this self-bestowal of meaning on existence as it cuts into the future exaggerate the discontinuity with the past and despoil the present of any lasting meaning? The past and the present, on this view, surrender all intrinsic value; their sole significance is that of serving as launching pads into the future. Certainly a case can be made today, in the West at any rate, for a repudiation of the theory of irreversible progress that gathered force at the time of the Enlightenment. If these contemporary reservations on the myth of progress can be sustained, they suggest that a reassessment of cultural symbols, including religious ones, is called for, but a reassessment that seeks whatever it is that grounds the whole phenomenon of symbolization. Must there not be, in short, some operating base that sustains the world of symbols, a matrix that is itself precisely nonsymbolic? A parallel case that might illustrate what is meant here arises in the mystery of human freedom. If such freedom, in all its finite limitations, is not anchored in something not free, something nonnegotiable (such as an ultimate destiny functioning teleologically on freedom, simply to offer one possibility), then it is difficult to see how freedom does not deteriorate into mere contingency. The purely contingent is a caricature

---

[51]This is a central thesis of Langdon Gilkey, *Naming the Whirlwind* (Indianapolis: Bobbs-Merrill, 1969).

of genuine freedom in that, while avoiding necessity, it lacks the ingredients of intelligence and love.

Still, a more serious reservation by far than the myth of progress surfaces in the fact that the sort of theology at work here tends to pursue transcend*ence* to the neglect of any acknowledgment of the Transcend*ent*. At least the latter's objective reality tends to become obscured; any possibility of its giving purpose and guidance is at least deferred. Thus, in often cryptic terms, the theistic foundations of Christianity become an open question. It can at least be seriously asked if the God of Schleiermacher is in fact personal. Ritschl's thought appears to confirm God's personhood out of a fear that Schleiermacher has not done service to it. Similar hesitancies are not unreasonable in face of Tillich's "God beyond Theism," identified only as the faceless "Ground of Being." For the Christian, these hesitancies are not at all mitigated by Tillich's oblique reservations on personal immortality.

The cautions here expressed on the reduction of the Trinity to a doctrine of the second rank and its transformation into a mere symbol by no means suggest that theology can dispense with symbolic language. This would be to miss entirely the invaluable insights and necessary correctives achieved in the sort of theology we have been considering. On the contrary, without a theory of symbolic speech, and a rich employment of symbols in its own exercise, genuine theology would suffer a serious truncation. Recent thought has made abundantly clear how deeply myth runs in all of us. Some things cannot be said in any other way. Also, there is no reason why trinitarian language cannot be *employed* in a symbolic way; conveying thereby, for example, God's ineffability. Rather the reservation expressed here regards the reduction of *all* theological language to the symbolic, the refusal of any other manner of speech—a conclusion implicit in Schleiermacher, but explicit in Tillich. This would appear to erode the symbol system of all verifiable objectivity where meaning is concerned. It means that in the religious realm one speaks not about God no matter how falteringly, but only about man's conscious questing for God. Symbolic meaning escapes a final arbitrariness only if it finds tether in what is not symbolic; the discovery of the latter controls the meaning that can arise symbolically and frees the symbol for its true creative function. The question then is: Can there be a source of religious meaning making possible a language other than the symbolic? A first reply to this question was forthcoming in a clarion call to Christian theologians in the 1920s from a Swiss parsonage in Basel.

[5]

NEO-MODAL TRINITARIANISM
The Uni-personal God of Three Eternal
Modes of Being

In Karl Barth's multivolumed *Church Dogmatics,*[1] the Trinity is treated in a *Prolegomenon* to the entire work, in what in fact amounts to a first half-volume of Volume One, entitled *The Doctrine of the Word of God.* This is in marked contrast with the practice of the immediate past wherein (as in Schleiermacher, e.g.) the doctrine was treated as a mere appendix to a systematic theology. It marks a return to the methodological key of Aquinas's *Summa theologiae* and Calvin's *Institutes.* Barth begins, then, by laying the foundation for God's relation to the world, a foundation in God himself prior to the world he was to create. In a proximate sense that foundation is God's free choice to exercise lordship over the world in the election of Jesus Christ. But that election is itself the trinitarian mystery; as Barth himself observes, "Originally God's election of many is a predestination not merely of man but of himself."[2] The ultimate foundation is thus trinitarian; the doctrine of the Trinity precedes the doctrine of creation and covenant and forms its presupposition. In such fashion, Barth sought the rehabilitation of Christian language, the reacquisition of its specific carrying power as the vehicle of God's word and not man's word at all. The changed theological climate had minimized two previously prevailing factors in method, namely, authority and reason, in favor of a third new factor which in fact was given primacy—experience. Experience had first gained a Cinderella-like role in the sixteenth century perhaps, but it came into

---

[1] *Die kirchliche Dogmatik,* 1st ed., 12 vols. (Zurich, 1932–)· Eng. transl., *Church Dogmatics,* G. W. Bromiley and T. F. Torrance, eds., 14 vols. (Edinburgh: T. & T. Clark, 1936–69); vol. I, part 1, *The Doctrine of the Word of God,* transl. G. T. Thomson (1936). Hereafter cited as *C.D.,* I/1.

[2] *Church Dogmatics,* vol. II, part 2, *The Doctrine of God,* transl. G. W. Bromiley et al. (1957), p. 3.

its own in the nineteenth. This was motivated by the search for relevance, sought in a gradual secularizing of the Gospel, under the aegis of the *Aufklärung*. Developments between the two great wars served to call the enterprise into question; later, a discovery of the part played by the Churches in the horrors attendant on World War II provoked a strong reaction against it. The reversal was signaled by the publication of Barth's *Commentary on Romans* in 1918, which in Karl Adam's phrase "fell like a bomb on the playground of theologians"; Barth's most lasting contribution remains his massive *Kirchliche Dogmatik*. Barth had come to see how radical the secularization had become, to appreciate what Colin Williams describes as secular man's concern "to understand life from within and to master life from below"[3] as precisely a moving of God out of the picture entirely.

The Neo-Orthodox movement, launched by Barth, was an attempt to recoup an earlier understanding of Scripture and the ancient Creeds such as Nicaea's, as those had been mediated through Reformation orthodoxy. The intentions of Luther, Melanchthon, Zwingli, and Calvin, where the doctrine of the Trinity is concerned, are sedimented in such authoritative documents as the *Confession of Augsburg*, prepared by Melanchthon in 1531; the *Formulary* and *Book of Concord* in, respectively, 1577 and 1580; the *Institutes* of Calvin in 1559; as well as the *Helvetic Confessions* of 1536 and the *Belgic Confession* of 1561. In Luther's own writings, the Trinity plays only a very minor theological role, serving largely to buttress his real concerns, which were those of faith and justification. But Melanchthon's *Augsburg Confession*, which influenced all later Reformational confessions including the Thirty-Nine Articles of the Anglican Church, makes explicit exactly what is being confessed. The paradigmatic character of that *Confession* justifies a lengthy citation:

> Our Churches teach with great unanimity that the decree of the Council of Nicaea concerning the Unity of the divine essence and concerning the Three Persons is true and should be believed without any doubting. That is to say, there is one divine essence, which is called and which is God. . . . Yet there are three Persons, of the same wisdom, and goodness, one creator and preserver of all things visible and invisible. The word "person" is to be understood as the Fathers employed

---

[3]*Faith in a Secular Age* (New York: Harper and Row, 1966), p.3.

the term in this connection, not as a part or a property of another but as that which exists of itself.[4]

The document goes on to condemn "all heresies which have sprung up against this article" including those which "impiously argue that the Word and the Holy Spirit are not distinct Persons, but that 'Word' signifies a spoken word and that 'Spirit' signifies motion in created things."[5] All this is evidence of a marked unanimity concerning the Trinity. Later differences in seventeenth-century Protestant Scholasticism (on more detailed questions) did not dislodge this foundational uniformity. Such differences did arise, for example, from the tendency of Reformed theologians, against the Evangelicals, to stress the distinction of natures in Christ. This led the former to eschew the term "person" in trinitarian discussion, in a preference for *"hypostasis,"* or *"subsistentia,"* or *"tropos hyparxeōs"* — a practice which the Lutherans interpreted as Sabellianistic, since this suggested to them that God had assumed a new mode of being in conjunction with the humanity. Among Lutherans themselves, the division between a *Kenōsis* (emptying) Christology and a *Krypsis* (concealing) Christology meant an obvious difference for the doctrine of the *Logos*. But it was doctrinal unity that prevailed until the antitrinitarianism latent in Pietism in Germany and Deism in England marked a first turning of the tide.

THE TRINITY AS MODES OF DIVINE SELF-MANIFESTATION: KARL BARTH

The coping stone of Karl Barth's theology is a theory of revelation as innovative and revolutionary in its own way as Schleiermacher's. Behind it lies a century of Idealist thought in Germany, a background to Barth's thought usually camouflaged under his reservations on the importation of philosophy into theology. Yet such negativity is not directed towards philosophy as such but only to its usurpation of what rightfully belongs to faith. Like Kant, Barth is doing away with science to make room for faith. Nonetheless, to theologize is to think, and Barth's thinking bears the unmistakable

---

[4]*Book of Concord,* transl. and ed. Theodore G. Tappert et al. (Philadelphia: Fortress Press, 1959), pp. 27–28; this is the so-called Invariata version of the *Augsburg Confession* published in the *Book of Concord* in 1580.

[5]Ibid.

imprint of German Idealism, despite his refusal to thematize the latter. The dominant feature of this outlook is an understanding of reality as modeled on the structure of human consciousness and on what is indigenous to that consciousness—the idea. Simply put, reality is ultimately viewed not in categories of Being but in those of Spirit. Being is classically looked upon as *analogical;* spirit allows for a more dynamic view of reality as *dialectical.* The former admits of a great chain of being (substances) running from the atomic world of matter, to separated substances, and thence to the divine. The latter plays upon the dipolar dynamism between infinite and finite consciousness; it tends to reduce matter and corporeality to precipitates of spirit and to highlight such characteristics of reality as temporality and becoming.

Earlier thought had tended to conceive of God as analogous to substance and accordingly looked upon revelation as the *action* of God towards men. The vantage point inherited by Barth meant a view of God more isomorphic to "occurrence," to "appearance," in the sense of the coming to pass of meaning within consciousness. God was less the agent of revelation than the pure event of revelation itself. Reformational disinclination to speak of a *Deus in se* also lent itself to this way of thinking of God—not as substance, nature or essence with an intrinsic intelligibility, but as pure happening. The difference lies in the correlative character of the latter category; it necessarily implies someone to whom and for whom something happens or eventuates. Thus, at one stroke, all human speech about the divine concerns only the *Deus pro nobis.*

But God for us is still God; the divine event transpires as something utterly free. This is the root of Barth's "dialectical theology"[6] (approximating the dialectics of Kierkegaard rather than that of Hegel), wherein every theological assertion implies immediate qualification by a counterstatement. In this way, faith resists all absorption by culture, bearing out Luther's saying that God even in his very revelation remains hidden *sub contraria specie.* With Bultmann, Barth affirms that God is subject only, never object.[7] He is known solely in his addressing us. All speculation about the God behind the revealed God is idle. But at this point Barth's original insight

---

[6]This dialectical character to theology, bespeaking its engagement with secular culture, is more pronounced in Barth's thought prior to the *Church Dogmatics.*

[7]*Church Dogmatics*, II/2, p. 438.

begins to show its force: it is part of revelation that what God is for us he is in himself. God is conceived as Event. What event? The event of revelation; God *is* revelation. He is the unknown and the unknowable who freely discloses himself to man. What God reveals is that he is free to reveal, that is to say, free to become God for man. Barth seemingly means this in the sense that revelation is a new occurrence even for God. As "event" rather than changeless essence, God can become something other than himself. This "other" is Jesus the Christ, whose election is the election of mankind. But the fullness of the mystery is reached only in the acknowledgment that God *remains himself* in the very act of becoming other than himself. In a word, the mystery of Christ is the mystery of the Trinity.

The Barthian Trinity is not a doctrine of the second rank, rationally fashioned to defend what has been revealed (as with Brunner), but is itself the very structure of revelation. It is an immediate implication of the revelatory event itself and so cannot be reduced to being a mere symbol functioning arbitrarily in our attempts to know that event. He does deny nonetheless that the New Testament text contains a doctrine of the Trinity as such or of any other doctrine for that matter.[8] The message of the New Testament is only that of God's lordship in Jesus. As integrated into a formal doctrine, then, the Trinity is a construct. But it is not a theoretic or theological construct on a second level of reflection. It is a construct that occurs as an act of faith, not of theology; it is an implication, but immediate in kind, of the New Testament message. It is not an inference *from* revelation, but something intrinsic to the latter upon the sort of analysis that is spontaneous to the believer. In Barth's own words, it is "exegesis . . . in the light of questions arising out of a later situation," thus apparently calling for continual reappropriation in language. "It belongs to the Church. It is a theologoumenon. It is a Dogma."[9]

What we grasp in faith on hearing the word proclaimed is the mystery that "God reveals himself." This means that God is himself the event of revelation because he is the subject (*God* reveals), the

---

[8]*C.D.*, I/1, p. 353: "The statement or statements about the Trinity of God cannot claim to be directly identical with the statement about revelation, or revelation itself." Similarly, on the Christological doctrine: "The dogma as such is not to be found in the Biblical texts. The dogma is an interpretation." Ibid., p. 475.

[9]Ibid., p. 431.

content (God reveals *himself*), and the very happening (God *reveals* himself). This follows from understanding that the faith phenomenon which occurs can only be regarded (precisely because it is faith) from God's perspective;[10] it does not surrender itself over to human reflection. God himself is at once the agent, the content, and the very being of this faith-reality which is revelation. Revelation is trinitarian, in other words. And, since the revelation-event *is* God, God is himself Trinity.

The most oft-quoted Barthian expression for the Trinity is the formula: God is Revealer, Revelation, and Revealedness.[11] These are equivalents for the New Testament symbols: Father, Son, and Spirit. God is the agent, the content, and the state of revelation. *God reveals, God reveals himself, God reveals through himself*—the Trinity thus appearing as the formal structure of that event which is God. Alternate triadic sets readily express the same truth: God is veiling, unveiling, and impartation; he is freedom, form, and historicity; he is Creator, Reconciler, and Redeemer; he is holiness, mercy, and love; liturgically, he is Good Friday, Easter, and Pentecost.[12] A *leitmotiv* of Barth's theology is the total otherness of God. Only the dialectical method enables us to acknowledge the paradoxical character of revelation; in it God makes himself known but precisely as the Unknown. This enables Barth, unlike Rahner and Moltmann, to distinguish between the immanent and the economic Trinity (the Cross, for example, enters into the latter but not the former). But Barth does so against the background of the constant theological principle: God corresponds to himself. Paradoxically, what God reveals of himself in Christ corresponds to what is true of God in himself, to the God hidden in the very revelation. As Father, Son, and Spirit, God is *our* God, antecedently in himself.[13] With this, Barth has recouped the truth of the centrality of the Trinity to Christian faith, its indispensability to the question of the meaning of human existence and salvation.

At this crucial point in his thought Barth faces squarely a question that lesser theologians tend by and large to bypass: the paradox of God's three-in-oneness. If we ask, "Three what?" we find only the tradition-honored reply of "three *persons*." But Barth aligns himself

[10] Ibid., p. 339.
[11] Ibid., p. 417.
[12] Ibid., pp. 382 and 415.
[13] Ibid., pp. 441 and 448.

with Augustine who takes "persons" as a mere convention of speech; to take it literally is to run the risk of tritheism. Barth shares Calvin's polemic against the term, the latter viewing *trois personnes* as suggestive of *trois marmousets* ("grotesque figures"). Melanchthon's preference for it appears to Barth as having "a somewhat suspicious ring."[14] The reason lies in the connotation the word acquires from Schleiermacher's time onward. Schleiermacher himself had used the concept in a way that advanced a form of Neo-Sabellianism. There, Trinity meant only three phenomenal forms behind which stood the one divine reality. "Personality" especially, as a nineteenth-century term, added to this ancient and medieval use of "person" the notion of self-consciousness. This precipitated two opposite courses of thought: (i) to eliminate the term entirely from speech about God on the grounds that as Absolute Spirit he transcended all limitation implicit in consciousness (Fichte and Strauss), or (ii) to continue to use the term but as divested of the new meaning it had acquired. In the ancient Church, somewhat the same problem had been resolved by transforming the Greek πρόσωπον into ὑπόστασις. Barth seeks to surmount the dilemma—of tritheism on the one hand when the connotation of self-consciousness is retained, and of mystification and meaninglessness on the other when it is denied— by substituting the phrase *"Seinsweisen"* (modes of being).[15] This is not only "a literal translation of τρόπος ὑπάρξεως, already in use in the early Church debates," but also registers the sense of ὑπόστασις insofar as it means *"subsistentia* (not *substantia),* i.e., mode of existence of one who exists."[16]

This doctrine of Barth is surely not "modalism" in its traditional senses but it does qualify for what might be called "modal trinitarianism." Why this might be so is clear from the intentions of the following quotation:

> The statement "God is one in three modes of being, Father, Son, and Holy Spirit" thus means that the one God, i.e., the one Lord, the *one personal* God, is what he is not in one mode only but—we appeal in support simply to the result of our analysis of the Biblical concept of revelation—in the mode of the Father, in the mode of the Son, in the mode of the Holy Spirit.[17]

---

[14]Ibid., p. 411, where Barth refers to both Calvin and Melanchthon.
[15]Ibid., p. 407.
[16]Ibid., p. 413.
[17]Ibid., p. 413 (emphasis added).

Barth has clearly cast his lot with the tradition of the Western Church. This means that the mind, unable to conceive oneness and threeness simultaneously, and thereby obligated to grant logical priority to one or the other, chooses to accord priority to the absolute oneness of God. The understanding of threeness is sought subsequently and expresses modalities of that oneness. A secondary confirmation of this Western approach is ready to hand in such doctrines as the *Filioque,* appropriation, and the commonness to the Persons of all *opera ad extra.*

> ... Three in oneness in God, so far from conveying a threat to, rather asserts the establishment of the Christian thought of the unity of God.
>   ... In our proof that the doctrine of the Trinity is rooted in Biblical revelation, we started from and always returned again to the revealed name *Yahweh-Kyrios,* which binds together the OT and NT. The doctrine of the Trinity itself neither is nor claims to be anything else than an explanatory confirmation of this name. The name is the name of an unique entity, of a single, unique Willer and Doer, whom Scripture designates as God.[18]

The *point de départ* then in reflective exploration of the Trinity is "the divine οὐσία, *essentia, natura,* or *substantia,*" which from the biblical standpoint is "that wherein *Yahweh-Kyrios* is the *person* whom he describes himself to be by this name, the name of the Lord" (emphasis supplied). It is to the one single essence of God that there "belongs what we call today the 'personality' of God ... [so that one speaks] ... not of three divine 'I's', but thrice of the one divine I."[19] What Barth is emphatic in not saying is that there can be any fourth reality behind the three who are Father, Son, and Spirit. It is untoward to speak of an absolute Person distinguishable from the three relative Persons.[20] And it is precisely by this move that Barth removes himself from any dalliance with classical modalism; on his grounds it is impossible to conceive the Three as phenomenal forms of the One Absolute Spirit. Yet in eschewing the term "persons" in preference for his own term "modes," thus avoiding the use in the plural of words connoting consciousness, Barth has to accept the

---

[18]Ibid., p. 400.
[19]Ibid., pp. 401–3.
[20]The contrary opinion was entertained by some Catholic scholastic theologians, e.g., R. Garrigou-Lagrange: "Deus *secundum se consideratus,* ac relationibus seu personis praeintellectis, est *subsistens,* est enim non solum Deitas, sed Deus. ..." *De Deo Trino et Creatore* (Rome: Marietti, 1951), p. 113.

consequences of a modal trinitarianism. At bottom, his God is one divine Person, whose divinity does not remain monadic but differentiates itself into three modes of existing. If we harken back to the Fathers (and not the least of Barth's virtues as a theologian is that his thought allows one to do this), we hear above all the echoes of Tertullian. The latter's trinitarian thought may be characterized as "Monarchial Trinitarianism"; God, the *Monarchia*, "economizes" himself into a triad.[21] This cannot be dismissed as mere Economic Trinitarianism. Not in Tertullian, because God is a Trinity not only in the economy but in himself, though seemingly Tertullian's thought would allow us to say he is Trinity in function of the economy. And even less so in Barth because he views God's differentiating of himself as occurring, not simply for the sake of the economy, but ultimately because, in becoming Lord for us, God is predestining himself. This interpretation gains credibility when one remembers that, for Barth, God is not changeless essence but pure event. How else is one to understand the following statement in the *Doctrine of the Word of God:* "The name of Father, Son, and Spirit means that God is the one God in a threefold repetition . . . in such a way that only in this repetition is He the one God"?[22] Barth immediately adds that this "implies no alteration in his Godhead." This precludes any understanding of the self-differentiation which is the event of God as if it were temporal. It is less certain that, logically, it precludes an eternal differentiation of the divine essence as such.

Barth's doctrine of the Trinity is free of any overt modalism, and it is also beyond the danger of subordinationism, i.e., in no way open to conceiving the Father as already the fullness of the one Godhead who subsequently (in a logical, not temporal sense) generates a Son and spirates a Spirit, with the implication that the latter are thus lesser divinities. But some compromise has to be allowed in denying to the Three in God the full prerogatives of personhood. Granting that self-consciousness is a prerequisite for subjectivity, Barth cannot allow that Father, Son, and Spirit are three subjectivities because of the way in which he locates consciousness on the side of essence and nature. A logical reflection of this is found in his rejection, in Christology, of the *Logos asarkos*. He does not mean

---

[21]See Chapter Two; also note Barth's use of the terms *dispositio* and *oeconomia* in *C.D.*, I/1, p. 407.

[22]Ibid., p. 402.

by this to deny that the *Logos* is eternal within God, only to insist that even there the *Logos* is preexistent not otherwise than as the *Deus pro nobis*, i.e., he is not preexistent apart from the flesh in which he is eternally predestined to become incarnate within history.

> In this context, we must not refer to the second 'person' of the Trinity as such, to the eternal Son or the eternal Word of God in abstracto, and therefore to the so-called λόγος 'ἄσαρκος. . . . In Himself and as such He is not *Deus pro nobis*, either ontologically or epistemologically . . . it is pointless, as it is impermissible, to return to the inner being and essence of God and especially to the second person of the Trinity as such, in such a way that we ascribe to this person another form than that which God himself has given in willing to reveal himself and to act outwards.[23]

At the same time, this Christology retains an Alexandrian character, it remains a Christology "from above," and so Barth is led to defend the *enhypostasis* doctrine against Von Harnack and Paul Althaus. But even here Barth appears to mean an existing of humanity in the *hypostasis* of the Word, not as any sort of ontological state but as the event of divine revelatory freedom.

Two critical questions for Barth suggest themselves at this juncture: (1) Does his doctrine of the Trinity enable him to do justice to God's transcendence of his creation and especially of his chosen economy of salvation? (2) Can he do justice to the trinitarian doctrine, theologically, without explicit development of the implications, especially the psychological ones, of the category "person"?

First Question. Barth has made abundantly clear that we encounter the Trinity only in the revealed economy, that there God reveals himself as a Trinity even *in se*, but that even in the inner divine life God is a Trinity for us. This appears to say that God is not triune in himself other than in a manner corresponding to the form in which he so appears to us. Or, perhaps it would be fairer to Barth's thought to say that we are not free to think of God as triune in any other form. Such trinitarianism is rooted in a strong incarnationalism, as indeed any doctrine of the Trinity must be. The assumption of humanity, in God himself becoming man, is the epistemological clue to the triple self-differentiation within divinity that constitutes the Trinity. It is difficult to see how it could be otherwise. But Barth's theology carries us beyond this; for him, the incarnational

---

[23]*Church Dogmatics*, IV/1, *The Doctrine of Reconciliation*, transl. G. W. Bromiley (1956), p. 52.

event enjoys not only an epistemological role but an ontological one as well. God's becoming Lord for us in time is *identical* with his inner-divine self-differentiation in eternity. Barth is certainly clear that the Incarnation is free in the sense that nothing on man's part can call it forth. Here he is in agreement with Kierkegaard and in opposition to Hegel, for whom the Incarnation is at least philosophically necessary in the sense that without it man himself would be unintelligible. If man were to make any claim on the Incarnation, exercise any control over it, God would cease to be the Sovereign Lord. Yet, Incarnation and Trinity are two aspects of the one mystery of God's so becoming Lord, of his freely becoming God for us.

It is precisely this that poses the dilemma. Either the Trinity need not be in the same sense that the Incarnation need not be, or the Incarnation is also necessary from God's side. In the former alternative, how can the Trinity any longer be the very structure of divine being, rather than something contingent? In the latter alternative, why are not both Incarnation and Trinity accessible to reason, as Hegel believed? This impasse in Barthian theology is simply the logical consequence of the refusal to speak (however falteringly) of an inner-divine Trinity that exists apart from all consideration of creation and restoration—granting that all awareness of such could only be by way of revelation. Barth has no Trinity immanent in God, which, while the foundation of the economic Trinity, is not *identical* with it. But only such an immanent Trinity allows one to speak of an eternal self-differentiation within God that is necessary, not in the sense of coercion or of an infraconscious natural resultancy, but in the sense of constituting God's very beingness, which could not be other than it is and yet is such in total freedom. Against this background, the Incarnation is free in a quite distinct manner, namely, as something that, in distinction from the trinitarian processions, is freely willed by God and need not be at all.

Second Question. Another reservation on Barth's trinitarianism focuses on his eschewing of the traditional term "persons" in favor of "modes of existing." Understanding the threeness of God as his modes of existing for us, both in time and in eternity, conveys something quite different from speaking of three *Persons* who exist as God—which latter has never been taken to mean three existences. It is this difference that Barth wishes to leave unsaid. His theology is a modal trinitarianism in that it prefers not to conceive of three really distinct subjectivities constituting the one Godhead. His work is a bulwark against the all too obvious dangers of the cryptic tritheism latent in such a way of thinking. It can hardly be questioned that, for Barth, all terms connoting the personal in God refer in fact to divinity grasped as essence, and thus can properly be used only in the singular.

> ... It is to the one single essence of God, which is not to be tripled by the doctrine of the Trinity, but emphatically to be recognized in its unity, that there also belongs what we call today the 'personality' of God.[24]

One of Barth's followers, Heinrich Ott, makes this even more explicit: ". . . God is in no sense 'three Persons'. He is one Person."[25] But then the modes appear to be in reality modes of the Person, i.e., freely chosen modalities of God as he acts (both in eternal self-differentiation and in temporal communication) through and by way of his nature. They thus become modes of God's acting in the mystery of a self-communicating revelation. True enough, this *is* God for Barth—granted his concept of revelation. But all divine action, entitatively considered, is self-identically the divine reality and not merely some accident thereof. The point is whether or not such action *towards the world* is not necessarily creative, that is, whether it does not require as its terminus the production of something that is *not* God, something creaturely. On the basis of this distinction it is fairly simple to distinguish between the God who acts creatively and the variety of creatures brought into being—but it precludes assigning any real modes intrinsic to the divine activity itself; all such modes exist only in our thinking and, as said of God, collapse into the simplicity of the divine nature. But this is the very problem with the expression "modes of being," suggesting as it does distinctions of essence, something that the more traditional category of "persons" avoids at the outset. Barth, of course, emphatically denies the possibility of distinctions within the divine essence.[26] The caution expressed here regards rather the inner logic of his trinitarian explanation. Whether the designation "persons" can be purified of all anthropomorphic and tritheistic implications, and rescued for a positive role in trinitarian theology, remains to be explored.[27]

The Holy Spirit. Karl Barth's treatment of the third divine person clarifies further his modal trinitarianism. Once again, the herme-

---

[24]*C.D.*, I/1, p. 403.
[25]*God* (Atlanta: John Knox Press, 1974), p. 60.
[26]*C.D.*, I/1, p. 402.
[27]See Chapter Eight.

neutical key is revelation. In his transcendent freedom, God is the one who is free: to reveal, to determine the form of that revelation, to effect the contingent mode of its happening. In each, God remains God, but as respectively Father, Son, and Spirit. The Holy Spirit is the reality of God in his freedom to be subjectively present to men, that is, enabling them from within to believe that Jesus is the Lord. The occurrence of revelation is "not a thing within the power of man"; it is "not identical with ourselves"; it is never "statements about the existence of man." Indeed, since revelation occurs "not on the ground of [our] knowledge and choice, but on the ground of [our] being known and chosen," it is more a case of "God meeting himself from man's end." Herein lies the identity of the third divine person who is "no less and nothing else than God himself . . . executing his claim as Lord on us." The Spirit brings no new revelation, but is only the impartation of the revelation which has assumed form in the Incarnate Word. Faith (*pistis*) is "a possibility coming from a mode of God's existence, a mode of existence which is on a level, in essential unity, with Him who in the NT is described as Father and Son."[28] Thus, the Spirit is not to be confused with Jesus Christ, the Son and the Word. The Spirit is a third element added to the other two. As communicating God's lordship, the Spirit is Redeemer, in contrast to the Word who is Reconciler. Once again: the dogma of the Spirit is not Scripture but exegesis; God does not become Spirit solely in the event of revelation but is so antecedently in himself and could "under no circumstances be regarded as a third 'person' in the modern sense of the concept, not a third spiritual subject, a third 'I', a third Lord, but only a third mode of existence of the one divine subject or Lord."[29]

The mode of divine existence which is the Spirit is one conveying the *contingency* of revelation, which need not happen and when it does happen is entirely the work of God. The sovereignty of God is thus preserved even in his revelation, which is an unveiling of the God who *by his nature* cannot be unveiled. This reintroduces the paradoxical element in Barthian thought: in revelation we confess God, not only as he becomes manifest in history, but even as he is antecedently in himself, yet with the awareness that he could be otherwise. This is reminiscent of Kierkegaard, suggesting as it does that God is the unknown beyond all reason and faith-knowledge.

---

[28]*C.D.*, I/1, pp. 516–20, 526–28.
[29]Ibid., p. 537.

The believer, without ever knowing God, confesses his lordship in the personal existential event of revelation. That is, the names Father, Son, and Holy Spirit do not furnish *content* for our conceiving the eternal relations within divinity. They offer only a formal framework for our conceptions; it is "the regularly recurring mutual relations of the three concepts respectively"[30] that enable us to think, first of a pure origin and then of two different issues. This hiddenness of God is what such terms as "generation" (of the Son) and "spiration" (of the Spirit) are intended to convey. They mean only that the relations internal to God are unlike his relations to world and to man, and remain ineffable.

THE TRINITY OF TEMPORAL UNSURPASSABILITY: ROBERT JENSON

Barth's influence has been both major and lasting. The work of his followers, in richly exploiting his original thought, has tended to throw into relief different features of his trinitarianism. Robert Jenson, for example, in *God after God*[31] focuses attention immediately on the implications of Barth's intent to speak of an *antireligious* God. If the God of Kierkegaard inhabits a realm beyond reason, the God of Barth dwells in a region beyond religion. It is precisely revelation, that is to say, the appearance of God in our midst as Son of the Father in the Spirit, that renders the religious quest (and its frequent instrument, natural theology) vain. "Trinity," then, is simply a way of identifying the God who is the God of Faith and so other than the God of religion. But it is legitimate to ask if this disillusionment with the God of religion is not protracted to where it assumes an a priori, determining role in what follows in Barth's theology. It is this very presupposition which appears to deliver to him his focal concept of revelation, for example. Here a concealed indebtedness to Schleiermacher comes to the surface. The impasse to which organized religion had come vis-à-vis the question of God led Schleier-

---

[30] Ibid., p. 418. Barth means here that the triadic content of the New Testament is "sublimated once more in the unity of the divine essence," so that "to these facts there are no analogies." Thus also: "And the Father is not only the Creator God, He is with the Son and the Spirit also the Reconciler God and the Redeemer God." Ibid., p. 453.

[31] Robert Jenson, *God after God* (Indianapolis and New York: Bobbs-Merrill, 1969), esp. chap. 7.

macher to discover (or to rediscover) the role of religious experience. Barth simply transposes that (via Kierkegaard) into an existential experience of the word of God creating faith. In Barth's well-known tripartite division of revelation into: (i) the proclaimed Word, (ii) the normative Word of the New Testament, and (iii) the Word experienced in faith—it is the last that plays the central role.[32] Schleiermacher began with the historical Jesus, finding in him evidence of a God immanent in human consciousness. Barth's *point de départ* is not Christ's experience but the believer's experience of God in the form of the Word. The Barthian God is a God who cuts across all religious mediation of himself. There is no neutral third area between the true God and man; not even the humanity of Christ can function as such. The God of faith is a living God, he is a God of present address to men. The power of this theological thinking has demonstrated itself, yet it remains a presupposition that determines everything else; a concept of revelation is thereby formative of an entire theology. This a priori character of Barthian thought gives it a certain gratuity. Moreover, since the gratuitousness arises entirely from faith, any recourse to reasoned discourse is foreclosed to begin with. God is left inaccessible from man's side; the initiative is God's alone with the result that the relationship to men is unilateral and irreversible. Barth continued to defend this stance in his later work against Feuerbach's reduction of theology to anthropology.[33] But it is here that the charge against Barth of fideism finds some warrant. And it is his doctrine of the Trinity that puts all this into a clear perspective, because he insists the Trinity is not *a* doctrine but the prolegomenon of all other doctrines.

Another way of expressing the same reservation is that, with Barth—as Jenson makes clear—"we must ask who God is *before* we ask whether he is or what he is."[34] He further indicates that such a question is impossible outside the encounter with Jesus the Christ. Thus, one can raise the question of the oneness of God's being prior to the trinitarian question only if one wishes to neglect entirely the revelation which comes only by way of the Christ-event. Yet this only particularizes the problem already indicated. How can the

---

[32]*C.D.*, I/1, chap. 1, no. 4, pp. 98–140.

[33]See *Protestant Thought* (New York: Simon & Schuster, 1969), pp. 353–61, esp. p. 358.

[34]Jenson, p. 97; this accurately represents Barth's own position in *C.D.*, I/1, p. 345.

encounter with the life and message of Jesus have any significance, other than the purely humanistic, unless one already has some general ideas of God, at the very least of man's openness to the transcendent? Without some previous awareness of the divine, what grounds are there for believing what Jesus says about God or for confessing his own implicit claim of divinity? Such a general idea cannot, of course, determine the content of the encounter with Christ and may itself be no more than the *question* about God. In the Barthian project, the question arises only from God's answer, which in this sense precedes it: "Men call upon God, *because* and only *because*, he has answered before they call."[35] But then revelation merely "happens," and is thereby a mysterious and mythic phenomenon; it lacks any point of reference to man's own being other than the one it itself creates. Tillich, and even Bultmann, in reaction to this, attempt to work out what is rather a correlation of man's question and God's response.[36]

Jenson, however, in his own development of Barthian thought, highlights an even greater problem that lies at the heart of that theology. At the very least, it lays bare a paradox that defies understanding. The mystery of God's triunity is precisely the mystery of God's becoming what is other than himself without ceasing to be himself. The divine act and event in question is, of course, revelation. And it is exactly "Barth's doctrine of the Trinity [which] identifies God as the One whose being is the occurrence for and among us of the history of death and resurrection in Jesus" (p. 106). This divine self-differentiation occurs within our history and antecedently in God himself. This means, as Jenson makes clear, that "without ceasing to be the eternal, God took time and made time his own"; God "takes the form of creation, time, to be the form of his eternity" (p. 128). Thus God not only "is this becoming . . . is an event," even more he is "a particular event . . . a free event," with the consequence that "the act of being God is a *decision*" (pp. 125–27). Far from being timeless, God is time, he is primal history. What Jenson has done with Barth's thought at this point is to collapse God's eternity into what is rather "temporal unsurpassability." What has

---

[35]*The Epistle to the Romans*, transl. E. C. Hoskyns (London: Oxford University Press, 1933), p. 383.

[36]P. Tillich, *Systematic Theology*, 2:13; R. Bultmann, "The Problem of 'Natural Theology'," in *Faith and Understanding*, transl. L. P. Smith (New York: Harper and Row, 1969), pp. 313–31.

enabled him to do so is the process of identifying the economic and the immanent Trinity, following Barth's insistence on the unity of the Trinity as it appears in history and as it constitutes the inner life of God. Jenson's conclusion at any rate cannot be mistaken: "We are not to say that . . . he himself is timeless" (p. 103); eternity is itself "movement away from what is left behind and toward what is to be" (p. 128).

This development of Barth's thought throws light on his puzzling teaching in *The Humanity of God*[37] concerning the preexistence, not of the *Logos* in Jesus, but of the humanity of Jesus, with its logical consequence that there is no time before the Incarnation. Jenson observes that "Barth has abolished the notion of the timeless being of God by putting the historical event of Jesus' existence for his Father and his brothers in the place formerly occupied by timelessness" (p. 132). In support of this he quotes the *Church Dogmatics* (adding his own emphasis): "God's eternity is the unity of Father, Son, and Spirit; the three modes *in their temporality* are the one God."[38] While this does not mean to say that God has no nature at all, it does suggest that he has no nature other than that consisting in the insurpassability of what has happened. God could have chosen his eternity to exist in some other form but did not.

It is one thing to view the Trinity as affording explanatory grounds for the mystery of creation and salvation—in this matter Barth's theology is illuminating indeed. It is another thing entirely to dissolve all distinction between the inner-divine Trinity and the Trinity of the dispensation. The suspicion remains that Barth's thought does this in not allowing that God is anything more than what he has revealed himself to be. In his sovereign freedom, God always remains free to be other than he is, but Barth does not give place to any *actual* "excessus" of divinity, beyond what the believer faintly grasps. Put differently—Barth's theology will not allow any speculation about a possible *Deus in se*; of such a God man cannot even begin to speak.

The pure contingency of revelation, in its happening and in its form, means that there is nothing divine behind this pure facticity, no higher principle. Barth is quite right in refusing to speak of a deity behind the three modes of divine being; there is no fourth

---

[37]*The Humanity of God*, transl. John Newton Thomas (Richmond, Va.: John Knox Press, 1960).

[38]Jenson, p. 128, quoting *Die kirchliche Dogmatik*, II/1, p. 687.

reality in God. But he disallows a Trinity constituting the deity as deity that is distinguishable from its chosen modes of self-communication to men. His inner-divine Trinity is the structure of the particular event which has happened and continues to happen. What occurs can only be grasped eschatologically, i.e., in the Spirit who makes to be real in us already that which, absolutely speaking, still lies ahead. But it is here that the reservation on Barth's trinitarianism, especially in the development given to it by Jenson, is so strongly felt. If the being of God is only this event in its facticity, then has not the notion of God as transcendent been emptied of all true content? Do we not then have to give to God a future of his own, quite as open as ours? And is he then any longer God? Jenson himself is prepared to take these risks, but he observes that Barth is deliberately ambiguous on the matter (p. 113). It is as far as Barth's thought can be stretched. But it leaves us with a huge question.

THE TRINITY AS THREE RELATIONS OF ONE PERSONHOOD: CLAUDE WELCH

Claude Welch's "Constructive Statement," which forms the concluding section of his book on the Trinity, *In This Name*,[39] adopts Barth's negative attitude towards the suitability of the concept "persons."

> Properly, it can be said that if we really wish to maintain historical continuity with what the doctrine of the Trinity has meant, we ought *not* to speak of God as "three persons".... I am increasingly persuaded that the most useful term for our purpose is "modes of being" (or "modes of existing," the two terms being taken here as interchangeable). (pp. 274, 276)

This position is defended against advocates of a "social analogy" for the Trinity, notably Lionel Thornton,[40] who argues that the three Persons achieve among themselves an "organic unity," and Leonard Hodgson,[41] who builds upon the notion of person as be-

---

[39]Claude Welch, *In This Name: The Doctrine of the Trinity in Contemporary Theology* (New York: Charles Scribner's Sons, 1952; London: SCM, 1953).

[40]Lionel S. Thornton, *The Incarnate Lord* (London: Longmans, Green, 1928).

[41]Leonard Hodgson, *The Doctrine of the Trinity* (New York: Charles Scribner's Sons, 1944).

speaking interpenetration rather than isolation and discreteness, so that it includes rather than excludes the others to which it is related. Both of these arguments for a divine *koinōnia* carry over onto God many of the modern connotations of personality. Thornton's explanation, as Welch notes, has an anthropomorphic ring; the Persons are reduced to being "parts" of the deity. In Hodgson's alternate explanation, it would seem that in the perfect instance of personhood there would be a tendency to absorb the distinctness of others. The notion of distinctness, of differentiation, of mutual exclusivity, expressed in medieval thought as the incommunicability of the person, is left unexplained. Hodgson, unlike Thornton, advocates the social analogy at the cost of neglecting the psychological analogy which in earlier theology functioned as a corrective to some of the untoward implications of the social model. Both explanations suffer from a failure to think in genuinely analogical ways when speaking of persons in God.

Charles Lowry[42] pursues this social analogy further and comes closer to the nerve of the problem by introducing the formula: "three centers of one consciousness." But he fails to supply the metaphysical details that might illuminate what that formula really could mean. At any rate, Welch treats it as a mere verbal solution and himself sides with Barth's position which requires that we speak of one divine Person.

> The name 'God' is a proper name, not a generic term. The name of the Father, Son, and Holy Spirit, into which we are baptized, is one name. (p. 252)

Understandably, then, Welch appropriates Bethune-Baker's conclusion that Tertullian's *"personae,"* as a translation of the Greek *prosōpa,* bears the meaning of role or function and "conveys the notion more of the environment than of the subject."[43] He makes his own the observation of Reinhold Niebuhr that what is really constitutive of personality is self-transcendence. This helps to explain Welch's uneasiness with the doctrine of *enhypostasis* and leads him to cite with approval D. M. Baillie's caution that to view Jesus as a divine subject is Apollinarianism (p. 266). Welch even enlists

---

[42]Charles W. Lowry, *The Trinity and Christian Devotion* (New York: Harper, 1946).
[43]J. F. Bethune-Baker, *An Introduction to the Early History of Christian Doctrine* (London: Methuen, 1929), p. 234; cited by Welch, p. 269.

Aquinas as one of those who eschew using the term "person" of God in its full sense, citing the latter's statement that it is the divine nature that subsists.[44] But he fails to observe that St. Thomas holds this to be true because nature is included *in obliquo* in the concept of divine person.

In the final analysis, Welch's own conclusion is that of three distinct relations within divinity constituting the one personhood of God.

> In saying this, we of course do not mean that God the Father is another person from God the Son or God the Spirit ... as present to us God is one Lord, one essence, one Thou, and therefore one in personality, but he is present to us as Father, Son, and Holy Spirit and therefore "He" in a threefold sense. (pp. 271–72)

A clear contribution in Welch's thought is his acknowledgment of theology's need to have recourse to the resources of metaphysics ("trinitarian philosophizing" but not "philosophic trinitarianism"), especially the categories of "relational being" or "subsistent relation" (p. 243). But he himself fails to carry this through to where the distinction between nature and person becomes a significant theological factor. One reservation to this overall view of his work, however, is called for. In an article published in 1967 Welch declared himself less confident of this trinitarian theology he had worked out in 1952.[45]

THE THOMIST TRINITY AFTER KANT: KARL RAHNER

Strange to relate, the movement of Neo-Orthodoxy in German Protestantism found an ally in German Catholic thought developing in an inverse direction, i.e., not away from the Liberalism introduced by Schleiermacher but, in a qualified sense, towards it. This direction was unavoidable after the Modernist crisis, in which the real problems were not so much solved as merely deferred through ecclesiastical intervention.[46] But the latter disciplinary action was

---

[44]Welch, pp. 278 and 191, citing Thomas Aquinas, *Summa theologiae*, I, q. 29, a. 4.

[45]See "Theology as Risk," *Frontline Theology*, ed. D. Peerman (Richmond, Va.: John Knox Press, 1967), p. 120.

[46]See the decree of the Holy Office *Lamentabile* and the papal encyclical *Pascendi*, both published in 1907 under Pius X; Denzinger-Schönmetzer, 3401–66 and 3475–500.

necessitated precisely because the intellectual resources were lacking which might have enabled Catholic thinkers to deal with the questions raised as genuine theological issues. Thus the questions perdured and continued to show themselves exigent of answers. A tentative probing began with the so-called *Nouvelle Théologie* of the 1940s (DeLubac, Daniélou, etc.). Vatican Council II signaled the beginning of the attempt to reappropriate Christian faith-content, not apart from the question, but precisely from within it. Joseph Maréchal had earlier provided a remote impetus for this move of Catholic theology into modernity by confronting the thought of Aquinas (as it had reasserted itself in the Neo-Thomist movement) with the *Critiques* of Kant.[47] This proved to be the most promising avenue of development, and its end product was the recasting of Thomism in "transcendentalist" terms, above all in the area of epistemology. The "transcendental turn," seeking to surmount the subject-object dichotomy in consciousness itself, meant in fact a quite different concept of being, with the focus now on spirit, meaning, subjectivity, temporality, and the dialectical movement of history.

The virtualities inherent in the new thinking inaugurated by Maréchal have come to full bloom in the theology of Karl Rahner— not there alone, but most markedly there. In his impressive system, the Trinity occupies a central and privileged place, as in the equally powerful system of Karl Barth. Indeed, Rahner reduces the complex richness of Christian theology to solely the three inseparable doctrines of: Trinity, Christ, and grace. This *ontological* order transposes as easily into an *anthropological* order: grace, Christ, and Trinity. But this is only to say that the Trinity simultaneously inaugurates and consummates everything else. The transposition of order, which occurs in our knowledge, simply illustrates Rahner's principle that theology *is* anthropology, but a Christian anthropology, that is to say, a doctrine of man *before God,* as precisely openness to God. And, in fact, Rahner makes the anthropological starting point his own. This is the transcendentalism at the heart of all his thought, inherited from the Germanic philosophies of consciousness, the tradition in which he stands, and filtered through Maréchal's accommodation of that to Thomism. Rahner's revision of Aquinas, centered on a

---

[47]Joseph Maréchal, *Le point de départ de la Métaphysique,* Leçons sur le développement historique et théorique du problème de la connaissance, cahier V, *Le Thomisme devant la Philosophie critique* (Brussels and Paris: Desclée, 1949).

theory of human knowing in his seminal work *Geist in Welt,*[48] is radical and represents a move considerably beyond Maréchal. The basic thrust of that work is furthered and altered into what amounts to a philosophy of religion in *Hörer des Wortes.*[49] The two works are the foundations for Rahner's addressing the concrete questions of theology in his massive *Schriften zur Theologie.*[50] The underlying themes of this impressive program have been recapitulated recently in the single volume *Foundations of Christian Faith* (1978).

Philosophical Presuppositions. The very title of what is still Rahner's major work, *Spirit in the World,* discloses what is from beginning to end the foundation stone of his thought—his conception of man, not as rational animal, but as embodied spirit. The data of Scripture and tradition are incorporated into and interpreted within the context of this transcendental anthropology, emerging therefrom into a systematic theology. Though Rahner treats this as a theological anthropology, it does not surrender thereby its philosophic character, but lives as a philosophizing within theology.[51] Without confusing the two orders or failing to distinguish between them, Rahner does steadfastly refuse to separate or allow any sort of radical dichotomy between faith and reason, grace and nature, theology and phi-

---

[48]*Geist in Welt,* 2nd ed. by J. B. Metz (Munich: Kosel-Verlag, 1957); *Spirit in the World,* transl. W. Dyck (New York: Herder and Herder, 1968), hereafter *S.W.* Originally done as a doctorate thesis at the University of Freiburg, it failed to win the approval of Martin Honecker (as mentor of the dissertation) on grounds of not being an accurate interpretation of Aquinas's metaphysics of knowledge, thus preventing Rahner's earning the degree.

[49]*Hörer des Wortes,* revised edition of J. B. Metz (Munich: Kosel-Verlag, 1963); Eng. ed., *Hearers of the Word,* transl. M. Richards (New York: Herder and Herder, 1969), hereafter *H.W.* Some reservations have been expressed on this translation; a good number of helpful corrections have been supplied by Andrew Tallon in "Spirit, Freedom, History," *The Thomist* 38, no. 4 (October 1974), pp. 908–36.

[50]*Schriften zur Theologie* (Einsiedeln-Zurich-Cologne: Benziger Verlag, 1954); Eng. ed., *Theological Investigations,* 20 vols. to date (Baltimore: Helicon Press, 1961–69; New York: Herder and Herder, 1971–73; New York: Seabury Press, 1974–), hereafter *T.I.*

[51]"A really *theological* question can only be put, however, if it is understood as being simultaneously a philosophical one.... 'Natural', 'philosophical' theology is first and last not one sphere of study side by side with revealed theology, as if both could be pursued quite independently of each other, but an internal factor of revealed theology itself; if philosophical theology, however, is transcendental anthropology, so is revealed theology too." "Theology and Anthropology," *T.I.,* vol. 9, p. 34.

losophy. In this, his project resembles the Augustinian "Christian wisdom," and it is closer in spirit to the exemplarism of Bonaventure than to the empiricism of Aquinas. At any rate, the consequence of this is that it is impossible to deal adequately with what he makes of the doctrine of the Trinity without adverting to his philosophic thought as it works within the light of faith.

Rahner's initial commitment to Transcendentalism means not only that man is viewed as spirit but that ultimately reality itself is conceived in terms of spirit. What is beneath spirit is a precipitate of spirit—for example what Aristotle calls prime matter, also the body, and the faculties of the soul.[52] If spirit in its finite conditions is to transcend itself this can only be by way of a movement which is at bottom receptive. Were this not so, there is no reason why finite spirit would not actively consummate itself, i.e., bring itself to full realization, immediately. This means the origination of the whole apparatus of sense out of spirit for this purpose. Here Rahner's speculative thought demands that spirit undergo an act of self-alienation in which its own being is posited as the act of being of what is not spirit, but matter. Then spirit's consciousness of itself becomes knowledge of the other, which in its receptive character enriches the limited being of created spirit and inaugurates its movement of self-transcendence. What is above finite spirit, on the other hand, is infinite spirit, which the believer names God. This spiritlike character of all reality endows it with a dialectical quality, isomorphic to the phenomenon of human consciousness. Spirit is not mere beingness, in the sense of what is other than nothing, but being as present to itself (*Bei-sich-sein*);[53] it is being in the dynamic process of coming to itself. But this coming to self demands the positing of the other in which spirit realizes itself and appropriates itself, thereby returning to itself. Being is thus luminous self-presence and so is, in its origins, one with knowing.[54] This original unity of being and know-

---

[52]See *S.W.*, pp. 279–80; on prime matter, see p. 80.

[53]*S.W.*, p. 68; see also "Current Problems in Christology," *T.I.*, vol. 1, p. 169 and "Some Implications of the Scholastic Concept of Uncreated Grace," ibid., p. 327.

[54]"Thus being and knowing exist in an original unity. . . . Being itself is the original, *unifying* unity of being and knowing in their *unification* in being-known." *S.W.*, pp. 68–69. "For St. Thomas, being and knowing are thus *unius generis;* they arise from a single, unified root, from an original unity. Being is knowing *in itself,* and knowing is the being-present-to-itself of the being of a thing—that is, that which is necessarily contained in the constitution of being, its reflection back into itself, its subjectivity." *H.W.*, p. 41.

ing explains the phenomenon of finite knowing. Man, though distanced from being in the finiteness of his existence, retains a mysterious preobjective, non-thematic "awareness" of being as such, as unlimited. This amounts to a sort of "foreknowledge" which constitutes the transcendental ground to consciousness; the prehending is itself primordial self-consciousness. As nonobjective, as only the horizon for objects, it emerges into explicit consciousness only in the apprehending of particular beings (and only subsequent to this can be thematized in reflexive consciousness). The turn to the act of "to be" is simultaneous with the turn to material things, and openness to God is only by way of immersion in the world. All concrete knowing, in and by way of the image or the concept, is thus the thematization of the foreknowing (the *Vorgriff*).[55] Such thematization as always inadequate to the latter unleashes the dynamism of an inexhaustible process of question, answer, new question, etc. In this metaphysics of knowing we do not grasp being as sedimented in a world extrinsic to consciousness (as in Aristotelian abstraction). Rather, our very constitution as spirit is already a preapprehension of being in a limitless way as the a priori condition making possible the categorical grasp of particular beings. Rahner is quick to make clear that this is not the combining of objects of knowledge under some more general point of view; it "cannot be the subsequent sum, but only the original unity of the possible objects."[56]

The *Vorgriff* means that in the conceptualizing act the knowing subject does not so much abstract being as "perform" it. Though appropriating the term "abstraction" from Aquinas, Rahner gives it a meaning quite different from any it has in the latter. The *intellectus agens* of St. Thomas becomes, in Rahner's thought, the faculty of the pregrasp of being.[57] It floods with its light of being the content of sensation, represented in the phantasm. Thus, abstraction (as *conversio ad phantasmata*) is a *synthetic* act; it is the coalescence of a sensible grasp of the particular with the *Vorgriff* which allows the determined content of the particular entity to appear in its beingness. The universal is achieved by grasping the content of sensation "in its dynamic orientation to the totality of all possible objects, to *esse* . . . . Insofar as it apprehends this material of sensibility within its anticipatory (*vorwegnehmenden*) dynamism to *esse*, it 'illuminates' this

[55]*S.W.*, pp. 142–45.
[56]*S.W.*, p. 145.
[57]*S.W.*, pp. 202–26; see also p. 225.

material . . . and thus lets the universal be known in the sensible."[58] The universal concept is not achieved in excising individual notes and concrete determinations of existence and attaining to an intelligible representation of what is understood of the essence, to an intentional surrogate of real (extramental) being. Thus Rahner is able to say once again that knowing is the self-presence of being, being in its subjectivity; it is not any sort of stretching out to a world extraneous to the spiritual knower.[59]

This brief *excursus* into Rahner's philosophical thought is necessary if his theology is to be explored in more than a superficial way. Its foundational character justifies at this point a brief critical word. At least attention should be called to two general questions that continue to assert themselves. First of all, the original unity of being and knowing seems at times to be transformed by Rahner into an identity. Such identity can be readily granted in the case of God, but in the realm of the finite it means collapsing being into meaning, metaphysics into cognitional theory. Welcome as the emphasis upon the subjectivity that lies at the heart of existence is, must this mean that things lacking their own subjective pole, i.e., incapable of knowledge, do not truly exist as beings, as exercising *their own* act of "to be"? Is there not a covert Idealism in Rahner's contention that, as only potentially intelligible, such entities come to actual intelligibility and so actual being only in and through man? It is at least questionable whether this does justice to the reality of matter and bodiliness in their own right (even if one is willing to allow that man's knowing of them is the bestowal upon them of meaning they cannot otherwise possess). If man is spirit in the world, he is not such in some angelic fashion, for his spirit is always the form of a body and naturally incapable of any understanding save in dependence upon the body.

Secondly, there is an obscurity regarding the being that is preapprehended. Is this God, even if not known as such? In *Hearers of the Word* Rahner does make the identification: "The preconcept is directed towards God";[60] something is understood insofar as it has

---

[58]*S.W.*, p. 225.

[59]"Some Implications of the Scholastic Concept of Uncreated Grace," *T.I.*, vol. 1, p. 327.

[60]*H.W.*, p. 64; Rahner adds here: "It does not aim directly at God, so as to present absolute being in its specific self, immediately and objectively"; thus it does not constitute a purely a priori proof of the existence of God.

its ground "in the absolute being of God";[61] limited knowledge is possible only "in virtue of the a priori, implicit affirmation of an asymptotically approached, infinite being, whom we call God."[62] But this seems to be a gratuitous postulation, a sudden leap from reason to faith. Elsewhere, Rahner is more consistent in maintaining that "the preconception given in transcendence is directed to the nameless" and that "the Whither of transcendence is always there as the nameless, the indefinable, the unattainable. It bestows itself upon us by refusing itself, by keeping silence, by staying afar."[63] Earlier, in *Spirit in the World,* he argued that the being seized in the preapprehension was *not* God: "For the *esse* apprehended in the preapprehension, . . . [is known] . . . as able to be limited . . . and as already limited."[64] This is misleading until he goes on to explain what it means, namely, that being is known as limited only in virtue of a pregrasp of *esse* as such. The terminus of the *Vorgriff* here appears to be the *esse* of the particular beings, but only insofar as such *esse* is *in itself* (i.e., apart from its particularization) unlimited. But why need this be anything more than the realm of pure possibility for knowledge, as Rahner himself implies in speaking of it as "the preapprehension of the unlimited scope of all the possible objects of thought altogether"?[65] In the end, there is little doubt that Rahner grounds our being and knowing in the absolute act of *to be* which is God. As a philosopher, he does justify speaking of an unlimited horizon to human knowing. But it is a horizon that, within philosophy at any rate, remains empty of content. What is critically questionable is the leap enabling Rahner to name that horizon "God." Rahner notes that from Plato to Hegel the horizon is that of the Forms or of Absolute Idea; that Kant was content to leave it a horizon set by sense intuition; that Heidegger gives it the negative infinity of the nothingness (*das Nichts*) which conceals Being (*Sein*) and out of which it unveils itself to man (*Alētheia*)—but he himself calls it God.[66] But even if our experience (understood by way of the

---

[61]*H.W.*, p. 97.

[62]"Science as a 'Confession'," *T.I.*, vol. 3, p. 388.

[63]"The Concept of Mystery in Catholic Theology," *T.I.*, vol. 4, pp. 50–52.

[64]*S.W.*, p. 180.

[65]*S.W.*, p. 209.

[66]*H.W.*; this reference to Heidegger does not appear in the translation by Michael Richards but can be found in the translation by Joseph Donceel which appears in *A Rahner Reader,* ed. Gerald McCool (New York: Seabury Press, 1975), p. 17.

transcendental method of reduction) testifies both to this primordial, anticipatory "knowing" and to a certain positivity on the part of what is thereby "known," this still leaves unexplained how it can be called God. This difficulty may not be insurmountable; Vincent Branick, for example, may be close to suggesting a way out in writing that "the *esse* in itself of the limited being is precisely the inconceivable contact-point between creature and God."[67] But the way in which *esse commune* and *esse divinum* are used interchangeably remains a vulnerable point in Rahner's thought at the very outset. Underlying these two general reservations is the question whether being for Rahner can be genuinely analogical (as he wishes to maintain) or whether in the final analysis it is not rather something univocal that is differentiated only dialectically. The suspicion persists that the being thematized in Rahner's *Vorgriff* is in fact only the unrestricted illuminating power of the intellect; if so, it cannot be common being.[68]

An Ontology of Symbolism. The significance of all this for theology is that it introduces Rahner's doctrine of the real symbol. All being is a dynamism of self-expression and self-communication, achieved in a universal process of symbolization.[69] Everything, to the extent that it is, seeks to come to full realization of itself by bringing its own being to expression in "another" that it posits over and against itself. When made into the domain of matter this amounts to embodiment or incarnation. This "other" is posited by the being seeking its fulfillment as its own real symbol. It is not a mere sign or cognitive pointer, but an ontological reality; not merely a symbolic representation (which is a derivative instance of symbol), but a symbolic reality. However, this realization of the self in and through the other—being giving itself away into the other to discover and appropriate itself there in knowledge and love—is constitutive of the very essence of the being in its coming to fulfillment. Thus, the mystery of being is such that it is one, but only in its very plurality,

---

[67] Vincent P. Branick, *An Ontology of Understanding: Karl Rahner's Metaphysics in the Context of Modern German Hermeneutics* (St. Louis: Marianist Communications Center, 1974), p. 141.

[68] James B. Reichmann has argued persuasively for this interpretation in "Transcendental Method and the Psychogenesis of Being," *The Thomist* 32, no. 4 (October 1968), pp. 449–508.

[69] "All beings are by their very nature symbolic, because they necessarily 'express' themselves in order to attain their own nature." "Theology of the Symbol," *T.I.*, vol. 4, p. 224.

i.e., it maintains itself precisely by resolving and disclosing itself into a plurality.[70] It is not a primordial oneness that diminishes itself as it splinters into a multiplicity.

But it is the doctrine of the Trinity that delivers this knowledge to us; Rahner expressly indicates this, referring to such knowledge as an "ontological ultimate."[71] The confession of Jesus' divinity leads to the realization that he is the real symbol of God in the world. As the condition for this, he is first of all the Word uttered by the Father as the Unoriginated God from all eternity within the depths of divinity. This inner-divine dynamism prolongates itself *ad extra* into the Void. God communicates himself a second time, this time to world. As a genuine *self*-communication, the communicated is the same divine *Logos* but now uttered into the spatiotemporal sphere. The consequence is the Word Incarnate, the Word existing as the man Jesus Christ. Thus, man is possible because the exteriorization of the Word is possible. Indeed, man is what eventuates if God choses to utter himself into the Void. Humanity, and thereby the rest of creation, are preconditions for the Incarnation because there must be a nature other than God's into which the Word can be spoken.

> God's creative act always drafts the creature as the paradigm of a possible utterance of himself.... The immanent self-utterance of God in his eternal fullness is the condition of the self-utterance of God outside himself, and the latter continues the former.[72]

Men other than Christ are by their very nature capable of and— through a subsequent gratuitous act of God's love that affects that nature existentially—called to that sonship towards the Father already achieved in Christ. The one difference is that other men realize accidentally (by grace) what Jesus is hypostatically (by ontic union); a difference reducible to the distinction between adoptive sonship and natural sonship. This phase of Rahner's suggestive theology admits of rich development: as the *Logos* is the real symbol within the divinity of God as Father, so Christ is the symbol of God in the world; the Church in turn is the symbol of Christ, and the Eucharist the symbol of the Church.

---

[70] "... a being is, of itself, independently of any comparison with anything else, plural in its unity." Ibid., p. 227.

[71] "Being *as* such, and hence *as* one (*ens* as *unum*), for the fulfillment of its being and its unity, emerges into a plurality—of which the supreme mode is the Trinity." Ibid., p. 228.

[72] "On the Theology of the Incarnation," *T.I.*, vol. 4, p. 115.

But there is another phase entirely, one rooted in the procession of the Third in God. Two self-expressions within God would make no sense. Rahner is thus forced to break out of the framework of symbolization and resort to another act of divine self-realization, that of self-appropriation. Self-communication by way of the Word consummates itself in a *redditio completa ad seipsum*, in a seizing of the self as expressed in its symbol. Spirit returns to itself by the prior giving away of itself to its real symbol; the coming-to-oneself (*Zu-sich-selbst-kommen*) is always a coming-from-another (*Von-einen-andern-herkommen*).[73] If Rahner's trinitarianism at this point is somewhat less convincing—and it is—it should be remembered that all trinitarian theologies suffer a similar impoverishment when it comes to explaining the Third Person within God. There is a certain retreat into obscurity here because it is not at all clear why loving appropriation of the self in the symbol demands positing a third reality which is neither the self nor its symbol, a third which in the Godhead is neither Father nor Son but *Pneuma*. Nonetheless, this latter phase of divine life in which God is not expressing but rather "receiving" himself is also prolongated to the world—necessarily so since the two are inseparable. The Father "appropriates" his own reality symbolically realized in Christ (at once the natural Christ and the mystical Christ that is Church) in the temporal mission of the Holy Spirit.

Rahner brings his thinking to a concise systematic statement in *The Trinity*[74] when he writes that what we are striving to speak of here is "one self-communication of God [that] occurs in *two* basic ways that belong together" (p. 88). Further clarification can be gained by understanding that these two phases of divine life, that of self-communication and of self-appropriation, are realized respectively by way of knowledge and by way of love. The basis for these assertions is what has been made manifest historically in the life of the Incarnate Word; thus Rahner's starting point is God's self-communication *to man*. That communication, constituting as it does the

---

[73]*S.W.*, p. 229.

[74]*The Trinity* (New York: Herder and Herder, 1970), translation by Joseph Donceel of "Der dreifaltige Gott als transzendenter Urgrund der Heilsgeschichte," which is vol. 2, chapter 5 of *Mysterium Salutis: Grundriss Heilsgeschichtlicher Dogmatik,* ed. Johannes Feiner and Magnus Löhrer (Einsiedeln: Benziger Verlag, 1967). In the text, page references in parentheses that follow are to this work.

economy of salvation, leads us to understand that creation itself is
in reality a moment of this salvational self-communication, insofar
as it posits the addressee, the personal recipient. The two moments
in God's approach to man within salvation history are inseparable
but distinct, and Rahner brings to light four double sets of their
distinguishing characteristics (p. 88).

God communicates himself:

in a first "moment"	in a second "moment"
as truth	as love
in history	grounding transcendence
being God's offer	bringing about man's acceptance
and man's origin	and man's absolute future

Identity of Economic and Immanent Trinity. The very possibility of
this self-communication of a God of absolute mystery is nowise
attainable by reason; it is merely accepted in its pure givenness in
a faith encounter with the Christ of a historical revelation. But part
of the content of that encounter is its character as made possible by
a *self*-communication of God. What the Christian encounters is nothing less than God himself, in the structure of his own being, that is
to say, precisely as triune. Thus, the Trinity that becomes manifest
in time, in sacred history, is not otherwise than the Trinity which
eternally is the deity itself. What the believer experiences in God's
dealing with man within history is not merely an analogue of the
inner-divine Trinity, a replica reflected within the creaturely sphere
that only conveys the truth that God is in himself three-personal.
"No adequate distinction can be made between the Trinity and the
doctrine of the economy of salvation" (p. 24). In Rahner's succinct
phrase: "The economic Trinity is the immanent Trinity, and the
immanent Trinity is the economic Trinity" (p. 25). Clearly enough,
God need not have chosen to communicate himself to the world;[75]
that he did so is a pure given that lies hidden in his transcendent
freedom and love. But having so elected, a certain inner necessity
prevails. God can communicate his own reality to a universe of time
and space only by becoming man; only the *Logos* within divinity can

---

[75]"'Christocentricity' . . . does not deny in any way that God *could* have
created a world without an Incarnation. . . ." "Christology within an Evolutionary View of the World," *T.I.,* vol. 5, p. 178.

become man;[76] the Incarnation of the Word cannot be without its consummation in the mission of the Spirit (as God's own act of receiving back the Word spoken into the Void). It also follows that the entire occurrence cannot be other than historical, though such particulars as "when" and "where" remain contingent. Rahner does safeguard God's freedom in becoming man against the implied necessity for such in Hegel's thought. But the way in which emphasis falls upon the Son as the auto-expression of God the Father, coupled with the insistence that only the Son could be God's self-expression (real symbol) into the Void, does strongly suggest that, prior to the Incarnation, the eternal Word is not so much the nonincarnate Word as the Word that is to become incarnate. It is a matter of a subtle shading of thought, but a significant one. Obviously, God wills to become man from all eternity. But Rahner's thinking appears to compromise a view of that utterly free act as *logically* subsequent to the unoriginate "structure" of God's very being as triune, that is, to God's very being as deity apart from all relation to the nondivine. Does not this overstate the continuity between the eternal procession and the temporal mission, by implying that the Second Divine Hypostasis *in virtue of his eternal generation* is the hypostasis, not only that can become man, but that is to become man? At the most, this is suggestive of a moral necessity, which, however, also may be questioned. The contrast can be more sharply drawn: Rahner finds an explanation for creation and redemption in God's very *being* as Trinity; earlier theology preferred to find only its possibility there and to leave its actual occurrence to the mysteriousness of God's altruistic *love*. The former does highlight the salvational import of the doctrine of the Trinity, and much of its power lies here. But does not this strict identification of "economic" and "immanent" Trinity exact a price of its own? Does it not compromise the utter transcendence of God's *creative* love? Rahner's trinitarianism stresses self-communication so far that *creatio ex nihilo* loses its full ontological density. It is the Christian understanding of creation that now becomes problematic. This hesitancy, in the face of his rich speculative endeavors, gains some vindication from another characteristic in his thinking. This is the repeated tendency

---

[76]"It will appear that on this point St. Augustine had too little understanding of the most ancient theology, which held that it is the Logos who appears and must appear if God wishes to show himself personally to the world." "Nature and Grace," *T.I.*, vol. 4, p. 177.

to explain as *formal* causality what an earlier theology had insisted could only be grasped as an instance of divine *efficient* causality, if an adequate distinction was to be maintained between Creator and creature. It is above all in a trinitarian context that Rahner defends this position, granting to each of the Divine Persons indwelling the soul in the grace-state the exercise of a distinct "quasi-formal causality" upon the soul, something "proper" to each of them rather than common.[77] The question that all of this raises is whether or not the traditional Christian understanding of creation has been altered into something closer to Hegel's understanding of the origin of the world. What that tradition leaves in the contingencies of divine love, Hegel reduces to "appearances" already determined by the essential structure of what appears.

Rejection of the Psychological Analogy. Rahner makes clear what he is doing: he is bypassing the psychological analogy by means of which the Trinity was explained from Augustine's time onward (until the radical reinterpretation of Schleiermacher), in favor of the earlier model operative in the speculation of the Greek Fathers. But, as noted earlier,[78] the dialectic of thought at work there had not yet freed itself of a certain subordinationism. This was perhaps inevitable because of the immediacy of religious experience focused upon the historical life and death of Jesus. Against the background of Old Testament piety, the One whom Jesus calls Father is taken as Yahweh-God. Jesus is the Son of God in an economic or functional sense, without the ontological question as yet intruding upon the Semitic consciousness. But that question is inevitable, and when it does urge itself upon believers, the first reaction is a pattern of reflection that tends to view the Word and the Spirit as the two arms of God held out to the world by the Father. Only the latter is *the* God (*auto-Theos* in Origen's sense); the Others are extensions of his divinity which are merely personified. What is correctly surmised is the derivative character of the Second and Third in God; what is incorrectly implied (though not intended) is that they have the Father's divinity by participation, and as a result that they possess a diminished divinity. The two Cappadocian Fathers, Gregory of Nazianzus and Gregory of Nyssa, do introduce the category of "relation," but it remains peripheral to their trinitarian thought. It

---

[77]See "Some Implications of the Scholastic Concept of Uncreated Grace," *T.I.*, vol. 1, pp. 319–46, esp. pp. 334ff.

[78]See a view of this development worked out in Chapter Two.

enables them, negatively, to oppose subordinationist tendencies without positively illuminating the mystery; its use is formalistic and abstract in the pejorative sense. With Augustine a fresh start is made in another thought-world entirely, one that seeks understanding in an exploration of the human psyche. Rahner refuses the move inaugurated by Augustine. His grounds for doing so are biblical; the believer first encounters the mystery in the history of Jesus of Nazareth, and so all attempts at understanding must begin there and not from any human, philosophical concept of knowledge and love. But he cannot do so without allowing a subtle subordinationism to reassert itself. In *The Trinity*, he argues that:

> The Bible and the Greeks would have us start from the one unoriginate God who is already Father even when nothing is known as yet about generation and spiration. (p. 17)

The same point is reaffirmed in "Theos in the New Testament":

> ὁ Θεός in the language of the New Testament signifies the Father . . . the concrete, individual uninterchangeable Person . . . who is in fact the Father, not the single divine nature that is seen subsisting in three hypostases, but the concrete Person who possesses the divine nature unoriginately.[79]

Rahner cites Michael Schmaus, confirming that this is the interpretation of the early Fathers and the Creeds, and adding the observation that "subordinationist ideas must not be associated with this mode of speech."[80] Certainly, there was no intention of subordinationism among orthodox Christian writers, and there were even declaimers that were explicit if inconsistent. But the inner logic of their thought—and so of Rahner's too—bears that connotation despite explicit disavowals. The system of thought being used as an instrument of explanation reaches a breaking point in face of the mystery itself. In the initial dialectical development of trinitarian theology this mode of thought was understandable and unavoidable (like the early stages of organic growth). The question that has to be faced is what its reintroduction does to our understanding of the mystery in its presently developing stage.

---

[79]"Theos in the New Testament," *T.I.*, vol. 1, p. 146.
[80]Ibid., p. 147.

Ways of Existing, Not Persons. Rahner himself is fully alert to the cryptic subordinationism towards which the logic of his trinitarianism tends at this point in its development and is quick to repudiate any such implication. He achieves this by allowing the earlier-employed categories of "self-communication" and "self-appropriation" to give way to the category of "relation." The latter more readily brings into relief the equality of the Three in God and the full identity of each with the Godhead. In line with Aquinas's development of Augustine, the real relations are understood as subsistent, but Rahner demurs at taking the further step and identifying these Subsistent Relations as "Persons" (*Personae*). All in all, four explanations for this can be found.[81] First, "person" is not a biblical concept to begin with, but a theological construct, and so can be set aside without jeopardizing the language of revelation. Secondly, the concept itself today cannot be unburdened of psychological connotations according to which it signifies an autonomous center of consciousness—which in a trinitarian context would mean three centers of consciousness, and so tritheism. Thirdly, in thinkers such as Aquinas, its proper meaning is metaphysical, not psychological; it is akin to the Greek term *hypostasis* and is used interchangeably with the Latin word *subsistentia,* which conveys not what subsists but the fact of subsisting. Fourthly, its employment in early Church Councils and Creeds is intended as a *logical* explanation, with the formal role of safeguarding a certain consistency in speech, and not as an ontic description of the mystery itself. The first of these reasons cannot be gainsaid, but the fourth is questionable in light of what would appear to be the intention of the early Church to address the Trinity precisely as a mystery *of salvation.* At any rate, it is in the second and third reasons that the heart of the matter lies.

By using the expression "ways of existing," however, Rahner has taken the edge off any suggestion that his thought bears an inherent tendency towards subordinationism. Yet, in the same instant, he has chosen not to exploit the category of "person" because of its implication of three divine subjectivities. Paradoxically, after observing in *The Trinity* that "the word 'person' happens to be there, it has been consecrated by the use of more than 1500 years, and there is really no better word which can be understood by all and would give rise to fewer misunderstandings" (p. 44), he himself insists strongly upon

---

[81]These are to be found scattered throughout *The Trinity.*

the need to replace it. He urges that "we consciously give up the explicit use of the concept of 'person' " (p. 101, n. 20). The term is not to be found in the New Testament's confession of the economic Trinity, nor among the early Fathers (p. 104); indeed, Scripture says nothing explicit about any doctrine of the immanent Trinity as such (p. 22). His own alternative is a preference for the formula "three relatively distinct ways of existing" or "ways of being" (p. 74). A bit further on, this is rendered as " 'distinct manners of subsisting' [which expression] has the advantage of not as easily insinuating as 'three persons' the multiplication of the essence and of the subjectivity" (p. 113).[82] In this, one hears both the τρόποι τῆς ὑπάρξεως of the Cappadocians and its equivalent in the theology of Karl Barth. This is surely not classical modalism, but it can justly be called a Modal Trinitarianism.

Summary. The above cursory summary of Rahner's trinitarianism leads to one very positive evaluation: it is an impressive recouping of the salvational import of the doctrine. At the same time, three felt reservations challenge the conclusiveness of his speculations. First, there is his foundational concept of being as dialectical; so viewed, being loses its analogical character and becomes in fact univocal. What this calls into question is an adequate understanding of creation *ex nihilo*, at least in causal terms. Secondly, there is the schematic thinking which represents the Father as the *Fons Divinitatis*, and the *Logos* and *Pneuma* as his auto-expression and self-repossession respectively. The latter are so characterized even vis-à-vis the world, with the result that only with difficulty can such thinking be purged of a subordinationist tendency. Thirdly, there is the refusal to allow any psychological dimension to the term "person," and thus the disavowal of distinct subjectivities within God. This more than all else is the crucial point in Rahner's understanding and explains its characterization here as a Modal Trinitarianism. It can be theologically weighed only by exploring the alternative possibility, an option which will be pursued in Chapter Nine. For now it will suffice to call attention to two questions to which Rahner's own position gives rise. Is it allowable to restrict the concept of personhood so much that it excludes the aspect of intersubjectivity? And is not the doing of this, in fact, a reification of "person," a reduction of it to another form of essence?

---

[82]Rahner notes here that this expression is not to be understood as "a 'modality' without which the substantially real might also exist." *The Trinity*, p. 112.

NEO-MODALISM: JOHN MACQUARRIE

What is meant by designating the thought of both Barth and Rahner "Modal Trinitarianism" can be clarified somewhat by contrasting it with a more explicit modalism, advocated by some contemporary Christian thinkers. John Macquarrie's procedure in *Principles of Christian Theology*[83] is representative of this. Macquarrie (the translator, with Edward Robinson, of Heidegger's *Sein und Zeit* into English) radicates his theology in a divinizing of Heidegger's concept of Being (*Sein*). God is not a being (*das Seiende*), even the supreme among beings, nor is he what all the beings have in common. He is the mysterious Source that unveils itself in the appearance of historical being to *Dasein*, the explanation that there are beings rather than nothing at all. Macquarrie, in suggesting that this Source can be best grasped by the term "Act" (p. 103), is in literal agreement with Aquinas. But the understanding is not the same at all because a radically different ontology is at work. Aquinas's metaphysics of being leads him to view God as Pure Act in the sense of Subsistent Being; Macquarrie's ontology of existence means by "Act" the *energeia* or pure process whereby the beings come to be (though he does maintain that this being-process is itself the *transcendens*; see p. 109). Also, Macquarrie declines to equate his own notion with Tillich's "Ground of Being," which he finds suggestive of static substance and thoroughly ambiguous (p. 100). This concept of God considerably qualifies what it means to call him the creator; creation is not the act of the First Cause producing a world *ex nihilo*, but "the dynamic 'letting be' (as we shall designate it) of the beings" (p. 99).

It is precisely this coalescence of being and becoming in the Transcendent that the Christian articulates with the symbol of the Trinity. The believer distances himself from monism on the one hand, and from polytheistic pluralism on the other, by confessing that the very structure of divine being is trinitarian. Macquarrie's translation of this symbol into the language of Heidegger's existential ontology reveals God to be at once Primordial Being (Father), Expressive Being (Son), and Unitive Being (Spirit) (pp. 182–84). These are not temporal modes of being but simultaneous and permanent ones. He makes a telling point in interpreting the transition in early Church

---

[83]John Macquarrie, *Principles of Christian Theology* (New York: Charles Scribner's Sons, 1966); in the text, page citations that follow in parentheses refer to this work.

usage from the Greek πρόσωπον to ὑπόστασις as intending permanency but not independence (p. 177).

Ultimately, Macquarrie stresses the paradoxical nature of the trinitarian formula. It seeks to express the identity in God of the stability of being with the dynamism of becoming. This allows for

a continuous line from philosophical theology's conception of God as holy Being to the full Christian doctrine of God as triune.

Holy Being, then, has let itself be known in the Christian community of faith under the trinitarian symbolism of Father, Son, and Holy Spirit, one God. (p. 181)

This occasions that "stretching of language which brings us into symbolism and its resulting paradoxes," especially illustrated in the use of "person," which is inappropriate when used nonsymbolically, for then it "always retains a separateness" and implies "an inevitable privacy and impenetrability"; if the word is employed, "the wisest course is to leave the meaning shadowy" (p. 177). But, here again, there is lacking the option of allowing an analogical power to the use of the term, with the result that its rich potential is left unexplored.

In the final analysis, then, it is the absoluteness of God that predominates in Macquarrie's theology. The starting point is a concept of deity as absolute, not in the sense of the *Monarchia* of the pre-Nicene Fathers, but after the fashion of Heidegger's *Sein*, i.e., as the *energeia* or pure process mysteriously grounding the coming into historical existence of finite beings and their appearance on the horizon of consciousness. Such divine Being in its absoluteness is at once primordial, expressive, and unitive; these are its dimensions or eternal modes. Insofar as the Trinity of faith—the Father, Son, and Holy Spirit—is only the rendering of this in Christian language, the doctrine assumes the character of a Neo-Modalism. What it falls short of is any explanation of *real* distinctions within God. The threefoldness of which it speaks is an essential triplicity, which if real does away with unity. Thus it appears to lack the element that gives a more orthodox aspect to the Modal Trinitarianism of Barth and Rahner. Macquarrie takes us far beyond the ancient modalism of Sabellius; also his thought has a more objective and ontic character than the transformation of Sabellius to be found, for example, in Schleiermacher. Nonetheless, in its own way, it fosters a conception of God that is more modalistic than anything else; it is modalism in the dress of existential ontology.

[6]
NEO-ECONOMIC TRINITARIANISM
The Eternal God of History

The movement in Christian reflection upon the Trinity, systematically presented as one from a Symbolic Trinitarianism (Chapter Four) to a Modal Trinitarianism (Chapter Five), represents only one front of the dialectical development taking place. A quite distinct alternative was not long in coming, one that finds its remote ancestry in the rehabilitation of Hegel and whose foremost proponents are Wolfhart Pannenberg and (differently) Jürgen Moltmann. It has arisen in large extent in reaction against the ahistorical element in the Dialectical Theology of the Barth-Bultmannian axis. By contrast, it views history not simply as the arena in which revelation occurs, but as identical with revelation. The Trinity is not, then, a doctrine based on historical events attributable to God, but is itself the underlying structure of history. This alternative position refuses to reduce the Trinity to a mere cognitive symbol, but resists at the same time the basis of the Barthian and Rahnerian defense of the doctrine. This latter based itself on the premise of a self-communicating God, i.e., an eternal God who differentiates *himself* in the revelational event (Barth), or in his own being apart from that event but as its precondition (Rahner). By contrast, Pannenberg and Moltmann work from the alternative premise that God is not eternal at all, in the sense of timelessness, but intrinsically historical in his very divinity. The structure of that historicity manifests a certain threefoldness, grasped philosophically in the triadic language of Hegel's dialectic and religiously in the trinitarian language of believers. If the Trinity expresses a differentiation within God, this is one that is not fully intelligible in itself apart from the differentiation that occurs historically and that redounds on what it means to speak of God as a Trinity in himself.

Pannenberg and Moltmann do not speak of an inner-divine Trinity distinguishable from that Trinity's free presentation of itself in the economy. Pannenberg (if not Moltmann) eschews a Christology from above in which a preexistent *Logos* descends into this world. In place of this mythic language of the early Fathers, he prefers one representing Jesus as a man who achieves the status of divine sonship historically, i.e., by way of his historical relationship with

God—with the strange but important qualification that, once achieved, such sonship shows itself to have always been the case. This is difficult to grasp and clearly has recourse to a radically novel concept of history. It appears to say that what transpires in time is already the structure of God's own being. Though God is given the attribute of eternity, this no longer bears the meaning of "timelessness" but functions as a code word for the coalescence of all time in the primordial time of God. This unfolds itself into a Neo-Economic Trinitarianism, differing from that of primitive Christianity (Justin Martyr, Tertullian, Irenaeus, etc.) only in that God does not *become* a Trinity solely in function of the economy. Rather, he is in himself trinitarian and thereby the ground of the process that is universal history. Obviously, a radically new understanding of history and time is operative here. To grasp it demands a brief *excursus* into the climate of Hegelian thought.

HISTORY AS TRIADIC: THE HEGELIAN HERITAGE

Hegel views the Christian confession of the Trinity as a way of conveying in religious language that God is Absolute Spirit (Father) who achieves consciousness finitely (as Son) and unites all differences in himself (as Spirit). Christianity asserts in the symbolic language of religion what philosophy comes to assert in the conceptual language of logical thought. The Incarnation is the revelation of a reconciliation that philosophy sees as the overcoming of the opposition between the infinite and the finite by their synthesis into absolute spirit.

The beginnings of Hegel's thought lie in his denial of Kant's noumenon, or thing-in-itself (*Ding an sich*). If it never appears in consciousness then it is meaningless to inquire about its existence; reality beyond consciousness is by definition unknown and unknowable. This leaves his phenomenal object free-floating, not tethered down by sense intuition of an extramental world. At the same time, its experienced otherness, and so its character as determined and finite, has to be explained. This brings to light a certain oscillation within consciousness, an interplay between the finitude of the known and the transcendence of such limitation on the part of the knowing subject. Hegel resolves this (in a concession to Idealism) by viewing reality itself not in terms of Being-in-Itself (substance), but in terms of Being-for-Itself, as absolute subject, or in his preferred term, Spirit (*Geist*). Spirit, as infinite creative life, comes to itself as self-conscious subject only by a process of self-othering that is in fact an alienation of itself. It posits a world which in its determinateness, as both conscious (man) and infraconscious (nature), is the negation of its own infinite indeterminateness. Then, in a negation of that negation, Spirit overcomes the estrangement in a higher synthetic unification. Were Spirit to remain opposed to the finite, it could not rise above being finite itself. The dialectical move is from identity to alienation to reconciliation or from abstract universality to particularity to concrete universality. The opposites are sublimated (*aufgehoben*) into a higher unity in which their differences are not lost but preserved. The differences of Being and Nothing, for example, are retained in the higher unity of Becoming. Spirit is absolute insofar as it attains to this status of the all-pervasive whole, the encompassing Ground of everything.

What dominates Hegel's thought in the end is the very dialectic itself, the pure process. It is a dialectic obedient to the laws of thought because the content of Spirit is Idea. The *logos* that Hegel seeks is not the essence of things (noumena), nor that of phenomenal objects (as for Kant and Husserl), but the essence (*Wesen*) of the intending process itself as transcendental. Objects within consciousness (from the Latin *ob-jicere*: to throw over against) are only objects for a subject; thus, truth and being are the same—in other words, reality is ultimately Being-for-Itself (*Geist*). Understanding and that which is understood are in themselves only abstract "moments" of the One Absolute Spirit, which cannot be without them. The finite is then a "moment" of Absolute Spirit, and the nonbeing of the finite is thereby revealed as the being of the Absolute.[1]

All of this means two correlative things: first, Spirit gains consciousness of itself only through finite human consciousness; and secondly, finite consciousness in so knowing itself transcends itself to where it becomes the self-consciousness of Absolute Spirit. Hegel expressly calls Absolute Spirit "God," adding that God is God only in achieving self-consciousness and personality in and as man. In a startling statement in both the *Lectures on the Philosophy of Religion* and the *Encyclopedia* he makes the implications of this explicit.

> Finite consciousness knows God only to the extent to which God knows himself in it.[2]

---

[1] *Hegel's Science of Logic*, transl. A. V. Miller (New York: Humanities Press, 1969), p. 443.

[2] *Lectures on the Philosophy of Religion*, vol. 2, transl. E. B. Speirs and J. B. Sanderson (New York: Humanities Press, 1962), p. 327.

His [God's] knowledge of Himself is moreover the self-knowledge of
man, and the knowledge that man has of God is continuous with the
knowledge that he has of himself in God.[3]

Enigmatic as this reads, one is hard put to absolve it of pantheistic
undertones. The distinctness of God and man is sublimated into a
higher unity that approximates a virtual identity. Or, if this is too
strong—in light of Hegel's own disavowal of pantheistic intentions,
in an allusion to Schelling—at least it puts into a favorable light the
judgment of Julius Müller that Hegel's Absolute is not the God of
Christianity but only an explanatory principle of philosophy, "only
the necessary principle of the world, which by means of the world
process brings about its own absoluteness."[4] This conclusion is
endorsed by Hegel's insistence upon the *logical* necessity of God's
creating a world; even divine freedom is determined by the necessary structure of the concept. The trinitarian implication of this is
that it is the very world process itself that constitutes the inner life
of God as Trinity. Even Pannenberg's benign interpretation of
Hegel notes that in the latter's essay on Fichte and Schelling, "the
trinitarian begetting of the Son and the Incarnation do seem in fact
to be the same here."[5]

More radically, Hegelianism did issue in atheism, in its so-called
Left Wing interpretation by Feuerbach especially. And the charge
was laid to Hegel himself. The younger Fichte wrote of Hegel's own
thought that "if the Absolute is actualized *only* in man's self-consciousness, if man, mankind, is God positing Himself into consciousness and realizing Himself there and there alone, then religion is
objectively nothing more than this divine-human mental process of
the ingress of the Idea into a finite self-consciousness to assume

[3]*Enzyklopädie der philosophischen Wissenschaften,* ed. by J. Hoffmeister
(Leipzig: Meiner, 1949), p. 481; this is vol. 5 of the projected 21 vol. critical
edition of the original *Werke* begun by G. Lasson and J. Hoffmeister in
1905.
[4]Julius Müller, *Die Christliche Lehre von der Sünde* (3rd ed., 1849), vol. 1,
p. 552; cited by Pannenberg in "The Significance of Christianity in the
Philosophy of Hegel," *The Idea of God and Human Freedom,* transl. R. A.
Wilson (Philadelphia: Westminster Press, 1973), p. 169.
[5]Pannenberg, p. 164, note 59, basing this conclusion on Hegel's *Über die
Differenz des Fichteschen und Schellingschen Systems der Philosophie* (Jena, 1801).

there a personal form."[6] Cornelio Fabro, who sees no way around this atheistic interpretation of Hegel, cites Friedrich Engels's satirical poem in which Hegel is made to declaim:

"All my life to science I devoted
And atheism with all my power promoted
Self-consciousness unto the throne I prodded
Hoping to see the old-time God ungodded."[7]

But it is one thing to note the logical implications in a thought system and quite something else again to draw the conclusion explicitly. Feuerbach did draw the atheistic conclusion, Hegel himself did not. But Hegel himself cannot be so easily absolved of the pantheistic charge. Pannenberg has made an impressive attempt to do so, but in the end his effort is less than convincing.[8] Hegel makes clear that in the representational language of religion man is *not* God; here the distinction is preserved. But in the conceptual language of philosophy the distinction disappears. The distinction is lived (ritually), but the identity is thought. But philosophy supersedes religion, granted that this is in the mode of *aufhebung* in which the symbolic truth reached by religion is both negated and preserved. Emil Fackenheim has argued persuasively for the Hegelian "middle," that is, for Hegel's insistence upon keeping the opposites in tension and not surrendering one to the other.[9] In this interpretation it is true to say both that the Trinity is preworldly and that it is the universal process occurring in time and space. The truth of the matter is that Hegel refuses to merge God and man into one, as does occur in the philosophy of Schelling. Yet, at the same time, one cannot get around his understanding that divinity is not actualized save in and as man, and his explicit statement in the *Phenomenology* that "the divine nature is the same as the human, and it is this unity that is intuitively apprehended."[10] In this sense it is pantheistic, albeit in a sophisticated and lofty way.

---

[6]I. H. Fichte, *Ueber die Christliche und Antichristliche Spekulation der Gegenwart* (Bonn, 1842), p. 21; cited by Cornelio Fabro, *God in Exile*, transl. and ed. Arthur Gibson (Westminster, Md.: Newman Press, 1968), p. 653, note 8.

[7]Fabro, p. 683.

[8]"The Significance of Christianity in the Philosophy of Hegel," *The Idea of God and Human Freedom*, pp. 144–77.

[9]Emil L. Fackenheim, *The Religious Dimension in Hegel's Thought* (Bloomington, Ind.: Indiana University Press, 1967).

[10]*The Phenomenology of Mind*, transl. J. B. Baillie (New York: Humanities Press, revised ed., 1931), p. 760.

The move from Kant to Hegel is one from subjectivity to history, from a conscious subject's structuring of its own world to the dialectic of Absolute Spirit unfolding itself within consciousness. History is a process of Spirit (as abstract identity) alienating itself in the positing of its concrete and limited other, thereby giving rise to the return movement of reconciliation. Hegel's illustrations of this are numerous and well known. The individual self is estranged in the objective, impersonal structures of society, and this precipitates its return to its true self, its elevation to fully developed personal life. He works it out (somewhat artificially) in the triadic move from Art to Religion to Philosophy, in which Spirit operates, respectively, by way of intuition, symbol, and concept. In the sphere of religion, Christianity is a higher synthesis of earlier opposed forms of religion; it is the unity of God and man in freedom arising above the subservience of man to fate and the gods of nature, on the one hand, and the assertion of autonomy over and against the divine on the other. But the basic law of the dialectic is the dispossession of the self in the other in order to gain the self's true being in love and freedom. And Hegel expressly declares that this is what the doctrine of the Trinity asserts:

> This eternal Idea, accordingly, finds expression in the Christian religion under the name of the Holy Trinity, and this is God himself, the eternal Triune God.[11]

God (the Father) disappears into the finite other (nature) in order to realize himself as finite consciousness (the Son) and bring about the perfect community of persons reconciled in love (the Holy Spirit).

But is not this philosophical trinitarianism? And is it not at a considerable remove from everything that Christianity has entertained about God as Trinity? Hegel's God is not the free creator of a world distinct from himself, a Divinity who is triune in his own inner being apart from that world. Rather, the world is a necessary stage in the dialectical becoming of the Absolute, explaining the sense in which the Absolute is triune. God is a Trinity in the necessary unfolding of history and does not transcend that process, because it *is* that process in its universality. In the final analysis, the judgment on Hegel that seems to prevail is the one that David F. Strauss offers on both the early Schelling and Hegel: "The Son is

---

[11]*Lectures on the Philosophy of Religion*, vol. 3, p. 11.

not a being above or beyond the world, but can only be the world or the finite consciousness itself."[12] Pannenberg, it is true, does call this interpretation into question, noting that there are statements in Hegel himself which contradict it and which do distinguish between the inner life of the Godhead and the act of creation. But this negation of earlier statements is characteristic of Hegel's dialectical thinking. Pannenberg himself is forced finally to neutralize his own absolution of Hegel from the charge of pantheism:

> Yet an irremediable ambiguity remains here, because for Hegel the distinction between the Absolute and the world, as the essence of the finite, cannot be the last word. The truly infinite cannot be thought of only as the opposite of the finite; it must also transcend this opposition, and be the unity of itself and the Other to which it gives rise.[13]

Some interpreters of Hegel, for example, R. C. Whittemore and Hans Küng, prefer on such grounds to view Hegel less as a pantheist than as a panentheist.[14] But, the latter designation better fits Whitehead and his followers, and gives rise to a somewhat different sort of trinitarianism. For Whiteheadians, God and world are coprinciples of reality that are not sublimated into a higher unity. While obviously cognate to Hegelianism, this position does not easily make room for the immanentism and monism indigenous to the latter system. Hegel's God, as Absolute Spirit, is not one pole of reality but the all-encompassing Whole.

THE TRINITY AS EVENT OF DIVINE FREEDOM: WOLFHART PANNENBERG

Wolfhart Pannenberg has established himself as a Christian theologian who argues powerfully for the reality of God against the various forms of atheism issuing from the Enlightenment. He does this, however, by accepting the critique of God begun by Feuerbach rather than fleeing from it into "biblical supranaturalism," as Barth does in his *Church Dogmatics,* or into an existential decision of faith,

---

[12]D. F. Strauss, *Die Christliche Glaubenslehre in ihre geschichtlicher Erscheinung und im Kampfe mit der modernen Wissenschaft* (Tübingen-Stuttgart, 1840–41), vol. 1, p. 490.
[13]Pannenberg, "Significance of Christianity in the Philosophy of Hegel," *The Idea of God and Human Freedom,* p. 168.
[14]R. C. Whittemore, "Hegel as Pantheist," *Studies in Hegel* (New Orleans, 1960); Hans Küng, *Incarnation de Dieu* (Paris: Desclée de Brouwer, 1973), a transl. by Elisabeth Galichet and Catherine Haas-Smets of Küng's *Menschwerdung Gottes* (Freiburg-im-Br., 1970).

as Bultmann wishes.[15] Pannenberg's starting point, then, is the anthropological one of man's consciousness of the infinite, which he views as not mere awareness of the limitlessness of man's own "essence" (Feuerbach), but as an ontological structure of man's being that presupposes an infinity transcending man's nature. "Against Feuerbach, this means that man is essentially referred to infinity, but is never already infinite in himself."[16] Pannenberg, moreover, goes a step further in denying that this can be interpreted as nothing more than the élan of human spirit towards an "empty transcendence." This latter is all that is allowed by Heidegger (for whom ultimately Being and Nothing coincide), and Jaspers (for whom the questionableness of existence is answered only by the Cipher), with the consequence for both that today we must remain silent about God. For Pannenberg, the perduring questionableness of human existence does not indicate that there are no answers and so ground nihilism (Sartre); nor is the question "disclosed exclusively in the light of the answer contained in God's revelation" (Barth, Bultmann, Tillich, Eberling); rather it is aimed at an answer, yet an answer which it anticipates and ever supersedes.[17] Nor is the answer, projected in the question, merely "a hypostatized ideal of the as yet unrealized essence of man"[18] (E. Bloch), but God as the source of the questionableness. Thus, man "already stands in the experience of the reality about which he is concerned in his question. . . ."[19]

But at this point a question surfaces: What is it that Pannenberg here designates as "God"? The answer lies in noting Pannenberg's indebtedness to Hegel. For Hegel too—as for Feuerbach—God is the essence of man. Not, however, in Feuerbach's sense of a divinized projection of human aspirations, nor in the sense that "God" is simply a label for whatever man makes of his own history, but in the sense of constituting man's destiny. That destiny, for Hegel, dawns on man in the concrete occurrences of history as the realization of Absolute Spirit or Idea, but in obedience to the necessary laws of logic. Religiously, this means that man's need for God makes the latter's unfolding of himself in revelation, as a trinitarian event, inevitable. Pannenberg feels compelled to break out of this closed

[15]Pannenberg, "Types of Atheism and Their Theological Significance," *Basic Questions in Theology,* vol. 2, transl. George H. Kehm (Philadelphia: Fortress Press, 1971), p. 199 (hereafter *B. Q. T.*).
[16]Ibid., p. 191.
[17]"The Question of God," *B. Q. T.,* vol. 2, pp. 201–33.
[18]*Das Prinzip Hoffnung* (Frankfurt, 1959), vol. 2, p. 1523.
[19]"The Question of God," *B.Q.T.,* vol. 2, p. 225.

system of Hegelian necessitarianism. He does so by introducing into his own thought an original element. In exploring this, it should be noted at the outset that he is speaking solely of the *Deus pro nobis* — of the *Deus in se,* nothing whatsoever can be said. God, in the former sense, is not the cosmic god of nature, sought by the Greeks and early Christian theology, but a God of revelation, of free self-disclosure. But that revelation is identified with history, not the primordial history (*Urgeschichte*) of which Karl Barth speaks, nor the salvation-history (*Heilsgeschichte*) of Oscar Cullmann, which is a privileged segment within time, but history in its full temporality and contingency. This coincidence of revelation and history as such leads to understanding history as, in fact, the history of the transmission of traditions. If the latter is interchangeable with revelation, it can be so only in its universality, as *Universalgeschichte.* Yet the successive character of history is such that it can be grasped in its totality only from its end. Since the end is not yet, history remains open and undecided. Yet when it is resolved, it will manifest itself as having been so all along. The future is thus a privileged segment of time; it has ontological priority over past and present. Moreover, it determines *retroactively* present history. This is so because history is the gradual establishment of the Reign of God, and God is himself the simultaneity of all time; this is what is meant by his eternity. Pannenberg identifies God with the exercise of his reign,[20] and the latter is history itself viewed from its end. It is in this sense that he is able to say that God does not yet exist—though when he does come to exist, it will be clear that he was all along.[21]

God, for Pannenberg, then, means history in its universality or as viewed from its consummation, that is to say, history insofar as it constitutes the unfolding of the being of God. This unfolding is not the appearing (phenomena) of reality (essence) that lies *behind* the appearances, because it is characterized by the pure contingency of God's action. This overcomes the necessitarianism of the Hegelian dialectic and corresponds rather to "the Biblical idea of God in his irrational freedom." It reintroduces the thinking of early Christian

---

[20]"The Deity of God is his Rule." *Theology and the Kingdom of God,* ed. Richard J. Neuhaus (Philadelphia: Westminster Press, 1969), p. 55 (hereafter *T. & K.G.*). "He is God only in the execution of this Lordship." "The God of Hope," *B. Q. T.,* vol. 2, p. 240.

[21]"Does this not mean that God is not yet, but is yet to be?" "The God of Hope," *B. Q. T.,* vol. 2, p. 242. "Thus, it is necessary to say that, in a restricted but important sense, God does not yet exist." *T. & K. G.,* p. 56.

theology, which "set the freedom of God above his 'nature'," and looked upon the divine, not as the immutable ground of the world, but as the "free Lord of history."[22] To underpin this philosophically, Pannenberg borrows from the thought of Heinrich Barth, finding grounds there for his own conclusion that appearance is the arrival *of the future.*[23] The stress is upon the radical contingency of events. Appearance must be the appearance of something, but what appears is not any sort of essence or Hegelian Idea in its timeless, logical structure. Hegel, it is true, had insisted upon the reciprocity of essence and appearance; the idea is actual only in the phenomenon. But he gave ontological priority to the former. Heinrich Barth reverses this order: the appearance asserts its ontological priority, and the *eidos* or essence arises out of it only in virtue of a process of interpretation. Phenomena, then, are always *anticipations* of further reality, of reality that lies *ahead*, and not the actualization of a form or structure that lies behind it (Plato) or is simultaneous with it (Hegel). The anticipation, when confronted with the anticipated, collapses in the face of the difference. Ronald D. Pasquariello observes that this is an instance of negative mediation in which "the ultimate exerts its power negatively because it is active and present in the breakdown of the anticipatory which is effected by the realized difference between the anticipation and the anticipated (the ultimate)."[24] This is further clarified in noting that "because it realizes itself, through man, as mere anticipation, the presence of the ultimate brings about the collapse of the anticipatory contingent in the production of a new synthesis which is in *continuity* with the previous anticipation in that, by a process of reflection, it preserves the first anticipation in the midst of its collapse" (p. 347). Significantly, Pasquariello adds that Pannenberg applies this negative dialectic "first to the relation of Jesus as Son to the Father, and subsequently . . . to the structure of the whole of reality. . . ." (p. 346). This proleptic character of reality means the continual arrival of the future as (ontologically) new being and (noetically) new truth.

---

[22]"The Appropriation of the Philosophical Concept of God as a Dogmatic Problem of Early Christian Theology," *B. Q. T.*, vol. 2, p. 179.

[23]"Appearance as the Arrival of the Future," *T. & K. G.*, pp. 127–43; the work inspiring Pannenberg's thought here is Heinrich Barth's two-volume *Philosophie der Erscheinung* (Basel, Stuttgart: Benno Schwabe, 1959).

[24]Ronald D. Pasquariello, "Pannenberg's Philosophical Foundations," *The Journal of Religion* 56, no. 4 (October 1976), pp. 346–47.

It would be difficult to exaggerate how radical and bold Pannenberg's thought is at this point or the novelty of what he is attempting. He is doing no less than reversing the direction of time. The future is the power determining the present. This is something quite other than Aristotle's principle of teleology. It is rather history, identified with deity, and unfolding from its end. The future is the coming reign of God that has appeared already in Jesus, not as an epiphany of God, but as a prolepsis of his lordship. That reign *is* God for us. Therefore, God is present in Jesus (identity), precisely as the One who is different from him (distinction).[25] In this fashion, Pannenberg radically reinterprets the definition of Chalcedon. Jesus is the coming to appearance of God; he is the concrete point in which the end of history appears. But Pannenberg's use of Heinrich Barth's transformation of Hegel enables him to insist that Jesus is of the essence of God.[26] The distinction between the Father and Jesus belongs to the divinity of God; that *historical* relationship characterizes the Godhead in its essence. Thus the being of God

> ... can be comprehended only as the unity of the Father with the Son and the Spirit, so that the revelation of the triune God is what brings the philosophical question to a genuine fulfillment for the first time.[27]

History is thus ingredient in the very being of God, at least of the God *pro nobis*, and that history is the history of Father, Son, and Spirit.

It is obvious that Pannenberg's project demands a reconceptualization of divinity. The equating of history in its totality with the coming reign of God makes it impossible any longer to conceive of God as immutable and as eternal in the sense of timeless. Pannenberg's concern for the tradition, however, means less a jettisoning of these attributes than a radical reinterpretation of them. Their older meaning is taken by him as conveying "propertylessness," thereby collapsing divinity into the formless infinity of Platonism. Immutability thus comes to mean rather "faithfulness"; eternity

---

[25]"Appearance as the Arrival of the Future," *T. & K. G.*, p. 135.

[26]"Just as the one completely obedient to the Father, he is the revealer of God's divinity and thus himself belongs inseparably to the essence of God." *Jesus: God and Man*, transl. L. L. Wilkins and D. A. Priebe (Philadelphia: Westminster Press, 1968), p. 336 (hereafter *J. G. and M.*). "Rather, as this man, Jesus is God. . . . he is one with God and thus is himself God." Ibid., p. 323.

[27]"The Appropriation of the Philosophical Concept of God as a Dogmatic Problem of Early Christian Theology," *B. Q. T.*, vol. 2, p. 182.

acquires the sense, not of timelessness (which "repeatedly forced the concept of God into an unbridgeable distance from the contingent changes of historical reality in which the salvation of men is decided"), but "lordship over time."[28] So reconstrued, eternity is no longer a manner of being that transcends all temporality and succession so as to include all time within itself in the surpassing form of its own timelessness (Thomas Aquinas), but is only the "unity of all time."[29] Pannenberg does misinterpret what the older tradition tried to say in this matter. He takes it, not as an implication of Pure Actuality which the tradition intended, but as the very opposite, as "the universal that is at rest in itself stand[ing] opposite time as the realm of meaningless change."[30] A curious corollary to this conception is Pannenberg's understanding of "the life that awakens in the resurrection of the dead [as] the same as the life we now lead on earth. . . . it is our present life as God sees it from his eternal present . . . [so that] . . . we are, in the present, already identical with the life to which we will be resurrected in the future."[31]

Pannenberg's trinitarianism is an issue of these foundational categories, preeminently his original but idiosyncratic view of history, in which the unity of history is understood from its end, and is seen thereby as continually dawning from the future; this enables him to identify revelation with universal history. Some reservation must be expressed, however, on the way in which this makes the future the privileged moment of time and empties the present and the past of meaning beyond that of opening up the future. Indeed, the future is made to be even the mode of God's being, implying that he is not a God of the present, but a coming God, yet to be. God, then, has not yet achieved his deity, which is identical with his rule, and this, in turn, fosters a view of the eschatological Kingdom in terms of a perfect historical society. If salvation is something more than historical achievement, for example, the overcoming of death bespoken in Christ's Resurrection, it remains true that "the achievement of a liberated society (or the rule of God) is the immediate center of the promise of the gospel."[32] Is God himself, then, the product of man's

[28]Ibid., p. 180.

[29]*What Is Man?*, transl. D. A. Priebe (Philadelphia: Westminster Press, 1970), p. 74.

[30]Ibid.

[31]Ibid., p. 80.

[32]Langdon Gilkey, *Reaping the Whirlwind* (New York: Seabury Press, 1976), p. 232.

history? If, on the contrary, it is rather God who influences the course of history from the eschatological future, then two questions remain unanswered. Why is not this a covert endowing of God with actuality—so that the mode of his being is no longer merely future, as that of a God who is not yet but will be? And why is not such a God the Lord of present history, in its achievements and in its failures, rather than a God who only summons to a radically new future? Pannenberg's impressive theology begs this latter question in equating the past with sin and the future with liberation, though not in so marked a fashion as does Moltmann's version of the same theology.

The Logos. Be that as it may, Pannenberg readily accepts the position that God is historical in his own being and, in this sense, a Trinity. Pannenberg transposes the basic Christological question from one of the unity of the divine and the human *in* Christ to one of the unity of Jesus with God. Both the unity and the distinction between Jesus and the Father are established on the grounds of the historical relationship. But the relationship belongs as such to the divinity of God; it is of the essence of deity.[33] The notion of "essence" in this context, however, is that of Feuerbach; its meaning is not "nature" or "species," but the common spirit emerging from the interaction of individuals in pursuit of their destiny. Pannenberg adds only that the essence is, in fact, the end of history anticipating itself in the present. What is important, at this point, is Pannenberg's disassociating himself from the classical doctrine of the preexistent *Logos.* Jesus is not the *Logos* of God in the sense of a distinct hypostasis existing alongside the Father. The traditional doctrine, dating from the second-century Apologists, does safeguard both the unity and the distinction within God; moreover, it explains God's mediation of creation through his Word. But it suffers serious limitations, deriving as it does from a conception of God as ground of the cosmos rather than as the free origin of contingent events. Its inner logic gives support to the subordinationism of Arius. More importantly, it lends itself to "the precarious loosening of the connection of the Son's divinity with Jesus of Nazareth, God's historical revelation."[34] Pannenberg himself does hold fast to Jesus' divinity and preexistence, but insists that this cannot be asserted as something "over against his earthly path." He is divine and preexistent precisely

---

[33]*J. G. and M.,* p. 130.
[34]Ibid., p. 165.

and formally as human and involved in temporality. The patristic *Logos* doctrine is no longer tenable; insofar as it presents itself as doctrine, its concepts are contradictory. The re-presentation of this attempted in Dialectical Theology, in which the Word is rather God's present address to man, does not fare any better; its value for Pannenberg is reduced to that of a useful metaphor. But this leaves him with a God who gains reality only in the revelatory events of history seen as the proleptic occurring of the end—albeit a destiny that will manifest itself at the end as always having been so. Trinitarian language, then, is neither doctrine (concepts), nor kerygma (proclamation), but doxology, which is essentially the language of worship of a God to be, couched in accounts of the concrete life and destiny of Jesus, proleptically understood.[35]

The Pneuma. Pannenberg's doctrine of the Holy Spirit is consistent with his understanding of the *Logos*.

> . . . The Spirit belongs essentially to the event of God's revelation and thus to the divinity of God himself . . . [thus] . . . God is not only Father and Son but Spirit as well. . . .[36]

But the *Pneuma* is not a Third in God—as is claimed, for example, in the theology of Karl Barth where the Spirit is distinct from the Son precisely because he makes possible belief in the Son's divinity. This is rooted in Barth's contention that revelation "is not a thing within the power of man. It can only be God's own reality if it does happen."[37] If the event of revelation is God himself, then he is manifested therein, not only as Father (Revealer), and as Word (the content of revelation), but as Spirit (the very happening of revelation). The Spirit thus has an identity distinct from that of Father and Son. In contrast to this, Pannenberg's pronounced emphasis upon the dialectic within history between God as Father and his Word of revelation makes a Third in God superfluous. The Spirit is not really other than the Word, but distinguishable only as a divine depth dimension within that Word. In virtue of that dimensionality, the *Logos* does not only confront us in its objectivity (as Word), but "takes us up into [God's] own reality"[38] (as Spirit). Faith, as such, rests upon the Word alone spoken in history and theoretically available to all; but there is a hidden power *in* the Word

---

[35] Ibid., p. 184.
[36] Ibid., p. 175.
[37] Barth, *Church Dogmatics,* I/1, p. 516.
[38] *J. G. and M.,* p. 175.

whereby it embraces the subjectivity of the believer in the latter's commitment to it. This amounts to an inversal of Barthian theology: the Spirit does not enable us to confess Christ's divinity; rather, believing such on the basis of the Word alone, we are then grasped by that Word as it extends itself towards our own subjectivity.

> ... the divinity of the Father and the Son, experienced as distinguished for the believer and thus as "objective," springs over through the Holy Spirit to embrace the subjectivity of the believer himself.[39]

What is at work in Pannenberg's thought at this point is a refusal of any such thing as immediate, nonobjective knowledge with definite content. All knowledge, including knowledge of God, is objective in some sense. But the knowledge of God, due to its unique content, mediates a suspension and absorption of its own objectivity, whereby it tends, not to indefiniteness, but to the nonobjectivity of God.[40] This power, latent in the Word itself (and so not coming to it from without), is articulated into faith-language by the Christian symbol "Holy Spirit." Recourse to nonobjective knowledge on the part of many theologians is a facile sidestepping of the real problems. Pannenberg's refusal of this is justified and points the way to genuine solutions. What is less certain is why this does not mark the way back to Neo-Orthodoxy.

Elsewhere, Pannenberg enters upon rich attempts to isolate, descriptively, the Holy Spirit's identity.[41] These center upon *Pneuma* as the New Testament name for "the actual presence of divine reality in Christian experience and in the Christian community." This, in turn, arises out of the Old Testament use of *Ruah Yahweh* to mean the ground of all life. Taken together, Spirit is a symbol for divine creativity, for God's life-giving activity extending to: (i) all life understood as sustained by breathing within a divine milieu, so that the breath of God *(Ruah Yahweh)* is an environment sustaining life like the air we breathe; and (ii) the new life of faith, especially resurrectional life, for it is the Spirit who raises Christ *(Rom. 8:11)*, and whose presence enables the Christian community to live from it in faith and hope *(Pneuma)*.

---

[39]Ibid., note 146.
[40]Ibid.
[41]"The Working of the Spirit in the Creation and in the People of God," *Spirit, Faith and Church*, W. Pannenberg, A. Dulles, and C. Braaten, eds. (Philadelphia: Westminster Press, 1970); "The Doctrine of the Spirit and the Task of a Theology of Nature," *Theology* 75, no. 619 (January 1972), pp. 8–21.

But, in all this, can the Holy Spirit any longer be understood as a distinct person within the Godhead? It is clear that Pannenberg prefers not to do so.

> The Patristic doctrine of the Trinity apparently sometimes all too rashly inferred a similar personal uniqueness for the Spirit from the personal uniqueness of the Son.[42]

Nonetheless, an implication of so thinking is that a dyadic concept of God predominates over a triadic or trinitarian one. The *Pneuma* is not a distinct divine person, though it remains true his reality is to be understood personally. The real significance of the traditional formula was meant to convey that God's action is not impersonal force but assumes a personal character in that rather than being coercive in kind it appeals to the freedom of believers and summons *them* to full personhood.

> The Spirit shows himself to be a personal reality by not extinguishing the personal character of human action through his activity but by letting personal life come to consummation through willing dedication.[43]

A somewhat similar appreciation of the Spirit is expressed by Hans Küng in his *Christ Sein*.[44] Pannenberg deepens its meaning in two ways. First, is the implication that the center of the believer's own "person" lies outside himself in God as Spirit, who is thereby also personal. Secondly, it should be noted that the Spirit's action is distinct from that of the Father and the Son and so justifies speaking of personal distinctions *within* divinity. That action he identifies as the Spirit's inducing in us the action of glorifying the Father and Son, an action that cannot be the Father's or the Son's own.[45] Once again, the trinitarian formula is rooted in the triadic character of God's historical revelatory action. One positive gain in Pannenberg's view of things is that it enables him to observe that awareness of the mystery of personhood is not something that arises out of ordinary experience or philosophical speculation, but rather is something delivered to mankind by God himself precisely in the act of faith encounter.[46] God's unveiling of himself in this triadic or trinitarian

---

[42]*J. G. and M.*, p. 178.
[43]Ibid., p. 177.
[44]Eng. ed., *On Being a Christian*, transl. E. Quinn (Garden City, N.Y.: Doubleday, 1976), pp. 303 and 650, note 14.
[45]*J. G. and M.*, p. 179.
[46]"Weighty evidence favors the idea of the personal having its origins in religious experience, in the encounter with divine reality." *T. & K. G.*, p. 58.

way is what first brings man face to face with the surpassing mystery of his own personhood. Thus, the danger is lessened of starting with an a priori concept of "person" and superimposing it upon God. But Pannenberg advances this as closing off any way of seeing the Holy Spirit as a distinct divine *hypostasis* or *subsistentia* within deity. Throughout, Pannenberg is eschewing a methodology that would take as its point of departure either the doctrine of the "processions" or that of inner-divine "relations." He sees no way around subordinationism with the former, nor around modalism with the latter.[47] This imposes upon him the task of seeking an alternative explanation of what tradition has meant by consistently defending the Spirit's personal distinction within God. It demands, in short, a new theory of the meaning of person, and this brings Pannenberg back to the thought of Hegel. Hegel's emphasis upon God as Spirit, and so as Subject, enabled him to defend God's personality against Spinoza and Fichte. Such a God is engaged in a dialectic of self-differentiation, an emptying out of himself into the other that explains both his own life and the being of the world. In trinitarian language, this means the Father positing his Word and the Spirit arising out of the tension between them as a synthesis of love. At the base of this dynamism, however, are autonomous "persons" opposing and so limiting one another. This calls into question the unity of God until it is realized that the fullness of personhood is achieved precisely in the relinquishing of autonomy and isolation in surrender

---

[47]*J. G. and M.*, p. 180. Pannenberg's understanding of how what was best in the tradition understood "procession" and "relation" leaves something to be desired and explains a somewhat facile dismissal of these notions on his part. For example, he observes that the second procession by way of a "breathing forth" (*spiratio*) of the Spirit—in contrast to the first procession as the Father's generation of the Son—"as such does not reveal any personal difference" (*J. G. and M.*, p. 178, note 151). Aquinas, however, offers an illuminating argument to the contrary, explaining that spiration as the movement of mutual love between Father and Son demands both their distinct personhoods (there is no love without the personal other, except metaphorically) and a personal character to the immanent *term* that is posited as the *res amoris* of love (i.e., not the lo*vers*, nor their lo*ving*, but the reality posited in genuine love); see *Summa theologiae*, I, q. 27, a. 4; q. 37, a. 1; IV *Summa contra gentiles*, 19; *Compendium theologiae*, 46. Pannenberg's understanding is true only if "breathing" is taken anthropomorphically. Again Pannenberg tends to view the doctrine of the relations as implying no more than relative distinctions within an essence, failing to grasp the significance of the relations as *subsistent* and so constituting the divine essence, not distinguishing it; the relations are distinct solely in regard to each other; see Aquinas, *Summa theologiae*, I, q. 28, a. 2 and esp. q. 29, a. 4.

to the other, out of which emerges a new and higher form of unity, one rooted beyond being in freedom and love, a unity that is not merely natural, but personal.

What is problematic in this appropriation of the Hegelian notion of person is its lack of ontological density; the concept of person appears to play a merely functional role in a purely conceptual system. Its use allows the threeness of God to collapse dialectically into a unity that either is abstract and impersonal in kind, or reduces to the moral unity of a divine *koinōnia*. In either case, the Trinity is an achievement of God's being, the dialectical realization of a unity of the three that is, in fact, a new, higher form of unity (triunity). Moreover, this achievement is *intrinsically* related to history, by which is meant temporal history and not only some inner-divine history or metahistory of God himself. Indeed, this self-realization of divinity is the very structure of history.

In brief summary: Pannenberg's trinitarianism does not allow that God is Three Persons. He is rather one Person, who posits historically a human person (the man Jesus) as his other, who belongs nonetheless to the essence of his divinity. He then acts personally through the human history of that other upon others (believers) as Spirit, bringing them to full personhood.

THE TRINITY AS EVENT OF THE CROSS: JÜRGEN MOLTMANN

Jürgen Moltmann shares with Pannenberg a dissatisfaction with the Neo-Orthodox movement and an agreement with the atheist critique against it. There is an acknowledgement at the very outset that it is quite impossible for men of contemporary experience to believe any longer in an omnipotent and gracious God; this is the God who is "dead." Such a stance calls for a reconceptualization of God more radical than that of Pannenberg. Moltmann has attempted this in a theological project spanning three continuous stages of development in three major works: *Theology of Hope* (1967); *The Crucified God* (1974); and *The Church in the Power of the Spirit* (1977).[48] Since then he has synthesized his trinitarian thought in a

---

[48]*Theology of Hope*, transl. J. W. Leitch (New York: Harper and Row, 1967); *The Crucified God*, transl. R. A. Wilson and J. Bowden (New York: Harper and Row, 1974); *The Church in the Power of the Spirit*, transl. M. Kohl (New York: Harper and Row, 1977) (hereafter *T. H., C. G.*, and *C. P. S.* respectively). Moltmann's *The Trinity and the Kingdom* was not available at the time this present volume went to press; in it his trinitarianism is both clarified and enriched but not basically altered.

1981 work entitled *The Trinity and the Kingdom*. His methodological key is eschatology; the content of that eschatology is trinitarian. This marks his consensus with Pannenberg; the difference lies in conceiving God, not as the power of the future positively operative on the present, but as the promise of a radically new future that contradicts the present. Pannenberg risks everything on the Resurrection of Christ; Moltmann does too, but with the important difference that this means precisely the Resurrection of the Crucified One.

Incorporating the atheist critique (that of Ernst Bloch above all) against a God of present efficacy, Moltmann saves Christian faith by deferring transcendence to the future; everything is predicated upon hope in God's promise of a future that will be different. *Theology of Hope* develops the thesis (never to be abandoned) that eschatology is the decisive element in Christianity. The consequence of this is an understanding that futurity is the very mode of God's being and that all theological statements have only a provisional character. Events by their very nature are open-ended, including the Christ-event. But Moltmann proposes this in a radical and original sense which emphasizes the discontinuity of the new with the old; indeed, the future continually overthrows and contradicts the present. *The Crucified God* defends this against any interpretation that reduces it to just one more theory of universal progress, that has merely added a negative element to the dialectic, by carrying it forward and deepening it on two counts. First, the theological key to this repudiation of present achievement is the cross of Christ understood as the suffering of God in his very deity. Secondly, the event of the cross is ingredient in the historical constitution (not the eternal origin) of the inner-divine Trinity. This is less a futurist eschatology, then, than a true *eschatologia crucis* whose inner structure is trinitarian. A third development in *The Church in the Power of the Spirit* argues for a view of the Christian Church not as institution or primal sacrament but as a movement actively and passively contributing to this divine trinitarian history. These shifts in thought, while marked with continuity, represent moves from (i) conceiving God as one whose being is future, to (ii) conceiving God as one whose being is trinitarian history, and finally to (iii) conceiving Church as the arena where such trinitarian history continues to be played out. Each of these three structural points in Moltmann's theology merits critical reflection.

(i) The first determinant in his thought is the pronounced eschatology which reverses the direction of time and gives the future a retroactive causality over the present.

In the historical meaning of time the past precedes the future and determines it, thus Jesus' crucifixion precedes his resurrection. In the eschatological meaning of time the last is first, and in a literal sense, the future of the resurrection precedes his crucifixion and determines its content.[49]

The same theme is central in Pannenberg, and the reservations registered there weigh against Moltmann as well. These are: first, a view of history that is not critically mediated but simply postulated on the basis of personal faith wherein an epistemological interpretation of biblical history as eschatology is less an explanation than an exposition of an a priori theory; mysteriously, the Christian simply experiences this as a given, as grace.[50] Secondly, there is an overly facile dismissal of the metaphysical tradition, a repudiation of the category of being as "static" without any advertence to its dimension as act; this is due to a preoccupation with the least illuminating elements in early Neo-Platonic and unreconstructed Aristotelian theology, and its consequence is a loss of balance in opting exclusively for categories of temporality. Thirdly, there is a failure to account really for the eternity of a God who "by the nature of his being is situated in the future" (E. Bloch); the suspicion persists here that a heightened experience of human transcendence is being hypostatized into the Transcendent.[51]

But Moltmann's view of time (in which the future, rather than the eternal, breaks into the present) has original elements that mark his difference from Pannenberg. Both men see history, insofar as it focuses upon Jesus the Christ, as the *promise* of God, rather than as a *theophany* of God—thus both escape Hegel's understanding of history as a completed totality. Yet, Moltmann remains ill at ease with Pannenberg's universalizing of history, worked out by means of Gadamer's "fusing of horizons" *(Horizontverschmelzung).*[52] This avoids the limitations of Hegelian history only by insisting upon the anticipatory character of what occurs. Moltmann prefers to see events, not as anticipating a future, but as negating the present in

---

[49]"The 'Crucified God'," *Interpretation* 26, no. 3 (July 1972), p. 286.

[50]See George Hunsinger, "The Crucified God and the Political Theology of Violence," Part I, *Heythrop Journal* 14, no. 3 (July 1973), p. 277.

[51]See, in support of this, Moltmann's article "The Future as a New Paradigm of Transcendence," *Concurrence* 1, no. 4 (Fall 1969), pp. 334–45.

[52]Hans-Georg Gadamer, *Truth and Method,* translation ed. by G. Barden and J. Cumming (New York: Seabury Press, 1975); a significant difference is that the role of language for Gadamer becomes that of understanding for Pannenberg.

order to break open the way to a totally unpredictable future. His future, as it comes to be, contradicts the present. The Christ-event is not a glimpse of the end of history; it is a starting point that catapults us into a future about which we have little more than negative clues. Moltmann's use of "promise" as a theological category does away with the traditional category of *Logos* that lingers in Pannenberg's thought.

Moltmann's inspiration here is surely Luther's dialectical principle of a God who is found under the form of his opposite. But Luther seemingly intended by this that the will of God appears paradoxically *in the context of* what is ungodly;[53] it is the experience of sin and our helplessness in face of it that brings us to accepting salvation in faith. Moltmann's language takes us beyond this—but are we to take his exaggerated expressions literally? Surely, we are not to believe in two Gods—not the Gnostic dualism of the "good" God versus the "alien" God; but not a Christian God who justifies over against one who condemns either! But does it make more sense to introduce a division within deity in which God overthrows the achievements of his own creative and redemptive love? If "God is love" (*I Jn.* 4:8), Moltmann has given that love a strong Hegelian quality in which it appears less as *agapē* that, creatively, lets the other be in its very otherness than as a dialectical overcoming of all otherness. In this latter, contrary to St. John, God is not love but seeks to become such.

(ii) The trinitarian element in Moltmann's eschatology, however, brings its originality to the fore, revealing that at its very heart lies the cross of Jesus.

> We must see the Trinity as event, the event of the cross, and then think of it as history open towards the eschatological.[54]

The crucifixion is an event between God and God, i.e., between the Father and the Son in their very deity, and not between God and his assumed humanity.[55] Already, then, the doctrine of the hypostatic union is set aside, although on the uncritical grounds of an a priori understanding of the Trinity.

---

[53]Richard Bauckham, "Moltmann's Eschatology of the Cross," *Scottish Journal of Theology* 30, no. 4 (August 1977), pp. 301–11.
[54]"The 'Crucified God'," p. 299.
[55]*C.G.*, p. 249.

In order to understand what happened between Jesus and his Father on the cross, we must abandon the doctrine of the two natures and with it any concept of God—metaphysical, moral, or political—that is assumed to have general validity. And we must begin to think in terms of the Trinity.[56]

Here, Jesus is not the incarnate God-man but, in the manner of Schleiermacher, the perfect man of God, whose consciousness of God's will for him determines his "divinity." Concretely, that will of God for him is his abandonment to death and destruction, which Jesus accepts in his passion. Moltmann works this out with power in grasping the deep meaning of *Mark* 15:34, in which Jesus quotes *Psalm* 22:1 and *First Corinthians* 5:21. This forsakenness (*paredōken*; *Rom.* 1:18) affects both Father and Son in such wise as to constitute them in their very distinctness within divinity—a distinction bespeaking at the same time, however, a unity in the mutuality of this surrender. This latter is Moltmann's way of saving the sense of *homoousion*.[57] God makes Jesus to be his divine Son in delivering him over to death, in which act God makes death to be a phenomenon *within himself*, freely choosing this to be the mode of his being. At the same time, in this divine event, God achieves his own identity precisely as Father (in the trinitarian sense). The "spirit" of this sacrifice goes out from Father and Son and becomes determinative of the eschatological future; insofar as it is at once divine and distinct from Father and Son, it constitutes God's identity as Holy Spirit.

Obviously, understanding the Trinity as originating in this way means leaving aside any notion of God as immutable. Nicaea meant only that God does not change as do creatures.

So then, God is not changeable as his creation is, but he is free to change himself and also free of his own volition to make himself subject to being changed by others.[58]

What God concretely wills is to enter into the heart of his creation and undergo suffering, a suffering that is the price of love. Love is an impossibility apart from the lover opening himself to the beloved so as to be passively affected by the latter. Thus the "nonsparing" in God affects the Father, too.

---

[56]"The 'Crucified God'," p. 288.
[57]*C. G.*, pp. 241–44.
[58]"The 'Crucified God'," p. 287.

> For a God who is incapable of suffering is a being who cannot be involved . . . . But the one who cannot suffer cannot love either. So he is also a loveless being.[59]

Why this should be so is not explained at all satisfactorily by Moltmann. Is it the nature of love as such to mean vulnerability to hurt? This is surely the case with love in any of its finite conditions. A love that can suffer is a love that can be enriched, in a word, a love that lacks fullness of being and to that extent is finite. If love bespeaks an affective identity with the beloved, and the latter is in a state of anguish, then the suffering of the loved one is visited upon the lover whose love is finite, whose love is by way of response to the goodness of the other rather than creative of it. But the self-giving of an infinite love would (in theory, at any rate) seemingly restore in a creative way the diminished being of the beloved, rather than succumb itself to the causes of the grief. This, of course, raises the further question of why a God of infinite love continues to allow his creatures to suffer. Here perhaps the most that can be said is that such suffering mysteriously takes upon itself a redemptive power. Puzzling as that may be, it at least rescues divinity from a necessary submission to evil. Moltmann appears to view the apathetic God of the tradition in terms of Aristotle's "Unmoved Mover," without noting the radical reconstruction such a concept underwent in medieval theology. More tellingly, his concept of love can be reconciled only with great difficulty with the New Testament's designation of divine love as *agapē*. Moltmann's love is rather of Hegelian provenance; he has, in fact, altered Hegel's dialectic of rational understanding into one of suffering. For Hegel, God empties himself out into his other (the Son), thereby diminishing himself and precipitating the move to abolish the difference. For Moltmann, God posits his other precisely in the act of abandonment and destruction, and then overcomes the difference in love that reconciles by way of sacrifice. In both instances, God is no longer a *theos apathēs*. Moltmann's Christian vision here should not be reduced to that of Process Theism, in spite of obvious similarities. It is not that man's negative response to God opens the latter to suffering; rather, in strictly trinitarian categories, Moltmann insists that it is God who freely creates suffering within himself. He does this by his self-emptying into the situation of man's godforsakenness, in the crucified Christ.

---

[59]*C. G.*, p. 222.

Thus, the recognition of God in the event of the cross means, inexorably, awareness of suffering and rejection as intrinsic to divine life.

But a trinitarian theology of the cross perceives God in the negative element and therefore the negative element in God, and in this dialectical way is panentheistic.[60]

Approximations to this dimension in Moltmann's theology can be found in such Catholic thinkers as Rahner, von Balthasar, Mühlen, and (somewhat differently) Küng.[61] All take seriously the truth that it is God who suffers and dies on Calvary. But there is an important difference, one that gains clearest expression, perhaps, in Rahner's essay where he insists that, while it is God who suffers and not just the manhood of Jesus, still he suffers in his "other" and not in himself. Moltmann does not pursue this qualification because he intends something more radical, namely, that suffering becomes a freely chosen attribute of God in his very deity.

The Trinity is thus the conceptual framework for understanding that the history of Jesus crucified and raised is the history of God. Thus, for Moltmann, God's very being is historical—not, however, out of need as is the case with creatures but out of the freedom of his superabundant love. From this it follows that no distinction is allowable between the immanent and the economic Trinity. Moltmann understands this in the sense that Christian theology is not allowed to speak of a humanless God, i.e., of any God in himself other than the one who grounds the historical events of crucifixion and resurrection. But does not this suggest a form of neomodalism, of successive and perduring modes of divine historical being? Moltmann suggests as much when he writes:

> Expressed in rather inadequate figurative language, God is transcendent as Father, immanent as Son, and as Spirit open to the future. . . . We must be careful not to picture the Trinity as a closed circle of perfect existence in heaven . . . and to think of the Spirit as return.[62]

The consistent disallowing of a conception of the Trinity as a strictly divine reality in the sense of an eternal preexistent *koinōnia*,

---

[60]Ibid., p. 277.

[61]K. Rahner, "On the Theology of the Incarnation," *Theological Investigations*, vol. 4, pp. 105–20; H. U. von Balthasar and A. Grillmeier, *Le Mystère pascal, Mysterium Salutis*, vol. 12 (Paris: Editions du Cerf, 1972); H. Mühlen, *Die Veränderlichkeit Gottes als Horizont einer zukünftigen Christologie* (Münster: Verlag Aschendorff, 1969); H. Küng, *Menschwerdung Gottes* (1970).

[62]"The 'Crucified God'," pp. 298–99.

in favor of an eschatological process towards the world, can be interpreted as carrying modalistic overtones. But the other side of the coin appears in Moltmann, too. Jesus, after all, preexists his abandonment by the Father, a rejection that requires his consent. At times, Father, Son, and Spirit are given an autonomy that appears tritheistic; their unity then reduces to no more than a unity of will. He writes, for example, that "God" is simply an a posteriori term for the unity of that event which transpires between the Father and the Son, out of which the Spirit originates. The deity develops out of and is constituted by that event:

> . . . as something which occurred between Father, Son, and Spirit and out of which the concept "God" is constituted, not only for men but also for God himself.[63]

Paradoxically, it is not unusual for trinitarian thought with modalistic strains to veer over into tritheism as a corrective maneuver. One explanation of this is the absence of any ontological density to the category "person." A truer estimate of Moltmann's trinitarianism than either modalism or tritheism, however, comes to the fore in his recourse to the term "panentheism" (with which he seeks to disavow pantheism). Trinity is thus the historical structure of God's being as it is intrinsically—though by an act of divine freedom—involved with and dependent upon the world. An illuminating instance of the rich use to which Moltmann is able to put this kind of thought appears in his contention that both Father and Son become different as a consequence of the Father's abandoning the Son to the cross and the Son's experience of that sacrifice. This is true also of the history of the Spirit, which manifests that God does not want to become one with himself without the new creation of humanity and the world through the Holy Spirit (see "The Trinitarian History of God," p. 644). Moltmann's version of panentheism, markedly Hegelian, is clearly to the fore here. Yet it exonerates God of needing creatures in order to fulfill his being as God; God's loving of the world can remain gratuitous. But it raises once again the question about the adequacy of Hegelian categories to illumine Christian revelation truly. More specifically, it urges the question as to whether Moltmann's thought does not dedivinize God in imputing suffering and death to him as intrinsic to his being (even as freely entered into) rather than leaving them as purely finite and creaturely characteristics from which God seeks to rescue us.

---

[63] Ibid., p. 269.

(iii) Moltmann's later theological move qualifies somewhat his earlier emphasis upon the negative element in present history and the deferring of transcendence to the future. *The Church in the Power of the Spirit* recaptures the sense of a God who is not only "ahead of us" but is also in present history with men; hope remains primary but greater scope is allowed for love. Still and all, the Church is not to be conceived as an institution or as a primal sacrament incarnating God's presence and providing a focus of human availability for grace. Baptism, ordained ministry, and eucharist recede into the background. The Church is rather a "movement," wholly provisional in kind, in which the dialectic of contradiction remains uppermost. It lives from the *memory* of the cross, without rendering that saving mystery present and operative. The character of the movement takes shape in the fostering of liberation from all forms of oppression, something creatively achieved in Christian *praxis*. At this point, Moltmann's eschatology moves close to a form of Christian Marxism and is not entirely immune to the charge of ideology.

The trinitarian character in all this, however, is pivotal; the movement itself is all the work of the Spirit. *Pneuma* is the Christian symbol for the Father's sacrifice of his Son as that goes out to mankind and becomes a formative influence in history.

> Out of what happened on the cross between the Father, who forsakes, and the Son, who is forsaken, that is, the loving Father and the loving Son, there proceeds the sacrifice itself, the Spirit who justifies the ungodly, rescues the forsaken, and raises the dead. From this we draw the thesis that God's being is historical and that God exists in this specific history of Jesus Christ.[64]

But this graphic way of describing "Holy Spirit" seemingly deprives the latter of full personhood. The Spirit is reduced to being the power of futurity insofar as that is a mode of God's own being. The *Pneuma* is not a *persona*—on some analogy with the ontological and psychological meaning of the word—but the personification of the divine element in the interaction of God and men; certainly "he" is not distinct from the Father and the Son precisely as a person. The feeling persists that New Testament *agapē* is giving way to Hegelian love as the dialectical drive towards abolition of otherness. Moltmann, of course, transposes this into the Christian context of Christ's suffering in which otherness is abandonment to destruction. Moltmann's Holy Spirit seems to be, then, a symbol devised from experiencing the phenomenon of life's striving to come to higher

---

[64] Ibid., pp. 293–94.

achievement by passing through the gates of death. Christians through the centuries, however, have tended to find hope for newness of life in God's efficacious presence here and now as Holy Spirit. If this notion of the Spirit tended to dominate Moltmann's earlier writings, it was later qualified. In the article "The Trinitarian History of God," and in fuller detail in his 1981 *The Trinity and the Kingdom,* he made explicit that the Holy Spirit is to be interpreted in both a dynamistic and a personalistic sense. In the latter work, he argues that the Spirit should be conceived of not only as "an energy proceeding from the Father or from the Son" but as a subject of that activity which is the glorifying and unifying of Father and Son (p. 126).

But even granting this personalistic conception of the Spirit, the panentheistic theme remains dominant. Human history is not, formally speaking, ours, assumed by God's unexacted and gracious love as his own; it is rather self-identically God's history. This one history is open-ended; the negotiation between Father and Son is unfinished; man's destiny remains undecided. The Church is the place where trinitarian history continues to be played out, a history to which man makes novel contributions not attributable to God. Ultimately, however, everything will collapse into divinity—when God will be "all in all" (*I Cor.* 15:28).[65] This seems an inconsistent element in Moltmann's impressive theology. The pronounced emphasis upon historicity as even the mode of divine being leaves unexplained why it suddenly all comes to an end. The principle of teleology, which he rejects, seems strangely to intrude itself at this point. And if history is to consummate itself in eternal life, why does not that end already make its mark, positively, upon our present? Again, if the content of divine history, as trinitarian, is death as a phenomenon within God (so that suffering is not in contradiction to love but its condition; and thus God is to be found in his opposite), then how does God any longer remain a God of love once suffering and death are overcome?

THE TRINITY AS GOD'S CONCRETE BEING-IN-REVELATION: GORDON KAUFMAN

Another contemporary version of Neo-Economic Trinitarianism is to be found in the theological program of Gordon Kaufman.[66] At

---

[65]*T. H.,* p. 224; *C. G.,* p. 277.
[66]Gordon D. Kaufman, *Systematic Theology: A Historicist Perspective* (New York: Charles Scribner's Sons, 1968); *God the Problem* (Cambridge, Mass.: Harvard University Press, 1972).

the very outset, he makes clear his intention to avoid both trinitarian orthodoxy and modalism.

> The more earthbound approach to theology developed in these pages enables us to avoid the error common to both modalism and orthodoxy, namely, their tendency to overlook the *relational* character of our knowledge of God. Both presupposed we can know God's inner essence *as it is in itself* or as it is known to himself, not simply as it is known to us. From this common premise they drew opposite conclusions. The orthodox held that God's inner essence is three-in-one; the modalists, that it is simple unity.[67]

On the one hand, the deity is not one substance subsisting as three really distinct "persons"; such a "cosmic committee of three" would amount to tritheism. Strangely enough, he interprets this traditional thought as asserting three separate and independent personalities, an excess it consistently repudiated. On the other hand, neither is the deity only three "modes," implying merely successive manifestations of God (modalism in its ancient Sabellian form) or merely a triadic structure in our knowledge of God (modalism in its modern epistemological form). But Kaufman also resists allowing his theology to tend by a logic of its own into what may be called a Neo-Modal Trinitarianism (see Chapter Five). He avoids this by transposing Karl Barth's notion of a God who is triune in his revelation entirely into the perspective of history. Barth himself had felt the necessity to appeal to metahistory *(Urgeschichte)*. Kaufman's God is a Trinity historically, and so his trinitarianism can be justly called Neo-Economic. It is instructive to follow in more detail the way in which he arrives at this position.

Kaufman begins with an emphasis upon the symbolic character of the doctrine of the Trinity: precisely as a doctrine, it is a human creation, a threefoldness in our knowledge of God arrived at through revelation. The Trinity is primarily a way in which we structure our knowledge, a knowledge which, in the revelatory encounter, grasps God as transcendent, historical, and historic in the symbols of Father, Son, and Holy Spirit.

> The first person signifies God's transcendence of the historical process at each point and in its entirety; the second person refers to his special involvement in the person-event Jesus Christ . . .; the third person designates his being in and with and under all events of history.[68]

---

[67]*Systematic Theology*, p. 100.
[68]Ibid., pp. 101–2.

This triplicity of symbolization, however, does not regard only our knowledge gained in revelation. Since it is true knowledge, it must reflect the situation with God himself. But here Kaufman's thought grows hesitant and introduces a subtle distinction. The refusal of modalism—a refusal which means that God is trinary not only in his appearances, nor only in our knowledge of him—does *not* mean that he is trinary in his very divineness and transcendence, but solely in his "bound-up-ness" with the world. Medieval theology had insisted on the simultaneity of God's transcendence and immanence; they were, so to speak, the two sides of one coin. Kaufman introduces a drastic disjunction: God's transcendence is ahistorical and about it we can say nothing; his immanence is achieved in an entirely historical way. That immanence is trinitarian in its mode; it is a structure of God's own being, but entirely an *extrinsic* structure.

> . . . there is no reason whatsoever to maintain that the structure of that external relationship which we perceive in our experience somehow directly mirrors a similar but more primordial threefold structure in the innermost recesses of the divine being.[69]

Revelation, then, because of its historical character, marks God's emergence out of the unknown transcendence of his inner being into his abiding presence *in a threefold manner* within history. But why in a threefold manner? Seemingly, this is rooted not in divine reality but in human reality as it exists in relationship with the divine. Human nature is (i) historical, yet seeks (ii) to transcend time, but (iii) from within time. Divinity thus "economizes" itself, in correspondence with the human condition, so that it exists vis-à-vis the world in this triune way.

> The doctrine of the Trinity, then, as developed through analysis of the historical character of revelation, is not an esoteric item of information about the peculiar internal structure of some transcendent being up in the heavens. Rather, it expresses the structure of history (as apprehended in Christian faith) in relation to its ground, and conversely, the way in which transcendent reality is bound up with history.[70]

This is "transcendence without mythology," in which the teleological model of transcendence is replaced by an interpersonal one, with a corresponding avoidance of all ontological language.[71] A cer-

---

[69]Ibid., p. 102, note 9.
[70]Ibid., p. 101.
[71]These constitute the subjects of chapters 3 and 4 of Kaufman's *God the Problem*.

tain threefoldness is indigenous to relationships between persons, in which there is a striving to rise above the limitations of time without denying temporality. This also characterizes God's initiatives towards men, but means that "the same one personal God is acting, not three independent personalities."[72] Kaufman's approach to God collapses the categories of being into those of temporality. The issue at this point is that "person," as said of God, ceases to be either a mere symbol or a strictly analogical concept; it becomes a historical category that is reductively univocal.

Kaufman's theology bears obvious affinities to the Symbolic Trinitarianism of Paul Tillich on the one hand (see Chapter Four) and to the Modal Trinitarianism of Karl Barth on the other (see Chapter Five). But he presses beyond these initial similarities with his pronounced emphasis upon the concrete historical character of God's "bound-up-ness" with the world. He avoids the Christian Hegelianism of Pannenberg and Moltmann, in which history (rather than the cosmos) is ontologized. But, in the final analysis, his remains a Neo-Economic Trinitarianism: God, relating historically to a world of men, "economizes" himself in a way that comes to expression as the doctrine of the Trinity. The Trinity is not a structure of God's eternal being, but of his being-in-revelation. Insofar as it might be conceived as a structure of God's own being, it remains an entirely extrinsic one.

CATHOLIC NEO-ECONOMIC TRINITARIANISM: PIET SCHOONENBERG

It was Martin Luther who inaugurated in a lasting way theology's break away from the employment of metaphysics in favor of a biblical understanding of God as a God of history. Catholic theology, by and large, has avoided the antimetaphysical stance on the grounds that God is the author also of man's rational nature, a defense that has become considerably more difficult today with the rise of critical thought in the era after Kant. Still, W. Schulz has pointed out how transcendental philosophy tends to conceive God in one of two ways, both of which enervate the trinitarian doctrine of its import.[73] The first views divinity in terms of absolute freedom

---

[72]*Systematic Theology*, p. 103.
[73]W. Schulz, *Der Gott der neuzeitlichen Metaphysik*, 3rd ed. (1957); cited by Walter Kasper, *Jesus the Christ*, transl. V. Green (New York: Paulist Press, 1976), p. 182.

that is the transcendental condition for finite freedom, which empties the Trinity of all significance whatsoever (Kant) or reduces it to a merely utilitarian "doctrine of the second rank" (Schleiermacher). The second opts for a panentheism in which finite realities are mere "moments" of the divine—here the Trinity is interpreted in a frankly modalistic way, in which God's being is historicized and Christ becomes a mere avatar of a divine process.

Karl Rahner, taking the Kantian critique seriously, has argued for the identity of the immanent and the economic Trinity.[74] Logically, however, this lends itself to advocacy of a Trinity of mediation. To forestall such a view, Rahner explains what he means in such wise that his position really amounts to a Catholic version of Modal Trinitarianism (see Chapter Five). That such is the case, is confirmed by his substitution of the term "modes" for that of "persons"—by which he means modes of *subsisting* rather than Barth's modes of *being*. This means the introduction of change into God, in a rejection of the principle of divine immutability as a superficial flight from the full implications of the faith-confession that "God became man" (Prologue of St. John's Gospel). Rahner describes the Incarnation, somewhat enigmatically, as God's "changing *in* another,"[75] something more than a change *of* the other by God, as his own assumed earthly reality. This suggests certain affinities with the theological project of Pannenberg and Moltmann. But there is a major difference—Rahner insists that what occurs in history is a mirror image of something eternal and constitutive of divinity apart from God's free act in creation and salvation. His searching thought in this area has to be put into the larger perspective of his theology, which repeatedly insists upon eternal processions and eternal relations, irrespective of world and history. Thus, this strain in Rahner's thought, while it does support a Trinity of mediation, does not justify classifying him as an advocate of Neo-Economic Trinitarianism. This is not so clearly the case, however, with other Catholic theologians—among whom are Hans Küng, possibly Walter Kasper, and certainly Piet Schoonenberg.

The Dutch Jesuit, Schoonenberg, stands explicitly in the ranks of those who eschew any speculative or "doctrinal" starting point. Little exception can be taken to his contention that the Trinity is a doc-

---

[74]*The Trinity*, transl. J. Donceel (New York: Herder and Herder, 1970), pp. 31–33.

[75]"On the Theology of the Incarnation," *Theological Investigations*, vol. 4, esp. pp. 113–14, note 3.

trine arising solely from the historical events centering on Jesus of Nazareth.

> In no respect do we conclude from the Trinity to Christ and to the Spirit given us, but always the other way around. . . . the divine preexistence of Christ can be determined only in the light of his earthly and glorified life.[76]

Strangely enough, however, Schoonenberg underestimates—as does Rahner also—the extent to which this is also true of the early Church Fathers, of Augustine, and of Aquinas; these latter attempts at systematization always presuppose the biblical record of salvation history. Apart from God's self-communication in Jesus of Nazareth, there is no way of affirming that God is triune. Schoonenberg makes this explicit—and if he means it in the epistemic order, one can hardly quarrel with it; there is simply no other avenue of knowledge leading to the revealed mystery. But he appears to intend something more than this. The Christ-event is a happening in which it is not only revealed that God is a Trinity; it is one in which he is constituted as Trinity.

> . . . [It] is not impossible that God becomes Trinity through communicating himself in a total way to, and being present in, the man Jesus as Word, and through being in the Church as Spirit. . . . I myself am convinced that the idea of God becoming triune through his salvific self-communications is possible. Therefore, I can go further than Karl Barth, who refers God's Trinity to a decision of God which, however, is a "primordial decision" . . . . I can see God becoming triune by a historical decision of himself.[77]

This is no denial of the immanent Trinity, of the truth that God is a Trinity in himself. But God *becomes* a Trinity, as something that occurs only out of his involvement in history. If this happens, some eternal structure within divinity must be its precondition. Thus Schoonenberg readily allows an eternal triadic structure to deity. Yet, only within history (which must be mediated through men as historical beings) does this triadic structure take on *personal* form.[78] What this might mean is fairly clear in the instance of Christ, whose personhood is explained by his humanity. At work here is Schoo-

---

[76]Piet Schoonenberg, "Trinität—der vollendete Bund: Thesen zur Lehre vom dreipersönlichen Gott," *Orientierung* 37 (1973), pp. 115–17.

[77]*The Christ*, transl. D. Couling (New York: Herder and Herder, 1971), pp. 85–86, note 16.

[78]"Continuîteit en herinterpretatie in de Drieëeheidsleer," *Tijdschrift voor Theologie* 14, no. 1 (January, February, March, 1974), pp. 54–72.

nenberg's Christology, with its well-known reversal of the Chalcedonian formula, at least as the latter came to be interpreted in light of the doctrine of *enhypostasis* worked out by Leontius of Byzantium. Schoonenberg stands this teaching of Leontius on its head.

> . . .[It] is primarily not the human nature which is enhypostatic in the divine person, but the divine nature in the human person.[79]

This understanding is, perhaps, less clear in the instances of the Father and the Spirit who are "persons" on the basis of relating in a personal way to the person of Christ (and through him to other human persons). On the basis of revelation, it is possible to grasp the mystery of God present among men in the twofold, mediated form of Word and Spirit. This, in turn, bespeaks a primal, nonmediated form of divine being, expressed in the name Yahweh, and eventually in the symbol Father. But only when the Word becomes enhypostatic in the humanity of Jesus does it exist as a person. And only on the basis of their relationship to that person are we justified in referring to the Father and Spirit as "persons" in their own way. Prior to this Christ-event, the eternal threeness of God lies only in our discernment of his modes of being vis-à-vis a world of men, modes which do not imply real distinctions in God, let alone personal ones. Distinction within the Godhead, then, is both eternal and temporal; but the distinction in the former instance is modal only, and solely in the latter instance is it personal. This is not mere Symbolic Trinitarianism (Chapter Two), because God really becomes a Trinity in his own reality; it is a version of Economic Trinitarianism because God becomes Trinity solely in function of the economy of salvation.

True enough, Schoonenberg's position demands change in God's inner being. He chooses not to see this as a problem and is content to say only that the change in question is in no sense univocal to that of creatures.[80] But in what sense is it any longer change, then? Logically speaking, can one attribute change to God, and at the same time deny to him what specifically makes change to be change in all its analogical modes? For something to change is for it to undergo alteration, implying that the subject of the change is in potency to

---

[79]*The Christ*, p. 87; see also p. 93 where Schoonenberg criticizes the idea that before the Incarnation "this Word was already there in his preexistent person"; and p. 90 where he prefers to say that "the transcendence of the Son of God [is] precisely in his manhood."

[80]Ibid., pp. 83ff., note 16, esp. p. 86.

the new act it can acquire (as in Aristotelian-Thomistic thought) or
that the subject in act perishes in order that its values can be prehended in a new self-creative act (as in the Whiteheadian system).
There seems to be no alternative: to speak of alteration from act to
act appears simply an attempt at an explanation that veils the fact
that the first state is potential to the second in one of the above two
ways. Thus, Schoonenberg's solution is merely a verbal sidestepping
of the problem. To maintain God becomes a Trinity in himself
makes no sense unless one is prepared to admit into God potency,
change, finitude, and temporality—as do the advocates of futurist
eschatology (for example, Pannenberg and Moltmann) and (differently) the process theists. There seems no problem in allowing *extrinsic* change in God; this would mean that when what God knows and
loves changes, then God's own knowledge and loving change *relative
to what has changed.* But this is not change in God's own ontic beingness; it is rather alteration in his cognitive and affective intentionality.[81] There still remains, of course, the problem of how ontic
immutability might be reconciled with intentional change. One
approach to a resolution might well lie with the distinction at issue
here, namely, that between "nature" and "person." It is this distinction that is the explanatory basis of both the doctrine of the Trinity
and that of the Incarnation. Person means being as pure existential
process, but occurring within the structures of what is known as
nature or essence and in such wise as to leave the latter intact. If
so, it is possible to hold that God remains immutable in his divinity,
while at the same time he wills to become on the level of personhood
the sort of God he chooses to be relationally, i.e., vis-à-vis his free
creatures—even to the point of choosing to accept determination
from his creatures.[82]

At this juncture, a quite positive contribution of Schoonenberg
should not go unnoticed. He allows that the term "person" as used
in the early trinitarian debates is not a clearly defined philosophical
category, but a kind of preconcept that is operative in all cultures.
It is at first a confessional symbol for believers rather than a theological category for reflective thought. This raises an important
question: Can one restrict the trinitarian sense of "person" to an

[81]For an illuminating development of this, see W. Norris Clarke, "A New
Look at the Immutability of God," in *God Knowable and Unknowable,* ed. R. J.
Roth (New York: Fordham University Press, 1973), pp. 43–72.
[82]An attempt at developing this can be found in W. J. Hill, "Does the World
Make a Difference to God?" *The Thomist* 38, no. 1 (January 1974), pp. 146–64.

ontological and objective meaning without extending to it a psychological and subjective meaning? The latter is commonly dismissed as tritheistic, but the former by itself falls victim to modalistic thinking. Thus, Schoonenberg is right: either one uses "person" with its psychological overtones or one jettisons it altogether.[83] This is not to say one must incorporate the psychological dimension in the way Schoonenberg himself does—that is, as finding its ground in the humanity of Jesus. An alternative lies open—one to be explored in Chapter Eight. The economic dimension in Schoonenberg's trinitarianism finds an echo in other Catholic theologians. Hans Küng evidences a similar marked resistance to the inroads of metaphysics and mythology, which he sees as making the doctrine into a "Hellenistic formula . . . [amounting to] . . . a kind of higher trinitarian mathematics . . . partly inconsistent . . . [and] . . . scarcely understood by modern man."[84] Whereas the doctrine is to be neither "thoughtlessly repeated [nor] thoughtlessly dismissed, but discriminatingly interpreted," Küng himself has no doubts that the future of the doctrine lies in a repudiation of such categories. Küng's project has twin roots: the first is his desire to recover, and make exclusive, a perspective that can be read immediately from the pages of the New Testament; the second is the interpretative framework of a Hegelian Christology, as proposed in his *Menschwerdung Gottes*.[85] The Christology offered in this latter work is the only theological explanation which Küng sees as leaving intact the original Christology of the Bible. There,

> [The] triadic formulas of the New Testament are meant to express, not an "immanent" but an "economic" theology of the Trinity, not an inner-divine (immanent) essential triunity in itself but a salvational-historical (economic) unity of Father, Son, and Spirit in their encounter with us. The New Testament is not concerned with God in himself, but with God for us, as he has acted on us through Jesus himself in the Spirit, on which the reality of our salvation depends.[86]

---

[83]"Continuïteit en herinterpretatie in de Drieëeheidsleer," English summary, p. 72.

[84]Hans Küng, *On Being a Christian*, p. 472.

[85]*Menschwerdung Gottes* (Freiburg-im-Br.: Herder, 1970); French ed., *Incarnation de Dieu*, transl. E. Galichet and C. Haas-Smets (Paris: Desclée de Brouwer, 1973).

[86]*On Being a Christian*, pp. 475–76.

To assert that Jesus is God, just as the Father is God, means not any unity of nature but a oneness achieved in "the revelation event and [a] revelational unity."

> Christologically defined, "truly God" means that the true man Jesus of Nazareth is the real revelation of the one true God.[87]

The deity of Jesus, in his real distinction from the Father, while not reducible to his human and earthly life, is unthinkable apart from that worldly humanity. Thus, the preexistence texts must be interpreted in light of this truth and not vice versa. Küng's "prolegomena to a future Christology,"[88] then, closes off any continuing relevance to the doctrine of hypostatic union. It rather opens the way to an Incarnation in which the Word achieves personhood historically. This, in its turn, allows for a doctrine of the Trinity that, reductively at least, is Neo-Economic.

Both Schoonenberg and Küng allow that only in the economy of salvation are the trinitarian distinctions personal; within the Godhead itself such distinctions are at the most modal in kind.[89] Walter Kasper refuses a Neo-Economic Trinitarianism in this sense, insisting that "there is no dark mystery of God *behind* his revelation," for in Jesus God reveals himself as "unfathomable and inexplicable love," as self-communicating love which "self-communication between the Father and the Son is the eternal nature of God himself."[90] Kasper's view, however, leaves unexplored the mystery of God's immutability and its reconciliation with an eternal, totally immanent self-communication. God's self-communication seems to be simultaneously and self-identically eternal and temporal. Accents of Hegel are heard here, though they are deeply Christianized ones—for example, the suggestion that the Incarnation, while free, retains a certain inevitability, at least the inevitability of love. This is at a remove from the Neo-Economic Trinitarianism of Schoonenberg and Küng, but it seemingly approaches that of Pannenberg.

---

[87]Ibid., p. 477.

[88]The subtitle to the French translation of Küng's *Menschwerdung Gottes* reads "Introduction à la pensée théologique de Hegel comme prolégomènes à une christologie future."

[89]This is implicit throughout Küng's *On Being a Christian;* it is explicit in Schoonenberg's *The Christ* (see, e.g., pp. 82–83).

[90]Walter Kasper, *Jesus the Christ,* p. 181.

[7]

THE TRINITY OF
CREATIVE BECOMING
The God of Panentheism

A recent and quite distinct theological phenomenon has come to prominence in what is loosely called Process Theism, a movement whose precursor is Alfred North Whitehead. Despite certain affinities, it represents a view of God as triune that remains distinct from that of Neo-Liberal Theology (the Trinity as cognitive symbol), on the one hand, and that of Futurist Eschatology (the Trinity as historical deity) on the other. Its difference from the former turns primarily on its acknowledging the need for metaphysics in any serious theological endeavor, albeit a neoclassical metaphysics which replaces Being with Becoming. It distances itself from the latter on two general points: (i) in viewing process as an ontological, and so universal, phenomenon which cannot be limited to the sphere of history, and (ii) more specifically, in advocating an idea of God that is dipolar rather than dialectical. These two characteristics combine to signal a break out of the tradition of German Idealist and Transcendental thought, with its basic category of a self-othering God. Insofar as this marks a move into realist philosophy (in the service of theology) it represents an amalgam of a revised Platonism and Anglo-Saxon empiricism.

Process theology, at any rate, when it does deal with the trinitarian doctrine does so with a whole new set of categories. But those categories express assumptions by and large inimical to the doctrine. The trinitarian conception of God proves, by and large, to be an embarrassment to a conception of God as a privileged agent in universal process, of which he is part. Questions on the nature and attributes of deity, on Christology, ecclesiology, eucharist, faith, reconciling love, justice, community, and sexuality have received ample treatment from process theologians. But the Trinity is seldom to be found among them. Most works in process theology do not include a single reference to "Trinity" in their indexes. Norman Pittenger does not even use the terms "Trinity," "Father," *Logos,* or

"Spirit" in an article entitled "Trinity and Process."[1] It is not included in the Christian themes given a process interpretation in Schubert Ogden's *Reality of God,* nor in the more systematic *Spirit and Forms of Love* of Daniel Day Williams.[2] John Cobb, who does deal with the Trinity in a recent book, finds it "more a source of confusion for theology than a help," and in the end unsatisfactory ". . . a mystification rather than a clarification of Christian belief."[3] A notable exception to this is available from Lewis S. Ford, but even here in the final analysis it is a matter of subordinating the Trinity to the all-determining concept of God as dipolar. Thus, an initial characteristic of Process Theism is a marked atrinitarianism.

GOD AS DYAD, NOT TRIAD: ALFRED NORTH WHITEHEAD

The ultimate category in Alfred Whitehead's philosophy of organism is Creativity, which however lacks all actuality itself and so is real only in its instantiations. These latter are not substances but "actual occasions" which are self-created and ever perishing in order to give way to the novel emerging occasion. Chief among them is God who, though a nontemporal or everlasting occasion, is not "an exception to all metaphysical principles [but] their chief exemplification."[4] Thus God is the "primordial nontemporal accident"[5] of Creativity; as is true of every actual entity, he is "a creature transcended by the creativity which it qualifies."[6] Thus, God and world are "both . . . in the grip of the ultimate metaphysical ground, the creative advance into novelty."[7]

---

[1]"Trinity and Process," *Theological Studies* 32, no. 2 (June 1971), pp. 290–96; the term "Trinity" does occur in his opening sentence but in citing an article by Anthony Kelly; also there is one use of the term "triune."

[2]Schubert Ogden, *The Reality of God* (New York: Harper and Row, 1963); Daniel Day Williams, *The Spirit and Forms of Love* (New York: Harper and Row, 1968).

[3]John B. Cobb, Jr., *Christ in a Pluralistic Age* (Philadelphia: Westminster Press, 1975), pp. 13 and 155.

[4]Alfred North Whitehead, *Process and Reality* (Macmillan, 1929) (hereafter cited as *P.R.* from the Harper Torchbook edition [New York, 1960] with identical pagination), p. 521.

[5]Ibid., p. 11.

[6]Ibid., p. 135.

[7]Ibid., p. 529.

An actual occasion's act of creating itself is limited by the raw material for this available in past, perished occasions, which it selectively "prehends." Still, Whitehead has reversed the vector of causality: what is existent has not been created by its ancestors, but has created itself by a novel combination of what its ancestors make available as data. The implications of this for a concept of God are far-reaching. For one, God then transcends the world not in his "unoriginateness" (the *agenētos* of the early Fathers), but in his act of unique self-creation. For another, the world also transcends God in its act of self-positing. Thus, there is mutual interdependence, each supplying to the other data which it transforms in its own novel way, thereby continually coming to new actuality. Granted, this is accomplished differently in either instance: God supplies initial aims or impulses in a conceptual manner to finite entities, while they rather make available to God their limited actualization of those impulses (an actualization implemented in a physical manner, in prehending the data objectively furnished by past occasions). Still and all, this means a duality at the heart of every existent entity in virtue of which it is simultaneously transcendent to the whole and immanent within the whole, at once absolute and relative, autonomous and dependent. This is simply expressed in an oft-repeated phrase of process thought: God is as much the effect of the world as its cause.

Whitehead's God is thus dipolar; the two dimensions to divinity he calls God's *primordial* nature and his *consequent* nature. In the former (wherein he is all-perfect, but nonactual and abstract) God contemplates "eternal objects," envisaging the optimal way in which they can be rendered actual in the cosmos. In the latter (wherein he is limited, but actual and concrete) God achieves status as an actual entity by preserving, in a selective and sublimating fashion, the continuing genuine accomplishments of the finite world.[8] God differs from other realities in that he is a nontemporal actual occasion, meaning that he stands outside the order of time in one dimension of his being, while simultaneously he is dependent upon it for achieving actuality in another.

This is, of course, an entirely philosophically elaborated idea of God. But it is one which at the very outset appears to close off all avenues to the Christian concept of God as a triunity of persons. It does this on two fronts: first, by reducing the dynamism of divine life to a polarity of natures, which obviates any notion of inner *self-*

---

[8]Ibid., pp. 521–24.

communication; secondly, by altering radically the meaning of "person." The first is rooted in the view of a fundamental and necessary reciprocity between God and world. Still, the relative primacy of God means that this basic relationship must somehow or other find its ground within God (and it is at this point that Whitehead is forced to allow that God is somehow unique among actual occasions). This Whitehead does by positing a dynamic polarity at the heart of divinity, but as a tension between God's nature as primordial and as consequent. It is thus clear why he explicitly notes that, in his system, God is a derivative notion. Without God so conceived, there is no way to explain why the creative process itself is never in jeopardy and why becoming is in the long run progressive rather than retrogressive. This ensures that God is not any self-enclosed Absolute but rather a privileged and perduring moment in creative process, a pure dynamism. But the dynamism is not that of a triadic self-communication; it is rather the dyadic interrelationship of actuality and possibility. This is at a considerable remove from the triune God of traditional Christianity. There, God as Father generates his Son, through whom and with whom he spirates forth their common Spirit, eternally and by nature rather than by choice—and then in imitation of his own trinitarian structure freely creates and redeems a world that is his nonnecessary creation. Here, God triggers the creative advance of the universe by envisaging what is both truly possible for the world and best in the given situation—and then achieves his own fullest actualization on the basis of what the world makes possible for him.

Secondly, Whitehead's thinking makes no allowance for personhood as an enduring metaphysical component of reality. In this system, it can designate no more than the remembered continuity of a cluster of conscious occasions, on which basis a kind of social identity can be claimed. There is nothing in the existent that remains actual and self-identical throughout change. There are only atomic occasions that perish and lose their identity in the very instant of achieving it. To speak of any existent as possessing a personal character is only to mark the sense of continuity it bears with its ancestors and of heterogeneity with other lines of concretion. Whitehead observes that "an enduring personality in the temporal world is a route of occasions in which the successors with some peculiar completeness sum up their predecessors."[9] Thus, by definition it is

---

[9] Ibid., p. 531.

realizable only in the context of temporality, whereas God is precisely the nontemporal actual occasion. On such grounds, Whitehead himself preferred to think of God as not a person. Others feel that it is possible to be faithful to his theism without following him on this particular conclusion. Charles Hartshorne, Schubert Ogden, and John Cobb depart from Whitehead's conclusion by introducing temporality into divinity.[10] But such a revision allows them to think of God as personal only in the sense that his constant self-becoming betrays a consistent and coherent pattern and is not a random, chaotic process. Some indication of how radically this alters the ordinary understanding of person is conveyed in the following words of Hartshorne: "I grant that God judges all acts, but on the understanding that the past self alone is judged for past acts, and the present self only for its present acts or intentions."[11] An immediate and ever novel process of self-constitution thus replaces an order in which constancy of change does not eliminate an underlying and perduring personal identity. The latter allows for a basic permanency at the heart of all movement, in which being offers an anchor to becoming. What is questionable in this alternative view of Whitehead is why it does not mean the collapse of freedom, as genuine self-determination, into a universe of radical contingency in which God alone supplies whatever *telos* is there.

At any rate, it is surely meaningless to speak, from this position, of a plurality of persons within divinity. More than that, what it means to speak of the loving interrelationship between God and men as transpiring on a personal level is considerably compromised. One is left with something closer to a world view in which the divine occasion and the worldly occasion are mere factors in a vast impersonal, cosmic process—in spite of the fact that such process involves values associated with love and genuine self-transcendence. In summary, then, this abbreviated look at Whitehead's dipolar God is adequate to convey that alien to it is any notion of distinct subjec-

---

[10]Charles Hartshorne, *The Divine Relativity: A Social Conception of God* (New Haven: Yale University Press, 1948), pp. 142ff.; Schubert Ogden, "Beyond Supernaturalism," *Religion in Life*, vol. 33 (Winter 1963–64), pp. 7–18; John B. Cobb, Jr., *A Christian Natural Theology* (Philadelphia: Westminster Press, 1965), pp. 185–92.

[11]*Philosophical Interrogations*, S. and B. Rome, eds. (New York: Holt, Rinehart, and Winston, 1964), p. 339. This volume contains answers to significant questions by six other contemporary religious thinkers in addition to Hartshorne.

tivities in the Godhead, of a preexistent personal *Logos*, and of incarnate divinity.

THE TRINITY AS GOD'S SOCIAL RELATIONS TO THE WORLD: CHARLES HARTSHORNE

To the extent that process theology takes the doctrine of the Trinity seriously, it does so, by and large, by viewing it as an early Christian way of symbolizing some aspect or other of God's dipolarity. This is obviously rather difficult to do since the triadic and dyadic conceptions appear more mutually exclusive than complementary. The efforts of Charles Hartshorne, however, to transform Whitehead's seminal thought into an integral natural theology suggested a way of doing this—one not pursued by Hartshorne himself but worked out by others who have carried the implications of his work into theology. Hartshorne seemingly interprets Whitehead's distinction between a primordial and a consequent nature in God as endangering the divine unity. He rescues that unity by stressing the consequent nature, finding God's full reality there, and reducing the primordial nature to the abstract preconditions for the consequent nature.[12] He notes, however, that "'abstract' does not mean unreal, but does mean real within something richer in determinations than the factor said to be abstract."[13] The one essence of God can be considered by us either abstractly or under the conditions of its actual existence. In the former, it is viewed as containing all possible forms of concretion in a conceptual way. In the latter, however, God is seen as actually luring the cosmos into a richer future and, at the same time, as realizing himself in dependence upon the world. As with all process thinkers, Hartshorne makes clear the distinction is entirely a rational one. There are not two natures in God, but our attempts to conceive of him demand acknowledging two dimensions to the one deity, two aspects interrelated in an organic and dynamic way. Hartshorne does inaugurate, nonetheless, a line of development distinct from Whitehead's own—one in which the

---

[12]See in particular Hartshorne, *The Divine Relativity* and *A Natural Theology for Our Time* (La Salle, Ill.: Open Court, 1967).

[13]"The Philosophy of Creative Synthesis," Symposium: Creativity as a Philosophical Category, *Journal of Philosophy* 55, no. 22 (October 23, 1958), p. 949.

primordial nature is less prominent a factor in God's total reality. Only the actual is fully real for Hartshorne; the possible is a Platonic realm of ideal forms that functions largely in an explanatory role. Whitehead, by contrast, preferred to view reality as constituted by the polar tension between possibility and actuality. There can be no doubt, at any rate, that Hartshorne accords a clear priority to the consequent nature:

> ... God ... must be conceived not as wholly absolute or immutable, but rather as supremely relative, "surrelative," although, or because of this superior relativity, containing an abstract character or essence in respect to which, but only in respect to which, he is indeed strictly absolute and immutable.[14]

This is but an application of the general principle that:

> ... the "relative" or changeable ... includes within itself and in value exceeds the nonrelative, immutable, independent, or "absolute," as the concrete includes and exceeds the abstract.[15]

It is on these grounds that one is enabled to speak "personally" of God, that is, on the basis of his acquiring social relations in his active and passive involvement with the world, something characteristic of his concrete nature. Hartshorne never explicitly addresses the question of the Trinity, thus one is venturing on thin ice in suggesting, in a purely speculative way, what sort of trinitarianism his thought logically allows for. But the shift he inaugurated in Whitehead's theism has had its theological consequences. His decided emphasis upon the concrete, the actual, and so the finite, meant that the question of God's transcendence and immanence, his absoluteness and his relativity, was in fact transferred to the domain of what is for Whitehead the consequent nature. In this, the primordial nature becomes the ontological condition for what is characteristic of God ontically. The former expresses the essential structure that makes possible the concrete actualizations of that structure. This is suggestive of the distinction between existentiality (*Existenzialität*) and existence (*Existenz*) and recalls Heidegger's *existenzial-existenziell* distinction.

At any rate, the level of divine being that Hartshorne's thought seeks to clarify is that which comes to light in its concrete historical engagement with men, precisely that recounted in the biblical nar-

---

[14]*The Divine Relativity,* Preface to original edition, p. ix.
[15]Ibid.

ration. Central to that record—especially in the New Testament account of the meeting of God in the man Jesus—is an awareness of God as present within a world and a history he transcends. The basic categories are dyadic, and this lends itself to the interpretative powers of process theology. In the Christian instance, the language concerns, on the one hand, Yahweh-God who is Creator and Father of all, and on the other, the Word of God, the Son of God, the Christ, and the Spirit. Only subsequently does the language become reductively trinitarian, when attention is given to the difference between God's acting in Jesus and his acting in other men; at this point, some distinction begins to be drawn between *Logos* and Spirit. Hartshorne's thought points this way, even though he himself does not explore such properly theological questions. The direction it gives is one in which God, precisely in his consequent nature, relates himself socially to the world in the threefold way of providing it with purpose (*Logos*), and with creative transforming love (Spirit), and yet remaining true to his own purposes (Father). The reservations felt towards Whitehead's theism weigh against Hartshorne's too—above all that of a God who appears to be more a finite cosmic deity than the God of Abraham, Isaac, and Jacob, not to say of Jesus the Christ. The strictly trinitarian implications of this, however, can be better pursued in the theological writers Hartshorne has inspired.

SPIRIT AS GOD'S UNIVERSAL IMMANENCE TO THE WORLD

Hartshorne's panentheistic concept of God is, of course, a philosophically elaborated one and as such it bears no necessary relation to the religious doctrine of the Trinity. The attempt to accommodate the latter within the concept gives evidence of a certain artificiality. It is the rational and dipolar conception that remains the controlling one, and to it the religious and trinitarian one must yield at crucial points. What Hartshorne bequeathed to his followers was a way of dealing with the Trinity on the basis of God's nature in its concreteness and actuality. In this perspective, it expresses a certain triplicity in the social relationships concretely established between God and man. God is called "Father" in virtue of that individualistic way in which he chooses to exist that owes nothing to any creature, even though it remains his actuality vis-à-vis the world. This is God in his hiddenness, as "sufficiently free of the world to be ever true to himself ... and his purposes, even in his involvement with the changing world."[16] This is not simply his abstract transcending of the world, but his transcending of it precisely in his choosing to love that world in the concrete way that is properly seen as "fatherly."

But the correlate to this is God's necessary immanence in the universe, and this is process theology's explanation of what Christians mean in calling God "Holy Spirit."[17] Process Theism is more comfortable in ordering the Trinity in a way that gives logical priority to the Spirit over the *Logos*. The reason for this is that God's immanence in the cosmos is universal; it regards all actual entities without exception and with equal intensity. This makes it somewhat more problematical to think in terms of a special presence in the case of Christ. The symbol "spirit" is a religious way of expressing this immanence because of the range of meaning the term bears. It conveys presence, intimate inexistence, the sense of an invisible source of inspiration, unity, and love—especially compassionate love. In calling his system a "philosophy of organism," Whitehead meant that it views reality as a vast organic interrelationship in which each event is somehow linked with every other.[18] This includes the event that is God, but his privileged mode of being explains that he alone is *directly* related to, and so present in, everything else. The other side of this panentheistic coin is, of course, that whatever is actual in the world is "maximally present in God."[19] But his far richer experience of such values means that he is able to entice and lure forward, in a persuasive and never coercive manner, the advancing universe, by offering to each occasion the impulse that represents the optimum value for it, given its concrete situation.[20] This is true, it might be noted, even if what is best for it is so low in value as to be, comparatively speaking, evil. This amounts to one element in process philosophy's explanation of evil in the world—

---

[16]Thomas W. Ogletree, "A Christological Assessment of Dipolar Theism," in *Process Philosophy and Christian Thought*, D. Brown, R. E. James, and G. Reeves, eds. (Indianapolis: Bobbs-Merrill, 1971), pp. 345–46.

[17]As illustrative of this, see David Griffin, "Holy Spirit: Compassion and Reverence for Being," pp. 107–20 and S. Palmer Pardington III, "The Holy Ghost Is Dead—the Holy Spirit Lives," pp. 121–32 in *Religious Experience and Process Theology*, ed. H. J. Cargas and B. Lee (New York: Paulist Press, 1976).

[18]*P. R.*, pp. 79–80.

[19]Hartshorne, "Redefining God," *The New Humanist* 7, no. 4 (July–August 1934), pp. 8–15.

[20]*P. R.*, p. 373.

the more fundamental element being the occasion's refusal to correspond with God's subjective aim for it. It is an account which does offer a rationale for the phenomenon of evil, but it can be asked if it does full justice to what is conveyed in the Christian category "sin," which takes more seriously the destructive power of human malice.

Nonetheless, the doctrine of the Spirit at work here derives from the notion of causal immanence that lies at the heart of process thinking. Whatever contributes to the shaping of an actual entity is truly present to and ingredient within it. This means everything that the self-constituting occasion prehends, in both its conceptual and physical feelings. Whitehead stresses the former because he sees God's initial aims for things as deriving from his primordial nature. Hartshorne lets the compass swing the other way, viewing initial aims concretely and so as shaped by God's own enriching experience. Theoretically, this matters little to working out a doctrine of the Spirit, except that most theological endeavors along this line find Hartshorne's thought more congenial to the biblical origins of the doctrine. What is important is the shared understanding that God not only acts directly on every occasion, but does so not from outside but from within, by way of entering into an occasion's actual constitution and as forming a dimension of its own reality.[21] This doctrine of causal immanence, whereby one event is actually within another, means that God works universally from what Teilhard de Chardin calls the "inside of things." It suggests what Christians mean in calling God "Spirit"—as, for example, in St. Paul's "You are on the spiritual level, if only God's Spirit dwells within you. . . . everyone moved by the Spirit is a son of God" (*Rom.* 8:9 and 14). It conveys the religious sense of the divine pervading all of reality. In summary, Spirit is a Christian way of naming God under the aspect of: (i) his loving presence; (ii) in its universality, i.e., as extending to all events and with equal intensity; and (iii) in its noncoercive efficacy (God determines everything without infringing on the freedom of things); (iv) as operative within the structures of both the cosmic and historical orders; yet (v) as ever superior to these orders in one sense, since the Spirit is always from the Father.

---

[21]See the essays already cited in note 17; also Bernard Meland, *The Realities of Faith* (New York: Oxford University Press, 1962).

But this cocreative identification with all entities of the world means that the divine Spirit must suffer all resulting diminutions and failed opportunities in that world. The latter are inevitable, if for no other reason than that, in John Knox's phrase, "a perfect historical event is a contradiction in terms." There is no gainsaying this hard truth, but process thought turns it to advantage. It merely serves to indicate that God himself is Love and not Power—not the Omnipotent One of classical theism, nor preeminently "the power over all that is," in Pannenberg's phrase. God's love is all the more genuine for arising out of an empathetic appreciation for the finite conditions of all that it loves. It is *compassionate* love that opens itself receptively to the world's deficient response to, and return of, that love.

The foregoing highlights certain advantages in this reconceptualization of God as Spirit. But certain reservations come to the surface also, and these deserve to be heard. Basically they are three. First, the only mode of God's immanence in things that can be argued for, in this coherent system, is an entirely *objective* one. The freedom with which an event creates itself means that whatever enters into its constitution must be a past occasion (that is, a perished occasion that is no longer actual) prehended by the present occasion as it posits itself. This is true even of so-called hybrid feelings—in which God's subjective aims for things, coming from God as his conceptual feelings, pass over into the physical feelings of the occasions which respond to them. This is clear in the understanding that the self-creative process means that one actual occasion cannot prehend another in its actuality.[22] Even God "does not know and hence cannot unify actual occasions as they are in the subjective immediacy of their own concrescent becoming."[23] The kind of inexistence of cause and effect at work here seems less intimate, intense, and efficacious than what is allowed for in Aristotle's doctrine of efficient causality. By contrast, this present explanation reduces God's acting to what is in fact the occasion's own physical feeling for God.[24]

---

[22]*P. R.*, pp. 36–37.

[23]Gene Reeves and Delwin Brown, "The Development of Process Theology," in *Process Philosophy and Christian Thought*, Introduction, p. 46.

[24]See, among others, Daniel Day Williams, "How Does God Act?" in *Process and Divinity*, ed. W. L. Reese and E. Freeman (La Salle, Ill.: Open Court, 1964), pp. 161–80.

Secondly, the divine love for the universe, in this explanation, seems to be at a considerable remove from what the New Testament means by *agapē*. The former, though compassionate in kind, remains more basically a love motivated by the need for self-fulfillment; this brings it closer to a form of Greek *erōs*. God loves the world finally, not for its sake, but for his own sake; he seeks in it raw material for his own enduring advancement.

Thirdly, the Holy Spirit, while personal, is not a distinct person within divinity. Holy Spirit is no longer the revealed name of a distinct subsistence within the mystery who is God but merely the designation of an attribute of God's nature as the Inclusive Concrete. One process theologian has given clear expression to this in calling for a jettisoning of the symbol "Holy Ghost," conjuring up as it does images of an otherworldly and supernatural being, in favor of "Holy Spirit" as a symbol for creative and transforming love working in the natural sphere.[25] This seems less a striving to understand the mystery than a facile dismissal of it. The net result is more an instance of faith yielding to rational analysis than an attempt at *intellectus fidei.*

THE WORD AS GOD'S SPECIAL AIMS FOR CHRIST: SCHUBERT OGDEN AND JOHN COBB, JR.

The unique manner in which process theology understands God in the simultaneity of his transcendence and immanence issues in an understanding of Christ as somehow a special instance of that immanence. By this is meant not an immanence that excludes the element of transcendence, but rather one that includes it. Nonetheless, the problem this sets is one of explaining how the divine presence in this instance can be special, and even unique, without compromising the universal presence of God as Spirit. Indigenous to the metaphysics of process thought is a view of all reality as on the same level, a repudiation, then, of the analogy of being.[26] Hart-

---

[25]See note 17, S. Palmer Pardington III; also note 21, B. Meland.

[26]". . . all reality is on the same level, however diverse its forms may be." John B. Cobb, Jr., "Christianity and Myth," *The Journal of Bible and Religion* (October 1965), pp. 314–20; now appearing as *The Journal of the American Academy of Religion* 33, no. 4 (October 1965).

shorne—maintaining that God's presence to the world is isomorphic to the presence of the human self to its body—looks upon Jesus as simply one organ of the world-body that registers, in an intense and localized way, the feeling that is the response of the whole organism. There are grounds for referring to this as a "naturalistic Christology," since he writes:

> Jesus appears to be the supreme symbol furnished to us by history of the notion of a God genuinely and literally "sympathetic" (incomparably more literally than any man ever is), receiving into his own experience the sufferings as well as the joys of the world.[27]

Don S. Browning gives a psychological interpretation to this, suggesting that what is a prereflective awareness of God in all men becomes fully thematic and manifest in Christ.[28] Common to all process Christologies, at any rate, is a denial that the difference is one of kind; on the contrary, it is one of degree only. It is a difference in the divine operation upon mankind that is one "of immeasurable degree, not of absolute kind," in the words of Norman Pittenger, with which Peter Hamilton concurs.[29] Still, some way of making this specialness intelligible is called for. This has come above all from two students of Hartshorne: Schubert Ogden and John B. Cobb, Jr.

Ogden approaches the question of the presence of God in Jesus in terms of a divine acting, but one that justifies saying that the history of Jesus is the decisive act of God, so that it is normative for other men and constitutes what is meant by revelation. A strength of Ogden's explanation is that his special act of God is given both a subjective and an objective character. If the subjective element lies in the intensity and totality of Jesus' human response to God's initial aims for him, the more significant objective element consists in the fact that the content of that aim amounts to a "re-presentation" of God's purposes for the world at large.

---

[27]*Reality as Social Process: Studies in Metaphysics and Religion* (Glencoe: Free Press; Boston: Beacon Press, 1953), p. 24.

[28]*Psychotherapy and Atonement* (Philadelphia: Westminster, 1966).

[29]Norman Pittenger, *The Incarnate Lord* (New York: Harper and Row, 1959), p. 285; Peter Hamilton, "Some Proposals for a Modern Christology," in *Christ for Us Today*, ed. N. Pittenger (London: SCM, 1968), p. 166.

... to say of any historical event that it is the "decisive" act of God can only mean that, in it, in distinction from all other historical events, the ultimate truth about our existence before God is normatively represented or revealed.[30]

There is, in other words, no difference in content; the intentions of God that gain expression in the life of Jesus are no different in kind than those operative in all men.

... There is not the slightest evidence that God has acted in Christ in any way different from the way in which he primordially acts in every other event.[31]

Where does the uniqueness lie, then? In its normative character, for one thing, as Ogden notes. But this only pushes the question back further. Why is what this man does normative? Not because God's initial aims for him are different. Not solely because of Jesus' richer response to those aims, either— this is only the subjective side to this special event. Seemingly, Ogden means that Jesus' particular words and actions gave an objective manifestation to God's common intentions, which thematized that aim and rendered it available in a new and still unsurpassed way. His life concretized uniquely the intelligibility inherent in God's overall plan for all entities; his deeds mediated objectively the *logos* of God in a manner that earned him special claim to that title, to being confessed as the *Logos* of God.

David Griffin suspects a certain inadequacy in this explanation, and suggests that one has to acknowledge a difference in the very "whatness" of God's action in Jesus.[32] He also offers an illuminating insight into why Ogden is reluctant to do so. This is due to the influence of Heidegger, via Bultmann, who denies any authentic possibilities for modern Western man (i.e., men of Christian origins) distinct from what are universal possibilities. Still and all, Griffin does not mean that the divine action in Christ is essentially different in the sense of intending anything specifically distinct from what is the case universally. It differs only individually, in virtue of the

---

[30]Schubert M. Ogden, *The Reality of God* (New York: Harper and Row, 1963), p. 184.

[31]"Bultmann's Project of Demythologization and the Problem of Theology and Philosophy," *Journal of Religion* 37, no. 3 (July 1957), p. 169.

[32]David Griffin, "Schubert Ogden's Christology and the Possibilities of Process Philosophy," in *Process Philosophy and Christian Thought*, pp. 351ff.

concrete historical background and context in which it becomes actual. Thus, the earthly life of Jesus cannot be thought to be unique in the sense of possessing, for example, a redemptive or reconciling power not found elsewhere. In the end, then, Griffin's position is not all that different from Ogden's: Jesus is called the *Logos* and Son of God because of the "special appropriateness" with which his life expresses the designs of God.

The possibilities inherent in this Christology, with its implicit trinitarianism, come more clearly to light in the detailed and painstaking work of John B. Cobb, Jr.[33] He begins by noting that if the mode of God's presence in all entities is identical, there is no way of defending the Christian claims of Christ's uniqueness and authority. Since one entity is present to another on the basis of being prehended by it, there must be something special in Jesus' prehending of God. Ultimately, the difference is twofold: (i) Jesus' prehension embraces not only the initial aim but includes as well a consciousness of its divine origin, and (ii) that prehension does not synthesize with all others but dominates them so as to form that center of his consciousness constituting his unique self or "I."[34] Initial aims for other occasions provide mere possibilities; in Jesus' case a part of the aim is the explicit recognition of its source, which explains the completeness of his adherence to that aim. But even this would not seem to distinguish Jesus from other great prophets. Thus, there is seemingly an additional and distinctive content to the aim itself:

> God's aim for Jesus was that he prehend God in terms of that which constitutes him as God—his lordship, his love, and his incomparable superiority of being and value.[35]

This brings us to the second, more suggestive, element in Cobb's explanation. Here, God's effective presence to Christ has a formal role to play regarding all his other prehensions, one which determines his structure of existence. Cobb understands the "I" of Jesus, that is to say, his selfhood, not as the psyche, or any sort of transcendental ego, but simply as the organizing center of psychic life, as the point at which there is achieved a sense of self-identity

[33]See esp. *A Christian Natural Theology* (Philadelphia: Westminster Press, 1969); *Christ in a Pluralistic Age* (Philadelphia: Westminster Press, 1975); and "A Whiteheadian Christology," in *Process Philosophy and Christian Thought*, pp. 382–98.
[34]"A Whiteheadian Christology," esp. pp. 383–94.
[35]Ibid., p. 393.

through time. But that organizing and self-identifying activity is nothing more than the succession of decisions whereby an occasion posits itself in its own unique actuality, through selecting which available data are to be formative in its chosen structure of existence. Thus the way in which he prehended God "constituted in Jesus the center from which everything else in his psychic life was integrated," which is only to say that "God's presence in Jesus constituted Jesus' essential selfhood."[36] All this enables Cobb to say that "Jesus' weighing of values—his perception of the relative importance of things and persons, of the self and others, of motives and actions, of past, present, and future—was from the perspective given in his prehension of God."[37] The value of Cobb's development—perhaps the most lucid available from any process Christologist—is that it appears to open a way towards rejoining the traditional faith-confession of Christians. The point of convergence is an understanding of the divine in Jesus as pertaining to the domain of personhood or *hypostasis*. The consequence of this is no displacement of the nature in its integral humanity. But the differences remain uppermost.

In the end, the gains offered by this sort of Christology for a revised trinitarianism appear overbalanced by insurmountable problems it brings in its wake. First, the presence of God in Christ—for all the attempts of Ogden, Griffin, Cobb, and others to give it a distinguishing character—is not *toto caelo* different from every other divine presence; it is generically, and even specifically, the same. This is a cardinal principle of all process thought. Ogden dismisses all talk about a divine presence and action differing from what is the common case as mythological. But the notion of causality operative within the process system imposes this restriction upon him. At the very beginning, any possibility of creation (in the proper sense of production *ex nihilo*), and so of a true creator-cause, is eliminated.[38] All causation is a matter of finite actualization which, while introducing novelty into the world, can do so only in a univocal or homogeneous line of development. Even God's influx into the world is less a vertical than a horizontal one; it is determined in the final analysis by conditions alien to itself. Ogden believes that to

---

[36]Ibid., pp. 393–94.

[37]Ibid., p. 393.

[38]"Whitehead vehemently rejected the notion of a transcendent creator God who by an act of the will called all things into being out of nothing. . . ." Cobb, *A Christian Natural Theology*, p. 215.

view God's acting in Christ as a pure divine initiative is gratuitous and in violation of the unity of God's being. But this fails to allow God his genuine transcendence (a transcendence that is absolute and not merely relative). And only this makes possible understanding that the difference lies not in God's acting, which *is* his being and so one—but in the diverse, nondivine effects that single causality brings about. When the Word became flesh, it was Jesus' *humanity* (and so ours) that was altered and transformed beyond anything that lay within its own resources.

The process doctrine of causal immanence does seek to explain that one entity is actually within another, and moreover, that God's privileged mode of being (due to his nontemporality) means that he is present within *all* other occasions. Cobb, however, dismisses the classical doctrine of causality (deriving from Aristotle) as not allowing this.[39] This is somewhat surprising in that usually it is understood as an explanation of causality precisely in terms of the presence of the cause within the effect. True enough, this inexistence is *virtual,* and not the *actual* one of process philosophy. But the latter can only be explained in terms of the present occasion's prehending act, and this makes it in fact the actuality of the emerging occasion, not the preceding occasion. What is actual is not the past event at all but the present event's re-expression of an earlier value. There can be no question of one actual occasion being in another. The older realism of Aristotelian vintage allows a *subjective* presence of predecessor to successor, one achieved in causal agency; Whiteheadian realism reduces that to an *objective* presence, reducible to extrinsic exemplarism. The latter not only fails to explain anything distinctive about God's presence in Christ, it diminishes the full force of God's universal immanence to his creation.

Secondly, this understanding of the divine immanence as an objective, prehended presence even in Jesus cannot be easily reconciled with the intentions of the formulas of Nicaea and Chalce-

---

[39]"A Whiteheadian Christology," p. 385. Lewis Ford expresses a different reservation on the classical notion of causality, asking "If the new were completely constituted by the old, in what sense would it be new?" "Process Trinitarianism," *Journal of the American Academy of Religion* 43, no. 2 (June 1975), p. 202. But this supposes that all causes function only univocally, positing always mere replicas of themselves, whereas Aristotle makes room for causation of an analogical kind in which new forms come into existence that were previously in the cause only virtually.

don. If God only furnished data for the Christ-event, then its occurrence is entirely a matter of the free human prehensions of the man Jesus. It is his self-constitution that renders the divine a factor in reality. God does not become man, rather man becomes more fully man by incorporating the richer experiences of God as part of his own reality. Cobb, acknowledging that "in Jesus we have to do with deity itself . . . [so that] . . . the Logos incarnate in Jesus is God himself," goes on to add that "Jesus is not 'consubstantial' with the Father."[40] When he writes that "Jesus was not the Logos as such but the Logos as incarnate, that is to say, Christ," he really means that Jesus was not divine, but exclusively human—"in *every* respect, without qualification, a human being."[41] But he is a man who can be said to have "incarnated" the Logos of God in the process of achieving his own personhood, which would not seem to go beyond the sense of giving objective expression to God's purposes for the world. Divinity is "hypostatic" in the humanity and, moreover, only in this objective way. (Cobb avoids saying that the Divinity incarnates itself in the humanity, or that the humanity is "hypostatic" in the Word of God; thus, he shies away from the title "Christ" because it tends to confuse Jesus with God.)[42] All of this surely relativizes the specialness of God's action in the life and death of Jesus; it is unique only factually and, in principle, can be reachieved elsewhere and even surpassed.

Lastly, even if process theology succeeds in making God's presence to the world in Christ unique, Jesus himself is now a perished occasion. To say that "Jesus even now continues to reveal God to us in new ways"[43] cannot be read to mean he actively mediates God to us; he is simply an item of the past available for our prehending activity. This is a far cry from the risen *Kyrios* of St. Paul—a title that dominates classical, medieval, and Reformational Christianity. It means, too, emptying out the Resurrection of Jesus of all meaning other than that of the preservation in God of the values Jesus once made actual.[44]

---

[40]*Christ in a Pluralistic Age,* p. 170.
[41]Ibid. (emphasis supplied).
[42]Ibid., p. 42.
[43]"A Whiteheadian Christology," p. 396.
[44]Whitehead describes God as "the ideal companion who transmutes what has been lost into a living fact within his own nature." *Religion in the Making* (New York: Macmillan, 1926), pp. 154–55.

In the final analysis, it is difficult to gainsay that process theology leaves one with the sense of authentic Christian faith capitulating to a rational system of explanation. It refuses what Aloys Grillmeier calls the *lectio difficilior* of the early Church, which, in groping for understanding, refused to surrender the mystery of God to the carrying power of the categories of reason. That understanding of the Christ-event led inexorably to the confession of the Trinity, to the mystery of a God who in his very oneness is Father, Son, and Spirit. Process theology suggests a revised understanding that reduces the Trinity to a symbolic way of saying that man, carried forward on the wave of Creativity, is not alone, but "coconstituted by the presence of God" as the Great Beckoner.

AN INTEGRAL PROCESS TRINITARIANISM: LEWIS S. FORD

A notable exception to the diffidence shown generally towards any explicit doctrine of the Trinity appears in a formal study of this Christian mystery by Lewis S. Ford.[45] The problem, as for any process thinker, is how to reconcile a Christian concept of God as triune with the concept in neoclassical metaphysics of God as dipolar. Most attempts to do this have simply concluded that the tripartite formulas found in the Bible and early Creeds represent primitive and inept—even if religiously satisfying—ways of symbolizing what is in fact only the dyadic structure of a God at once absolute and relative. Cyril Richardson has done this, working exclusively from the biblical categories themselves (see Chapter Four); Charles Hartshorne has done the same in a philosophical milieu by suggesting that the Trinity images a subset of social relations to the world adopted by God in his concrete being. Ford, by contrast, eschews this facile dismissal of the doctrine and works through a far more intricate explanation. The solution at which he arrives actually demands *two* distinct trinitarian doctrines, but they are intimately connected and he fuses them together into one integral explanation. The first is of biblical origin; the second is one that the biblical Trinity merely points to and that itself arises out of a more refined speculation upon the creedal formula. In this there is something reminiscent of Hegel, that is, of religious truth being sublimated in philosophical truth.

---

[45]Lewis S. Ford, "Process Trinitarianism." See note 39.

Believers confess, on the basis of God's contingent activities towards the world, that God is Father, *Logos,* and Spirit. Ford contends that by this they mean God in what Whitehead calls his primordial nature.

> The Father is constituted by the primordial nature as it expresses the nature and activity of God, the Logos as it provides emergent possibilities for the on-going creation of the world, and the Spirit as it expresses the immanence of God within every creature as its particular creative possibility.[46]

It is noteworthy that he always names the second member of the triad *Logos* and never Son. Nonetheless, Ford's approach is unique among process thinkers in refusing the simplistic and anthropomorphic procedure of locating the Trinity in God's consequent nature, where it merely symbolizes the set of actual, contingent, somewhat extrinsic relationships that God chooses to adopt towards men. Ford goes further in reducing the threefold relationality discerned there back to God in his primordiality. This is possible only if the primordial nature is seen not as just the abstract precondition for God's actuality, but a true nature in God that has to be held in rational distinction from the consequent nature. In this, Ford is being faithful to Whitehead's own thought and disclaiming the interpretation put upon it by Hartshorne. The two "natures" exist in intimate interaction, and the primordial nature, far from designating God merely abstractly, or as "in himself" apart from his involvement with the world, expresses his aboriginal immanence in the world. The primordial nature, as "the complete, timeless ordering of all formal structures,"[47] makes the world a possibility. What the religious experiences at the origin of Christianity made apparent was a triadic structure within God as primordial, expressing: (i) first, his conceptual envisagement of true possibilities for the world (the symbol Father); (ii) secondly, the "bodying forth [of] a new emergence in the creative advance of the world,"[48] one transcending human possibilities and so creating a new structure of existence (the

---

[46]Ibid., p. 205.
[47]Ibid.
[48]Ibid., p. 204. An *emergent* is "a creative breakthrough ... a novelty inexplicable in terms of previous levels of the evolutionary process" in contrast to a mere *resultant,* which is "a new quality wholly explicable in terms of its antecedents"—a distinction Ford borrows from Lloyd Morgan; see p. 202.

symbol *Logos*); and (iii) thirdly, his immanence within every creature in supplying to it initial aims for its particular creative possibilities (the symbol Spirit). This gave expression to a God encountered as acting through the Word (in Jesus) and the Spirit (in all men), revealing the Father as the source whence they originate.

Once again, the Christian doctrine of the Trinity is seen as expressing God's immanence within a world that he continues to transcend. But it stops short of a full explanation of reality because it leaves unexplored the other side of the metaphysical coin. This is the truth that entities other than God, in their own way, transcend the divine and are immanent within it. It is Creativity that is the ultimate metaphysical category, not God. The latter is an actual entity, whereas Creativity is neither actual nor existent. God instantiates Creativity in his way, as its chief exemplification, but so do nondivine entities in their way in virtue of their decision of creative self-positing. What God introduces into being is not a world of determined actualities, but a realm of genuine possibility. Actual occasions create themselves (thus "creation," in its usual sense, is an inappropriate term for God's action) and so shape reality in novel ways not controlled by God. This provides data for God's physical, rather than conceptual, experience determining how he is able to constitute himself in the actuality of his consequent nature. These considerations bring us to the second, complementary way in which Ford seeks to revise the conceptualization of the Trinity.

Beyond providing initial aims for the world by way of his primordial nature, God responds to the actual values realized in the world. This response, while passive and receptive in kind, retains a creative character; it is an instantiation of Creativity on another level. It is not an inert and disinterested acceptance and retention of what the world offers, but a selective transformation by God of what the world renders available to his experience. It betokens an intimate copresence of God and worldly entities—not so much now by way of God's immanence in the world as by way of the world's immanence in God. This profound and startling awareness Ford finds conveyed indistinctly in early Christian use of the symbol "Spirit." If so, that divine name designates the consequent nature of God, i.e., God as lovingly involved with finite occasions precisely as, in their own actuality, they transcend God in enriching his actual experience. "Holy Spirit," then, is a mode of religious speech about God that refers not to his pure initiatives towards men but to his continuing loving response to the limited initiatives of men towards one another and himself. The term seeks to express God in his

temporal involvement with worldly entities. By this Ford means that
the genuine possibilities available in the initial aims supplied by
God's primordial nature are partially conditioned by the subsequent
response of his consequent nature to the values that the world
chooses to actualize. Both are activities of God under the rubric of
"Spirit"—but the latter instance is the more profound and illuminating.

What then of the other two members of the Trinity? The contrast
of *Logos* and *Pneuma* is easiest. If Spirit conveys the world's immanence in God, *Logos* conveys God's immanence in the world. Though
the two are simultaneous, we tend to think of the latter as having
logical priority—thus the traditional trinitarian order is observed.
It might be noted that Ford not only does away with the *Filioque*
(the doctrine of the Spirit's origin from the Son), but leaves no
opening for any doctrine of procession within divinity. At this point,
Ford has simply suggested that Spirit primarily symbolizes God in
his consequent nature and that *Logos* represents a corresponding
awareness of God in his primordial nature.

> . . . The Logos pre-eminently symbolizes and exemplifies that [pri-
> mordial] nature. For Logos is structure and order, and the primordial
> nature is the complete, timeless ordering of all formal structures. . . .
> From this perspective we may say that the Logos *is* the primordial
> nature, while Father and Spirit point to other aspects of God which are
> revealed to us through the primordial nature. With respect to this one
> nature, the Logos is central, the other two are peripheral.[49]

Does this leave the first person of the Trinity unaccounted for?
Not when we recall that there can be no word without a speaker,
that word necessarily entails its inner, dynamic source.

> Insofar as the Word symbolizes the whole of the primordial nature,
> the symbol Father is freed to point to the ultimate transcendent source
> of this manifest structure. For Whitehead this is the primordial envis-
> agement, that nontemporal act of divine self-creation which issues forth
> as the complete ordering of all eternal objects which is the primordial
> nature.[50]

The Father is thus God in that nontemporal act whereby he creates himself, i.e., constitutes his own nature as primordial. The *Logos*
is God in his atemporal act of envisaging creative possibilities for

---

[49]Ibid., pp. 205–6.
[50]Ibid., p. 206.

the world, or God as primordial nature. The Spirit is God in his temporal act of responding to the actual world he experiences by way of his consequent nature. Put differently: as Father, God transcends the world; as *Logos*, he is immanent within it; as Spirit, he is responsive to the world that transcends him. Ford's conclusion is clear and concise.

> Thus in the final analysis we must assent to an ultimate triunity of principles defining the divine life: the divine creative act nontemporally generating the primordial nature, from which proceeds the consequent nature as implicated in the categoreal conditions established by the primordial envisagement.[51]

Not without significance in the above citation is the use of the word "principles" and the avoidance of the term "persons." Ford understands that the meaning intended by what we translate as "person" in the creedal formulas is "a formally distinct aspect or principle or mode of functioning for a single unitary actuality."[52] In doing this, he transforms "person" into a misleading synonym for "nature," at least the sense of nature intended by Whitehead in speaking of the primordial and consequent natures of God. Some commentators on Whitehead make much of his occasional reference to a third nature in God, called the "superjective nature," which describes God's pouring back into the world values which he has already received and transformed in the experiences ascribed to his consequent nature.[53] If Whitehead intends this consistently then it might be possible to draw a rather neat parallel in which Father, *Logos*, and Spirit are viewed as biblical names for, respectively, the primordial, consequent, and superjective natures in God. Ford, however, argues exegetically that Whitehead uses "superjective" only to designate one function of the primordial nature.[54] Thus, his own position is more subtle than this perhaps overly facile one. No matter. He still equates person and nature—precisely what the early Councils of the Church insisted upon distinguishing; a distinction, moreover, on which turned their theological understanding of the mystery of both Christ and Trinity. The import of Ford's alteration is that it makes it no longer possible to see the trinitarian distinctions

---

[51]Ibid., p. 213.
[52]Ibid., p. 207.
[53]See Whitehead, *Process and Reality*, p. 135.
[54]"Process Trinitarianism," p. 207, note 16.

as *real* in contrast to all other distinctions introduced into the divine nature as purely *rational.* Ford acknowledges that his triunity of principles cannot be interpreted as "implying a plurality of subjects in personal interaction within the Godhead."[55] Three persons in the sense of three centers of consciousness would mean three substances, three instances of substantial unity. Counterpoised to the category of "person" or "hypostasis" in primitive Christianity is Whitehead's category of subjectivity or individuality. God achieves "innermost subjectivity," which is his hiddenness, his autonomy from the world, precisely in his nontemporal act of self-creation. This suggests a correspondence with the Father's identity as Father in the eternal generation of his Son. But Ford, in refusing to refer to the generated one as Son and retaining only the impersonal title of *Logos,* indicates how differently he understands the parallel. Insofar as God is acknowledged as personal, then, he is *one* person. Solely the biblical name Father refers to God in his personhood. In the end, Ford's interpretation of the God of Christian experience in Whiteheadian categories is unitarian, not trinitarian. It represents a unipersonal God who interacts with the world on the basis of his own dipolarity of nature. Ford is then forced to see the attempts of the early Church at a reflective understanding as the attributing of distinct subjectivity to these two "natures," over and above the subjectivity given to God as Father. In so doing, he concludes that believers succeeded in safeguarding God's transcendence of the world, but failed to make explicit the world's transcendence of God. Their doctrine of the Holy Spirit, however, he interprets as some faint surmising of this latter truth.

THE TRINITY AS PROCESS IN CATHOLIC THOUGHT: WALTER STOKES AND ANTHONY KELLY

Catholic theology, by and large, responds sympathetically to the intentions and religious motivations of process thinkers, especially in their endeavors to modify metaphysical thinking at the very point where it appears inadequate to Christian religious experience. It is, perhaps, on the question of the Trinity that the convergence is most significant. This is because the Catholic tradition (and indeed the

---

[55]Ibid., p. 207.

Christian tradition generally) has overwhelmingly conceived the Trinity in terms of a divine dynamism that is process in the purest sense of the term. The focus of belief in God as triune is exclusively the historical life of Jesus of Nazareth confessed as God's own mighty deed in history. Jesus is confessed as at once of divine status and yet "sent" into the world by God, as "from" the Father and "of" the Father. He is the only begotten Son of the Father, he proceeds forth as the Word uttered by God. Later confessional formulas will represent him as "generated" and "begotten"—the Greek term *agennētos* being reserved for the Father.[56] The third Person in turn "proceeds" as *Pneuma* from the Father (Council of Constantinople I), and in the Western Church from the Son as well (*Filioque*). Moreover, the dynamism consummates itself in the "return" of the Son to his unoriginate Source, as the "firstborn among many brethren." Likewise, the Spirit's mission of witnessing to Christ terminates through the Son at the Father, a mission in which he bears back with him the just in whose souls he dwells. The primitive images of the early Fathers witness to this processive character—for example, the depiction in Greek iconography of Son and Spirit as the two hands of God held out towards the world. The more rigorous logic of Aquinas seizes on this divine process as the dominant structural element of his *Summa theologiae:* the mystery of being is creation as the *exitus* and *reditus* of all things from and to God, which cannot be understood unless one allows for an eternal process within God as its ground.[57] At any rate, the doctrine of the Trinity has always

---

[56]Eventually, in the Arian disputes, both Father and Son are said to be *agenētos,* in the sense of "not created," and then recourse is had to the different term *agennētos* ("unbegotten") said of the Father but denied of the Son who is rather *gennētos* ("begotten"); see J.N.D. Kelly, *Early Christian Doctrines,* 5th ed. (London: Adam and Charles Black, 1977), p. 229.

[57]". . . Cognitio divinarum Personarum fuit necessaria nobis dupliciter. Uno modo, ad recte sentiendum de creatione rerum." *Summa theologiae,* I, q. 32, a. 1, ad 3. "Etiam processiones Personarum sunt causa et ratio creationis aliquo modo." Ibid., q. 45, a. 7, ad 3. "Sicut trames a fluvio derivatur, ita processus temporalis creaturarum ab aeterno processu Personarum." I *Sent.,* Prol. "Sicut igitur dictum est, quod processio personarum est ratio productionis creaturarum a primo principio, ita etiam est eadem processio ratio redeundi in finem, quia per Filium et Spiritum sanctum sicut et conditi sumus, ita etiam et fini ultimo conjungimur. . . ." I *Sent.,* d. 14, q. 2, a. 2, Solutio. It is this point that explains why the treatise on creation is subsequent to that on the Trinity.

precluded any notion of God as a self-enclosed Absolute. Rather, it undergirds God's communication with men; it explains how God is in the world and the world is in God.

But this convergence with process theology is a conditioned one. The reason is that, without exception, process theology views the Trinity as the divine dimension to a necessary cosmic process between God and world. The resistance to this in mainstream Catholic thought is on the grounds that it makes the process itself (Whitehead's Creativity) ultimate, rather than God. As subordinate to the ongoing process, God is affected ontically by the world, becomes finite, mutable, and temporal; in short, loses his true transcendence and ceases to be the God of Christian experience. Catholic trinitarianism has defended the alternate thesis that the Trinity constitutes an eternal process within divinity that is nowise dependent upon a universe of creatures. Succinctly put: it argues for an understanding of the Trinity as an inner-divine process *without mutation* in God's being, thus as process in an eminent sense.

The parting of the ways, then, occurs on the basis of a different understanding of what it means to say that God is transcendent. The disciples of Whitehead feel this arises from man's experience of himself as free creator of the world: if novelty is uppermost in this, it does include an intuition of some transcendent source of order, of relative permanency in creative advance. This is God interacting with the world (in Whitehead's phrase: not *before* the world but *with* the world), but solely in a finite way because only the finite can be actual and intelligible. By contrast, Catholic thought arises out of a background that well-nigh universally asserts the infinity of God as that of pure actuality. Some caution seems called for, however, in the overly facile tendency to identify this concept of deity with the Perfect Being, immutable and necessary, of Greek rational philosophy. Christian thought attempted to distance itself from this rationalism on two counts: first, in using the Greek categories only against the predominating background of the biblical view of a living God intervening in the concrete history of man; secondly, in always complementing the resulting conception with the confession that such a God was also a triunity of Persons. True enough, the passion for intelligibility meant, historically, an overemphasis upon the categories of nature and substance, a consciousness of cosmos to the neglect of history, a preference for the universal and the necessary over the individual and undetermined. It would be anachronistic to ascribe to an earlier epoch in thought an explicit awareness of a dimension to reality that is the peculiar discovery of the present age.

But both the patristic and the medieval period knew the need to sustain the dialectical tension between Hellenistic and Semitic categories as something that could not be rationalized away.[58] In the better efforts at theological systematization throughout both these periods there is an inner spirit to the thought that may suffer from, but does not capitulate to, the restrictions inherent in the only categories available for expression of mystery.

Necessity and immutability were affirmed as characteristics of God's *nature*, of his being in its formal structure, and so in its intelligibility and conceptualizability. Beyond this concept lay the divine reality itself as a realm of transcendent freedom, of self-determination by way of love, in which God becomes the kind of God he chooses to be in his chosen relationality with men. This is the realm above all that is brought to light in God's self-revelation to men. What the believer encounters is more the God *who* exists than *what* exists, i.e., than the nature by which he exists. And it is on this level (of freedom, subjectivity, and personhood) that God's unveiling of himself as a community of persons occurs. The awareness of God as tripersonal arose out of an encounter with God that remained open beyond the finitizing conceptual process. At work was analogy—but an analogy of persons more than of things. Still and all, the awareness that person is precisely not nature (a difference that is real, moreover, in the finite order) demanded distinguishing the two at least conceptually. The concept of the one is not the concept of the other, any more than the concept of justice is the concept of mercy, in spite of their real coincidence in God. This makes possible the assertion that God is immutable in his nature and at the same time self-determining in the free decisions of his person(s). This latter domain of freedom means the exclusion of all coercion from without; it does not mean the collapse of intrinsic necessity into mere contingency. God's transcendent liberty works in two ways: (i) he does freely what he cannot not do (e.g., know everything that possibly can be, love everything that actually is, generate the eternal Son, "breathe forth" the Spirit); and (ii) in the same act he does freely what he need not do (e.g., create a world, create this world rather than some other, etc.). This underscores the necessity of understanding that God's activity transcends our limiting and dicho-

---

[58]See Anthony J. Kelly, "To Know the Mystery: The Theologian in the Presence of the Revealed God," *The Thomist* 32, no. 1 (January 1968), pp. 1–66; 32, no. 2 (April 1968), pp. 171–200.

tomizing categories that set necessity in opposition to liberty. At the same time, it does not cease to be genuine freedom and reduce itself to mere natural spontaneity; that is to say, it occurs by way of conscious knowledge and decision.

Walter Stokes, in a series of seminal studies, has suggested a way of surmounting the impasse between process theology and theology appealing to the Catholic tradition.[59] He notes that the alternatives are those between:

> . . . a philosophy of creative act which excludes the philosophy of the real relation of God to the world and a modal philosophy which demands reciprocal relations between God and the world.[60]

The opposition can be overcome, he argues, by opting for a " 'third position'—a philosophy of creative act with real but asymmetrical relations between God and world." Stokes is thus setting aside the contention of Aquinas that God's total otherness makes him free of all *real* relations to the world, so that he bears towards it only a relation devised in our understanding (a *relatio rationis*), justified by the creature's real dependence upon God.[61] A real relation in God to the creature ceases to be a problem (for Stokes) as long as God is understood as not acquiring thereby any new perfection. Thus it appears legitimate to say that God alters, that God waits upon the free response of the creature to his initiatives, is truly a God of history—without the kind of mutation that would spell an increment in his own ontic reality. But this last reservation is exactly what the doctrine of God's *relatio rationis* sought to safeguard. And so, its rejection by Stokes weakens an integral doctrine of God. In

---

[59]Walter E. Stokes, "Freedom as Perfection: Whitehead, Thomas and Augustine," *Proceedings of the American Catholic Philosophical Association* 36 (1962), pp. 134–42; "Is God Really Related to the World?" ibid. 39 (1965), pp. 145–50; "A Whiteheadian Reflection on God's Relation to the World," *Process Theology*, ed. Ewert H. Cousins (New York: Newman Press, 1971), pp. 137–52; "God for Today and Tomorrow," in *Process Philosophy and Christian Thought*, pp. 244–63.

[60]"God for Today and Tomorrow," p. 257. In "Is God Really Related to the World?" Stokes attributes this citation to K. Schmitz, "Weiss and Creation," *Review of Metaphysics* 18, no. 1 (September 1964), pp. 147ff.; it is misprinted in "A Whiteheadian Reflection . . ." (p. 254) to read the very opposite of what is intended.

[61]The most explicit treatment of this can be found in II *Summa contra gentiles*, 11–14; the teaching remains unaltered in the *Summa theologiae*. However, see I, q. 13, a. 7, ad 4; and on the divine knowledge, q. 14; on the divine love, q. 19; see also *De potentia*, q. 7, aa. 8–11.

Aquinas's system, borrowed as it is from Aristotle, a real relation in God can mean only one of two things. Either it is an accidental increment to his essence, and so the acquisition of a new perfection specified by the terminus of the relation, or it is the nature itself essentially relativized into one more this-worldly entity.[62] Aquinas is quite clear that this is no denial of God's *actual* relation to the world—in creating, knowing, loving, redeeming, becoming incarnate, etc.[63] It is only the denial that such relations are real in the precise sense of bespeaking an ontic determination of deity, a passive dependence upon creatures.

But the doctrine of the *relatio rationis* does not close off genuine becoming in God on quite another level. It is possible for the understanding to move from the ontic order to the intentional order of knowing and loving, from the realm of essence and cosmos to that of personhood and freedom.[64] But it is the doctrine of the Trinity, the knowledge of God's being as intrinsically processive, in which the *Logos* and the *Pneuma* are posited in acts of divine self-knowing and self-loving, that is the key to this understanding. The reason for this is that it makes possible the dialectic of person and nature. In the divine sphere, unlike the creaturely, the two are really identical, but there is a need to hold them in conceptual distinction. It is impossible to speak of God as person(s) unless one ascribes to him also a nature; the very concept of person demands some nature that is personified. Similarly, even though essence and existence are identical in God, it makes no sense to say that God has no essence.

---

[62]Developed most clearly by Aquinas in II *Summa contra gentiles*, 12: "Huiusmodi autem relationes quae sunt ad suos effectus, realiter in Deo esse non possunt. Non enim in eo esse possent sicut accidentia in subiecto: cum in ipsum nullum sit accidens. . . . Nec etiam possent esse ipsa Dei substantia." For the further elaboration, see W. J. Hill, "Does the World Make a Difference to God?" *The Thomist* 38, no. 1 (January 1974), pp. 154ff.; also *Knowing the Unknown God* (New York: Philosophical Library, 1971), pp. 177ff.

[63]The entire corpus of Aquinas's writing would be unintelligible apart from these causal relationships which are obviously not left in the realm of possibility. Hartshorne's statement that from this denial of a real relation to the world "it follows that God does not know or love or will us, his creatures" (*The Divine Relativity*, p. 16) is his conclusion, not that of St. Thomas.

[64]An indication of implicit grounds for this move in the work of Aquinas himself can be found in J. B. Metz, *Christliche Anthropozentrik* (Munich: Kosel, 1962). For an elaboration of it, see W. J. Hill, "Does the World Make a Difference to God?"

This would make it impossible to speak of him at all, and so one must rather say that God's essence is his existence. The point argued for here, at any rate, is that an integral conception of God demands asserting that God is both absolute and relative, immutable and ever changing. But he is the former in virtue of what answers to the concept of nature and the latter in virtue of what is conveyed by the category of person. "Person" thus bears an existential overtone; it does not bespeak structure, essentiality, attributes, perfection, etc. Thus, in the human domain we designate the person by a proper name, not by a noun. Ultimately, it signifies the unique subject exercising the act of existence within a common nature. Thus it points to what is distinct in a purely relational way. It conveys, then, relation, and in its infinite instance, pure or subsistent relation. It is the dynamic, ever-changing act of relating which is the positing of the self in its unique subjectivity.

There is, of course, an enormous problem concealed in the solution being here suggested, namely, that of the real identity of nature (which as such includes knowing and loving) and person in divinity. More will be said about this later. For now it will suffice to repeat that it is the conceptual distinction that enables us to speak about the mystery who is God in this paradoxical way. It is one way of explaining how Catholic trinitarianism might appropriate a line of development stemming from Whitehead and Hartshorne, with one major reservation of its own. At any rate, it is the doctrine of the Trinity—the mystery of three Persons at once really distinct from each other and yet identical with the one divine essence—that affords an alternative way of incorporating the insight of process theists that God is at once absolute and relative.

Catholic trinitarianism, then, shows itself open to a God who is intrinsically processive (it could not do otherwise), but stops short of extending this into any sort of panentheism. One of the richer instances of this is to be found in the work of Karl Rahner (see Chapter Five). His position pivots on two truths: first, that of the identity of the economic and immanent Trinity; secondly, that of a God who himself changes, but in the other. Both of these mark some approximation to the position worked out within process trinitarianism. The former thesis enables believers to confess the Trinity in the very place of its revelation, man's history. The latter thesis indicates that the very possibility of there being a Trinity within the economy of salvation lies in a prior inner-divine process of self-othering. But Rahner's trinitarian doctrine suffers an impoverishment in its failure to appeal to the psychological analogy. It is the absence of this that explains his express intention of speaking, not of "persons," but rather of "modes of subsisting." Anthony Kelly has drawn attention to this missing element in Rahner's thought, observing that "without this [the psychological-image approach] it is difficult to see how he does in fact radicate the economic Trinity in the immanence of God."[65] This is a muted reservation, however, because apart from it Kelly does allow with Rahner that "man is the outcome of a prior process in God whereby God has determined to communicate himself to creation."[66]

Without the psychological model Rahner's trinitarianism remains profound but takes on something of the character of mystification; at the least, the desire for greater clarity in explaining the self-othering process in God seems a legitimate one. The power of the model drawn from the workings of the human psyche is that it provides the clue for the move in understanding from analogies in the cosmological order to analogies in the anthropological order. It is from within human subjectivity that the Trinity can be most richly clarified, from within that mysterious realm wherein the self achieves its own unique identity in freedom and love. It is here that man can recognize himself as the *imago Dei*. Use of the psychological analogy does not, of course, "solve" the mystery; its methodological function is limited to illumining what remains as mystery—as Kelly notes.[67] Perhaps we can say it only "deepens the darkness," but that is a gain for understanding. The suppleness of analogy, used to speak of the transcendent, is that it designates the divine reality, without conceiving it, that is, without encompassing deity within the confines of a finite concept.[68] It works in such wise as to recognize that it leaves a great deal unexplained in the reality it can only name relationally from creatures.

Recourse to the psychological analogy also represents a point of convergence with process trinitarianism, since its doctrine of God relies heavily upon the model of human subjectivity. But the difference is that thinkers such as Ogden and Cobb incorporate also the

[65]Anthony J. Kelly, "Trinity and Process," *Theological Studies* 31, no. 3 (September 1970), p. 400.

[66]Ibid., p. 403.

[67]Ibid., p. 398, note 12. Kelly cites Aquinas to the effect that the model drawn from human psychology in no wise demonstrates the Trinity; see *Summa theologiae*, I, q. 32, a. 1, ad 2; *De potentia*, q. 9, a. 5; IV *Summa contra gentiles*, 1.

[68]For a fuller treatment of this understanding of analogical talk about God, see W. J. Hill, *Knowing the Unknown God*, chap. 4.

finite elements of human subjectivity into divinity. What is being suggested here is rather a purging of all aspects of finitude, a speaking of God in a strictly analogical way and not in a fashion that is reductively univocal. Then the expressive word spoken in knowledge, and the unitive "spirit" proceeding from love, can found the language game of transcendental analogy, in which one can speak of God as ever changing in the domain of personal relationships— and this, paradoxically, even as one simultaneously affirms the immutability of God's nature.

The reservations expressed in the foregoing consideration of process trinitarianism can be briefly summarized.

(1) First there are the underlying philosophical assumptions, above all a *Weltanschauung* in which the foundational components of reality are not perduring yet temporal substances but atomic and discrete "moments" of existence, ever-perishing occasions—a view in which ultimate reality is no longer Being but Becoming.

(2) Secondly there are problems of a general theological kind, notably:

    (i) the replacing of revealed theology with what is only a natural theology in which reason is the decisive norm even for what is called revelation, with a corresponding relativizing of the historical Jesus;

   (ii) a concept of God as a panentheistic cosmic deity whose infinity and eternity are compromised by a view of God as also finite and temporal;

  (iii) a denial of God as creator, with a corresponding weakening of his causal relation to the world, in which God's knowledge is determined by creatures, and his love is ultimately *erōs,* motivated by self-fulfillment, rather than the altruistic *agapē* of the New Testament;

  (iv) a rejection of such theological doctrines as Incarnation, Resurrection, Redemption, Eternal Life, etc., at least in their recognizable Christian meanings.

(3) Thirdly there is the specific problem of the reinterpretation of the Christian Trinity, which is reduced to a linguistic symbol for expressing the transcendence-immanence of a dipolar God, in necessary relation to the world—an interpretation which asserts itself finally as unitarian rather than trinitarian in disallowing any real distinction in God of a personal kind.

[8]

THE TRINITY AS COMMUNITY
The God of an Interpersonal *Koinōnia*

The foregoing four models of the Trinity (Chapters Four through Seven) have in common a tendency to stress the divine unity to the point of perhaps failing to account adequately for real plurality. There is available, however, a radical alternative to this, consisting in the simple reversal of such an approach by seeking to explain unity only after taking real plurality in God as a point of departure.

THE SOCIAL MODEL OF THE TRINITY: WILLIAM HASKER

William Hasker has taken a significant venture in this direction in arguing for a view of the Trinity as a society of persons or individuals. He explicitly concludes to:

> . . . three Subjects, each of whom is really distinct from the other two and is the Subject of his own distinct experiences in the unity of the one divine nature and life.[1]

Clearly, he is accepting all the implications of a psychological understanding of person or self. But the problem remains of why such a multiplication of subjects does not mean a corresponding multiplication of natures. Hasker thinks to escape the dilemma by employing the term "person" somewhat as it is understood in P. F. Strawson's philosophy of mind.[2] There, nature is a sort of ontological ground for the self, determining the kind of experiences the self can undergo; it is "the real capacity or the real potentiality for having such experiences."[3] The relation between person and nature is thus that of actual experiences (of which there are three in God) to the abstract formal structure possible for such experiences (which

---

[1] William Hasker, "Tri-Unity," *Journal of Religion* 50, no. 1 (January 1970), pp. 1–32.

[2] See P. F. Strawson, *Individuals* (London: Methuen, 1959).

[3] Hasker, p. 24.

is one). While the suggestive intent of this proposal should not be lightly set aside, it can be seriously questioned whether it does justice to the ontic unity of divinity. Put very simply, the unity Hasker gives to the divine nature is only generic in kind. While allowing that the nature of God is *common* to all three persons, this dissolves any real *identity* of that nature with the persons, singly or severally. On reflection, it would appear that Hasker lacks any genuine concept of person; he speaks only of nature in the concrete (the individual) and nature in the abstract (the common nature). Limiting the usage of nature to the latter sense makes it into a conceptual abstraction—in spite of Hasker's wish and declared intention of not doing so—which is thereby universalized and unified for its three possessors. The inexorable logic of this position does lead to understanding the members of the Trinity as "participating in" or "sharing" a single nature, rather than being identified in a real and ontic way with it. If this is so, then how is it possible to avoid the implication of tritheism? Hasker's instinct for a social analogy is correct; it is his categories of explanation that play him false—above all, the lack of a concept of personality that goes beyond the purely psychological order.

GOD AS THREE CONSCIOUSNESSES: JOSEPH BRACKEN

The possibilities inherent in Hasker's insight have been further explored in a suggestive study by Joseph Bracken.[4] The result is a different version of the same basic position: a conviction that the doctrine of the Trinity shows God to be a social reality, a unity in community that is in effect a divine *koinōnia* of interpersonal relationships. His argument, succinctly, is that beyond and surpassing the substantial unity, which Aristotle contrasts with mere accidental unity, lies social unity, which is unity of a higher order. Aristotle himself betrays some suspicion of this when he allows that the State is superior to the individual as the whole to the part.[5] Another confirmation comes from the work of Max Scheler, who draws attention to the intrinsic orientation of "I" to "We." Scheler, moreover, emphasizes the superiority of this sort of unity when he affords it

---

[4]Joseph A. Bracken, "The Holy Trinity as a Community of Divine Persons," *Heythrop Journal* 15, nos. 2 & 3 (April & July, 1974), pp. 166–82, 257–70.
[5]Aristotle, *Politics*, I. 2. 1253a20; cited by Bracken, p. 171.

the highest place in his four ascending grades of unity progressing from (i) the herd, to (ii) the family, to (iii) larger impersonal societies, and finally to (iv) strictly personal societies.[6]

But Bracken's own understanding of this unity and of the kind of plurality it allows within itself is a radical one. It enables him to speak of the Three in God as "individuals" (a term usually signifying the several who possess a similar or common nature) and to posit within the Godhead not one consciousness, one mind, and one will, but three.

If this communitarian hypothesis for the Trinity be acceptable, then each of the three divine persons would possess his own consciousness, hence have a mind and will proper to himself.[7]

Their mutual knowing and giving of self to the others "would eliminate any reason for discord or dissension" and guarantee a unity at least in the sense of "unanimity."[8]

It is at this juncture that Bracken's thought gives one pause. And it is here that Rahner's trinitarianism can serve as a caution and corrective; in the spirit of the earlier work of Karl Barth, he warns against thinking in terms of "several spiritual centers of activity, of several subjectivities and liberties," and urges substituting the formula "three distinct manners of subsisting" for "three persons."[9] Still and all, there is a logical flaw in Rahner's own thought and Bracken astutely perceives it when he writes:

The term 'person' therefore, as used to describe the distinct reality of Father, Son and Spirit within the immanent Trinity, cannot simply be abandoned without at the same time calling into question the real distinction of persons within the economic Trinity.[10]

In short, there is an inconsistency in Rahner's treatment of the economic Trinity, on the one hand, and the immanent Trinity on the other. In the former (worked out largely in a christological context) he does use to advantage personalist categories, but with the result that the Trinity occasionally appears to assume a subordinationist form. In the latter, these same categories take on an impersonalist nuance, but at the cost of suggesting a modalistic Trinity. At the

---

[6]M. Scheler, *Der Formalismus in der Ethik und die materiale Wertethik*, 4th ed. (Bern, 1954), pp. 529–38; see Bracken, pp. 177–78.

[7]Bracken, p. 181.

[8]Ibid.

[9]K. Rahner, *The Trinity* (New York: Herder and Herder, 1970), pp. 106 and 113.

[10]Bracken, p. 258.

bottom of this inconsistency lies (it seems to me) a key difficulty—namely, a tendency covertly to reify the idea of person. Within the economy of salvation, plurality and distinction are emphasized to the point of approximating three agents who possess the divine nature in individually distinct ways. The same distinction, when used of the inner-divine Trinity, obviously calls for some qualification, one in which the threeness is muted into a modal distinction, into three distinct manners of divinity's subsisting.

Whatever be the case, we are left with two differing models of the Trinity—one of which is shaded towards Modal Trinitarianism (Rahner's), the other of which does not logically escape the shadow of tritheism (Bracken's). Reservations have already been expressed on the former (Chapter Five). In the case of the latter, it is not at all clear how the unity defended is anything more than a higher form of *accidental* unity, a social aggregate of individuals as nuclear units. The question is whether it can be understood as a genuine ontic unity, something that can bear the weight of Nicaea's *homoousion*. Bracken himself confirms a suspicion that it cannot, when he observes that the number three said of God (which he properly understands as number in the transcendental sense and not in the predicamental sense) is "ideal," but could conceivably be greater or lesser.[11] This surely betokens a unity that does not surpass the accidental; it is *per accidens* that God is a triunity. Still, in defense of his position, he does meet successfully two objections against it: first, by indicating that a person in the Godhead has no reality proper to itself over and above that of the divine nature; and secondly, by showing that the freedom with which the persons constitute themselves a community is no denial of an inner natural necessity (i.e., a necessity that is not extrinsic coercion).[12] It can readily be admitted with Bracken that, in attempting to speak of the Divine Persons, "one is not . . . committed to an understanding of their ontological tri-unity as reductively the unity of physical substance."[13] But his alternative, in which the name "God" is only a common or communitarian term, leaves something to be desired.

Bracken himself draws attention to what might well be a source for supplying this missing dimension. The German theologian Walter Brugger, accepting that ontic unity is either substantial or accidental, distinguishes two quite different kinds of accidental unity,

---

[11]Bracken, p. 179, note 1.
[12]Ibid., pp. 179–81.
[13]Ibid., p. 179.

which he labels as *"esse in alio uno"* and *"esse in alio pluribus."*[14] The former rests upon existence in some substance as a subject that it modifies in some fashion. The latter is not a mere random aggregate, but a unification of many substances which transcends the unity radicated in substantial form because it is achieved in the conscious exercise of knowledge and love, in the deployment of freedom. Granted that in Aristotle's categories this remains an accidental unity, it does in fact engage a level of reality not formally encompassed by his predicaments, and so its accidentality is only analogous to that of properties inhering in a substance or to mere moral unity of discrete entities. If this unity is less basic than other forms of accidental unity, it is of a higher order—much as to know and to love are higher modes of being than merely to exist, yet without bespeaking any extrinsic additions to being. In this sense, a moral unity of freely committed beings is greater than the physical or substantial unity of infrarational things. This is so in the finite order; the extension of this truth to the divine level carries with it the further dimension that such unity in God need not be, indeed cannot be, conceived as accidental or merely moral at all. Nothing prevents its being understood as constituting the divine nature in a unity that is fully ontic, without being reduced to the order of physical or cosmological substances. Brugger's reflections seem to capture a dimension lacking in Bracken's thought. It opens the way to what, in Heideggerian terms, can be called *Mit-Sein* (being with) that lies beyond both *Dasein* (mere being there) and *Sein* (the being process). It is a unity that allows, and even demands, a plurality at its core.

Still and all, the sort of unity towards which these two explanations reach (both Bracken's and Brugger's) needs to be grounded and explained as a genuine ontic unity. One way in which this might be done is on the basis of a concept of personhood as a true metaphysical principle of the real order. This hinges on an understanding of existence as act, existential act exercised by a subject (the existent) in and through a nature, from which even as an individual nature it is distinguished (and really distinguished in the finite realm).[15] Two irreducible unities are involved here: substantial unity bestowed by the substantial form rendering the entity *capable* of

[14]Walter Brugger, "Das Mitsein: Eine Erweiterung der scholastischen Kategorienlehre," *Scholastik* 21 (1956), pp. 371–75. (Title of journal was changed beginning with vol. 41 in 1966 to *Theologie und Philosophie*.)
[15]See Chapter Three for the origins of this in Thomas Aquinas.

existing as this kind of thing, and existential unity achieved in the supposit's actual exercising of its unique act of "to be." This latter accounts for uniqueness within a common nature—"individuality" in things lacking conscious self-determination, "personality" in natures capable of such self-constitution. Of course, there are not two kinds of unity in God; the divine essence *is* the divine existence and they represent a single unity. It is only that, in speech about God, recourse has to be had to two formally distinct *concepts* of unity.

The upshot of this is that the concept "person"—if it is to do service in speech about the Trinity—cannot be employed merely as a psychological category; its ontological rooting needs to be made manifest and taken into account. At the same time, the notion cannot be dismissed as merely a metaphysical one; it must carry with it the psychological dimension. Piet Schoonenberg has made a rather convincing case for this. In a brief English summary of his article written in Dutch, he writes:

> So, we cannot say that Scholastic theology was (and is) right in saying that there are three divine persons, using an ontological concept of person, while modern theology, using the psychological concept, denies that there are three persons in God. Therefore, theologians either maintain the threeness of persons, even in the modern, psychological sense of the word, and enlarge it by a dialogical elaboration, or they drop the whole concept of person and speak of "modes of being" (Karl Barth) or "modes of subsistence" (Karl Rahner). The present author is afraid that in the first attitude there is a danger of tritheism and in the second the position of the Church over against modalism is not maintained.[16]

At any rate, exception can be taken quite legitimately to Rahner's contention that person, in its contemporary signification, can no longer be employed theologically to convey unity in Christ and plurality within the Trinity. The Council of Chalcedon had professed in Christ one *prosōpon* and *hypostasis*, rendered in Latin as one *personam* and *subsistentiam*.[17] The undertones of this are, of course, strongly ontological, but there is no reason whatsoever for supposing that the nuance given to "person" in contemporary usage is not a development of what *hypostasis* and *subsistentia* seek to convey. In affirming monosubjectivism in Christ, Chalcedon does explicitly deny monophysitism. This is unintelligible unless the human nature,

[16]Piet Schoonenberg, "Continuïteit en herinterpretatie in de Drieëeheidsleer," *Tijdschrift voor Theologie* 14, no. 1 (January, February, March, 1974), p. 72.
[17]Denzinger-Schönmetzer, *Enchiridion Symbolorum*, 301–2.

and the subject who exists by way of that nature, are really different. Why then could not the same categories (i.e., *natura* and *persona*) be used, on the basis of a purely conceptual distinction, to affirm at once the single nature and its three divine subjects?

Bracken speaks rather of three consciousnesses, three minds, and three wills. But surely this reduces the oneness of God to a mere moral unity, to something that does not go beyond unanimity. It would seem closer to the mark to speak of consciousness, mind, and will as properties of the divine nature, and so as indistinguishable in their own being. It remains true that we must speak of them as distinct, but this is due solely to the limited powers of our finite conceiving intelligences. But there remain three who are conscious, three who know, and three who love; these are the three *Hypostases* or Persons who retain their distinct identities, in a personal sense, as pure subjects of the act of existing, knowing, and loving. In this fashion, they "personify" in three really, yet only relatively, distinct ways the single divine being and acting. To speak of "three centers of consciousness" is to limit personhood to the order of psychological phenomena. It is possible to speak of three subjects of one consciousness only if the subjectivity in question is seen as metaphysical in kind. But this, in turn, is kept from verging over into a subtle form of modalism by expanding it to where psychological personality is understood as grounded in, as precontained virtually within, metaphysical suppositality or personhood.

Rahner's option leads him to deny *mutual* love between the Father and the Son because "this would presuppose two acts."[18] But why could it not be the one act of two persons—in which the fullness of love demands not only lover and beloved (subject and object, agent and patient), but two who love and are loved in a single self-identical act of loving? If so, then the Father loves as Father (i.e., paternally) and the Son loves as Son (i.e., filially), with the distinction being entirely on the level of that relationality. So understood, an ontological precondition to love would be persons—in the plural; a person existing in isolation without others would be incapable of love save in a diminished sense of the word. The very phenomenon of love would be the mutual relationality in which each person constitutes itself in freely relating to the other in its very otherness. And, indeed, in the divine instance, the loving relationality would issue forth into a third person, the personification of that very love. This

---

[18]*The Trinity*, p. 106.

safeguards numerical and existential identity of each Person, and of all the Persons, with the divine nature and activity. Rahner's view appears to confuse essential love in God with notional love.[19] The former is activity and so a prerogative of the essence; the latter is a pure "regarding" that brings one into the realm of personal distinctions. If the difference be adverted to, it is not necessary to conclude, as does Rahner, that if the Son loves the Father this could only be by way of another essential act in God. Rather, it is an instance of the mutual interpersonal relationality at the heart of the mystery of uncreated love. In such pure relating the self is posited in freedom, and its correlate, the personally other, is allowed to be in its pure otherness (that is, as another self, not simply another individual instantiation of the same essence). Such relationality is a pure "being towards" or "being with" another, that is transcendent to causal relationships, there being a communitarian dimension to deity, a *koinōnia* within the Godhead.

The closest approximation to the foregoing view of the Trinity among contemporary theologians is to be found in Bernard Lonergan's 1964 Latin work, *De Deo Trino*.[20] Bracken himself cites a passage that succinctly and clearly encapsulates Lonergan's understanding.

> Father, Son, and Holy Spirit are in virtue of one real consciousness three subjects conscious of themselves, of one another, and of their act [of being] both notional and essential.[21]

He takes exception, however, to Lonergan's intent on the grounds that looked at this way Father, Son, and Spirit "together constitute only a single conscious self in virtue of being one God." If that is indeed what Lonergan means, then it is true he offers us only a verbal solution. There is not another reality or self behind the Trinity; there is not (so to speak) an absolute person beyond the three relative persons. Such an interpretation of Lonergan does lead to the conclusion that the Father is a self "in the sense required by the antecedent concept of the divine nature: one who actively knows and loves himself and others," whereas the Son and Spirit "are not selves in this same sense."[22] But this does not appear to be what

---

[19]For a more detailed explanation, see Chapter Three.
[20]Bernard J. F. Lonergan, *De Deo Trino*, 2 vols. (Rome: Pontificia Universitas Gregoriana, 1964).
[21]Ibid., Pars II, p. 186; cited by Bracken, p. 261.
[22]Bracken, p. 262.

Lonergan, in fact, means. Bracken's reading, if true, would alter the distinction between the Persons into a difference; it would differentiate them essentially. But in truth, the distinction between the Father and the Word is not a distinction between knower and known (as Bracken supposes), but rather one between Speaker and Spoken as a purely relational phenomenon within a single act of knowing. And the same is true of Father and Son vis-à-vis the mysterious occurrence of love. All three Persons know and are known, love and are loved—but by a unitary act in which even the knowing and the loving are really identical. This, at any rate, is an alternative reading of Lonergan and seems closer to what he himself intends. Its force lies in its capacity to safeguard a single divine consciousness without compromising the assertion that there are three in God who are conscious. This avoids the dilemma of the position developed by Hasker and, with more sophistication but still some ambiguity, by Bracken. Nevertheless, it points to a resolution only in a very general sense. What is still lacking is an explanation of what sense it makes to speak of Three who are conscious by way of a single consciousness. The distinction of Persons still stands in need of clarification.

THE TRINITY AS COMMUNITY OF LOVE: RICHARD OF ST. VICTOR

The social doctrine of the Trinity can claim a rich inheritance from the past, and the search for its roots there proves to be most instructive. It was Augustine who determined the course of Western trinitarianism with his psychological analogy of memory, understanding, and will. This development reached its fullest expression when Aquinas transposed it into a metaphysics of faith. But this imaging of the Trinity in man's soul led to Augustine's further doctrine, in the context of his exemplarism, of the soul's mystical ascent to the triune God, an ascent in which love assumes the primary role (see Chapter Two). This strain of Augustine's thought readily found an echo in twelfth-century monastic theology, above all in one of its finest representatives, Richard of St. Victor[23] (+1173). In the latter's hands it opened up a whole new approach to the Trinity—one whose influence was to be felt by such major medieval thinkers as

---

[23]Richard of St. Victor, *De Trinitate* (Migne: *PL* 196 887–992); a critical text has been edited by Jean Ribailler (Paris: Vrin, 1958).

Alexander of Hales and Bonaventure.[24] Michael Schmaus has noted that there are only two major trinitarian theories in the medieval theological world: the Augustinian, mediated by Anselm and Peter Lombard and culminating in Aquinas; and the one inaugurated by Richard of St. Victor, which finds its fullest expression in Bonaventure.[25] In Richard's own original development, however, this sort of theology retains a unique character from which others tend to shy away. This is its suggestion of a social model for the Trinity, quite possibly the most penetrating to be found anywhere.

Richard's starting point was the Neo-Platonic and Augustinian one of God as the *Summum Bonum*, which highest goodness he identifies as love. This he takes as so self-evident to experience that it does not need to be argued for. But love in its perfect state is personal and self-transcending. In short, it is personal love of the other, called by the medievals charity. Richard's reflections upon such love are not ontological but psychological and anthropological, which gives to him an immediate relevance to present-day theological concerns. His thought finds its matrix in experience, albeit an experience that for twelfth-century man already has faith as an inner ingredient. In light of the dogma of a three-personal God, Christian experience discovers that interpersonal love provides the most illuminating insight into that mystery.[26] What Richard does, in brief, is deduce the Trinity from the essence of God as love, on the basis of our Christian experience of love. Such bold and impressive thinking has received merited attention of late from, among others, Ewert Cousins.[27] The latter draws attention to "the very complex and subtle dialectic at work between experience, reason, and faith," by which Richard provides "the basic building materials for a comprehensive theology of interpersonal relations."[28] The dogmatic foundation for

---

[24]Alexander of Hales, *S. Theol.*, I, q. 42, Membrum 1 (in the critical edition of B. Klumper, Lib. I, Inquisitio 2, Tract. unicus, q. 1); Bonaventure, *Itinerarium mentis in Deum*, c. 6, n. 2.

[25]Michael Schmaus, *Der liber propugnatorius des Thomas Angelicus und die Lehrunterschiede zwischen Thomas von Aquin und Duns Scotus*, vol. 2, *Die trinitärischen Lehrunterschiede* (Münster: Aschendorff, 1930). It is worthy of note that Aquinas in his earlier commentary on the *Sentences* did pursue Richard's approach (*I Sent.*, d. 2, q. 1, a. 4), only to abandon it later.

[26]Richard's trinitarian analysis of love is to be found in Book III of his *De Trinitate;* for his observations on method, see the Introduction and Book I.

[27]Ewert Cousins, "A Theology of Interpersonal Relations," *Thought* 45, no. 176 (Spring 1970), pp. 56–82.

[28]Ibid., pp. 65, 82.

this is the truth that the inner life of the Trinity is the archetype of the universe, so that "the higher one mounts into the life of God ... the deeper one penetrates into the mystery of the human person."[29] Richard's vision is that of God as a community of persons; he stands initially in opposition to Greek emanationism, but within the Western tradition he opens the way to a social rather than a psychological model for thinking about the Trinity.

At the same time, certain cautions are called for. Richard believes that on the basis of experience we can be led to discover "necessary reasons" for the Trinity.[30] In this, he is overly sanguine concerning the power of reason even in its transformation by faith. Moreover, he neglects the totally *analogical* way in which human love reflects divine love. These are telling criticisms and indicate an exaggeration of the anthropological element in his theology. But, more importantly, they should not obscure what is positive and illuminating in his thought.

The basic principle of the Victorine—namely, that genuine love is self-transcending, and infinite love infinitely so—issues directly in two further truths. First, such love is love *for another* and thus always supposes at least two persons, and secondly, once such duality of love is achieved, it further consummates itself in the mutual love of a third person. Regarding the former, Richard echoes Gregory the Great to the effect that love of self is love only in a very diminished form and falls short of the full perfection of love that is self-transcending charity.

> Yet no one is said, strictly speaking, to have charity in view of his own private love of himself. Love must be directed to another in order for it to be charity. Where there is only one person, charity cannot exist.[31]

Charity, then, always presupposes the personally other. But since God's love is infinite it demands another who is infinite; the creaturely other will not suffice. An adequate concept of divine love means quite simply, then, at least two persons *within divinity*. Such love is not intelligible as mere self-regarding or as love for the creature alone. In the latter instance, the love is intensively infinite as God's act, but the object of such love is incapable of receiving it in an infinite mode. Thus, God cannot love his creature *objectively* as much as he loves himself—that is, whereas he wills to himself an

---

[29]Ibid., pp. 65, 69.
[30]*De Trinitate*, I, cc. 4–5.
[31]Ibid., III, c. 2; translation of Ewert Cousins, p. 60.

infinite good, he wills to the creature only its particular finite goodness—and accordingly such love falls short of unconditioned perfection. What the fullness of charity demands is nothing less than
"a person of equal dignity and therefore a divine person."[32] Richard
finds confirmation for this in another way of arguing for it: perfect
love requires a return of the love offered; the lover should be loved
as much as he loves, but no creature can return to God an infinite
love.

Beyond this lies the second truth: the self-transcending character
of genuine love demands a third person. In the purity of its motivation it precludes every shadow of egoism, of selfish aggrandize-
ment. But the love of two alone runs just that risk; there is the
danger that selfishness, or at least a complacency, in which each is
sated with the love given and the love received, will prevail. Charity,
in its highest reaches, breaks out of this isolation in the shared love
for a third. Here, the love of two persons is not simply mutual, but
coalesces into *one* love, i.e., a common love for another that establishes them in the profoundest of unions. This reveals a penetrating
insight into the altruistic character of love. The lover wishes to share
with another (a third person) his own joy in the beloved, and this
can only be by way of that third person's own love for the beloved.
At the same time, the generosity of love is such that the lover wishes
for another who is loved by the beloved as much as he himself is.
This expansiveness of love can also be expressed in terms of the
lover's wish that the beloved share in his (the lover's) own active
loving that is not a return of love first offered—and this calls for
a third as its recipient. It is difficult to be clearer than Richard
himself:

> When one gives love to another and when he alone loves the other
> alone, there is love certainly, but not shared love. When two love each
> other and give to each other their most ardent affection, and when the
> affection of the first flows to the second, and that of the second to the
> first, moving, as it were, in different directions, there is love on both
> sides certainly; but there is not shared love. Strictly speaking, there is
> shared love when two persons love a third in a harmony of affection
> and a community of love, and when the loves of the two converge in
> the single flame of love they have for the third. From this, then, it is
> evident that shared love would not have a place in the divinity, if there
> were only two persons and not a third.[33]

---

[32] Ibid.
[33] Ibid., c. 19; translation of Ewert Cousins, p. 79.

This mysterious triplicity at the heart of love closes the circle and is the consummation of love. Thus it does not open to a fourth. All that remains in God's case is the possible opening towards a universe of creatures.

The trinitarian implications of this are obvious; indeed, it is from the very beginning precisely an instance of trinitarian theology. Richard's confession of the dogma of the Trinity is what illumines for him the deepest character of human love. The Christian experiences the latter for what it is because the human soul is (as Augustine notes in Book VIII of his *De Trinitate*) an image of the Trinity. Human love is interpersonal in kind because its archetype is the divine community of Father, Son, and Holy Spirit.

The phenomenology of love that undergirds Richard of St. Victor's methodology—by which is meant a love in which nature and grace coalesce and are undifferentiated—betrays a glaring weakness at one point. It reduces to the conviction that, if perfect love manifests a personal plurality (indeed, a triplicity) as its presupposition, then the Trinity can be inferred rationally from an analysis of this love. This provides the Victorine with what he considers a "necessary reason" for the Trinity—a view in which theologians, almost unanimously, have not acquiesced. Usually the authority of Aquinas is cited to the contrary:[34] while human love does demand a plurality of persons, this is due to its finite, limited character, on which basis each individual needs to share the goodness realized by others as a complement to its own—thus community is indigenous to the human condition. Such, however, is not the case with divine love that, as purely actual, is already infinite, all-perfect, and incapable of increment. But the force of this counterargument is frequently carried beyond its own limits. Aquinas is inquiring if the Trinity can be demonstrated by reason and, concluding that it cannot, cites Richard's argument as failing in this regard. But he does not mean to imply that the Victorine's speculations are without value as a theological act which, for Aquinas, functions not *ad demonstrationem fidei* but only *ad manifestationem fidei*.[35] True, Aquinas does not choose to follow the direction in which the thought of his twelfth-

---

[34]*Summa theologiae*, I, q. 32, a. 1, ad 2um.

[35]Ibid.: "Primo ergo modo potest induci ratio ad probandum Deum esse unum et similia. Sed secundo modo se habet ratio quae inducitur ad manifestationem Trinitatis; quia, scilicet, Trinitate posita, congruunt huiusmodi rationes, non tamen ita quod per has rationes sufficienter probetur trinitas personarum." See also *In Boetii De Trinitate*, q. 2, a. 1, ad 5um, and *In De divinis nominibus*, q. 2, a. 1.

century predecessor points and opts instead for a quite distinct trinitarianism, one rooted in the eruption of *Ipsum Esse* rather than in
something demanded by the nature of love as such. Still, the position
he does work out for himself in fact lends credence to the alternate
position taken by Richard of St. Victor. Discussing the intelligible
emanation of the Word in God, Aquinas notes that the production
of the inner word in human cognition offers a faint analogical parallel to what faith affirms in God.[36] But our production of the concept is *ex indigentia*—without it, what can be known remains unab-
stracted from matter, and in the case of immaterial reality, not
intelligibly present to the intellect—none of which holds in God's
case. Recognition of this, however, does not preclude God's speaking
his Word *ex abundantia*, out of the mysterious fecundity of divine
knowing. We cannot argue from our own concepts to God's
uncreated Word, much less to the personal character of the latter.
But the former can offer some aid in a limited understanding of
what God has revealed. There is no reason why Richard of St. Victor's grounding of the Trinity in divine love cannot be purged of
its apologetic element and made to function analogously to Aquinas's grounding of the Trinity in the dynamism of divine knowing
and loving.

The integral position of Richard of St. Victor sometimes appears
to say that the Father first loves himself, then extends this love to
the Son, and finally enters with the Son into a shared love for the
Pneuma. Richard uses terminology that encourages this view, speaking of *amor privatus, amor mutuus,* and *amor consummatus,* in which
the respective objects are the self, the equal other (*condignus*), and
the third loved in common (*condilectus*).[37] But this lends itself to
approximating his thought to Greek emanationism, with its subordinationist undertone. The implication is not entirely lacking of the
coming into being of the Son and Spirit depending upon the
Father's will. It tempts one to look upon the First Person, the *fons
divinitatis*, as a Father prior to his generating the Son (though not
in a temporal sense), as one who generates his Son as the other
upon whom he can lavish his love. This points up a certain inconsistency in Richard's thought, but it can also be somewhat misleading. In light of his overall method, his emphasis seems to fall, not
upon love as a dynamism giving rise to the Word and the *Pneuma*,
but upon the very nature of love as presupposing an inner relation-

---

[36]See *Summa theologiae*, q. 27, a. 1.
[37]*De Trinitate*, III.

ality that is personal in kind. This is his primal and dominating principle to which the doctrine of the processions is subordinate. The universal tradition on the invariant order among the Persons demanded that he give consideration to the processions. But there his system reaches an impasse, because while love may well require a plurality of persons as its condition, it does not explain the origin of such a plurality. If the processions also constitute a structure indigenous to love, then it is difficult to explain that the Father is without origin, that the Son arises from the Father alone, and that the Spirit's origin is from Father and Son (at least in the Western tradition that Richard represents). That is, it is difficult to maintain a distinct personal identity for each of the Three. One is inclined to think of one person who reproduces himself twice over. What does it mean, for example, to give the Second Person the proper name of "Word" unless he is understood to take origin by way of intellectual emanation? Pseudo-Dionysius explained distinction exclusively in terms of origin, an explanation that is patently subordinationist. Augustine inaugurated the tendency to reconceive this in terms of relation. Richard of St. Victor goes the way of Augustine and leaves the doctrine of the processions gratuitously asserted but inadequately explained. Aquinas would find later another way, conceiving the relations dynamically as notional acts grounded in the processions.

Pannenberg notes with approval how the perspective introduced by Richard of St. Victor enhances the personal character of the Three in God in face of the tendency to compromise that distinctness in the development that runs from Augustine's psychological analogies to Barth's "modes of being."[38] However, he goes on, rightly, to observe that Richard's social doctrine emphasizes the autonomy to the point of putting into jeopardy the divine unity. This insight into the shortcoming in the Victorine's theology is born of Pannenberg's own commitment to Hegelian trinitarianism. It leads him to accuse Richard of failing to derive God's unity from the very reciprocity of the Persons. But the Hegelian explanation really grants an even more radical autonomy to the Divine Three, who only subsequently achieve a unity in virtue of a mutual self-surrender. This is unity in a diminished sense—more congenial to rational grasp, perhaps, but far less than a unity of Persons who are self-identically one nature. With the canon of St. Victor, at least, we are still able to think of the unity in this way. What he contributes

---

[38]W. Pannenberg, *Jesus: God and Man*, p. 181.

beyond this is the possibility of conceiving that unity of nature as a dynamic one grounded in a community of Persons.

THE TRINITY AS A SINGLE SHARED CONSCIOUSNESS: HERIBERT MÜHLEN

The monastic theology of Richard of St. Victor has provided the key for a fresh and original start on the mystery of the Trinity by the German Catholic theologian Heribert Mühlen. Following an earlier work (*Una Mystica Persona: Eine Person in vielen Personen*) in which he views the Church as a reality in the Holy Spirit, he has sought in a subsequent work (*Der heilige Geist als Person*) to explore the distinct identity of the Spirit.[39] His initial assumption is that the categories of classical theology serve admirably to throw light on how Father and Son gain real distinctness on the basis of an eternal divine generation, which is an intellectual emanation of Word from Speaker. But they fail to do similar service where the Third Person is concerned; here the distinct identity of the latter is only asserted or posited. The failure to achieve any satisfying theological explanation in this case lies in the transition from divine knowledge to divine love when one attempts to speak of the *Pneuma* in God. Love evidences a more elusive character, a greater resistance to conceptual clarification. More specifically, it does not readily manifest a counterpart to the concept or word in knowledge, i.e., some reality distinct from the knower (or lover) and the known (or loved) that springs to origin within the occurrence. Mühlen's way around this impasse is simply to jettison the traditional theological procedure and to substitute in its place insights deriving from contemporary investigations into the phenomenon of human beings in the discourse situation. If some reservation can legitimately be felt on this radical and somewhat arbitrary break in continuity of method, the resources to which Mühlen turns do deliver a network of truths that prove illuminating for trinitarian theology. A phenomenology of human consciousness readily underscores that linguisticality is an essential structure of man's being. Moreover, speech is itself a relational phenomenon; it demands both speaker and the one spoken

---

[39]Heribert Mühlen, *Una Mystica Persona: Eine Person in vielen Personen* (Paderborn: F. Schoningh, 1964); French transl. by A. Liefooghe, M. Massart, and R. Virrion, *L'Esprit dans L'Église*, 2 vols. (Paris: Editions du Cerf, 1969); *Der heilige Geist als Person. In der Trinität bei der Inkarnation und im Gnadenbund: Ich, du, wir*, 2nd ed. (Münster: Verlag Aschendorff, 1967).

to. Indeed, the communication and self-revelation are more important than the subject spoken about, which supplies only the material content of an interpersonal act. This secures at least one element in earlier trinitarian thought at the very outset—namely, the understanding of person as relation. Borrowing the speculative investigations into language of Wilhelm von Humboldt, Mühlen is able to conclude that the basic structure of discourse is that of an I-Thou relationality. In obvious ways, this can be appropriated in aid of understanding the Father-Son relationship within the Trinity; all that need be added is that such relationships in God are subsistent. But the Trinity is not a dipolarity but precisely a tripolarity. Thus, this dual relationship at the heart of consciousness offers only a first step in illumining the mystery. A third member can be introduced into the discourse situation if the speech is not about some neutral infrapersonal matter but about another person: the "I" addresses the "Thou" about "Him" or "Her." But, even so, the third remains only the subject matter or content of the speaking and is not incorporated as a dialogic partner in the communication; he is spoken about but not to. At this juncture, Mühlen appeals to the phenomenological explorations of Dietrich von Hildebrand.[40] The latter, acknowledging that the "I" and the "Thou" stand in opposition to one another, observes that that very opposition initiates a further dynamism in which the two combine into one. This latter phenomenon is expressed by the pronoun "We," for in it the "I" and the "Thou" are united in the common address of a third person. Thus, there comes into being a tripartite interpersonal situation. This ingenious way of making room for the Third Person in God can appeal to something perhaps not all that different in medieval theology. This is Aquinas's subtle but important distinction to the effect that there are two who spirate forth the *Pneuma* in God, but only one spiration (*duo spirantes, non autem duo spiratores propter unam spirationem*).[41] Mühlen puts this somewhat differently in indicating that the Spirit has no being apart from the "We" relation existing between Father and Son.

Mühlen's project is, indeed, a rich exploitation of the thought of Richard of St. Victor, though it contributes a genuine originality of its own. All in all, it is possibly the best available development to date of the social model of the Trinity. Its basic premise is that

[40]Dietrich von Hildebrand, *Die Metaphysik der Gemeinschaft* (Regensburg: Habbel, 1954).
[41]*Summa theologiae*, I, q. 36, a. 4, ad 7.

something of the structure of God's being comes to light from an analysis of the structure of man's being in discourse. What is new in comparison with previous theological explanations is that it transposes the analogy between God and creature from the static domain of nature to the more dynamic sphere of communication, from individual self-knowledge and self-love to interpersonal exchange. The very suggestiveness of this kind of trinitarian thinking invites critical reflection. Joseph Bracken—developing his own view as a counterposition to Rahner, Lonergan, and Mühlen—rightly observes that Mühlen espouses an explanation that allows for one divine consciousness or self (*Selbst*) shared in three distinct but related ways. But it is precisely this to which Bracken takes exception, seeing it as a withdrawal by Mühlen from the consequences of his own bold thought.[42] What the latter's thought really means is that the single consciousness is in fact radicated in only one of the Divine Persons, with the result that the full personhood of the others is compromised. In the final analysis, only the Father is the divine self in an unambiguous sense. The Son is only a "Thou" addressed by the Father, never an "I" addressing him. Similarly, the Spirit, addressed by Father and Son as in unison they form a "We" relationship, seemingly does not address them in return. (Mühlen, it should be said, does attempt to allow for some sort of reciprocity in address, but the attempt seems arbitrary and inconsistent with the logic of his system; at least it draws attention to inherent limitations in discourse as a working analogy.) But Mühlen is unwilling to let go the traditional understanding of the divine unity as substantial in kind. Bracken prefers to seek a genuine "unity of persons in community ... [who are] ... bound together indissolubly through mutual knowledge and love."[43] Then what needs to be reconceived is not the category of "person" but that of "nature"! This raises the question as to what is available as an alternative to the concept of nature appropriated, purified, and adapted by Christian thinkers in trinitarian discussions down through the ages. Seemingly there are only two: (i) that indigenous to Idealist thought where it conveys the abstract, ideal possibilities for an evolving reality; or (ii) that which reduces to a unity in only a moral and accidental sense. The first delivers a doctrine of the Trinity perhaps best represented today by Pannenberg (Chapter Six) or, differently, process theology (Chapter Seven). The second dissolves the unity of God into a loose aggre-

---

[42]See Bracken, pp. 266ff.
[43]Ibid., p. 268.

gation in which the Divine Persons are reduced to being rather individuals of a common nature, not of a numerically identical nature. It is overly anthropomorphic, skirts perilously close to a covert tritheism, and is difficult to reconcile with the notion of transcendence that underlies both the Old and New Testaments.

Mühlen, in the opening pages of his book, disavows any conception of the members of the Trinity as subsistent centers of operation within the nature.[44] Bracken, by contrast, wishes to affirm that this is precisely the case. Surely, they could not be centers of *essential* operation, of operation in the strict sense that is causal in kind and productive of an effect that is transitively posited with its own finite nature and created being. Mühlen is right in disallowing this; Bracken does not intend (I think) to affirm a distinct center of this sort of operation either, but then it is not clear what he does mean. Both authors fail to advert to another sort of operation entirely— namely, *notional* activity that is non-causal and gives rise to an immanent term that is not distinct in nature at all and so remains uncreated. Distinct centers of essential operation means natures that are at least numerically distinct; distinct centers of notional activity means only an interpersonal relationality at the heart of a single nature. Notional activity is the sheer exercise of the act of "to be" as a subsistent relationality. It is pure relation in the mode of substance; that is, it is neither a nature that is essentially relative to another (called by the Scholastics transcendental relation), nor an accidental acquisition of a substance (known to the Scholastics as predicamental relation).

Nonetheless, if Mühlen's trinitarianism can be rescued from the charge Bracken lays against it—namely, that it fails to render an intelligible account of the mystery by insisting upon a single consciousness and self—it is not without difficulties of its own. The Scylla and Charybdis of trinitarianism are modalism on one side and subordinationism on the other. Mühlen succeeds (perhaps more than any other contemporary writer) in avoiding coming to grief on either shore. There is, after all, no dead center here; no theology entirely succeeds in holding the two horizons in focus at once, and the most that seems possible is a dialectical move of the mind shuttling between the two, maintaining a certain tension without capitulating to either extreme. How, then, does Mühlen go about integrating these two dimensions to the mystery?

---

[44]Mühlen, *Der heilige Geist als Person,* pp. 2 and 3; cited by Bracken, p. 268.

First of all, the impression is given that the Three in God are inexplicably already there as a given structure of divinity. Whatever explanations are sought fail to account for order and distinctness of identity; this is a concession to the Western tradition at the expense of the Eastern. It is an approach more marked in Richard of St. Victor, moderated by Mühlen when he transposes the Victorine's exclusive concern with love into what is rather an exploration of speech, of the discourse situation.

But that very transition initiates an "about-face." It enables Mühlen to identify the Father as the "I" who speaks, the Son as the "Thou" spoken to, and the Holy Spirit as the "We" representing their speaking in unison. Is our conceiving of the Trinity, then, to be in terms of a Father who as the *fons divinitatis* is already a person prior to addressing the Son? And are the Father and Son already persons apart from their shared addressing of the Spirit? Is Mühlen, in short, reverting to Greek emanationism with its at least implicit connotation of subordinationism? Possibly to some degree this is the case. But the analogy of the discourse situation does not adequately explain the *origin* of the latter two persons and so their distinctness from the Father and from each other. It does not encompass the *generation* of the Son, the speaking *of* the Word in contrast to speaking *to* another. Nor does it explain the procession of the *Pneuma* as a spiration, that is, his origin as the immanent term of love. Indeed, the impression remains that (for Mühlen) the Spirit signifies the Father and the Son in their togetherness, rather than a distinct person within the Godhead. What is slighted here is a distinguishing of the Persons on the basis of their distinct processions—one by way of knowing, the other by way of love.

In the end, what predominates in Mühlen's illuminating trinitarianism is the first emphasis, that is, the stress upon relationality to the neglect of origin. This insures his thinking against any tritheistic or subordinationist interpretation—a safeguard that is less clear in Bracken's case. It does go far towards explaining triplicity in God and, moreover, one that is personal in kind and so constitutive of genuine triunity. But its explanatory power ends here. Because subsistent relationality is not consistently grounded in eternal origins it leaves inadequately explained the distinct personal identity of the Three confessed in Christian faith as Father, Word, and *Pneuma*.

SUMMARY

The groundwork for a social doctrine of the Trinity was laid by Richard of St. Victor's analysis of divine love as demanding, as its precondition, three coequal Persons. Joseph Bracken's expansion of this into a doctrine of "three divine consciousnesses," for all its boldness, does not clearly avoid succumbing to a covert tritheism. Heribert Mühlen advances the approach in attempting a phenomenology of discourse in which the Divine Three answer to the relationality conveyed by the pronouns "I," "Thou," and "We." This advocacy of "one divine consciousness shared in three distinct but related ways" does safeguard the unity of God. It is less certain that it secures the genuine personal distinction of Father, Son, and Spirit. Still and all, this manner of thinking about the Trinity, whatever its shortcomings, does illumine the mystery, and its suggestiveness needs to be pursued. It represents a rich line of development that, negatively, serves as corrective to all forms of subordinationism and, positively, opens the way to engrafting the psychological and social aspects of personhood upon the purely ontological aspect. The implications of this will be pursued, though in a differing context, in the chapter that follows.

PART THREE

FOCUS
Theology as Re-trieve *(Wiederholung)*

[9]

THE TRINITY AS MYSTERY IN GOD

To attempt to achieve a focus is to seek a clearer view of things, in overcoming the hypermetropic view that looks only to the background and the myopic view that is entirely taken up with the foreground. Obviously, this depends on the vantage point of the one observing. The result will not be an equal clarification for others who look out from a different stance upon the horizon. Thus, a certain individuality of vision is unavoidable; any focus will possess a tentative character that allows for some shifting. It is only hoped that what follows will enable others to achieve their own focus more readily. One conviction, however, is that a certain fusing of the two horizons cannot be avoided—the horizon of tradition, which historically shapes the present, and that of contemporary critical thought that seeks to appropriate the truth for itself—not, that is, if the historicity of man and of his thought is to be taken seriously. Such a fusion may well serve, moreover, not only to clarify ancient truths but as a point of departure for new understanding and new truths.

PROLEGOMENA

A Methodological Prenote

Without pursuing the important question of method either in detail or in depth, certain methodological observations are in order at this point. It will suffice for present purposes to indicate summarily five general characteristics of the methodology that will be at work in what follows.

Situation within Faith. At the outset it should be noted that the specifically theological enterprise is, from the very beginning, situated within the intentionality of faith. Otherwise it ceases to be theology even in a foundational sense and becomes rather philosophy seeking to utter the name of God that lies beyond its reach. Christian faith, in its distinction from theology, is an encounter with the living God arising out of the religious dimension ingredient, often at a hidden depth, within ordinary experience. Such religious experience is an interaction between the person (who as believer exists only

241

within the community) and the totality of his environment, including thus the vast network of symbols with which to interpret experience that is mediated to him by living tradition. Strictly speaking, the experience is not faith but only supplies the matrix within which it occurs. Faith itself is the hearing of the Word that comes only from God—a Word that sounds within human experience but cannot be derived therefrom. As God's Word, its very utterance, as well as any possibility of hearing it, is entirely the unexacted gift of God. Such an occurrence demands two distinct elements: the formal one of an inner illumination that is personal (not private) in kind, and the material one of the outer word of historical revelation that is publicly available.[1] At bottom, then, faith involves an awareness that is cognitive in kind—even though the knowledge is elicited under pressure of forces that are not themselves cognitive, but rather conative and affective in kind. But all genuine knowledge terminates at what actually exists; and faith (on this view) is said to be knowledge of God himself.[2] The object of faith, then, is no less than God in his very godness, a conclusion expressed in Aquinas's phrase that "faith terminates not at assertions but at reality."[3] But as an object of knowledge the existent is within the consciousness of the knower with a mode of existence different from that which it enjoys in its own reality.[4] Faith reaches to God solely on the basis of his own unveiling of himself, which is humanly attainable only insofar as it embodies itself in the symbols indigenous to human knowing. The latter can bear only an intelligibility that is finite, and they are incapable of representing what transcends the created order. Thus, even

---

[1] See Thomas Aquinas who distinguishes in faith the (i) "causam interiorem quae movet hominem interius" from the (ii) "quidem exterius inducens" (*Summa theologiae*, II–II, q. 6, a. 1); the former is "interiori instinctu Dei invitantis" (ibid., q. 2, a. 9, ad 3), or "instinctus interior impellens et movens ad credendum" (*In Joann.*, cap. 6, lect. 5); the latter are rather the material objects of faith, the events known "ex auditu" (*Rom.* 10:17), "verborum significantium ea quae sunt fidei" (*Summa theologiae*, II–II, q. 1, a. 4, ad 4).

[2] Thomas Aquinas: "Omnis cognitio terminatur ad existens, id est ad aliquam naturam participantem esse." *In Col.*, cap. 1, lect. 4. On faith's attaining to God himself, see *Summa theologiae*, I–II, q. 62, a. 1, and II–II, q. 1, a. 1, where both the formal and material object of faith is said to be God as the "Prima Veritas."

[3] *Summa theologiae*, II–II, q. 1, a. 2, ad 2.

[4] Ibid., I, q. 44, a. 3, ad 3: ". . . non tamen oportet quod res eundem modum habeant in essendo quem intellectus habet in intelligendo."

in the act of faith God remains a *Deus Incognitus*.[5] Our faith-symbols can designate him (without representing him) only in the indirect, entirely relational, and partial fashion proper to analogy. God's action in all this supplies not only the inner interpretative light, but also the events to be interpreted in their full historicity. This latter reaches its apex in God's utterance of his Word as this man, Jesus the Christ. Insofar as faith is a living encounter with God, and Jesus mediates that encounter, faith is an adhering primarily to the person of Jesus and only secondarily to his teachings and doctrines.[6] What follows from all this is that experience cannot be narrowly defined as something over and against faith, as if the latter can only be imported into experience in an extrinsic and illegitimate way. At the same time, the Christian finds himself at the interior of a sphere of experience not universally shared. Still, if God is "the power over all that is" (Pannenberg), obviously, some touchstone is to be found in other experience—that of Western theistic religion, that of Eastern nontheistic religion, and that of secular experience that oftentimes deserves the name "religious."

Seeking Rational Understanding. Theology is not faith; its concern is not to hear the Word in obedience but to seek its intelligibility. To believe is, spontaneously, to seek to understand; indeed, the former is a primordial, unclarified and unthematized understanding that is itself an *élan* towards reflective thought. Pascal's dictum that "to think rightly is the first of all moral duties" holds true not only in the domain of ethics. Theology in seeking the intelligibility of faith is thus a rational procedure, critical in its methodology, and lays claim to the canons of rigorous science in its own right—though obviously not in the sense of the strictly empirical sciences. This is only to say that theology is the introduction of reason into the sphere of faith—in which the procedures native to reason are left intact and cannot be violated within the range of their own competency, but now function within the perspective of the higher wisdom that is faith.

---

[5]See Aquinas, *In Col.*, cap. 1, lect. 4: "Deus autem est Ipsum Esse non participatum, ergo est incognitus."

[6]See Aquinas, *In Joann.*, cap. 1, lect. 1: "Quoad nos vero principium est ipse Christus inquantum Verbum caro factum est, idest secundum eius Incarnationem." *Summa theologiae*, II–II, q. 11, a. 1: ". . . principale videtur esse et quasi finis in unaquaque credulitate ille cuius dicto assentitur; quasi autem secundaria sunt ea quae quis tenendo vult alicui assentire . . . assentit Christo in his quae vere ad eius doctrinam pertinent."

Origins in Experience. Encounter with the living God, if genuine, occurs only in the present, regardless of how it may be shaped by the past or open to the future. Theology's radication in lived faith demands, then, that it attend to present Christian experience as a locus for the truth it seeks to articulate. Experience in its concreteness serves as a corrective to the abstractive tendencies of reason. As long as it is not restricted unduly to the narrow notion of it adopted in strict empiricism, experience discloses the real world around us— especially as it assumes a public and shared character. Moreover, understood as an interaction between the subject and his funded environment,[7] it acts as a buffer against theories of naive realism on the one hand and idealism on the other. Experience, however, being experience of a conscious subject with its own presuppositions and aspirations, is never a pure datum but always interpreted experience. It is here that religious experience—less as a special kind of experience than as "a depth dimension to ordinary experience" (L. Gilkey)—even as it gives birth to theology looks to that very theology for cognitive and objective norms of interpretation. What theology seeks to do is to mediate the submission of such experience to the interpreting Word of God—for which it needs among other things a theory of experience. Thus, the theologian seeks clues within experience to the God who lies beyond it. Gilkey has made a case for discerning such clues within secular experience in its very secularity, where they remain, however, largely covert, implicit, and often negative.[8] But this is a function of theology in its foundational role; it is the theologian who, already having heard the Word of God, is enabled to discern these references to the Transcendent, in the light of that Word. Thus, in spite of beginning with human experience, theology does not derive a doctrine of God from its analysis of the structure of man's being. Neither is the Bible normative because it is an ideal articulation of common experience at a certain religious depth (thus, it is reductionistic to diminish theology to "story"), but because it articulates revelation. But the Bible as a collection of books is only the literary record of revelation, which occurred (and occurs) within consciousness and so in experience. God is already ingredient in human experience, either

---

[7]See John E. Smith, *The Analogy of Experience* (New York: Harper and Row, 1973), for a detailed development of this theory of religious experience.

[8]Langdon Gilkey, *Naming the Whirlwind: The Renewal of God Language* (Indianapolis: Bobbs-Merrill, 1969).

implicitly or explicitly (not as an object directly experienced in itself, but only as a point of reference for what is experienced); but it is God himself who has disclosed this. Theology, then, resists all reduction to religious anthropology.

Hermeneutical Function. What the foregoing leads to is an explicit awareness of the hermeneutical character of theology. One of its primary roles is to function interpretatively on the transmitted texts and symbols of Christianity. Reason, deployed in the service of faith, in reflecting upon faith-experience mediated by its symbols, is not a *tabula rasa.* Contemporary thought no longer entertains the illusion of presuppositionless thought—an illusion prevalent during the Enlightenment, and one for which Husserl, perhaps its last defender, sought new grounds. To some degree man is a coconstitutor of his conscious world. But such constituting activity derives from the structure of man's being as being-in-a-world, and far from being arbitrary it rests upon some sort of isomorphic relation between consciousness and its given world. What it does away with is a naive objectivism, approaching a kind of physicalism, with the prejudice that man is a mere passive receptor of a world of objects. The flaw underlying this latter notion is the failure to recognize the immanent character of intellectual activity. Aristotle's recognition of this led him to view intellection not as action at all, but as something reducible to the category of quality.[9]

At any rate, theology's hermeneutical task involves another fusing of two horizons—this time the present horizon of the interpreter and the past horizon of the text (Gadamer). This defines theology's function as more than mere repetition of the past and as other than a search for novel solutions to present dilemmas. At the same time, it stresses the genuine historical character of living tradition, on which basis every interpretation is limited to what is possible from the vantage point of the present and so is in principle surpassable. This qualifies all theological findings as tentative and provisional in kind, as ever approximating (ideally at least) closer and closer to truth.

Yet, it is a failure to allow theology to collapse into historicism and relativism. It is not clear how Gadamer's method can be safe-

---

[9]*Nous* for Aristotle is not an *ousia* with a form or structure of its own but an indeterminate power (*dynaton*) that knows by being acted upon by its object, the *noēton*. It has no form of its own because it is the place (*topos*) in which forms are received, i.e., in which universals are actualized; see *De Anima,* bk. III, chap. 4; 429a10–29.

guarded against this, and so some sort of qualified use of it seems called for in theology. Pannenberg has attempted this, but by recourse to an idiosyncratic notion of history as the arrival of the future from its end. Whatever is said of his attempt, he is at least right in noting that the future about which theology thinks cannot be an open future in every sense, one that is directionless, utterly contingent, and so finally unintelligible. God's acts in history do have a once-and-for-all character which sets the horizon for human freedom and so for history; otherwise, it is the human project that is ultimate, and all meaning derives from man. This means that even the embodiment of God's truth in its various cultural forms displays at its interior a dimension of truth as immutable. As William Vander Marck has asked, "What is so dreadful about timeless and immutable truth?"[10] The expression has become a shibboleth by which some writers disassociate themselves from that disdain for the historical alleged against certain nineteenth-century thinkers. Granted, such truth becomes available to man only as it is incarnated in event and language that are by nature ever varying. Moreover, the truth and its form (*vêtement*) or expression can never be separated—as if one could peel away the outer appearances and discover a disembodied and transcultural truth at its core. But the impossibility of a real separation is no denial of grounds for a *distinction*. Nevertheless, the complexity of the theological endeavor is such that it can never be reduced simply to hermeneutics.

Constructive Use of Speculative Reason. Lastly, since theology seeks, through its analysis of experience and its hermeneutics of text and symbols, an encounter of the intelligence with the living God, it takes upon itself a constructive task. This consists above all in entering upon a dialogue with the subject matter itself of the religious experience as mediated and thematized through the symbols of the community. In this, thought enters upon its proper task of seeking understanding, of searching out the inner intelligibility of things. Theology cannot remain bound to an empiricism because what it strives to understand does not directly and in itself come to appearance on the phenomenal horizon of consciousness. But neither can it proceed in an a priori fashion, imposing the constructs of reason upon reality, thereby reducing theology to logicism or to the rational

---

[10]"Faith: What It Is Depends on What It Relates To," *Recherches de Théologie ancienne et médiévale* 43 (January–December, 1976), p. 164.

analysis of ideas,[11] because it is a science of the real. Rather, some place has to be made for deploying the speculative powers of reason in the service of faith. Any theology that fails to do so atrophies. Theology, then, must live with the paradox of utilizing the full resources of speculative reason in its projection towards an unknown God who manifests himself only in the contingent events of history. Clearly this calls for certain cautions: for example, acknowledging the realism of faith and so not mistaking the abstract for the concrete, the representation for the reality. Only with Descartes is the starting point of thought taken to be the representation rather than the reality, with the initial concern being certainty rather than truth. This false start can be remedied by distinguishing knowledge about the abstract from abstract knowledge of the concrete—the latter being the mind's way of penetrating into the depths of the complex but unified real. But it is in turning to metaphysics that theology finds its richest resource, some theory of being that it must rethink within its own perspective. Here options are available and no exclusive claims to truth can be made. Still, if theology is to illumine its subject at any depth and with any consistency, some informed choice has to be made. The avoidance of metaphysics by the theologian means a failure of nerve and superficiality in his project. Here, as an *apologia* for this present theological effort, it need only be said that a realist ontology cannot be ruled out of court as a viable option for the theologian over and against the antimetaphysical stance of empiricism and linguistic analysis, and the differing philosophies of idealism, of the neoclassical metaphysics of process thought, and that of existential ontology. Further, since eclecticism is in the long run self-defeating, it is still possible to make a case for what is meant by Moderate Realism rather than for the Critical Realism of post-Kantian origin. The latter remains a rich and vital alternative, but thus far has produced only one systematic theology (that of Karl Rahner) and one major work on method (that of Bernard Lonergan); apart from these, it has contented itself with the call for revisional theology.

---

[11]Such an a priori element is evident in the thought of Charles Hartshorne when he refers to the divine essence as "really the entirety of what we can know *a priori* about reality." *The Logic of Perfection, and Other Essays in Neo-Classical Metaphysics* (La Salle, Ill.: Open Court, 1962), p. 102. The remark is made concerning philosophy, not theology. Nonetheless, Hartshorne marks a crucial difference in his thought from that of Whitehead, who leans more towards combining rational procedure with a flexible empiricism.

There are strengths in this option for a realist ontology that cannot be easily gainsaid. Primary among them, perhaps, is the real differentiation between essence and existence—something lacking in all the above-mentioned alternatives, including (despite denials to the contrary) Critical Realism. The real distinction enables one to differentiate essence, as form or structure, from existence (*esse*) as the exercise of "to be," as the essence's act of be-ing.[12] Existence is here not mere givenness, or facticity (*ens in actu*), but actuality as the exercise of be-ing, taken not as a noun but as a participle (*ens ut actus*). It betokens an intelligibility of a radically different order than that of essence or nature—thus engaging the intelligence in a quite distinct activity, that of judgment rather than simple apprehension. It is the latter activity that gives rise to the concept, whose role in knowing is thus immediately limited. It is restricted to expressing the formal intelligibility of the real and is not able to enclose within its representative power the act of existing. Existence, as act, cannot be thematically grasped by way of the conceptualizing act; it can only be lived intentionally in the act of judging. The act of an entity, its "to be" (*esse*), becomes the act of the knowing intelligence, its "to know" (*intelligere*). (That actual existence is grasped only in the judgment need not lead to denying that in a subsequent reflection upon the judgment, by a second-level operation of the mind, it is possible to express being in that construct which is the metaphysically achieved concept of being.) The theological import of this philosophical stance is manifold: it radically alters what one means by analogy; it allows God to be construed as Pure Act rather than as form or essence; it safeguards God's transcendence over the world in disallowing any conceptual representation of him (quite as much as does Barthian theology), while explaining the simultaneity of his immanence in the world (as readily as does process theology); it demands a subject exercising the act of existence which issues in the notion of "person" as a metaphysical component, thus opening up the realm of freedom and so of history, and thereby balancing off

---

[12]Among the clearer texts of Aquinas on this central point are: *Summa theologiae,* I, q. 4, a. 1, ad 3: "Ipsum esse est perfectissimum omnium: comparatur enim ad omnia ut actus. Nihil enim habet actualitatem, nisi inquantum est: unde ipsum esse est actualitas omnium rerum, et etiam ipsarum formarum." III *Summa contra gentiles,* 66: "Quod autem est in omnibus effectibus perfectissimum est esse; quaelibet enim natura vel forma perficitur per hoc quod est actu: et comparatur ad esse in actu sicut potentia ad actum ipsum."

objectivist exaggerations with recognition of the role played by the subjectivity of the believer.

The apophatic character of this thinking—which maintains that a proper concept of God is an impossibility—does not deny the indispensability of the concept, nor its limited power of attaining to the real. Our concepts do afford a formal perspective in which it is possible to discourse about God—in the purely relational way proper to analogy.[13] Some faint intelligibility is shed on a God who remains unknown as the Pure Act of "To Be." That we cannot know the mode of divine being (or better, its modelessness) does spell poverty, but does not invalidate such a limited knowing. Knowing that we cannot know God in himself is thus not a negative factor in theology but a positive one.

There are, of course, further epistemological and anthropological considerations underlying all this. That such a metaphysics can come to light implies that man's own being is structured in such a way that it stands in strict relationship to being itself. The beingness of the beings can unveil itself to man (as, at the same time, it conceals itself) only on the basis of an a priori structure to human being that is an orientation to being itself. This makes room for some sort of immediate and intuitive seizing of being prior to all reflective thought, a pure given that amounts to being's presence-ing of itself to prepredicative experience. Ambrose McNicholl, in a 1977 article, indicates the implication of this:

> . . . reality is primarily existence; and existence is prior, in the order of actuality, to both subject and object, since both are real only in virtue of their existence; while what is first known is neither subject nor object but existence as actuating all that is real. This kind of knowing is indeed simple, immediate, and direct; and, as we have seen, is best described as pre-logical and even pre-conceptual, without however ceasing to be truly intellectual.[14]

Intimations of this basic intuitional act that grounds all subsequent conceptual and discursive acts are conveyed in a variety of ways in contemporary thought: in the "primal thinking" of Heidegger, the constituting intuitions of phenomenology, the tacit understanding of Polanyi, the ordinary language discourse of Wittgenstein, the *Vorgriff* of Rahner, the "transcendental notion" of Lonergan, etc.

---

[13]See W. J. Hill, *Knowing the Unknown God* (New York: Philosophical Library, 1971), chap. 4, for an attempt to develop this line of thought.

[14]"Heidegger: Problem and Pre-Grasp," *Irish Theological Quarterly* 44, no. 3 (1977), p. 224.

McNicholl goes on to discern two approximations to this in the thought of Aquinas. The first is his doctrine of the mind's intuition of first principles, which constitutes understanding (*intellectus*) in its distinction from reasoning (*ratio*), and whose basis is man's nature in its spiritual rather than rational aspect.[15] The second is his principle that what the intellect first knows in knowing anything at all is the beingness of such beings.[16] This betokens a primal orientation and openness of finite spirit to the real in its existential actuality that precedes all abstractive activity. All explicit knowledge demands the concept (as every act of existence demands the essence which exists); the latter for all its inadequacy points to reality in its entirety, but in virtue of a prelogical, premetaphysical, preconceptual (or better, nonconceptual) implicit, yet conscious, seizure of the real. Knowing, thus conceived, assumes a dynamic character—a dynamism understood as subjective in kind by Joseph Maréchal and his followers, notably Rahner, Coreth, and Lonergan; but as more markedly objective by Schillebeeckx, borrowing from the "implicit intuition" theory of Dominic de Petter.[16a]

For theology, this means constraints on procedures that are abstract and rational, involving conceptualization, deduction and induction, in favor of procedures that emphasize the subjective, personal, intuitive, experiential, and affective. This counterbalances "notional" knowledge with "real" knowledge (in Newman's terminology), or *la pensée pensée* with *la pensée pensante* (in Blondel's distinction). What this serves to bring home is that the reason which functions at the heart of theology never does so *ad probandum fidem* but solely *ad manifestationem fidei*.

A systematic theology of the Trinity, then, cannot be only hermeneutics in the sense of mere reflection on the corpus of sacred Scripture; nor simply dogmatics, in starting with the orthodox formula of the Church whose meaning it then seeks to explain. It will rather be a rational exploration, at once critical and constructive, but working within the intentionality of faith. Its immediate focus

---

[15]McNicholl cites the following texts: *Summa theologiae*, I, q. 79, aa. 8 & 12; I–II, q. 91, a. 2, ad 2; q. 100, a. 1; II–II, q. 8, a. 1, ad 2; *De veritate*, q. 15, a. 1.

[16]McNicholl cites: *Summa theologiae*, I, q. 5, a. 2; q. 79, a. 7; I–II, q. 94, a. 2; *In XII Metaphysicorum*, I, lect. 2, no. 46; IV, lect. 6, no. 605; *De veritate*, q. 1, a. 1; q. 21, a. 4, ad 4.

[16a]After an early advocacy of de Petter's "implicit intuition" (see *Revelation and Theology*, vol. 2, pp. 18ff.) Schillebeeckx has recently indicated his abandonment of the theory (see *Jesus: An Experiment in Christology*, p. 618).

will be the experience of contemporary faith as this gains expression in the symbols of the Christian community. The norm for theology's interpretation of such symbols will be the experience of the primitive Christian community brought to language in the New Testament as the inspired account of a people's faith in God's act in history, centering upon the life, death, and Resurrection of Jesus the Christ. By this is meant the Gospel as read in the Church—which reading represents the authentic hearing of the Word, and yet ever remains subject to that Gospel as its norm and, where some approach to certitude is possible, to exegesis and biblical scholarship. Finally, the mediation of the Gospel so understood throughout living tradition means that there is no overleaping of history, no starting afresh, for example, with the first century of the Christian era; there is only the demanding process of reaching back through history, with the aid of historical scholarship, to origins. Only then, and in this way, can theology seek creatively to open the way to the future.

The Trinitarian Problem

Contemporary Christians by and large do not appropriate God for themselves in a specifically trinitarian way. Yet both worship and thought remain replete with symbols expressing God as triune— symbols, however, that remain at a certain remove from actual life. The very origins of Christian faith—centered upon Jesus confessed as the Lord, a term with explicit overtones of divinity—explain the inevitable tension that demanded at first two distinct ways of symbolizing God as he enters newly into historical relationship with men. The first continued the Old Testament sense of Yahweh-God; the second conveyed this same God (not another) as mysteriously available in this man, Jesus—to whom were quickly given titles suggestive of this in a variety of ways: *Christos*, Son of Man, Son of God, *Kyrios*, *Logos*, etc. Contemporaneous with this, the community's experience of God's continuing activity in its midst, after the disappearance of Jesus from this earthly scene and his constitution as the *Kyrios* at the right hand of the Father, issued in a third symbol, somewhat more ambiguous and ambivalent in its meaning—that of *Pneuma* or Paraclete.

Moreover, the direct evidence does not favor thinking that this tripartite way of invoking God was explicitly understood as a mere process of symbolization, i.e., something characteristic of our way of knowing God but without any objective referent in divinity itself. At least *prima facie* the burden of proof falls rather on one who would urge an interpretation to the contrary. Without threading out the differences in meaning between the three symbols, or how they are interrelated, early believers understood themselves in an uncomplicated way to be addressing the Godhead which was itself, however mysteriously, Father, Son, and Spirit. This unexamined differentiation is constant in the New Testament: the Father is somehow not the Son yet both are given the prerogative of divinity; when Paul calls Jesus θεός, this is not exactly the same as speaking of ὁ θεός (*the* God), but certainly is not meant to suggest polytheism. The case is far more difficult with the use of *Pneuma*, but by the time of the writing of the Fourth Gospel, there is no confusing the Spirit with either Father or *Logos*-Son. The early baptismal formulas are all tripartite; God is always invoked in a threefold manner, never in the unitary way of the Old Testament, nor as twofold or fourfold. Yet in all of this the unity of God is never so much as broached as a question; it is the one sole Godhead who is worshipped, not simply in a threefold manner but as somehow threefold in himself.

Belief can operate on the level of such undifferentiated consciousness only so long; inevitably it must pose questions for reflective thought. Early attempts at resolution evolve from Economic Trinitarianism to Greek subordinationism to Latin modalism. Inadequate as these are, they reveal a dialectic at work in this thinking upon faith. The dialectic is in fact a dogmatic development leading to the awareness that Father, Word, and Spirit are not just simply names for God but convey for a Semitic mentality something similar to what the Greek mind registered with *ousia*. In both cases there is an underlying connotation of the dynamic, signifying less static essence or the definition of something than nature as operative, as bearing impact, thus approximating power and so the nature as acting subject. Gradual development moved through the category *prosōpon* to that of *hypostasis*, the latter at first not adequately distinguished from *ousia* and so confused in the West with the Latin *substantia*. With the Cappadocians, however, the distinction is made, even if imperfectly understood, and the formula of "three *hypostases* of one *ousia*" became the orthodox one. Shortly thereafter, the Greek term *prosōpon* is rendered in Latin translations of the proceedings at Chalcedon as *persona* (literally deriving, apparently, from *per sonare*, "to sound through," referring to the actor's mask conventionally representing a historical or mythical personage), while *hypostasis* becomes in Latin *subsistentia* (the concrete reality existing in a way proper to substance). Using these orthodox elements from tradition, Augustine in the West was able to make a fresh start, thinking through the mystery in a new key that set up what was, in fact, the beginning of a new stage in the dialectic going on—one that resisted the remnants of Eastern subordinationism but did not entirely avoid modalistic nuances of its own. Aquinas was Augustine's heir, in a later age when the *Patres* gave way to the *Doctores*. The "school" approach of the latter meant two things: first, an intellectual synthesis of sufficient depth to surmount, for the first time, the tension created by the existence of two formulas—that of the East and that of the West; secondly, a resolution of such metaphysical density that, in lesser hands, it was quickly divorced from concrete Christian living and tended to become in time religiously sterile.

But now the second stage in the dialectical process had been fully reached, one proper to theological science, even if unfortunately its religious power was overlooked and soon truncated. It was now possible to say in what sense God was one and in what sense three, and thereby to negotiate between subordinationism and modalism in their extreme forms. But for all their careful nuancing, these two stages of resolution—the Patristic and the Scholastic—never lost a strong doxological character; they served the exigencies of explanation only in subordination to worship and love. The Trinity was looked upon not as a problem to be solved, but as a mystery to be adored. Confession of it demanded that one think upon it, but this was recognized as a thinking out of what could not be grasped adequately in thought. The whole movement of notional theology was towards consummation in mystical theology. Such being the case, it was inevitable that the mystery would reassert itself in such manner as to transcend the tentative resolution, to break out of the categories that provided a totally inadequate noetic hold on the mystery.

The occasion for this was the dawn of modernity, an era shaped by the divorce between faith and reason inaugurated in the late-medieval, pre-Reformational period, and no longer questioned after Kant's *Critiques*. Reason, which had gradually come to be understood as distinct from faith and not to be confused with it, was now given rather its autonomy—a different state of affairs entirely. Faith was prohibited from illumining speculative reason in theology's search for the inner intelligibility of God's Word; theology was banished to the realm of the practical (morals) and the positive (the data of Scripture and tradition). Theology could no longer urge its claim to being a science "subalternated" to the divine science. This was partly because it no longer understood its primary source, the Scriptures, as *in its own distinctive way* subalternated to the revelation it articu-

lates. Earlier the Bible had been treated less positivistically, as a
depository of divine truths rather than as the record of a people's
search for the ultimate meaning of existence, initiated by the hearing of God's Word.

From Schleiermacher onwards, at any rate, considerations of the
Trinity assume a rationalistic rather than an intellectualist character;
the spirit at work is critical and views its subject not as mystery but
as problem. When the problem proves to be one that does not yield
to rational analysis, the tendency is to reason it away. The crisis
came when philosophies of consciousness and the development of
psychology as an empirical science gave to the term "person" a
meaning that vitiated its traditional use in the trinitarian formula.
If person means a center of consciousness, radicated in an autonomous exercise of freedom, then it makes little sense to speak of
three Persons of the one Godhead—especially since person, so conceived, is frequently understood as self-creating (thus Spinoza, and
later Fichte, contend that God's eternity precludes any conception
of him as personal), and as finite by definition because of the limitations imposed by other persons. Also, the notion of nature as a
correlate of person undergoes considerable alteration; it is no longer
the essential structure by which the person exists, determining the
ways in which it can act, but a historical product of the person
subject to ongoing transformation and bespeaking the open realm
of what is possible for persons in society. This frees the person from
many constraints arising from its rooting in a cosmos obedient to
the laws of matter; it tends to dismiss the chthonic element in human
reality, suggesting at times an "angelized" version of man. Lastly,
the relationality inherent in personhood is construed as a necessarily
temporal one and so unimaginable outside of history. It issues in a
view of reality as ultimately not Being but Creative Becoming, with
(frequently) connotations of subjectivity in the pejorative sense of
Heidegger's use of the term.

This state of affairs demands that the traditional trinitarian formula undergo a radical revision. Otherwise, triunity gives way to
tritheism, for three persons in the present acceptance of the term
means simply three gods. Either that, or the doctrine refers merely
to our knowledge as it thematizes God in a threefold manner. Or,
in another alternative, it is recognized as purely mythic, without any
anchorage or point of reference in anything known in a nonmythic
way. Karl Barth accordingly concludes that one must speak of God
as a single person, given what the word means today. Karl Rahner
argues for a Catholic version of the same position in insisting that

hypostasis and *subsistentia* did not mean in their original trinitarian and christological context what person means in contemporary speech. But there are reasons (as we have seen) for dissatisfaction with their alternatives, for an uneasiness that the door is thereby opened to a covert and subtle form of neomodalism. Is it so certain that the term person, even with its new layer of meaning, can no longer function to explain plurality in God? Is there not perhaps a connotation in the word as originally used that is essential to understanding the Trinity and that is lacking in such expressions as "modes of existing" (Barth) and "modes of subsisting" (Rahner)? That connotation alters radically what one means in talk about the Trinity because it allows for real distinction, not below the level of consciousness, but precisely within consciousness and so on the level of subjectivity. Moreover, no new term seems available in any of our languages with which to convey its specific intelligibility. Thus, one can argue that the term simply cannot be jettisoned in theological discourse. Its meaning has indeed evolved, thanks to researches in both psychology and philosophical anthropology, and now discloses explicitly a world of meaning that previously went unnoticed. But a genuine theology remains open to truth originating in other disciplines, e.g., in the empirical and social sciences as well as in the humanities (*Geisteswissenschaften*). More to the point, a case can be made for viewing this as a development of what was virtually contained in and dimly expressed by the Greek term *hypostasis* and its Latin equivalent *persona*. The contemporary use of person, in spite of the misunderstanding it can well give rise to, offers on the other hand certain advantages to the theologian of the Trinity. Notably these are: (i) its extension to consciousness, of self and others; (ii) its greater emphasis on relationality; and (iii) its focus on intersubjectivity. Ancient uses of the concept did not include these, but did not expressly exclude them either; a contemporary theology must appropriate them. Briefly put, the traditional understanding conveyed by *hypostasis*, without relinquishing any of its metaphysical density, must be deepened and expanded to where it incorporates the psychological sense. Two factors can mitigate any risk of anthropomorphism in this: (i) the retention of the underlying metaphysical dimension, and (ii) an explicit awareness of the strictly analogical character of the language at work.

Three "Moves" of Understanding in a Speculative Theology of the Trinity

From Unity to Triunity. All attempts on the part of the finite intelligence to grapple with the issue of God must acknowledge at the very outset a limitation that cannot be overcome. This is the need to distinguish formalities within what is itself utterly simple and transcends all distinctions made by the mind. The ground for asserting the divine simplicity is nothing more than the awareness that any composition of parts is indicative of a lack of fullness in being. The components of a composed being must be in some sort of structured relationship to one another (e.g., matter to form, potency to act, etc.) on which basis each is limited by its correlate, so that the composite itself is necessarily a limited being. Clearly enough, a concept of God as Being Itself is operative here, one whose critical grounding lies in the awareness that a world of empirical and phenomenal objects demands for its intelligibility Pure Being, necessarily existing, in which the originated and contingent beings exist by participation. This represents a metaphysical option to conceiving God as Pure Becoming. But it is an option that remains viable and can be argued for as persuasively as can its alternative. Philosophical reservations on a God of Becoming arise from considering that such a conception reduces God to being a cosmic deity, finite in his being, dependent upon the world, and subordinate to something more ultimate—for example, to the God-world process itself, or to what is conveyed in the category of "Creativity." Theological caveats are felt because such a concept of divinity seemingly washes all meaning out of what is meant by Creator and creation, by redemption, agapeic love, resurrection, etc.

But the Christian theologian is aware at the very outset (in a way as yet unexamined theologically) that the reality of God is at once One and Three. Thus, any critical dealing with this paradox (which has no parallel in the phenomenal order) calls for the mind to distinguish what faith confesses as in reality beyond all such distinction. The theologian must isolate unity from plurality in divinity in the attempt to discern in what sense God is one and in what sense he is three. Further, its own logical constitution would seem to dictate the order in which the mind can most fruitfully do this. This is the instinctive *démarche* of intelligence that moves from seeking to understand the divine reality in its unity to entering subsequently upon the attempt to understand the divine plurality on the level of personhood. The justification for this order, rather than the reverse, is simply that God's identity can only be approached by way of analogy with what prevails in the world of creatures. There, the concept of unity enjoys a logical priority over multiplicity; it is possible to grasp things in their plurality only on the basis of first becoming aware of the unity of each of those entities that go to make up that diversity. This does not, of course, deny that there is a dialectical movement at work in which the mind returns from the notion of plurality to a deepening grasp of unity. It should be noted that this seeking to know God by way of analogy holds true universally, in the domain of faith as well as that of reason.

This is not, of course, an order within God but solely an order of intelligibility for a mind that thinks rationally; thus, the theologian who proceeds this way must constantly bear in mind that the God who is One in being *is* three Persons. There are only two alternatives to this procedure: one is to consider divinity simultaneously in its unity and plurality; the other is to inverse the order and explore the unity in light of a prior reflection upon the Trinity.[17] But the first sacrifices both clarity and depth of understanding, doing inadequate service to what are distinct questions for the mind. In this option, the way in which nature and person are interrelated is not given its full intelligibility apart from a verbal assertion of the real identity of the two; the triunity too readily appears as a mere formal structure. The second alternative procedure tends to assume what is really the question, namely, how anything can be asserted of God in the plural; this is the real question because no unitary existent in our experience can be more than one subject or individual. It unavoidably exaggerates the trinitarian distinctions into differences that are absolute and not exclusively relative.

From the Trinity in God to the Trinity in the World. While some light can be shed upon the mystery of the Trinity by approaching it from a prior consideration of God's unity and simplicity, it cannot be forgotten that this is a theological procedure that arises only out of a prior faith that already confesses God's revelation of himself as a Trinity in history. If the way of discovery has no other starting point than this faith rooted in history (so that, apart from revelation, even suggestions that God might be a plurality of persons do not arise), the attempt at a reflective understanding of what is "given" religiously runs rather in an inverse direction. If God reveals himself, then what is revealed, its content, is measured by what God is in himself. To insist that God cannot be known except by indirection from creation and revelation is not to say that we know only God's

---

[17]Aquinas, it will be recalled, attempted three different methods—a simultaneous consideration in I *Sentences;* a radical separation of the two treatises in Books I and IV of the *Summa contra gentiles,* and finally a treatment in the *Summa theologiae,* I, in which the Trinity is immediately subsequent to a reflection on the One God, but forms with it one integral theological treatise. See Chapter Three.

effects, and nothing about God himself, other than the set of attitudes he has chosen to adopt towards men. If the God whom men
encounter in salvation history is the living God in his very reality,
then he is God as Trinity. What confronts the believer in Christian
experience is not a mere reflection or some created facsimile of the
Trinity.[18] Rather, the divine persons themselves confront us with
their infinite life. At the same time, unless that infinite life is
mediated under conditions of finitude it remains inaccessible to
men; thus it comes to us only from within events of history, and so
to the extent of, and after the manner of, God's loving dispositions
towards men. Yet God in his very deity is not identified with history
nor with those concrete attitudes of love he freely chooses vis-à-vis
mankind—even though these latter alone supply us with some clues
as to who he might be. Thus, a deeper reflective understanding of
the mystery that lays hold of the believer in Christian experience
proceeds from some attempt to think, in faith, upon what that mystery might be in itself. The particulars of God's offer of salvation
to man in history spell some inchoate awareness of the identity of
the God who saves, and this in turn illumines hidden dimensions to
the mystery of salvation. There can be no room here for arbitrary
speculation because the search for understanding originates only
with faith, remains normed by faith, always suffers the limitations
of a knowledge that is inadequate, faltering, and ambiguous because
it is not a proper knowledge but one that proceeds only by way of
analogy with created reflections of a God who ever remains
unknown. At most there occurs a deepening of the darkness, but it
is one that paradoxically illumines.

Two Complementary Stages in Trinitarian Theology. God's triunity is
best approached from his essential unity. But the mind's attempt to
grasp that triunity demands in turn that it approach the Trinity
proper in two distinct stages. The two levels of procedure are inseparable but logically distinct and complementary. The first marks
theology's appropriation of metaphysics, the second its appropriation of psychology. The overall method, however, remains theolog-

---

[18]Thus, the Trinity in the economy of salvation *is* the immanent Trinity.
This is, perhaps, the central thesis of Rahner's trinitarianism. However, he
identifies the two in an emphatic way that tends to obscure all distinction,
maintaining, for example, that the Word is eternally uttered by the Father
precisely as the Word to be uttered into the Void. The inner-divine Trinity,
however, need not appear within space and time, and if it does, the nature
and condition of its appearance are contingent upon God's freely chosen
plan for the economy that could be different than it is.

ical because reason, without surrendering its own autonomy, is here functioning within the perspective of belief. Also, what is under investigation ultimately is not being (metaphysics), nor *psychē* (psychology), but divinity. In both procedures what is sought is a concept of person that might throw some faint light on the Trinity. But what is yielded in the prior stage is the ontological dimension to that concept, while in the latter stage it is the psychological dimension that comes to light. To put it differently, theology in a first move seeks to understand the divine essence as fecund, explaining an immanent plurality—then, in a second, complementary move, begins with persons who act in order to explain such divine fecundity.

An integral speculative theology of Trinity, then, involves three interrelated phases: first, unity as ground of the Trinity; secondly, the Trinity in itself as real plurality; thirdly, that plurality as personal. These three phases will now be explored, leaving the Trinity as it relates to a world of nature and grace for the next chapter.

PHASE ONE—BEING AS ACT: GROUND OF THE TRINITY

What exactly is entailed in inferring the beingness of God from a universe of finitude and contingency? The entities of such a world pose for intelligence a twofold wonderment: that something is at all, and the distinct question of what sort of thing it is. The structure of the finite evidences a real distinction between what is (essence) and the fact that it is (existence), with existence as not another form or quiddity but the *act* of the essence.[19] The givenness of a thing's existing cannot be thematized (directly) in the concept because existing possesses an intelligibility of another order entirely. Consciousness of something existing is not the conceptual grasp of what sort of thing it is but the *judgment* that it is—in which act judgment is understood, not as the mental synthesis of concepts, as in the forming of the proposition, but the real synthesis of concept and existent,

---

[19]This is clearly the teaching of Aquinas; see, for example, *Summa theologiae*, I, q. 54, a. 3: "... in every created thing essence is distinct from to-be (*esse*) and is compared to the latter as potentiality to act." I *Summa contra gentiles*, 22: "Being ... is the name of an act, for a thing is not said to be because it is in potency but because it is in act."

as in the assertion.[20] This leads to the discovery that existence is not mere facticity, not the phenomenon of simply "being there," but is the exercise of the act of "to be" by the existent; the subject "is" as, analogously, the singer sings and the runner runs. But this structure to worldly being spells determination and limitation, both entitatively and noetically. The conceptual perspective onto the divine that it offers, then, is one in which such limitation must first be denied of God in a *via negativa*. This allows God to be conceived subsequently as the creative source of such being who transcends all its limitations. This, in effect, is to affirm the deity as the Pure Act of Be-ing, unreceived by any constricting essence; he is Being Itself (*Ipsum Esse*) rather than any conceivable mode of being. The significance of conceiving God as Be-ing Itself (the hyphen serving to convey the participial form of the term) is that it locates God noetically beyond all concepts. Concepts may function to *designate* God, otherwise we must fall silent altogether, but not to *represent* him. Thus, God's be-ing lies beyond the expressive power contained either in the concept of Being (taken now grammatically as a noun), or in the concept of Becoming, as well. This surmounts at once a basic difficulty in speech about God: use of the concept being (as a substantive) suggests a static divinity that is a self-enclosed Absolute; use of the concept becoming, by contrast, introduces into God the imperfection of change and dependence. The former is Aristotle's notion of divinity; the latter is Whitehead's. The worldly process that characterizes all creaturely existence does not reveal that God himself is a God of process; rather it mirrors forth, faintly, that God's being is not something static, akin to essence, but a dynamism expressed as actuality.

---

[20]"All that judgment adds to the question for reflection is the 'Yes' or 'No', the 'is' or 'is not'." Bernard J. F. Lonergan, *Insight*, rev. ed. (London: Longmans Green; New York: Philosophical Library, 1958), p. 366. This role of judgment is pivotal in the system of Aquinas who writes: "This word 'is' ... simply taken, signifies something enjoying the act of being (*in actu esse*) and so it signifies after the manner of a verb ... and thus, as a consequence of this, the word 'is' signifies composition." *In I Perihermeneias*, lect. 5, no. 22 (ed. Spiazzi, no. 73). For views of how judgment grasps existence, differing from that of Lonergan, see Ambrose McNicholl, "On Judging," *The Thomist* 38, no. 4 (October 1974), pp. 768–825; "On Judging Existence," *The Thomist* 43, no. 4 (October 1979), pp. 507–80; F. D. Wilhelmsen, "The Priority of Judgment over Question: Reflections on Transcendental Thomism," *International Philosophical Quarterly* 14, no. 4 (December 1974), pp. 475-93.

But if divine being is act, it further reveals itself as *intentionality*. If the reality of God is construed as pure actuality, as the fullness of be-ing rather than as infinite essence or substance, then it readily follows that divinity is a pure dynamism, transcendent to all forms of finite becoming. Such a dynamism cannot be chaotic, unintelligible, utterly without meaning. Thus, it points up that being in its depths is an intentionality. Formally speaking, this latent intentionality comes to light in the concept of being only as in its ground. It achieves explicit articulation in the concepts of knowing and loving as these activities give form and structure to the being of spirit. The more perfect the being, the more perfectly does it assume the form of knowledge and love; in God all three are self-identical, distinguished only by the finite mind that attempts to think them. The divine "to be" is thus identified simultaneously as "to know" and "to love." But the conceptual distinction makes explicit the latent intentionality; to know and to love is to know and to love *something* or *someone*. A subject-object dichotomy comes to light that is not expressed in the concept being.[21]

What God knows and loves is not *really* other than himself (setting aside for a moment the question of creatures) but only *formally* so. He knows his own divinity but under the formality of truth; he loves his own divinity but under the formality of goodness. Yet this unleashes a spiritual dynamism in which God not only *is* himself, but knows himself and loves himself in what is divine life. Moreover, that *élan vital* in its interiority manifests what can be rendered imaginatively only as of a circular character. The knowing of the other implies a certain psychic distance (even when it is the self that is known, there is required an objectification as "other," otherwise knowledge loses all meaning); what is known has to be granted its otherness as ob-ject over against the knower now constituted as subject. Loving appears rather as a recoil movement; the lover overcomes the cognitive distance in rejoining the other to himself, but without absorbing its otherness. If being is the ground of the knowing-loving, there is also an ontological order between the phenom-

---

[21]Without this objectifying, knowledge loses its character as an act of intentional assimilation; it need not bespeak *real* distinction between knower and known but only formal distinction. Even in the case of our knowledge of God, Pannenberg has observed astutely that God's nonobjectivity "is itself mediated through an objective knowledge of God," otherwise it means mere general indefiniteness. *Jesus: God and Man*, p. 175, note 146.

enon of knowledge and that of love.[22] In knowledge lies the very possibility of love, but the latter arises out of the mystery of awareness only as a spontaneous recoil that brings the known in its very otherness back to its primordial source—being.

PHASE TWO—PLURALITY AS REAL: THE METAPHYSICAL DIMENSION OF PERSON

The spontaneous emanation of being into knowing and loving means not only something that is known and loved but beyond this a mysterious "eruption" or "effusion" that issues in and brings to origin a term that remains entirely at the interior of such spiritual activity and yet is posited as distinct from the knower and lover.[23] Such an immanent term is the psychic inexistence of, respectively, the known (by way of the concept) and the beloved (by way of the *élan* of love). These terms in the depths of thought and love are really distinct from the knower-lover, from what is known and loved, and from the knowing and loving activity. They proceed forth not after the fashion of an operation elicited by a subject (*per modum operationis*), but as a real and perduring "product" of that activity (*per modum operati*) that emanates forth and qualifies the being of the subject in the richness of its spiritual dynamism. Thus, at the heart of being lies an expansive process of self-diffusion, a latent plurality that enriches an entity by enabling it to transcend its unity as static and isolating. The existent can surmount its own limitations by opening itself out to existences other than its own. But it achieves this not merely by some kind of exterior increment to its own reality, but immanently by an enriching transformation of its own inner beingness.

These two inner qualifications which arise, in one instance by way of knowledge and in the other by way of love, are distinct and cannot be reduced to one another any more than can the concepts

---

[22] Aquinas, *Summa theologiae*, I, q. 27, a. 3, ad 3. Lonergan expresses a reservation on this noting that ". . . the major exception to the Latin tag [*nihil amatum nisi praecognitum*] is God's gift of his love flooding our hearts." *Method in Theology*, p. 122.

[23] Aquinas, *Summa theologiae*, I, q. 27, esp. aa. 1 & 3. These effusions or emanations were known to the Scholastics by the technical term "processions," from *procedere* in the Latin version of the Bible, used to signify the temporal coming into the world of the *Logos* and the Spirit, and so signaling to the theologian an eternal coming forth in God.

of knowledge and love themselves. In the former procession by way of knowledge, being displays itself as indigenously self-expressive; in the latter procession by way of love, being manifests itself as rather self-unitive. The real term brought forth in the prior activity is an expression, a reproduction of what the knower has become in knowing the known (thus, the idea is the *conceptus* of the known in the "womb" of the knower). The terminus in love, by contrast, is not an imaging at all, but an impulse, a conative *élan* that orients the lover, through the cognitive symbol, out towards union with the beloved in the latter's own otherness.[24] It is that qualification of the lover's being, *qua* lover, that is not the act of love but the state of love, the affective presence of the beloved in the intentions of the lover which founds the *exstasis* of love that is its self-transcending character.

The import of these intelligible emanations is that they posit *relationality* at the core of existence.[25] If, in the human sphere, this is a relationality of each individual existent to others, still, as achieved by way of thought and love, it is accomplished first of all within the psyche, at the interior of consciousness. Were this not so, knowing and loving would lose their immanence and suffer reduction to the mere transitive activity and passivity of infraconscious "things." But the hallmark of spirit is precisely this interiority of life. Such relationality also bespeaks *opposition*; since it is a relationship between a

---

[24]Since the term coming to origin within love comes forth as Spirit rather than as Word in understanding, the procession is called "spiration" rather than (intellectual) "generation." In a further linguistic nicety, just as *intelligere* (to understand) is distinguished from *dicere* (to bring to interior expression what is understood), so *amare* (to love) is distinguished from *spirare* (to breathe forth a perduring impulse towards the beloved). Ceslaus Velecky distinguishes *amare* from *spirare* as "the act by which the lover fixes his attention upon the beloved [differs from] the act of conscious endorsement of the affective preference which leads to a permanent union between the lover and the beloved." *Saint Thomas Aquinas Summa Theologiae,* 61 vols. (London: Eyre & Spottiswoode; New York: McGraw-Hill, 1964-81), vol. 6, *The Trinity* (1965), Appendix 5, p. 140. What is important is that there is a real term posited by the spirative act, one that remains immanent to the consciousnesses of the lovers—in spite of a poverty of language in the attempt to name this term. This makes it somewhat more plausible to think of the Holy Spirit as a person, unlike Pannenberg's understanding that "in contrast to the Father-Son relationship, 'breathing' as such does not reveal any personal difference." *Jesus: God and Man,* p. 178, note 151.
[25]Aquinas, *Summa theologiae,* I, q. 28. Logical development here proceeds from processions (q. 27) to relations that are real, mutually opposed, and thereby really distinct from one another.

source and a term (e.g., speaker and word, lover and the perduring impulse to the beloved arising out of the love), they mutually exclude one another. Opposition, however, is on the basis of origin; the principle can never be in every respect the principled. The source that engenders the word can never be identified with the word spoken; lovers cannot be identified with what emanates from them as a reality springing forth from their loving. Thus spirit is possessed of a certain immanent creativity, such that in the fullness of its being it realizes a plurality within itself that is not inimical to its metaphysical unity. It is itself the unleashing of a dynamism that issues in intrinsic *distinction* that does not call into question the oneness rooted in its essence and existence. Because knowing and loving are real in God, so are the emanations at the heart of such activity, and so are the relations established thereby. But more to the point, granting the opposition between the terms of the relationships, there necessarily follows a real distinction between them. In their very intelligibility, paternity and filiation are mutually exclusive, unlike (for example) such absolute attributes as knowledge and love, or justice and mercy. But within divinity the distinction is exclusively a relative one, based solely upon the giving and taking of origin. In the finite order, relativity never subsists; it is never pure but always the accidental qualification of an existent. There, relative distinction implies a certain absoluteness because the term posited is the effect of some causal efficacy and acquires its own individual existence as an accident.

But are not the trinitarian implications of all this remote indeed? In principle, at least, unaided reason can discern these terms within the intentionality of spirit. Yet, needless to say, this by no means implies that the Trinity of Persons can be deduced from an analysis of pure actuality. There are lacking grounds for affirming that such distinctions are real in God; even more gratuitous is any suggestion that the terms of the distinctions might be personal. Still, what all this can afford to theological reason, working under the light of faith, is an a posteriori analogy for talking about the Trinity. The distinctions within conscious intentionality can serve to introduce the concept of relationality into God-talk—a relationality that, as one of mutual opposition, can render intelligible distinctions that are not intrinsically inimical to unity.

This way of theologically elaborating what is confessed in faith begins by shedding some light upon the fecundity or fructification of the divine essence as a pure dynamism at once self-expressive and self-unitive. The unity of God is identically a plurality in virtue of the self-communicative power of Being Itself. Moreover, because these emanations within divinity are from within the intentionality of pure spirit, they should not be looked upon as "natural" emanations, in the sense of being the necessary and spontaneous resultancy of a nature.[26] They are not analogous to the fashion in which light and heat come forth from the sun, for example. Thus, it is possible to understand the terms immanent to divine knowing and loving as not mere properties of the divine essence, as not distinct in a way reducible to the order of essences. Because these are processions proper to the operations of spirit, emanations solely of the intelligible order, they open the way for the mind at least to entertain the possibility of distinctions within God that are real and yet do not contravene the divine unity and simplicity. This latter point is strengthened somewhat with the realization that, in God, the Word and the Spirit do not come to origin out of divine need or by way of overcoming deficiency. Such is the case in finite knowledge and love, which are ways of transcending the limitations of individual selfhood. The eruptions within Pure Act, however, represent the richness of overflow; they reflect not indigence of being but abundance of being. Thus they are the ontological precondition in God of creation—which, because it occurs by way of the Word and the Spirit, is not a necessary or natural emanation of God's substance but entirely the freely willed consequence of God's love.

That which takes origin in divine self-knowing is designated, in the symbols of faith, as Word, Image, and (because it proceeds out of the substance of God by way of an imitation or reproduction) Son. The term proceeding in divine self-loving is rather named Spirit (*Pneuma*) and (designating his role towards men) Paraclete. Both stand in opposition—an opposition that is exclusively relative and nowise absolute—to their primordial source which, as itself without origin, is grasped in the symbol of Father. These oppositions, however, are founded in origins—thus they prevail solely between originator and originated, between principle and term.

---

[26]Suarez, for example, treats the processions as the mere natural fecundity of the divine essence, issuing therefrom after the fashion of properties from an essence; *De Trinitate*, lib. I, c. 8, n. 5. Louis Billot maintains that they are not genuine actions that are always productive of either an immanent or a transitive term, even though we cannot designate them in any other fashion; *De Deo Uno et Trino*, 4th ed. (Rome, 1902), thesis 38, ad 1. One caution on referring to these as true actions is that no agency in the sense of efficient causality is thereby implied; they are *notional* acts and so the pure act of relating.

Accordingly, Father and Son are really distinct; to be the Father is precisely not to be the Son. Further, Father and Son are really distinct from the *Pneuma* because they together are the principle whence comes forth the Spirit as term of their mutual love. Thus, the Son is really distinct from the Spirit because he, and not the Father alone, gives origin to the Spirit (*Filioque*).[27] Real distinction in God, then, is threefold, but exclusively relative. These relationships of mutual opposition mean there can be no confusion of the *relata,* one with another—yet there is no logical impediment to understanding them as constituting one identical essence because the distinctions are not on the plane of essence at all.

On these grounds, reason under the light of faith can contemplate the possibility that these relationships in God are subsistent in and of themselves. They do not inhere in "subjects" other than themselves, nor (properly speaking) do they inhere in the divine substance. The category "relation," in its own distinctive character, conveys only pure order to another. As an accident, of course, it depends upon some subject of inherence. But there is no reason why the mind cannot abstract from this latter aspect and consider the relation merely as subsisting, since inherence is not intrinsic to its definition. The relations in God then are not "in relation to" the divine nature at all (except in the abstractions of finite thought); rather they bespeak simple identity therewith. Each subsisting relation *is* God and all three of them together *are* God. Positing real relations in God explains two things then. It explains distinction (this is relation in its formal and specific sense as pure *esse ad,* as pure order *to* another). But it also explains how such relations do not violate the divine simplicity (this is relation in its less restrictive, quasi-generic sense as *esse in,* as expressing something having being and actuality in God). Both of these fall short of suggesting that distinction in God is *personal* in kind. How then is the transition to person effected?

There is a third way to consider relation. It can be viewed, not precisely as relation, i.e., in the very exercise of relating (this explains plurality in God); not precisely as identified with essence (this explains that the Three are the one God); but precisely as hypostasis, i.e., after the fashion of what subsists distinctly within

---

[27]On these grounds, if the Spirit were not from the Son there would be no way of accounting for their distinction (unless the Son were said to be from the Spirit, which has no basis in tradition).

divinity.[28] The distinction, if subtle, is revealing; it brings to light the notion of person as a metaphysical principle. Person in God signifies a distinctly Subsisting Relation. An at least remote analogue to this is available from the human sphere. There, the human person, taken in its metaphysical ground, is a unique existent within a common nature; it subsists relationally. Its existence in matter means that it also assumes a distinctness that is quantified and bodily, which constitutes man not only a person but also an individual, i.e., a discrete instance of a common nature. This latter has no place in the divine order; the three divine Persons do not share a common nature, but are that nature singly and collectively in total identity. At this point, the metaphysically elaborated concept of person begins to approach—or to recoup—what the Greeks sought to signify by *hypostasis*. That term meant to convey, not subjectivity, as does the term person in its present-day usage, but something closer to objectivity. It bore the sense of a concrete presentation of an essence, with connotations of existence and actuality as opposed to form or idea, and eventually found expression in the alternative phrase "modes of existing" (*tropoi hyparxeōs*). *Hypostasis* was rendered in Latin as *subsistentia;* but the Greek word was used somewhat interchangeably with the less exact term *prosōpon,* which was put into Latin as *persona.* Thus, the orthodox formula in the West came to read "Three *Persons* of one substance." *Persona* is used in the early Councils of the Church to make explicit what was only implicit in the New Testament—but the transition was from a religious symbol to a theological concept.

The logical moves in the foregoing development have traced the following sequence: from (i) Be-ing, to (ii) Knowing-Loving, to (iii) immanent processions, to (iv) really distinct terms, identified as (v) Subsistent Relations, that answer to (vi) the concept of person in the metaphysical sense. This phase of trinitarian thought represents a triumph of Western trinitarianism; it stands impoverished without some recovery of the contribution coming from Eastern trinitarianism. Thus, it is only the beginning of understanding theology's

---

[28]Aquinas, *Summa theologiae,* I, q. 29, a. 4. This article is the quintessence of Thomas's understanding: "The term 'person' signifies relation directly and essence obliquely, but not relation under its precise formality of relation but insofar as it bears a signification like that of hypostasis. *At the same time,* it signifies essence directly and relation obliquely, insofar as essence is identical with hypostasis" (my translation, with emphasis supplied: Aquinas is not expressing a preference for one formula over the other but indicating that the mind must hold the two in dialectical tension).

attempt to illumine the mystery of the Trinity. Left to itself, it can too readily be interpreted as an essentialism, in which the Three are relative aspects of divinity—a position most clearly represented by Anselm's appropriation of Augustinian trinitarianism. Unless it is complemented by a second phase of thought, it cannot easily be cleared of the charge of tending logically towards modalism. This very procedure in its first phase raises a whole set of posterior questions. What does person, in this metaphysical sense of being a distinctly subsisting relation explaining distinction in God, have to do with person as a center and subject of consciousness? If there is no convergence at all then seemingly God is one person in the contemporary sense of the word. If his threefoldness is understood as realized in the latter sense, then why is this not to use person in an equivocal sense and, moreover, one that implies tritheism? On either view the Trinity is compromised. If divine persons are subsistent relations grounded in the processions or eternal origins as true conscious actions, who are the subjects of these originative acts called generation and spiration? Obviously, they cannot be persons as formally constituted by relations subsequent to such actions.

PHASE THREE—PLURALITY AS PERSONAL: THE PSYCHOLOGICAL DIMENSION OF PERSON

Theological thought is thus brought by a dialectic proper to itself to rethink the Trinity in another register. The initial *point de départ* was the dynamism of being as self-expressive in knowing and self-unitive in loving, concluding to real plurality in God. Now a reversal of this needs to be made, a transfer to a new starting point, namely, that of a plurality of persons who act knowingly and lovingly, yet so as to constitute thereby one sole God. The focus now shifts to the subjects exercising the act of "to be," "to know," and "to love." This calls for acknowledging at the very beginning that God is not a thing, a mere object, an impersonal force, the mere ground of being—but a conscious, knowing, loving, creating, revealing, saving God who enters into an I-Thou dialogue with man in history. Pannenberg has made the suggestive point that only subsequent to this awareness does man discover the mystery of his own finite personhood.[29] Reason, even without faith, can readily grant that God's

---

[29]"The Question of God," *Basic Questions in Theology*, pp. 228–29; *Theology and the Kingdom of God*, pp. 57–58.

being is personal—but that is to affirm a single absolute personhood, and does not so much as suggest a triunity of persons. But
theological reason, proceeding in light of the faith-confession that
God is a Trinity, gains an insight that enables it to reach two possible
conclusions. First, it can be understood that the single, absolute
"person" of God is in actuality only an abstraction. Secondly, it is
possible to render that abstraction concrete and real by identifying
it with the One confessed as the first person within the Trinity, with
the *fons divinitatis* who is the origin of the other two persons and
himself without origin.[30] The abstractive element in this procedure
is entirely legitimate for a mind that cannot grapple with transcendent being in any other way. More specifically, this maneuver would
appear to be an instance of "appropriation," in which what is known
to be common to all three persons is predicated as if it were the
prerogative of one among them. This is a language device of believers that seeks in a paradoxical way to suggest the personal identity
of the members of the Trinity, but it is one that has always functioned in tradition. The need of recourse to such a device, which
violates to a degree the logic of ordinary discourse, lies in the elu-
siveness of the person that cannot be captured in a concept and can
only be described by the characteristic ways in which a given person
appropriates a common nature, unveiling himself in the externality
of that nature. At any rate, an awareness of the kind of knowing
act that is going on makes it possible to understand that, in reality,
there is no absolute person of divinity; there are only the relative
Three. There is not some fourth reality "behind," as it were, the
Father, Word, and *Pneuma;* there is no divine nature subsistent in
itself in addition to the three Persons. On these grounds, it is possible to maintain that the New Testament is in fact frequently speaking of the Father when it uses a common name for divinity such as
Theos or Lord. Rahner, it is true, makes a somewhat similar point—
but with a significant difference.[31] He does not suggest that the
New Testament is implicitly employing what in later development
is called the law of appropriation. The omission is not as minor as
might at first seem because it has the effect, in Rahner's thought,
of endowing the Father with a covert priority, of suggesting that he
is himself the *Monarchia.*

---

[30]See Emil Bailleux, "La réciprocité dans la Trinité," *Revue Thomiste* 74,
no. 3 (July–September 1974), pp. 365–66.
[31]"Theos in the New Testament," *Theological Investigations,* vol. 1, pp.
79–148.

Consciousness in God is a prerogative of the divine nature, but by definition it calls for a subject or subjects who exercise such consciousness. Since God is a Trinity, these subjects are in reality threefold: Father, Son, and Spirit. All three persons know the divine truth and love the divine goodness and thereby are themselves known and loved. This constitutes *essential* consciousness, knowledge, and love. But that selfsame consciousness is also interpersonal in kind; it bespeaks activity exclusive to each person in its relationality to the other two, something distinctive rather than common in which the very identity of the person consists. This is *notional* consciousness, knowledge, and love (so called because it "notifies" or gives notice of the Three in their personal identities). Consciousness in God, in short, is at once essential and personal; the former establishes the persons in their unity, the latter establishes them in their distinction. In the single act of eternal knowing, then, it is necessary to understand that *God* (or the Father by appropriation) knows and that at the very heart of such knowing, the *Father*, in an act that is proper to him and not appropriated, utters his Word or generates his Son. Moreover, in an act not really distinct from the knowing, *God* loves, and at the interior of that loving, the *Father* and the *Word* "breathe forth" their personal love as the Spirit—in a notional activity common to them, but not shared by the Spirit, called spiration. The notional action characteristic of the second person is that of being uttered or generated by the Father and with him of spirating forth the Spirit. This is one and the same notional action, and the first designation of it uses a passive grammatical form only because we have no other way of thinking or speaking about it; it is in fact true action, though one transcending efficiency. Similarly, the Spirit's personal action is that of proceeding forth from the Father and the Son without giving origin. Thus the Spirit's action represents a consummation of this dynamism of spirit in the sense of a return to the primordial personal source.

It is important to note that the Father is a divine subject who simultaneously (in time and in nature) relates himself not only to the Son but also to the *Pneuma*. There is no priority of the Son's origin to that of the Spirit. By the same token, the Father is not *before* the Son and the Spirit as if he were a distinct person antecedently to speaking the Word and spirating the *Pneuma*. There is no succession or priority among the divine persons; to think so is a capitulation to Neo-Platonic emanationism. There is, of course, a real *order* among the trinitarian members—founded in the *logical* order between being-knowing-loving. (The intelligibility of love, for example, bespeaks a prior formality which is awareness; moreover, unlike knowledge, it demands as its condition the existence of two persons). But this order is nothing more than their personal identities, their distinction, their relations of origin. It means that the Father is without origin, the Son is *from* the Father, and the Spirit is *from* them both; it does not mean that any one of them is constituted a person apart from such relating or, as it were, prior to it.

Thus, if the dynamism of pure act gives rise to real relations in God which subsist, those subsistent relations are in turn *subjects* of actions at once essential (constituting their unity) and notional (constituting their distinction). But these notional actions, precisely because they are not essential actions, are in fact nothing more than the pure relating. They are the very relations themselves, understood formally as relations whose whole being is *esse ad* or pure order to the personally other. By way of illustration, to be Father and Son is simply to interrelate respectively in a paternal and a filial way. This relating is not mere awareness but is love, and so in its mutuality it is established as the bringing forth of the Spirit as the mutual personal love between Father and Son, as their personal Communion.

If God's being is personal then it is to be expected that the intentionality of that being is also personal in kind. This renders it at least somewhat intelligible to see divine knowing as terminating not simply at the divine essence in its infinite intelligibility, but as giving origin beyond this to the personally other, as the self-communication, the self-othering of the One who knows. What is intended in transcendent knowing is both an expression of *what* is known and another to be with (*mit-sein*) the one *who* knows. Similarly, in transcendent love, the intentionality regards not only the divine goodness but gives origin to another who is the "bond," the *élan vital* between the lovers, in personifying the unexactedness and pure gratuity of mutual love.

In this exploration into the Trinity, it is the formal distinction between nature and person—first worked out at Chalcedon in a christological context, but in answer to a problem first raised at Nicaea in a trinitarian context—that remains irreducible and the key to theological discourse. The trinitarian use of the distinction is twofold: it enables one to speak of an absolute and a relative dimension in God's being while recognizing that he transcends our finite notions of both absoluteness and relativity; it allows one also to differentiate between a *principium quod* and a *principium quo*, i.e., between the subject who acts and the nature by which it acts. A first phase of thought has attempted to show that the category "person" bears a metaphysical dimension (distinct subsistence), while a second, complementary phase adds a necessary psychological dimension (center of consciousness). The latter makes it possible to say that the immanent terms in God are also principles, distinct subjects of notional acts. It marks an approximation to what the term person means in contemporary usage—an approximation, nevertheless, that never can be more than analogous. Relation remains the operative concept: it is first a principle of distinction; it is secondly also a formal reason for unity—but precisely now an interpersonal unity. The persons in God thus constitute a divine intersubjectivity: Father, Son, and Spirit are three centers of consciousness in community, in mutual communication. The members of the Trinity are now seen as constituting a community of persons in pure reciprocity, as subjects and centers of one divine conscious life. Each person is constituted what might analogously be called an "I" in self-awareness of its own unique identity, but only by way of rapport to the other two persons as a non-self; indeed, it is in virtue of that free interplay, wherein each person disposes himself towards the others in knowing and loving, that each person gains his unique identity. The Greek Fathers made much of *perichorēsis* (literally: "dancing around") to suggest this togetherness, this joyous "sharing" of divine life. The term was rendered in Latin as both *circuminsessio* (the coexistence and inexistence of each person in the other two: "I am in the Father and the Father is in me"; *Jn.* 14:11) and *circumincessio* (the vital circulation or mutual interflow of divine life). In this sense, the Trinity is a divine *koinōnia:* Three who are conscious by way of one essential consciousness, constituting a divine reciprocity that is an interpersonal and intersubjective unity. As personal, that reciprocity belongs to the sphere of transcendent freedom. Liberty is a property of the divine nature but it is exercised only by the persons, who within the Trinity interrelate one to another in the pure creativity of uncreated freedom and love.

This is the inner-divine Trinity. It remains to be seen (in a subsequent chapter) if the speculative procedure at work here is able to restore a trinitarian dimension to God's deeds in creating and saving a world.

THE TRINITY AS MYSTERY
OF SALVATION

God's revelation of himself as a Trinity precludes any subsequent understanding of him as a self-enclosed Absolute; henceforth he is manifest—primordially, in his own being—as a self-communicating deity. If in his own reality he is a communicating plenitude, then the mystery not only of salvation but of creation also is thereby illumined.[1] The full understanding of creaturehood itself is disclosed in the light of the Trinity, for only thus is it clear that world or universe—that is, the mystery of the communication of being outside of God to what apart from that communication is only the Void—bears a trinitarian imprint. This immediately throws into relief two significant truths: (i) the world is posited *freely* by God and does not proceed forth from his substance by any sort of necessary emanation, and (ii) the motivation in such giving of origin (and thereby the world's destiny) lies in the sphere of *love*.[2] The first is an implication of the eternal utterance of the Word in God, as a conscious, free, intelligible act; the second is an implication of the breathing forth of the *Pneuma* as the mutual love of the Father and Son.

Still, the very existence of the Trinity is disclosed not in creation but in faith-encounter with God centered upon Jesus of Nazareth. This is a religious experience of God acting within history whose articulation into language appropriates God in the threefold symbol of Father, *Logos*, and Spirit. God, otherwise ineffable, declares who he is in his dealings with men in Christ—namely, a gracious and saving God. Thus, the trinitarian implications of creation are sec-

---

[1] Aquinas, for example, explains that "just as the procession of the Persons explains the production of creatures from the first principle, so the same procession explains their return thereto as to their destiny." I *Sent.*, d. 14, q. 2, a. 2; see also *Summa theologiae*, I, q. 32, a. 2, ad 3.

[2] The Father "loves himself and every creature by the Holy Spirit inasmuch as the Holy Spirit proceeds as Love for that primordial goodness explaining the Father's love for himself and every creature." Aquinas, *Summa theologiae*, I, q. 37, a. 2, ad 3.

ondary to, and derivative from, the Trinity as it is manifest in the order of salvation, the *oikonomia*. The God who can save from the nothingness of sin is a God who can make to be from the nothingness of nonbeing. Belief in the saving Trinity brings the insight that the world is not just a brute and contingent fact, but a mystery ·vhose consummation lies in the depths of inner-trinitarian life. If the God who comes with the offer of salvation for lost mankind comes as Trinity, and is the sole God there is, then it is the Trinity that has called the world out of nothingness in the first place. Creation is itself in its depths a trinitarian mystery—even if the marks of the Trinity upon it are covert and become overt only in the events of salvation.

A METHODOLOGICAL NOTE

This order of knowing, however, is one indigenous to *religious* consciousness; *theological* consciousness, by contrast, alters this epistemic order somewhat. The former moves from the Trinity encountered in the events of saving history to the inner-divine Trinity and thence to an awareness of the Trinity operative in creation. The latter in its reflective act seeks the order of things in themselves rather than that involved in our discovery of them; it seeks to approximate (obviously in a highly limited way) something of the standpoint of God himself. This is dictated by its search for intelligibility; that God is a Trinity in himself "explains" the trinitarian characteristics first of creation and then of salvation—granted that the Trinity is manifest merely inchoatively in the former and fully so only in salvation history. In doing this, theological knowing does not repudiate or replace the order proper to faith in its origination. Rather, it preserves it and ever retains it as the norm of its own reflections. But the truth here so surpasses the capacities of the finite mind that it cannot be grasped from one perspective alone. The historical order is a "given," yet the mind natively seeks for its transtemporal intelligible ground. Theology doubles back, as it were, on the spontaneous movement of faith in a complementary move of its own in order to look out on the mystery from an opposite stance upon the horizon. This procedure is not entirely unique to theology; illustrations of something analogous to it can be found elsewhere. Heidegger's *Kehre* ("reversal") for example—in which a shift is made from *Dasein's* projection of Being in his *Sein und Zeit* to Being's giving of itself to *Dasein* in his later works—is cognate to it. Here, a reversal of direction is not a denial of what was said earlier but an inner dynamic of thinking (*Denken*) in the process of accomplishing itself. William Richardson reflects Heidegger's own understanding in calling this "a metamorphosis that is as much controlled by an internal unity as it is dictated by an intrinsic necessity."[3] It is an instance of the circular winding way inevitable for one who follows the path of truth in the thinking of Being.

CREATION AND INCARNATION

The significance of what has just been said comes to light against the background of two differing explanations of how creation relates to Incarnation. One views creation as a mere condition for God's personal communication of himself as Word and Spirit. Because God intends to communicate himself into the Void, he calls man into being to supply the nature in which his Word is to become incarnate and the history which is to be the milieu of his Spirit.[4] The alternative stance gives logical priority to God's intention to communicate not himself but a created participation in his own being, which, through man, is personal in its own finite way. On this view, God's ultimate purpose is not self-enactment, but the giving of origin to a nondivine world that would have meaning in and of itself. In its human dimension, such a world would be personal and so a reflection of the Trinity that God is—but as what Aquinas calls an image of representation rather than as an image of conformity.[5] Man would mirror forth God, but in the sphere of his own human, nondivine reality. God's self-communication (as logically subsequent to this) would represent a new gratuitousness (the New Creation of St. Paul) on his part, in which divine love now comes to the rescue of a world alienated from its true being by what is conveyed in the Christian symbol "sin." This is not a case of sin entering in as something unforeseen to alter God's original pur-

---

[3]*Heidegger: Through Phenomenology to Thought* (The Hague: Martinus Nijhoff, 1963), p. 16.

[4]See Karl Rahner, esp. in "The Theology of the Symbol," *Theological Investigations*, vol. 4, pp. 221–52. Here the Word Incarnate is the absolute symbol of God in the world, and "the symbol strictly speaking (symbolic reality) is the self-realization of a being in the other, which is constitutive of its essence" (p. 234).

[5]*De veritate*, q. 10, a. 7; Aquinas explains this as the difference between an image *secundum analogiam* and *secundum conformitatem*, and offers as an example the way the sense in relation to its object (e.g., color) imitates the intellect in relation to its intelligible object versus the manner in which the intellect, in knowing, images in an intentional way what it understands.

poses; rather sin is foreseen as an inevitable yet free consequence of a liberty that in its finitude cannot be its own norm. The sin is attributable to man alone, nowise to God; yet the divine intention to create includes the will to save from the consequences of fallible liberty. It intends this by the personal self-communication in which the Father sends into the world his *Logos* and *Pneuma*, making the human project his own.

An integral theology cannot hold to one of these two positions in complete isolation from the other. Whichever option carries the day for a given theologian, the other needs to be held in dialectical tension with it. The opposition between the two explanations does mean that one of them has to be primary and formally determinative, but the truth in the alternative theory can serve as a corrective against overstatement. The second of the two positions indicated above makes clear that God could have created a world without personally communicating himself to it even though he chose to do otherwise. With it the transcendence of divine freedom is secured; God is not subjected to moral constraints. Such a theory gives meaning to creaturely existence in its own right (not apart from God, but apart from his assuming the human countenance in the missions of his Son and Spirit), and thereby saves the pure unexactedness of God's saving love. This subsequent salvation history is then a second gratuity, the order of grace; it is something beyond the free gift which is existence. The creature by its very existence shares in being and goodness that is found in God as in its source, yet the perfections in question remain the creature's own, proper to its own level of existence, even though derived from God. In contrast to this, the New Being by grace means entry into God's being *as it is proper to him*, i.e., entrance into the uncreated divine life of Father, Son, and Spirit—possible to the creature only as the term of its intentionality of knowledge and love. To speak of this as a new level of being— which can never be natural to man, i.e., never due to his nature because "natural" only to God—is not to suggest its rarity. It is not to imply that mankind ever existed concretely without it, as if a state of pure nature preexisted its transformation by grace. At the same time, the first position, concerning God's creative purposes, explains that God's motivation in giving origin to a world—in which man as God's image is paramount—is nothing less than the intention to consummate it by bringing it into the sphere of uncreated love which is his own inner trinitarian life. At bottom, the determination as to which of these two views is to predominate turns on the question whether God's creative activity is self-enactment ultimately or altruistic self-communication. If a preference for the latter appears here, that option rests on two convictions: (i) first, it is the inner-divine Trinity that constitutes and consummates God's self-enactment; and (ii) secondly, the universe of creatures exists ultimately not for God's sake but for the creatures' own sake, even though the latter find fulfillment in giving glory to God (thus, the divine love that summons the world into being and saves it from itself is what the New Testament means by *agapē*).

In any case, both creation and salvation are trinitarian mysteries, though differently so. This is to say that in the Word and in the Spirit eternally proceeding within divinity there is to be discerned both an *essential* and a *personal* dimension. Taken essentially, the processions manifest the creativity of the divine nature and bespeak exemplarity towards a possible creation. Succinctly put, this leads to the conclusion that if there is a world, it must reflect God's imitability already perfectly expressed in the Word, and its destiny or consummation must lie in love already achieved in the Spirit. Taken personally, the processions ground the interrelationality and self-disposability of the persons as ultimate subjects within divinity, and so they betoken God's chosen relationship as one of personal self-communication to a world of finite persons. To illustrate: in the former way, the Second in God is the Word "through whom all things are made" (*Jn.* 1:3); in the latter way, he is the Word "made flesh . . . to dwell among us" (*Jn.* 1:14). The first renders intelligible a universe of *natures* (including man's, gifted as it is with the attributes of knowledge and love) with their enduring structures. The second speaks rather of a universe of finite *persons* who achieve themselves, within the limits of their natures, in free relating to one another and to the uncreated persons of God. These are not two different worlds but one world, distinguishable nonetheless as nature and cosmos on the one side and as person and history on the other. The inseparability and unity of the two aspects is but a reflection of the truth that the Three in God are at once the sole divine nature and the distinct subjects of that nature.

But the presence of the Trinity, as operative both in creation and in salvation, means not only an awareness of plurality within God but some clue as to the distinctive identity of those who constitute it. There are no concepts with which to grasp persons, but we need to give them names. Thus, it is not enough merely to acknowledge distinct subsisting relations in the depths of the Godhead, nor to add that such relations subsist in the intersubjectivity of a divine *koinōnia*. Some way of discriminating their personal characteristics seems called for. Awareness of the unique personal identity of another is accomplished largely by way of a symbolizing activity.

Because the person is precisely not essence it remains recalcitrant to conceptualizing and categorizing activity. Symbols are endowed with an evocative power lacking to the more precise concept, a "tensive" quality (Wheelwright) which demands a constant creative act of interpretation and explains why symbols can never be exhaustively rendered into literal terms. Distinctively personal encounter occurs only within the mystery of freedom, and here symbols serve well both to mediate and to express the essentially projective and future-oriented character of the encounter between personal freedoms, to "make room" for the freedom that lies at its base.

Still, if the persons of the Trinity are present as such in the created universe, that presence has to be mediated to men. Earthly realities need to be appropriated in which the members of the Trinity can "appear," realities which do have their natures that the mind can apprehend and which can serve as loci for man's encounter with the divine subjects. (To allow that the divine persons are really present in themselves is not to grant that such presence is unmediated.) What follows from this is that the names used to designate the members of the Trinity are taken from earthly realities, from what are attributes ox natures—but they function not as concepts (to define essences) but as symbols (to name the personal). Fatherhood in the finite order, for example, signifies a relationship between persons (and so Father can be used as a proper name), but only in virtue of attributes that convene to nature, such as the biological act of reproduction and material individualization. Yet there are no distinctions of the order of nature whatsoever between the Three in God. How then is it possible even to begin to surmise their unique identities?

ORDER WITHOUT SUBORDINATION

Early Greek trinitarianism sought the identities of the persons by treating the distinctions as if they were of the order of nature. Primarily, this meant viewing the *Monarchia* as realized in the First Person alone. The Word and Spirit, because derived from the Father, were viewed as subordinate to him in spite of their status as divine. The Three constituted a divine hierarchy, in which the divinity of the Second and Third in God was understood on the basis of reducing their beingness back to its origin out of the very substance of the Father. In the late seventh century a council of Toledo was to speak of the Father as *"fons et origo totius Trinitatis,"*[6]

---

[6]Denzinger-Schönmetzer, 525.

but in early Greek speculation this took the form of seeing the Father as the *divinitas fontalis* apart from Son and *Pneuma*. The latter two persons were distinguished between themselves on the basis of a different manner of proceeding forth from the First. This could not fail to suggest, in a covert way at least, that the distinction between the divine persons was reducible to one of kind or nature—even when from Origen onward all notion of temporal succession is eliminated. If this approach did offer some explanation of distinction, it did so at the cost of unity and equality. What is unmistakably at work in all this is the thought of Neo-Platonism—clearly evident in Origen's recourse to emanationism, and culminating in heterodoxy with Arius—which betrays itself at this point as unable to bear the weight of the Christian mystery.

The Cappadocians in the late fourth century overturned this subordinationist outlook and the earlier forms of Monarchianism and opened the way to use of the category of relation. But a price was paid for this achievement. It carried in its wake, especially as it made common cause with the reaction against Arianism, a tendency to isolate the economy of salvation from the inner life of God. *Theologia* proper became a contemplative reflection upon the mystery of God's hidden and ineffable being and evinced an understandable preference for the *via negativa*. The *oikonomia* gave rise to quite another concern, that of reflecting upon the utterly free dispositions that God chose to adopt towards men, his deeds *ad extra* in the sphere economized by the divine will. A disastrous consequence of this was a growing tendency to treat the trinitarian dimension of salvation history as something arbitrarily willed by God.

The surmounting of this impasse—between a trinitarianism of an Origenist inspiration and one inaugurated by the Cappadocians—demanded attending to the concept of order. The trinitarianism of Basil and the two Gregories is in the *homoousios* spirit of Nicaea and is markedly anti-Arian. Advancing beyond Nicaea, however, they draw the distinction that Nicaea did not—that between *ousia* and *hypostasis*. With the latter concept they are able to explain distinction in God that is not inimical to the divine simplicity. But beyond this, their overriding concern is with defending the consubstantiality of the three *hypostases*. In doing this, they allowed order between the Persons to be obscured. This is not surprising when one considers that the prevailing thought-pattern in the background of their own thought is Neo-Platonic participationism, in which order means a hierarchy of superior to inferior. Against any importation of this into trinitarian thinking they stand firm. Too readily this tends to insinuate that only the Father is divine by essence. The Son and the

Spirit are then apt to be thought of as divine in virtue of their unique rapport to their Source (a rapport not shared by creatures). This is tantamount to saying they are divine in a participatory way. The Cappadocians put to rest this kind of thinking, insisting upon the total equality of the Three in God. But they do this only by minimizing and neutralizing the implications of order within the Godhead. The result is that the identities of the persons become blurred and their distinct roles outside of God lost sight of. They are content to view the distinction between the *Logos* and the Spirit, and *a fortiori* their distinction from the Father, as a ministerial or functional one within salvation history, neglecting thereby the full import of the truth that this is characteristic of divine being in itself.

Augustine takes his clue from the line of thought begun by the Cappadocians and attempts to deepen it by delving into the inner working of the human psyche. Memory, understanding, and love of self provide some insight into how the Three in God might be one at the heart of the divine unity without losing their purely relative distinctness. This was, in effect, an attempt at affirming order, but it was limited to the psychological sphere. What it succeeded in bringing to light was an order *within the person*, but not an order *between persons*. Moreover, as Père Le Guillou has astutely observed, Augustine's overriding interest was christological rather than trinitarian; it was the mystery of the divine and the human in Jesus that concerned him above all.[7] It is the eternal *Logos* that assumes humanity—but in order to constitute himself the sacrament of God for men, rather than to be the Son living out on earth his trinitarian relationship to the Father. This seems true enough, though perhaps Le Guillou makes too little of Augustine's development of the temporal missions. The latter books of the *De Trinitate* do attempt a development in which the order of Word and Spirit to the unoriginate Father renders intelligible their distinct roles in history and even in nature. Still, the sacramental character of the Incarnation predominates in Augustine; if this is more balanced in the fifth-century Augustine, it becomes more pronounced in medieval Augustinianism.

It is difficult to deny that Anselm's interpretation of Augustine has strong modalistic overtones. He views the immanent acts *of the essence* as founding the relations, which thus appear to constitute the persons as an *essential* relationality in God. The relations represent

---

[7] M.-J. Le Guillou, *Le Mystère du Père* (Paris: Fayard, 1973), p. 107.

a certain fecundity of the divine essence since they come to be by way of originating acts (processions) of that nature. On such a basis, Anselm's thought cannot easily accommodate a doctrine of the missions. In Aquinas the case is quite different—there the relations constitute the persons only when understood as hypostatic, that is, as *principia quod*, or ultimate subjects, of the divine act of be-ing, who, through the essence as a *principium quo*, posit acts at once essential and notional or personal.[8] This is not simply a starting point arbitrarily posited, because relation signifies person, not formally as explaining distinction (relation as relation), nor as designating divinity (relation as identical with essence), but precisely as hypostatic or subsisting, i.e., as the concrete, purely actual subject(s) who *is* God. Thus, it is not a question of *either* the person having logical priority over the nature, *or* the essence enjoying such priority over the person. It is rather the case of a mutual or reciprocal priority; we cannot think them simultaneously and so dialectically must give priority now to the one point of view, now to the other.

The import of this is that it enables one to think of the Father as the first subject in God and so of the Word and Spirit as having their subjectivity derivatively from the unoriginate Father. The Spirit, in turn, is also derivative from the Son, but only because the Son has received from the Father that in virtue of which he is the principle of the Spirit. Thus, among the divine persons there prevails order—but order without succession of any kind, whether of time, of nature, or of thought. The order is real; that we can think of it only as successive is due to the limits of finite understanding and has no grounds within God. It is a *pure* order, without any preexisting elements to be ordered, or any elements subsequent to the ordering. The members of the Trinity are therefore equal, identical with the divine nature, and one in their essential actions *ad intra* and in all actions *ad extra*. Only in their personal acts *ad intra* are they distinct, and such activity is that of a pure relating. Yet that relationality is entirely an ordered one. The Father alone is without origin; the Son is from the Father; the Spirit is from the Father and the Son. In the liturgy, we do not pray to the persons singly, nor

<hr/>

[8]Observing the niceties of speech, Aquinas notes that action cannot be predicated of the essence designated by abstract names; when the name is a concrete one, e.g., "God," then the proper supposition of the essential name is person—thus, the impropriety of saying that the essence proceeds, or that the Son proceeds, from the essence rather than from the Father, etc.; see *Summa theologiae*, I, q. 39, aa. 5 & 6.

in any other order: we pray only *to* the Father, *through* the Son, *in* the Holy Spirit. The logical key to all this is the irreducibility of the distinction expressed in various sets of concepts: *ousia/hypostasis*, essence/relation, and nature/person. It enables Aquinas to make the doctrine of the missions—whereby the Father sends his Son into the world and then, through the Son, his Spirit—a centrally operative and illuminating principle in his systematic thought. Thus in his *Summa theologiae* a treatment of the immanent Trinity (I, qq. 29–42) culminates in consideration of the economic Trinity (I, q. 43), and the latter is formally determinative of the treatises to follow on creation, man, grace, Christ, Church, etc. It represents a theological insight that made an earlier appearance in Irenaeus and Tertullian. While not missing entirely in Augustine, this trinitarian mode of thinking tends to give way there to one that prefers to emphasize the mystery of sacramentality.

PRESENCE OF THE TRINITY: THEORY OF "APPROPRIATIONS"

If, then, there is a universe "outside" of God freely posited by him, it is a world summoned into being by the Three who are God. It is the Trinity that creates, and both that creative act and its product are an extension or prolongation of the eternal self-communication that is God. Every divine action vis-à-vis the world is thus trinitarian in kind. But there is a difference between this universal presence of the Trinity and that uniquely accomplished in the events of Incarnation and Pentecost. This can be expressed as the difference between a presence of the Trinity and a specifically trinitarian presence. In the divine creative act the Three act as one yet it remains true there are Three who so act. Their distinction as Source, Word, and Bond does not collapse into an act of a unitarian God. The Father creates as the ultimate Source of that temporal utterance into the Void which is the prolongation of his eternal utterance; the Word creates as the exemplar of the creature, thus explaining that the latter mirrors forth some aspect of the divine being; the Spirit creates as the motivating force of the world's coming to be, which is its destiny of being drawn up into the love of Father and Son. This is the richness of meaning caught in the ancient Greek formula of faith that spoke of all things being "from the Father, through the Son, and in the Spirit." But this means that the creature brought forth must bear within itself an impress of the

Three who called it out of nothingness. This signation or imprint is obviously mysterious and hidden; it can be acknowledged solely in light of what the believer becomes aware of in the Christ-event. But at least some suggestiveness is conveyed in the tripartite mystery of beingness and origin, of specificity of nature, and of that dynamism of activity whereby everything strives for its maturation and consummation. Where self-conscious beings are concerned it seemingly assumes the form of power, knowledge, and love. If this tridimensionality is rooted in man's nature, it assumes a personal character because that nature is real only in the person who exercises its act of existing. Nonetheless the ground for this threefold structure—in both the human and the infrahuman sphere—is the personal triunity in God; and this is what it points to, tenuously, for faith.

What is at work here, in fact, is that linguistic device, to which believers resort in speaking of the Trinity, called the theory of "appropriation." What is in reality a common prerogative of the trinitarian members is predicated of one alone to manifest his personal uniqueness in the Godhead. But this cannot be done arbitrarily; some mysterious affinity between the person and an action *ad extra*, or an essential attribute, lies at the base of this kind of speech. The rose in full blossom suggests tongues of flame because the imagination grasps this mysterious affinity at the heart of diversity. Indeed, when employed formally, an appropriation made to one divine person cannot be made to another in exactly the same way. In ordinary human discourse, concepts expressive of certain modes of acting or particular characteristics of nature are commonly used to designate the person so acting or so qualified. In such cases, the concept appears to be used symbolically to mediate and articulate the encounter with the person who unveils himself this way in the phenomenon of intersubjectivity. Thus, I encounter my friend in his very personhood but only in and through what he says and does, in the way he freely chooses to reveal himself through the medium of nature. Consciousness moves from apprehension to encounter, from concept to symbol, from an implicit metaphysics of being to symbolism of person. Appropriation is justified because of the awareness in faith that the divine persons, in the singularity of their unique identities, are involved *as such* in the creative act and so with all creaturely being, whose inner structure mirrors forth mysteriously a personal order in God.

The purpose of appropriation is simply the humanizing of the mystery by bringing it into the sphere of human language in the sole way possible. It is quite to be expected that warrant for so doing is found in the very language of Scripture and liturgy, which abound in instances of appropriation—these being, after all, the arenas of narrating and celebrating personal encounter. Epistemologically, the need for recourse to this sort of language device is due to the limitations of human knowing as it involves conversion to the sense phantasm. More philosophically, it resides in the way personhood transcends the nature it personifies, and resists all grasp in direct language categories. Beyond all this lies the hiddenness of the Mystery itself in the incomprehensibility of a multipersoned God. There is, in short, a peculiar logic at work here in which the *appropriatum*, signifying God's nature or operation, lies more within the range of our limited consciousnesses but which, through the symbolizing power of an intelligence open to revelation, can give anchorage to speech about what otherwise lies beyond our ken.

TRINITARIAN PRESENCE: THE MISSIONS

It is solely the Christ-event that leads the believing intelligence into the mystery of God's tri-personhood. The christological confession—namely, that in Jesus we have to do with God himself, who, as very God, "became flesh and dwelt among us"—signals the awareness that God's uncreated and eternal being is itself primordially a mystery of inner-communication. In Christ, he has communicated to us no less than his very self, and so we are beyond even *creatio ex nihilo*. Yet Jesus is not God *tout court*, a point conveyed well in G.W.H. Lampe's paradoxical phrase that the early Church came eventually to say "Jesus is God," but never "God is Jesus."[9] (The former, it might be noted, came about with the transition from "Son of God" to "God the Son"). Jesus is God *as man*, in the form of a man. This latter was not taken in the mainstream of Christian tradition in any Docetist sense as implying only "in the guise of a man," rather than meaning that God became in truth this particular historical man of Nazareth. He is of divine status in virtue of being the Son of God sent into the world, the Word of God uttered into time and space. In either case the unavoidable implication is that of an eternal utterance by the One who is not spoken but only speaks, of a Father who generates his Son beyond time. The full import of

---

[9]G.W.H. Lampe, *God as Spirit*, The Bampton Lectures 1976 (Oxford: Clarendon Press, 1977).

this is that the Incarnation is a prolongation into the world of the eternal procession of the Son from the Father. So viewed, the Incarnation gains its fullest intelligibility when seen ultimately as trinitarian.

This note sounds clearly in the Christology of Irenaeus, which is otherwise somewhat primitive. By contrast, a quite different note is struck in the Christology of Augustine, whose influence came to prevail, especially in the West, over that of the author of the *Adversus Haereses*. Augustine's thought—at least the syncretic Augustinianism that claims his inspiration—locates the core of mystery in the Incarnation as the rapport between the divine and the human. This is the insight on which a whole theology is built, one that views Christ as the primal sacrament of God, in which the humanity functions to render the Godhead visible and available to men. Everything that Christ does in his earthly life is thus redemptive from sin and a moral example to mankind. The illuminative power of this religious insight can hardly be exaggerated. Moreover, the historical context in which Augustine is working needs to be taken into account. Against the inroads of Arianism he wishes to deny that Christ belongs ultimately in the ranks of the creature; against a monophysitic tendency coming from the Alexandrians he wishes to avoid thinking in terms of a mere epiphany of the Godhead in humanity. The way out lay with a rich development of sacramentality, in which the humanity is the instrument of God, the external sign that bears us efficaciously to an invisible God. But what unavoidably recedes into the background in this focus upon Incarnation is trinitarian mission. As noted earlier, Augustine himself does not entirely neglect this dimension, but as a theological factor it does come to occupy second place, subordinate to sacramentality as the dominant concept. The union of the two natures in Christ tends (in Augustine) to obscure the person in whom they are united. Irenaeus's thought—otherwise so poverty-stricken in comparison with Augustine's—keeps this in focus precisely because it looks upon salvation history as mirroring forth God's inner being. The Son of God becomes the Son of Man in order to recapitulate in himself God's original plan. The One who comes is the Son of God for the very reason that he comes to make men adoptive sons of the selfsame Father who sends him. Theology that developed in the Reformation tradition noticeably shied away from this sort of thinking. The result was a need to explain how what transpired in Jesus could be salvation *for me,* a dilemma that Luther resolves with a new understanding of the subjective certitude of faith. Even today, so-called Christologies "from below" face the same difficulty; Pannenberg, for example, continues Luther's teaching on Christ's sufferings as vicarious punishment for our sins.[10]

An integral trinitarianism is, of course, not only christological but pneumatological. The personal relating of Father and Son is above all a disposition of love, an "achieving" of personhood in a pure giving to the other in the mysterious creativity of love; it is love that bears a paternal character in one and a filial character in the other. Because that love is the mutual love of two who are distinct in person, it issues in another *hypostasis*, the *Pneuma*, who is the hypostatic "bond" or "nexus" between them. This Third in God answers now not to "I" or "Thou" but to what is expressed with the pronoun "We."[11] God's being is a dynamism which brings forth the *personally* other in order that such being might consummate itself in love. The Father's love for his natural Son in eternity is thus the origin of the Spirit, the motivation for creation, and the explanation of God's love for his adoptive children. The love of adoptive sons is but the prolongation of the Father's love for his eternal Son, and thus is indigenously a trinitarian mystery. It is then a love accomplished in and by the Holy Spirit, who thus plays in the economy a role determined by his personal identity in God. The Father sends the Spirit to us through his Son and through the Incarnation of the latter: he is "the Spirit of the adoption of sons whereby we cry out 'Abba, Father'" (*Rom.* 8:15). The Son receives from the Father that whereby he can release upon us the Advocate. In his redemptive death he "returns" the Spirit (so to speak) to the Father, that Spirit whereby he is loved by the Father, the Spirit already poured out on others. In this way, we can say (imaginatively) that the Spirit, returning to the Father, carries in his wake all those constituted adoptive sons of that Father. But, there is even more: the Father returns the Spirit (to continue to speak imaginatively) once more to his "only begotten Son"—who is nonetheless the "firstborn among many brethren" (*Rom.* 8:29). In his glorified humanity "at God's right hand [where] he stands and pleads for us" (*Rom.* 8:34), he sends the Paraclete upon the New Creation, to those who are "heirs of God and coheirs with Christ" (*Rom.* 8:17).

---

[10]*Jesus: God and Man*, pp. 258–80.

[11]For a development of this line of thought, see Heribert Mühlen, *Der heilige Geist als Person*, 2nd ed. (Münster, 1966).

PNEUMA AS "PERSON" OF THE NEW CREATION

What has been said makes it clear that the divine persons themselves, in their hypostatic distinctness, are present within the economy of salvation. This is not merely a presence of God who happens to be triune, in which the trinitarian dimension is explained by appropriation. It is rather a *proper* presence of two Persons in virtue of their being sent into history; the Father is not sent, yet is present—this is demanded by the inseparability of the Three, as well as by the doctrine of *perichorēsis*—as the One who sends. If the proper role of the Word in salvation is clear enough, because of its concrete and visible appearance in the individual humanity of Jesus, that of the Spirit is not nearly so evident. Yet the weight of Christian tradition has tended to suggest that, analogous to the way in which the Word is exclusively present in the humanity of Jesus (the others are there, but only the Word is there as the *persona* of that humanity), the Holy Spirit is present in a way proper to himself in the hearts of believers, constituting them as the New Creation of God. The divine presence in one mission is an incarnate one proper to the Word; that in the other mission is an ecclesial one proper to the Paraclete. The effect of the former is *manifestive* of God; the effect of the latter is rather *unitive* to God. But both effects are trinitarian in mode. Each can be proper to the respective member of the Trinity because there is no operation *ad extra* involved. The Word's personification of Jesus' humanity is not the doing of something in the order of efficient causality, but rather an actualization in the order of personal being. The work of Wittgenstein cautions against attempting to speak of the mystery of intentional activity in the categories of causal activity, and the anthropology of Karl Rahner stresses a personal becoming in which the dynamism of spirit outreaches the limits of causal explanation.[12] This suggests the possibility of personal communication at the heart of causal activity that cannot be apart from causality, but that cannot be explained in causal terms alone. What we are speaking of here can be reduced to the order of formal causality (the form actualizes by its very presence), as long as it is understood that person is not a form but

---

[12]For two suggestive pursuits of this line of thinking, see David B. Burrell, *Aquinas—God and Action* (Notre Dame, Ind.: University of Notre Dame Press, 1979), and Andrew Tallon's study of Rahner's anthropology, *Personal Becoming, The Thomist* 43, no. 1 (January 1979), entire issue, pp. 1–177.

merely actualizes in a way analogous to that of form.[13] Person is
that which exercises the act of "to be," and both person and existence remain radically unknowable to us—unlike predicates expressing form, properties, nature, essence, etc. We can only assert the
former—e.g., "Matthew does exist"; "He is Matthew not Mark."
Thus, we can only declare the phenomenon of personification in
terms of what is known to us, i.e., the mode of causality proper to
form. Aquinas insists, for example, that *esse* (to be) is not a *form*, and
yet speaks of it as *formalissimus* (most formal), suggesting that we can
gain some insight into the way it confers being, on analogy with the
way the soul gives life to the body.[14]

Just so, the Holy Spirit's gathering together of believers is not an
agent causality but the very relating in love which constitutes his
distinctive personhood. A divine efficacy is, of course, also at work
here, but that is the common operation of the persons. It produces
real effects and transformations within created natures, but as a
precondition for contact and encounter of created persons with God
in intersubjectivity. This interrelationality of the trinitarian members
with the world is real, yet does not involve them in change. The
divine immutability excludes all change insofar as the latter involves
transition from potency to act. To introduce such into God is to
render him no longer transcendent over a world of potency/act composition, no longer God. To insist that God's being lies beyond all
change, in the sense of a transition from potency to act—even in
his actual knowing, loving, and acting upon the world—is only to
insist that Pure Act means to name what transcends the conditions
of finitude in which alone we come to any knowledge of act. It is
not to deny that—in another sphere, that of relationship as *personal*
and beyond the relationship rooted in substance and causality—God
can will to be affected by the responses of other persons whose
freedom is creaturely, without acquiring in himself perfection he

---

[13]For an explanation of how the Word's actualization of the humanity is
reductively "a purely terminative formal causality," see Kevin F. O'Shea,
"The Human Activity of the Word," *The Thomist* 22, no. 2 (April 1959), pp.
143–232.

[14]*Summa theologiae*, I, q. 8, a. 1: "Esse autem est illud quod est magis
intimum cuilibet et quod profundius omnibus inest, cum sit formale res-
pectu omnium quae in re sunt." The body-soul metaphor is used in ad 2.

previously lacked.[15] It is no denial that, in his transcendent power and freedom, he can choose to be the kind of God he will be, in dialogic relationship with men. The archetype for this is love within the Trinity, as it is at once essential (constituting divinity) and relational (distinguishing the persons). Its mysteriousness reduces to that of spirit itself, as intentionality.

The symbolism unleashed in this understanding of the trinitarian missions has been richly mined by the Christian imagination. A long tradition has looked upon the humanity of Jesus as the great sacrament of God, as the *Ursakrament,* a view fostered by Rahner's explanation of the "real symbol." But a further enrichment is possible (which Rahner pursues) by viewing the humanity as the symbol rather of the Word, thus making the trinitarian dimension explicit. It is then possible to comprehend the Church, not so much in the usual way as the sacrament of Christ, but as the sacrament of the Spirit. Heribert Mühlen's *Una Mystica Persona: Eine Person in vielen Personen* is an illuminating development of this line of thought, and it has been explored further (with some reservations) as an alternative model of the Church by Avery Dulles.[16] But the category of sacrament here ought not to obscure the perhaps richer category of "communion." The latter serves to underscore the trinitarian constituent in this mystery of God's dealing with men. Inspiration for this vision of things comes from many sources but nowhere is it said better than in Cyprian's description of the Church as "a people united by the unity of the Father, Son, and Holy Spirit."[17] This trinitarian view by no means denies the dimension of sacramentality

---

[15]For previous explorations of this theme, see W. J. Hill, "Does the World Make a Difference to God?" *The Thomist* 38, no. 1 (January 1974), pp. 146–64; "Does God Know the Future?" *Theological Studies* 36, no. 1 (March 1975), pp. 3–18; and "The Eucharist as Eschatological Presence," *Communio* 4, no. 4 (Winter 1977), pp. 305–20. Another noteworthy contribution to the question along similar lines is W. Norris Clarke, "A New Look at the Immutability of God," *God Knowable and Unknowable,* ed. R.J. Roth (New York: Fordham University Press, 1973), pp. 43–72; also *The Philosophical Approach to God,* ed. W.E. Ray (Winston-Salem, N.C.: Wake Forest University Press, 1979), esp. p. 104.

[16]Mühlen's *Una Mystica Persona: Eine Person in vielen Personen* (Paderborn: F. Schöningh, 1964) has been translated into French as *L'Esprit dans L'Église* (Paris: Cerf, 1969); further development of this theme can be found *passim* in his later work, *Der heilige Geist als Person,* 2nd ed. (Münster, 1966). Avery Dulles, *Models of the Church* (Garden City, N.Y.: Doubleday, 1974), esp. pp. 51ff.

[17]*De Orat. dominica,* 23; Migne: *PL* 4 556A.

in an integral concept of Church, but it does suggest a theological subordination of sacrament to communion—parallel to the way in which christological explorations are enriched when logically (not genetically) subordinated to trinitarian ones. When a view of the Church as sacrament predominates, at any rate, the trinitarian complement emphasizes the reality dimension (the *res tantum*) which is the believer's participation in trinitarian life. The communion at issue here is both that of man with God and that of man with man. It is a communion of love, and the love in question is identically a love for God and for other men; one cannot be achieved without the other. However, since the objects—God and man—are not to be confused, the problem of priority arises. But the priorities in this case are reversing ones. *Quoad se,* the love of God comes first and is the formal condition for loving the neighbor; *quoad nos,* a love of neighbor is the condition for our being able to love God. Union with God is then the formal element, the determining motive, in our union with other men, even if other men are first of all required as the "material" for its enactment. But this union with God takes upon itself a specifically trinitarian mode: it is communion with the Father, through the Son, and in the Spirit. It is a communion of adoptive sons with the Father, accomplished historically through the temporal mission of the natural Son, and transhistorically in the temporal mission of the *Pneuma.* It is not that the Spirit does not come within history, but that he "breathes where he will" in an invisible way. The *Logos* works through the unique freedom of Jesus and so through his individual history; the *Pneuma* through the communal freedom of all believers and so through continuing history that cannot yet be finally thematized. What the Spirit effects is perhaps less unity than union, since it is interpersonal in kind, that is, one in which finite personhood is not absorbed or suppressed but "let be" in all its otherness as not-God and as freely self-constituting. In short, it is not ontic in kind (as a union of natures) but "hypostatic" (as a union of persons). It is on the level of spirit in its intentionality of knowing and loving.

Two immediate implications of this advent of the Trinity into human history by way of their missions should be noted at this point.

(i) *Nature-Grace Distinction.* This knowing and loving communion with the divine persons is the unexacted gift of God and nowise ingredient in the structures of man's own natural being. On our part, there is only gracious acceptance of God's knowing and loving of us as an extension of his eternal knowing and loving of himself.

A condition for this is God's previous positing of a universe of free creatures able to know and love the truth and goodness proportionate to their own level of existence in finite imitation of divine being. Beyond this is another giving not exigent in the first; this holds true even in fact of the truth that God would not have created man had he not intended to transfinalize human existence to a destiny with himself in his own Godhead. This new donative act is God's *self*-communication to the creature, in which he appropriates its nature and its history as his own, accomplished in the *Logos* ("and the Word became flesh"; *Jn.* 1:14) and in the *Pneuma* ("the Advocate, the Holy Spirit, whom the Father will send in my name"; *Jn.* 14:26). Here, man is enabled to enter into intersubjective union with God in the depths of his own uncreated trinitarian life—with the Father, Son, and Spirit who can only be communicated to the world as God. In creation, (apart from grace) by contrast, all that is possible is man's imitation, in a way proper to the structures of his natural being and person, of God in his nature known by reason as the first source and last end of creatures. This is only to note the necessity of maintaining the real distinction between what have been designated traditionally as the order of nature and the order of grace. Both are gratuitous—since no one can make a claim upon his own coming into existence—but differently so. On the level of nature, man participates in the divine being, but as it is imitable in finite ways; on the level of grace, he participates even in the uncreated mode of that being proper to God. To say that everything is grace (thus denying the distinction) is tantamount to saying that nothing is grace and is to render the word meaningless. This is clearer in the case of faith where to believe obviously presupposes credibility, which is judgment on a level prior to faith.[18] At the same time, to insist upon the gratuitousness of an order above the givenness of natural existence is to mark its formal distinction, not its historical separability from the latter. It is not to imply the rarity of grace, nor to suggest that it is not offered to all men; it is not to suggest that men were ever without grace.

(ii) *Indwelling of the Spirit.* Secondly, man's union with the triune God is ascribed to the Holy Spirit not as an appropriation but as proper to the Third Person. The mere presence of the *Pneuma* means loving union with God because the Third in God is personal love. He is himself the union of Father and Son and so if given to

---

[18]The observation is that of Aquinas; see *Summa theologiae*, II–II, q. 1, a. 4, ad 2.

men makes them to be, by his very personal presence, sharers in divine trinitarian life. What the Spirit accomplishes is a union of all believers with his own person, analogous to the union of the *Logos* with the single humanity of Jesus. The comparison is only analogous since the differences between the two are many and radical. Most obvious is that the union in Christ is of the ontic order; it is a union of natures though achieved on the level of person. Union with the *Pneuma*, by contrast, is not ontic in kind but intentional; it is not between natures but between persons who are united in a knowing-loving that forms them into the *ekklēsia* of God.

Among theological explanations regarding the manner of this abiding of the Spirit, the predominant one today is that inspired by Maurice de la Taille's theory of the incarnational union as "created actuation by Uncreated Act."[19] Rahner has worked out the application of this theory to the union in grace in more careful detail than others.[20] His explanation turns upon a presence of all three Persons in the soul as "quasi-formal causes" of salvational life. Some of the early Greek Fathers had conceived of this special sanctifying presence of God as the exclusive prerogative of the Spirit. Rahner does not pursue this possibility of a preeminent presence of the Spirit and is more concerned with insisting that all three Persons are present, each in a distinctive way. Others have emphasized the special role of the Spirit to the point of making the inhabitation exclusive to the Third Person—not denying thereby a presence of Father and *Logos* but reducing their presence to something derivative from that of the Spirit, and explained by the inseparability of the Three.[21]

This theory is well known and has been argued for and contested in numerous other studies. Thus it will suffice for present purposes to register a reservation on the category "quasi-formal causality." Certainly, it is necessary to understand these trinitarian presences

---

[19]Maurice de la Taille, "Actuation créée par Acte Incréée," *Recherches de Science Religieuse* 18 (1928), pp. 253–68.

[20]"Some Implications of the Scholastic Concept of Uncreated Grace," *Theological Investigations*, vol. 1, pp. 319–46. A similar theory was advanced independently by Malachi J. Donnelly esp. in "The Inhabitation of the Holy Spirit," *Proceedings of the Catholic Theological Society of America* (New York, 1949). For a detailed response to Rahner, see W. J. Hill, "Uncreated Grace: A Critique of Karl Rahner," *The Thomist* 26, single complete issue of 1963, entitled *Vatican II: The Theological Dimension*, pp. 333–56.

[21]David Coffey, "The Gift of the Holy Spirit," *Irish Theological Quarterly* 38, no. 3 (July 1971), pp. 202–23; Robert Faricy, "The Trinitarian Indwelling," *The Thomist* 35, no. 3 (July 1971), pp. 369–404.

as proper and distinctive to each of the Three and not to dismiss them as mere instances of appropriation. Some kind of personal communication and distinct intersubjective relationship needs to be allowed. But to explain this in terms of a quasi-formal influx of a divine person risks reducing the role of person to that of form. A person cannot be a form in any proper sense. Form belongs rather to the realm of essence and is a determinative principle of composite being which can be "had" only as constituting an intrinsic aspect of the receiving subject's own being. Divine being, however, as the pure act of "to be," is transcendent over all form; moreover, it is transcendent over all composition (ontological or logical) so that it cannot enter into composition with the creature.[22] The prefix "quasi" means to avoid all such implication, conveying the notion of a form that does not inform but only actuates. The explanation of Rahner and others, then, does not intend to suggest that a divine *hypostasis* exerts some kind of formal, hence essential, determination, but only that a divine person by its very presence renders the soul actual or existent vis-à-vis itself. To actuate means to render existent, either simply so (to be rather than to not-be) or in some determinate way (to be in this way rather than in some other way). And this is exactly what person is and does: it signifies the ultimate subject of the act of existing whereby some nature is, either absolutely or in some qualified way. But the correlative concept of nature, either substantial or accidental, is indispensable.

Thus, the *Logos* renders the humanity of Jesus existent, but as enhypostatic in that Word; the Word of God communicates existence *simpliciter* to that humanity so that it exists as the humanity of God. Here is indeed a genuine instance of an actuation that is not an information. Obviously the union with the Trinity in grace cannot be of this sort. In Rahner's theory it is explained as one in which the Persons function as "quasi-forms" affecting the soul in an ontological way; since there is no question here of other instances of the hypostatic union, this can only be accidental in kind. This single created actuation—created grace in short—really involves (for Rahner) three modally distinct terms within the soul, each a created affecting of the soul by a distinct divine Person. But this cannot be accounted for by the mere presence of the uncreated Persons; if so, such created actuation would be surreptitiously an information despite Rahner's disclaimer to the contrary, i.e., it would make God a structural element in the intrinsic constitution

---

[22] Aquinas, *Summa theologiae*, I, q. 3.

of the finite. (This is not true in the case of the Incarnation because there the humanity has no existence of its own prior to and apart from that given to it by the Word.) But the transformation of the soul at issue here rather has to be accounted for in terms of some created quality or form intrinsic to the soul. This demands, of course, a logically prior presence of the Trinity in the soul, but under the formality of exercising a common causality. What is at work here is better seen as a common agency of all three Persons than as what Rahner ambiguously terms "quasi-formal" causality. Once energized with a created participation in God's own nature, the soul is then able to relate to the uncreated Persons precisely as distinct subject-terms of its own knowing and loving. This is in marked contrast with Rahner's explanation wherein distinct relations to the Three in God are achieved in the ontic order prior to all knowing and loving.

In accord with Rahner's theory is his preference for speaking of the immanent Trinity in terms of "three distinct modes of subsisting" rather than of three persons.[23] Such thought is not entirely free of an Idealist cast: Being is Spirit, and Spirit (God) posits the other (man) *as its own reality*, rather than as a reality that exists in its own right as creature (see Chapter Five). Idealist thought tends to be essentialistic, reducing efficient causality to emanation, replacing analogy with dialectics in the knowing of God, and seemingly reifying the notion of person, i.e., seeing the latter as something that exists in its own right rather than solely by way of some nature.

At any rate, Rahner gives uncreated grace *logical* priority over created grace (there can be no question as to its ontological priority); grace is first of all the very presence of the Persons, formally as Three rather than causally as one, before it is a transformation of the soul that orients the finite person towards the Trinity. Yet it is only when created grace is allowed its prior function—as created gift—that the persons are freed to be seen precisely as persons. A "quasi-formal causality" theory leaves the soul passive and inoperative in the union with God which thereby loses its dynamic dialogic character. A richer concept is that of a pure relationality between infinite Persons and finite persons which can occur only within the perspective of a common nature—one subsistent in God in which rational creatures participate through the gift of grace. Thus, it

---

[23]See *The Trinity* (New York: Herder and Herder, 1970), pp. 112–13. In *Encyclopedia of Theology: The Concise Sacramentum Mundi*, ed. by Rahner (New York: Seabury Press, 1975), p. 1770, he prefers "ways of subsisting."

would seem advisable to surmount the difficulties in the above explanation by transferring the discussion from the ontological order to the intentional order, wherein the persons are regarded not after the fashion of quasi-forms but simply as "terms" in knowing and loving. In this way all *causal* activity upon finite persons is exercised by the Three through the commonality of their nature. Then, at the interior of this causal scheme, the persons communicate themselves in the sense of offering themselves to be known and loved in their personal distinctness. This is accomplished by an extension of their inner relating to one another to include finite persons and is the import of Aquinas's teaching that "the Holy Spirit is the love whereby the Father loves the Son, and also the love whereby he loves the creature."[24] This obviates any proper causality on the part of the Persons and yet allows for a truly interpersonal union with them in their hypostatic uniqueness.

At this point, what is at best a pure speculation might be ventured. Trinitarian relating (as noted earlier in Chapter Nine) is conceivable as notional acts of distinct divine subjects. Personality means relationality to others. On the human level this occurs in the depths of freedom wherein the person is not simply a given but something continuously achieved as the subject's enactment of self. Intersubjectivity is thus dependent upon the degree to which persons unveil, communicate, and commit themselves to others—as well as choose to respond to the self-bestowal of others. There is surely no reason why such personal becoming cannot be undergone in relationality to the three Persons of divinity. But is there any reason to deny that God himself, remaining immutable in his nature, can choose *to become on the level of personhood?* May not God choose to relate as he will to a community of finite persons with the free intentionality of intimate knowing and loving, becoming towards men the kind of God his love elects? God's love lets the finite person be in its very otherness, in its freedom and becoming. As it enacts itself, God's awareness of it must alter; he must come to know and love what he did not know and love before as actual in a finite way. This seemingly bespeaks a "becoming" in God within the domain of intentionality analogous at least to the personal becoming of men—once again, however, without implying acquisition by God of intrinsic perfection previously lacking to him. Perhaps to try and speak of becoming in God in this fashion—that is to say, in trinitarian terms which allow such becoming in the interpersonal order of intention-

---

[24]I *Sent.*, d. 14, q. 1, a. 1, sol.

ality while at the same time denying it in the ontic order of God's immutable nature—is to attempt to say too much. Wittgenstein warns us of things that cannot be said and of the need at such times to remain silent. And this echoes the "agnosticism" of Aquinas's tract on God: "Because we are unable to know what God is but only what he is not, we are able to reflect only upon the ways in which God is not, rather than the ways in which he is" (*Summa theologiae*, I, prologue to question 3). But at least we can say: should this loving exchange be at all a possibility, its language will be rooted in a symbolism of person rather than a metaphysics of being. Such language is at bottom prayer; it is the speech of mystics and prophets rather than of theologians.

Nonetheless, if such a personal relating of the divine Persons to men is possible, it must respect the order that prevails within the immanent Trinity. The Father can communicate himself only through the Son and in the Spirit. Indeed, just as for the Father and Son to communicate themselves *ad intra* is to spirate the *Pneuma*, so to communicate themselves *ad extra* is to give the Spirit as Gift. Seemingly, an implication of this is that the graced soul relates to the Trinity in inverse order: first to the Spirit, then to the Son, and lastly to the Father. If so, this explains the preeminence given to the Spirit in all questions of God's *presence*. Of the Spirit alone it can be said that in relating to him we are bound to God in the union of love which always retains a certain priority in our relationships to God.[25] What this suggests is a priority of the Spirit over the Son in the missions *ad extra*. The ground for this is simply the primacy of divine love in all negotiations with creatures. The Bible symbolically identifies the One who hovers over the Void at creation, and who is thus the source of revelation through the cosmos, as the Spirit. The infancy narratives employ the image of the Spirit overshadowing Mary at the conception of Jesus. If God's becoming man is a grace-event, having no motivation beyond that of God's love for mankind, then the first gift extended to us is divine love itself, which in trinitarian terms is that person of love who is the *Pneuma*. Our adoption as sons, in its turn, is likewise inaugurated by the Spirit who cries out in us "*Abba,* Father" (*Romans* 8:15), the Spirit-inspired prayer of Jesus himself in the garden of Gethsemane.

---

[25]Note can be taken here of Aquinas's observation that "the very act of believing is an act of the intellect assenting to divine truth but under a propulsion coming from the will moved by God through grace." *Summa theologiae*, II–II, q. 2, a. 9.

IDENTITY OF THE *PNEUMA*-PARACLETE: FURTHER CLUES

Spirit as Divine Immanence. "Spirit" is a central symbol in biblical literature and nearly always bears a divine connotation, as in the *Ruah Yahweh* of the Old Testament and the Holy Spirit *(Pneuma Hagion)* of the New. In differentiation from other names for the deity, it conveys the sense of God's immanence within history and (derivative from this) within creation. As *divine* immanence it carries the prevailing notion of presence by way of creative and transforming power. *Ruah* and *Pneuma,* in spite of significant differences, agree in denoting God as active and effective, and moreover, in a fashion proper to God alone. *Genesis* (1:2) explicitly describes the *Ruah Yahweh* as creative, and the Psalms (e.g., 104:29) refer to it in the imagery of life-giving breath. If it usually occurs as a transient activity of God, this is to forestall any interpretation of the *Ruah* as a sustaining power indigenous to nature, rather than as an intervention of God from beyond the universe of creatures. Most frequently, this divine presence plays a prophetic role. This shifts attention to the future and allows the Spirit to be seen eventually in a Messianic and eschatological context. This becomes pronounced in the New Testament, in which the Spirit is the Spirit "of Jesus" *(Acts* 16:7; *Phil.* 1:19), "of Christ" *(Rom.* 8:9), and "of the Son" *(Gal.* 4:6), who is himself the eschatological prophet and the bearer of the Spirit. While the christological context is new, it would seem (clearly from Luke at any rate) that the Spirit is not other than what the Old Testament knows as *Ruah Yahweh.*[26]

Paul thinks in terms of this Spirit as now embodied in the risen Christ *(sōma pneumatikon; I Cor.* 15:44)—significantly, his identification of the Spirit with Christ is never an identification with the historical Jesus—but it is still the power of God poured forth from there upon believers. In both Paul and John, *pneuma* means the sphere of God's saving influence, set over against *sarx* as the realm of what has not come under that power. Although Spirit occasionally appears as an impersonal noun in both Testaments, it is hardly questionable that oftentimes it is clearly meant to be taken person-

---

[26]See Eduard Schweizer, "The Spirit of Power," *Interpretation* 6, no. 3 (July 1952): "The distinction between this and the Old Testament Jewish concept rests only in the fact that here this power is no longer given to individuals, but to the whole community" (p. 268).

ally, but then only as a symbol for the transcendent agency of God and certainly not as expressing a personhood somehow distinct within the Godhead. Any explicit suggestion of a real distinction in person of Spirit from Yahweh-God or the Father, as well as from Christ, is lacking. Only in the relatively late Fourth Gospel, overlaid with Church constructions, is it reasonable to detect—on such basis as John's reference to "another Paraclete" (*Jn.* 1:16; *I Jn.* 2:1)—an implicit opening to such an understanding. What is rather the case is that *Pneuma* in the New Testament is a symbolic expression articulating a people's religious experience of God's active immanence within their history. It does not take cognizance of a later alien and speculative question concerning distinct personhood. But, as symbol, neither is its evocative power closed off to such later ventures of understanding. Edmund Dobbin makes this point in observing that the symbolic character of the term explains its use as both an impersonal and personal category and "ought to caution us against an exclusive and premature application of either category to this mystery."[27] The meaning that does well up spontaneously with the symbol is that of "an experience of being taken hold of by a mysterious power, of being overwhelmed or inspired or directed or moved by a supernatural force"; thus "for Paul *Pneuma* is a term which is symbolically expressive of the divine power which is the source of the new life experienced through faith in the risen Christ"; while in John that experience is not merely attributed to the Spirit but actually identified with the Spirit (4:10; 7:39; 20:22).[28] In New Testament usage, then, Holy Spirit conveys the immanence of God, an active presence taken as identical with God's own personal reality, but it remains neutral as yet to the question concerning a distinct *hypostasis* in God.

Spirit as Source of Life. Pannenberg, exploiting further this approach to the Holy Spirit in terms of divine immanence and active presence, notes that the biblical use of "spirit" pivots on the phe-

---

[27]"Towards a Theology of the Holy Spirit," *Heythrop Journal* 17, no. 1 (January 1976), p. 18. Part II of this article appeared in the subsequent issue (April 1976), pp. 129–49.

[28]Dobbin, pp. 16 & 17, citing from J.D.G. Dunn, "I Corinthians 15:45— Last Adam, Life-giving Spirit." *Christ and the Spirit in the New Testament,* ed. B. Lindars & B. Smalley (Cambridge: At the University Press, 1973), pp. 127–41.

nomenon of life.[29] Life is a function of spirit; it is not a property of the organism but something accruing gratuitously to the organism from spirit as the origin of all life. Thus, the implication of divinity is uppermost from the very beginning. The human spirit is an off-shoot of the uncreated and creative Spirit who "breathed into his [man's] nostrils the breath of life" (*Gen.* 2:7); the identical Hebrew term *ruah* is used for both. Psalm 104 proclaims "when you send forth your spirit (breathe into them), they recover" (v. 29). Christian usage in the New Testament simply appropriates this in a more particular way, most specifically in understanding life as above all the new life given to the resurrected body of Christ by the Spirit, making it a *sōma pneumatikon* (*I Cor.* 15:44), and promised to us. Pannenberg thus adopts the Pauline view which, in effect, identifies the Holy Spirit with the new life already actual in the risen Christ. That life is life in unity with the origin of all life; moreover, it is one that manifests its creative (life-giving) resources *historically.* Man achieves the newness of life held out to him by God in terms of his temporality; such newness of life is identical with the future. Spirit then means God, present in the depths of man's being, luring him to self-transcendence, in the sense of calling him out of the present into the future. Here Pannenberg is using Spirit to symbolize both God's immanence and his transcendence. Man is summoned from within but to the beyond. Transcending the limits of present existence is precisely participating in the Holy Spirit.

What Pannenberg describes, however, is more the Christian's participation in divine love, as essential and identical with God's nature, rather than union with a distinct divine *hypostasis.* It is an explanation which tends to reduce the Trinity to the formal structure of God's historical dealing with mankind. It illumines what earlier theology had sought to express by *appropriating* essential divine love to the Third Person. But it neutralizes the specifically trinitarian dimension: the *Pneuma* is God and so personal, but not a distinct person in God; the love at issue is not the mutual love of Father and Son that is itself hypostatic. The believer, surrendered to that love, is not thereby an adoptive son of the Father with the eternal Son in their Spirit. The sharer in God's gratuitous and saving love has

---

[29]Wolfhart Pannenberg, "The Working of the Spirit in the Creation and in the People of God," Wolfhart Pannenberg, Avery Dulles, and Carl Braaten, *Spirit, Faith and Church* (Philadelphia: Westminster Press, 1970); also W. Pannenberg, "The Doctrine of the Spirit and the Task of a Theology of Nature," *Theology* 75, no. 619 (January 1972), pp. 8–21.

newness of life, but is not brought thereby into the life of the divine *koinōnia*. Pannenberg attempts to compensate for this by minimizing the distinction between divine and human spirit; that distinction is blurred almost to the point of obliteration once the Holy Spirit takes root in man.[30] If he can defend this against a proclivity towards pantheism—on the grounds that the drive to self-transcendence is not natural to man—he seemingly has to settle for a panentheistic bias that obscures the distinction between spirit in its finite and its infinite modes. Much of this can be laid to Pannenberg's tendency to view causality in terms of the future's impinging upon the present, a view that leads ultimately to a historical merging of the finite and the infinite. This precludes any view of the Holy Spirit and the human spirit as absolutely distinct in their respective personhoods. Yet only in this way can the unity between them not impinge upon the autonomy and creatureliness of finite persons. Seemingly, it makes more sense to speak of an intentional unity in affective knowledge and love, that is, a true interpersonal relationship. On this view, what Pannenberg considers as an assimilation of finite and infinite spirit can be seen rather as the creature's participation in the divine *nature* by way of grace, in which the creature far from being absorbed comes to its full maturity as finite person.

Spirit as Distinct Personal Presence. The Fourth Gospel's use of Paraclete as a synonym for *Pneuma* is an initial clue that the Spirit might be distinct from Father and Son. As masculine in gender, the name, usually translated as "Advocate," or "One who pleads," implies a personal agency that is lacking in the neuter name *Pneuma*. (In some Syriac versions, the Greek *Pneuma* is rendered rather by a name that is feminine in gender.) Moreover, John's reference to *"another* Paraclete" (14:16) suggests one who is other than Christ in the nature of his mission and so is a personal agent. But this is clearly a gradual development and was not so understood from the beginning. There is next to nothing by way of an explicit doctrine of the Spirit in the Synoptics, and not only there, but in Paul and John as well, the word is frequently used in an impersonal sense. John himself apparently offers an explanation for this when he writes that "there was no Spirit as yet because Jesus had not yet been glorified" (7:39). The Spirit, in short, is the "Spirit of Jesus" (*Acts* 16:7); it signifies the continuation of all that Jesus stands for but less by way of per-

---

[30]"The Working of the Spirit in the Creation and in the People of God," p. 21.

sonal presence than by way of power or energy stemming from the now glorified Lord. This suggests a simple identification of the Spirit with the mode of existence Christ enjoys after his death. But, in fact, that identity is not made explicitly, if one looks to the overarching import of the New Testament. The centrality that Luke affords the Ascension, for example, indicates that for him Jesus is no longer with men on earth; he is not "spiritually" present in this world, but is in glory at the right hand of the Father both personally and (if we attend to the Easter stories) corporally. It is the Spirit who is present to believers. The Spirit is the One who descended upon Jesus before the Ascension to make possible his saving mission, and now after the Ascension descends upon the Church to entrust it with that same mission. Jesus, who was in his earthly ministry the bearer of the Spirit, is now rather the sender of the Spirit.

"Spirit" conveys for all the New Testament writers the sense of divine agency, that is to say, an agency that in the final analysis is not other than God himself. From the beginning, that agency (and so the Spirit as either that agency or its source) is understood as personal; it is God himself encountering and communicating with men on the level of consciousness. Luke's religious thought manifests a subtlety that does not allow him simply to identify this Spirit with the *Logos* in Jesus; the Spirit is "another" from the risen Christ. As Christians experience the workings of the Spirit within the community, as its history brings it into novel situations, this awareness of the distinct identity of the Spirit becomes more pronounced. And this experience leads gradually to an awareness of distinction, not only from the Son whose work he continues, but also from the Father who sends him through the Son. God's active presence in history—a history whose horizon has been set by the Resurrection of Jesus, but which remains an open history and a human project—is not in the "person" of the Father but in the "person" of the Spirit. The differentiation of the *Logos* from the Father was easier to grasp—because of the appearance of the former in and as the man Jesus. But if this leads to understanding that the *Logos* is God without being the Father, then the way is open to seeing the Spirit as a Third in God. The only viable alternative to this would seem to be the atrinitarian one which makes the humanity alone the ground for distinguishing Father and Son. Attempts to explain this growing faith-awareness on the part of early Christians are varied; noteworthy among them, however, is one that turns on viewing the emerging Church as the new *Shekinah Yahweh*, the dwelling place of God (see Chapter One).

Mission of the Spirit: Three Traits. The work of the Spirit is distinctive in a variety of ways. It will suffice for present purposes to single out, briefly, three such distinguishing characteristics that suggest the Spirit's own identity. These are the marks of interiority, anonymity, and community formation. (i) First, the mission of the Spirit, who comes unbidden and "breathes where he will," is accomplished, in contrast to that of the Word made visible flesh, in inwardness and invisibility. Unlike the *Logos*, the *Pneuma* is not the Father's self-expression, is not in Rahner's phrase the "real symbol" of the Father. As *Spiritus*, his office is that of inspiration—a forceful but nonviolent motion that, though coming from without, moves in accord with principles that are interior and spontaneous, in concert with our liberty. We are aware of another at work within us; we live from a personal center that is not our own self (Pannenberg), when, in St. Paul's phrase, the Spirit "lays fast hold of us" (*synantilambanomai*). This trait of inwardness or interiority by no means suggests anything private in the Spirit's activity; rather, it implies that what does transpire does so on a deeply personal level, but of persons in relation. Whereas the Word uttered to men is marked by a certain objectivity and historical givenness that confronts the mind, the role of the Spirit appears more as an appropriation of the subjectivities of men who, having heard that Word, face the open future.

(ii) Secondly, the mission is accomplished in a certain anonymity. The Spirit has no doctrine of his own; he effaces himself, as it were, behind *the* Word. "When the Spirit of truth comes . . . he will not be speaking as from himself but will say only what he has learnt" (*Jn.* 16:13). His role is not the expressive, manifestive, thematic one proper to Word or Image, but the motivational and unitive one proper to love and commitment. As the Spirit unites the eternal Son and the Father so does he unite adoptive sons to the Father, through the only-begotten Son, in the freedom of love. If the Son is made manifest and humanly available in the earthly life of Jesus, the impulses coming from the Spirit gain visibility rather by way of the symbols of the ecclesial community—though, even here, the material content of such articulation, its cognitive referent, remains christological. Fully human existence demands not only word but silence, not only speech but listening; we seek not only to grasp ultimate truth in form and concept, but to allow that truth to grasp us in formlessness and evocative symbol. The former looks to the Word identified as this man Jesus; the latter looks rather to the Spirit who "groans within us" in anonymity.

This anonymity makes understandable that the Spirit appears at times to be identical with human freedom in historical deployment towards its fulfillment. What obviates this confusion between the Holy Spirit and our spirit is reflection upon the unexactedness of that fulfillment. St. Paul's reference to the advent of the *Pneuma* as a "pledge" or "earnest" points to the distinctness of the Spirit as a sort of down payment towards his actualizing within the histories of our spirits what God has already accomplished in the history of his Incarnate Son. At the same time, our obedience to the Spirit's "laying hold of us" is always consciously and freely ratified and so makes us in a sense "co-creators" of our own history as what Paul calls a "new creation." What we receive from the Spirit is less a given than a summons to appropriate the salvation offered historically in and through our free choices; thus is the Spirit ever the Spirit of freedom.

(iii) Lastly, the effect of the Spirit's presence among us is the binding into community. As the oneness in love of the Father and Son, the Spirit is the unitive source of the oneness of believers with God and so with one another. He is a Presence, but an active, living, efficacious presence, creative of a fellowship of love. The reality of personhood lies in relationality, and the divine *Pneuma* achieves this on both a vertical and a horizontal level, bringing men into the sharing of a common life which (in imitation of the Trinity) is a unity in plurality. We become persons in relation by virtue of the very presence of the one Holy Spirit who binds Christians to the Father through Christ and thereby to one another. Thus Peter Lombard, as also some of the Eastern Fathers, thought that our love for God (*caritas, agapē*) is not a created gift at all, but the very person of the uncreated Spirit.

GIFTS OF THE SPIRIT: THE ECCLESIAL CONTEXT

Medieval theology of the Spirit was elaborated largely in terms of what St. Paul calls "the gifts of the Spirit" (*I Cor.* 1:7) and gave birth to an ingenious construction based on an interpretation of *Isaiah* 11:2-3, in light of scattered references throughout the New Testament to particular effects ascribed to the Holy Spirit. Aquinas notes that the predominant characteristic of the New Law or Covenant in general is "the very grace of the Holy Spirit . . . in which its whole power consists."[31] The Gifts were understood as concrete and specific particularizations of this grace. Their sevenfold number meant

---

[31]*Summa theologiae,* I–II, q. 106, a. 1.

to convey only a symbolic plenitude; though Isaiah lists only six, a seventh was taken from verse 4 to accord with the biblical number seven. They were categorized as created dispositions of the soul, energizing the converted consciousness so as to make possible its intersubjective encounter with the Trinity, its responsiveness to the Creator-Spirit who "breathes where he will." The Gifts amounted to habits of docility (the medieval sense of "habit" being "aptitude" and "inclination"; and docility coming from the Latin *docere*) whereby the soul remained open to promptings of divine origin. This affecting of the soul rendered possible a level of intentionality that surpassed the strictly human. Thus, the Gifts were distinguished from even the infused virtues in that the former functioned in an intuitive way whereas the latter depended upon the processes of rational, discursive deliberation. To take but one example, the Gift of Wisdom was taken to be a knowing by connaturality, arising out of a love for God in which the very love acts as a formal medium for the knowledge; it was a love-knowledge, akin to the sort of knowing at work in aesthetic experience but surpassing that in virtue of its being an awareness of person. Aquinas called it a "quasi-experiential knowledge" because it welled up from the very presentiality of the beloved; Bonaventure described it with the illuminating word "contuition."

These perduring dispositions of the Christian heart resulted from the common causality of the divine Persons, but betrayed a mysterious affinity to the distinct hypostatic characters of each of the Three. Theology's discernment of these affinities was a creative instance of the theory of appropriation, worked out on the basis of an exemplarity whereby the distinctions between the Persons were imprinted upon the graced soul. Strictly speaking, a person acts *according to* an exemplar but his own personhood, precisely because it is something other than form, cannot function *as* an exemplar. We are here obviously up against the limits of language. But one way of dealing with the distinction between Word and Spirit, for example, is by shifting to an alien key and declaring that distinction to be *something like* the distinction between knowledge and love. The mystery of person, as well as that of existence, exceeds whatever cognitive hold we have on it; we speak of both in terms of what is better known, namely, form, whereas they are in truth something more elusive, that is, the subject of the form and the act whereby it is.

More to the point, however, is that these transformations of the soul that held it in a state of readiness towards the initiatives of divinity made possible an objective encounter with the divine persons themselves—objective, because they were reached to, through the Gifts, as terms of knowledge and love.[32] The *Letter to the Romans* (5:5) suggests both these aspects (that of exemplarity appropriated to a divine person and of personal indwelling of a divine person that is not merely appropriated) when it speaks of "the love of God poured out in our hearts by the Holy Spirit, who is given to us." This living in consort with the Trinity is rooted ultimately in charity as love of friendship for God. But that love, as a grace, is in its source the Holy Spirit as the mutual and personal love between Father and Son. Thus, a certain preeminence attaches to the indwelling presence of the Spirit. Aquinas, for one, makes clear that this presence of the Spirit is not a mere appropriation; the love in question, then, is not essential divine love but love *proceeding*, relational love, or love as a divine *hypostasis*. It is "Love taken as comprising the proper name of the Holy Spirit, just as Word is the proper name of the Son."[33] This amounts then to a "possession" of the soul by the Spirit, who moves it after the fashion of an "interior instinct," analogous to the instinct of nature.[34] The horizons of finite liberty are now opened out onto the horizons of uncreated liberty. Clearly at work here is an understanding of the finite person that is far removed from that which becomes dominant in the West after Descartes, in which the human person is an isolated self or empirical ego.

---

[32]This represents the common teaching of medieval theologians. Thus Aquinas speaks of the missions as terminating in "a special presence [of the persons sent] that is in accord with the nature of an intelligent being, in whom God is said to be present as the known in the knower and the beloved in the lover." *Summa theologiae*, I, q. 43, a. 3. This presence is formally of the intentional order, not of the ontic order.

[33]Ibid., q. 37, a. 1; later in treating of the missions, Aquinas makes clear that God's love is both created grace and uncreated grace: "Saving grace not only enables the rational creature to function according to a created benefaction, but even to enjoy a loving union with a divine person." Ibid., q. 43, a. 3, ad 1.

[34]In commenting on *Romans* 8:14, Aquinas observes that "the spiritual man is inclined to act, not primarily from the movement of his own will, but from the prompting of the Holy Spirit (*ex instinctu Spiritus Sancti*)." *In Ep. ad Romanos*, VIII, lect. 3. For a detailed development of Aquinas's understanding of how the Spirit moves by way of the Gifts, see Edward D. O'Connor, *The Gifts of the Spirit*, vol. 24 of *St. Thomas Aquinas Summa Theologiae* (London: Eyre & Spottiswoode; New York: McGraw-Hill, 1973), Appendices 4, 5, & 6.

But this medieval theology of the Gifts, for all its richness, suffered two significant limitations: it was looked upon as a phenomenon restricted to the soul of the individual believer; and it was articulated solely within the framework of an Aristotelian psychology of the soul and its faculties. Lacking was a philosophical environment that could carry the discussion beyond the cosmological and psychological orders into the social and historical orders. Anthony Kelly has attempted to supply this development, suggesting two promising lines of thought: (i) first, an understanding of the Gifts, in the context of a different cognitional theory, transposing them from the faculty psychology of Aristotle and Aquinas to the "horizon analysis" of Lonergan and others; (ii) secondly, an awareness of the activity of the Holy Spirit as having its locus not in the individual but within the communal sphere of the ecclesial community.[35] The first of these recommendations enables theology to break out of the narrow confines of psychology. It enables Lonergan, for example, to speak of grace, not as an entitative habit of the soul, but as the finite person's entrance into "a world of immediacy" with God, as being in love with Transcendent Personal Mystery.[36] This highlights the receptive sharing in divine spontaneity as a "conversion" in which there occurs a deployment of liberty that is radically new in being exercised on a vertical rather than horizontal plane. Such categories make clearer to the contemporary mind, perhaps, the surmounting of perspectives humanly available to man, the dismantling of former horizons, that can take place in existential response to the Spirit.

But Kelly's second suggestion is even more to the point—namely, that the doctrine of the Gifts can be more richly exploited in an ecclesial context. Here, the consciousness whose horizon is transformed by the Spirit is communal rather than individual. The *Pneuma* both transforms natures and unites the persons of such natures to himself. But the first achievement is only appropriated to the Third Person whereas the second is proper to him, an immediate effect of his mere presence. Clearly, both workings of the Spirit are something real only within believers, but it is real within them not as individuals but as persons. The former concept bespeaks only discrete instantiations of a common nature, and its

---

[35]Anthony J. Kelly, "The Gifts of the Spirit: Aquinas and the Modern Context," *The Thomist* 38, no. 2 (April 1974), pp. 193–231.

[36]Bernard J. F. Lonergan, *Method in Theology* (New York: Herder and Herder, 1972), p. 112.

root is matter; the latter bespeaks unique subjects who freely relate to others within a shared nature, thereby constituting social reality, and its root is spirit. The Holy Spirit is active within believers, then, as they constitute the community of believers which is the New Creation, the *ekklēsia*. In uniting men to God, the Spirit unites them to one another. In this way, the outpouring of the Spirit appears as the very constitution of the people of God as a community of trinitarian love. That outpouring is at once the sending of the Spirit by Father and Son and the Spirit's forming of the assembly of saved mankind. The New Creation is thus the immanence of God to humanity; that immanence, however, is the special prerogative of the Holy Spirit.

What the ecclesial perspective allows, in man's ongoing encounter with the living God, is a shift of emphasis to historicity and futurity. The domain of the Spirit is that of community, of a people's history; the sphere where his promptings are felt is that of corporate faith and love in which a people, graced with the power of self-determination, give shape to the future. The Holy Spirit thus means a capacity for self-transcendence, which, through the history of God's people, reaches beyond the boundaries of Christianity to universal history.

THE TRINITY AND NON-CHRISTIAN RELIGIOUS EXPERIENCE

If the Trinity is indeed a mystery of salvation, and if the will of God, who "wants everyone to be saved and reach full knowledge of the truth" (*I Tim.* 2:4), is truly salvific—then non-Christian religions raise a question that cannot be blithely ignored. If the God confessed by Christians is "the power over all that is" (Pannenberg) and not a god among the gods but the sole God there is, and if that God is a Trinity—then it should be possible to discern some semblance of that triunity in all religious experience that is genuine. Yet such experience outside Christianity is not expressed in trinitarian terms. Part of the explanation lies in the distinction between religious experience and its articulation into symbol and idea. It must be granted that the former allows for encounter with God in which some elements remain anonymous and do not find their way into formulations. If the encounter is genuine, however, as in authentic prayer, this bespeaks a divine initiative in which God can communicate himself only as he is. The life of grace, then, means an experience of the tripersonal God. No attempt will be made in what follows to explore such experience in depth or detail. This has already been done elsewhere by those versed in, and in some cases committed to, such experiences. Yet very few attempts have been made to relate Christianity to other religions from an explicitly trinitarian perspective. Among exceptions to this are two notable studies by Raimundo Panikkar and Ewert Cousins.[37] Concern here will be limited therefore to the problem raised by the absence of any trinitarian dimension to such religious phenomena—in light of the Christian understanding that it is precisely God's triunity that explains his self-communication to men.

Hinduism and Buddhism. If reality discloses itself to human consciousness, and reality is grounded in a tripersonal God, then the symbols that mediate and articulate such disclosure must speak, however anonymously, of Father, Son, and Spirit. This dictates Panikkar's conclusion that:

> It is simply an unwarranted overstatement to affirm that the trinitarian conception of the Ultimate, and with it of the whole of reality, is an exlusive Christian insight or revelation.[38]

Panikkar feels able to confirm this thesis on the basis of his own appreciation of (especially) Hindu religion. The feeling persists that his instinct is right and that the doctrine of the Trinity offers richest promise as a meeting ground of the religions, that it is the "juncture where the authentic spiritual dimensions of all religions meet" (p. 42). Yet in spite of his religious sensitivity, this appears at times overly sanguine—granted that both of the great religious traditions of the East, Buddhism and Hinduism, tend to shy away from any notion of deity as personal, much less tripersonal. On the other hand, that very reluctance can serve as a caveat against the Western

---

[37] Raimundo Panikkar, *The Trinity and the Religious Experience of Man* (New York: Maryknoll, Orbis Books; London: Darton, Longman, and Todd, 1973); Ewert Cousins, "The Trinity and World Religions," *Journal of Ecumenical Studies* 7 (1970), pp. 476–98. For comparative studies in areas other than the trinitarian, see the bibliography by J. Masson, "Le Chrétien devant le Yoga et le Zen," *Nouvelle Revue Théologique* 94 (1972), pp. 384–99. Helpful studies are William Johnston, "Zen and Christian Mysticism," *International Philosophical Quarterly* 7, no. 3 (September 1976), pp. 441–69, and Kakichi Kadowaki, "Ways of Knowing: A Buddhist-Thomist Dialogue," *International Philosophical Quarterly* 6, no. 4 (December 1966), pp. 574–95; significant in the area of Christology is John B. Cobb, Jr., *Christ in a Pluralistic Age* (Philadelphia: Westminster Press, 1975).

[38] Panikkar, p. viii.

temptation to indulge in anthropomorphic thought; and, if it does, it may neutralize to some degree what otherwise would be an insurmountable difference. The metaphysical and psychological concept "person" has in Western thought a precision and density that is lacking in Oriental philosophy. Still, both major language groups (of Buddhist and Hindu religion) know the pronouns "I," "you," "he," "she," "we," etc., and yet eschew their applicability to the divine. This, however, is less a specific denial that God is personal than a denial of *all* concretion and determination to deity. The lesson for Christians in this is to remind us that God is more truly transpersonal. James Dupuis has suggested that this is indeed the intentionality of Eastern religion by noting that the Hindu doctrine of the *Trimūrti*, for example, posits plurality in God; while this plurality appears as one of modes on the level of concepts, the Hindu believer goes on to personify it.[39] Nothing prohibits a Christian from interpreting this as an approach to the mystery of the Trinity at the level of mythological expression, an experience of the divine presence in the cosmos in which there occurs what might be called "a religious presentiment" of the Trinity.

As illustrative of this, Dupuis observes that the *Nirguna Brahman* of Hindu religion is described in the *Saccidānanda* as the divine *by* himself (*Sat*), *in* himself (*Sit*), and *for* himself (*Ānanda*).[40] This vividly calls to mind the "above all, through all, in all" of *Ephesians* 4:6, which has a long history of trinitarian application. Panikkar reads this Pauline text as presenting the Father, Son, and Spirit as respectively divine Source, Being, and Return—a reading in which its parallels to the Hindu text are clear. Panikkar himself, however, prefers to make a different adaptation. He suggests that the apophatic Absolute of Buddhism, the totally other that lies beyond both affirmation and negation, answers to what the Christian symbolizes as God the Father ("above all"). Similarly, the All of Hinduism, simultaneously transcending everything and immanent within (indeed, identical with) everything, approximates the Holy Spirit of Christians ("in all").[41] This opens up the possibility that other religions encounter divinity under a formality that Christians symbolize as one or another of the Three who are the Trinity. This is not to imply, of course, that the Persons, who are God inseparably, enter

[39]James Dupuis, *Jesus Christ and His Spirit* (Bangalore: Theological Publications in India, 1977), pp. 174–75.
[40]Ibid., p. 175.
[41]Panikkar, chapter II.

the limited religious experience of men in isolation from each other. Christian faith offers an immediate obstacle to such thinking—but the same faith opens the way to allowing for an experience of the divine in which there occurs in an anonymous way something parallel to what Christians explain as appropriation.

Surely, these are authentic religious experiences. As such, their origins are anthropological in the sense that the starting point must be man even if the terminal point is God. Moreover, part of the content of the experiences may well be their origination from God. A problem does arise, nonetheless, with the formulation of the experience. Here the basic mystery in Eastern religions appears to be the intersection of the infinite and the finite, that is, God's otherness from and yet proximity to man. This is to suggest that the Buddhist and Hindu concepts of deity turn, less upon trinitarian notions, than upon the transcendence-immanence axis, with the apophatic element seemingly more pronounced in Buddhism, while immanence and totality predominate in Hinduism. They converge in a flight from dualism, viewing God in theandric terms that affirm reality as at once completely divine and completely human. Such a God is: nonpersonal, necessarily related to the world, never without men, not creator of the world but ingredient within it, Spirit but never Word, beyond all possibility of incarnation, etc.

This reminds us of the radical differences that remain between Christianity and Eastern religions; this is certainly true where concepts of deity are concerned and suggests that the underlying experiences may manifest corresponding differences. Panikkar himself indicates that this Eastern theandric concept of God is in fact an alternative to the doctrine of the Trinity. The emphatic tendency in Buddhism and Hinduism continues to resist viewing the Absolute as a God who is Father, Son, and Spirit *in se*: "God is only God for the creature and with reference to it. God is not [God] for himself. . . . Without us and apart from our relation to him God would not be [God]" (p. 26). Such a notion asks "whether an exclusively personal conception of the godhead does justice to it" (p. 28), partly because it looks upon person as a category properly applicable only to humans and signifying "radical solitariness" (p. 51). From this it follows that "an immanent God cannot be a God-person, [someone] with whom I could have [personal] relationship, a God-Other" (p. 31).

Still, such religious experience remains an encounter with the God who is a Trinity, even if it is not an experience of God as Trinity. As such, it can contribute to a deepened understanding of what the Christian does, and does not, mean in confessing God as tripersonal.

For one thing, it can serve to disabuse Christians of false notions of divine personhood—here its role is much like the positive function of atheism in dispelling false ideas of deity. This is a caution against an anthropomorphic understanding of person when said of God, a particular temptation for those who confess the incarnation of God. Panikkar issues a caution that has to be taken seriously, "The thirst for *immanence* is the driving force behind personalism and its great temptation is anthropomorphism" (p. 24). To designate the eternal Word as the *hypostasis* of Jesus' humanity is not to attribute the traits of human personality to God. It is to speak in the only way we can, namely analogously, whether in a literal or figurative mode, about what remains unknown in itself; it is to name God relationally, that is, from the vantage point of what we do know, precisely because he remains unknown and unknowable in himself. Such words *truly* refer to divine reality (the symbols are not their own referent), but the nature of that reality eludes us. Eastern religion reminds us of this and sharpens our sense of how tenuous a cognitive hold we have upon the mystery who is God. By such routes, we are led to see that God is more transpersonal than personal, perhaps more illuminatingly spoken of as the Person(s) of persons, rather than simply as person.

Person is not a univocal concept; the divine Three are not distinct as mere individuations of a common nature—each of them is person in a unique sense, designated only by their proper names. Proper names identify but they do not represent because their referent is something self-positing, something that is a self-enactment out of the unfathomable depths of freedom. If the Christian confesses God as Word, the Hindu vision of Spirit reminds us that silence is the source of speech, that the Word originates from the Father who is not Utterance. Hindu literature draws attention to what it calls "egolessness," and this can serve to guard against the usurpations of the false self, the "ego," especially in our interpersonal relationships with God. In face of a Western fascination with the phenomenon of knowing that highlights the subject-object polarity, this Eastern attitude makes room for a primal, objectless awareness, in which consciousness stands open and receptive towards reality as it "gives itself" as gift. Anthony Kelly relates this to Heidegger's *Gelassenheit*: a detachment, a releasement from manipulative thinking for the sake of a contemplative stance towards the ultimately real that is a quite different experience of human intentionality.[42] By such primal

---

[42]Anthony Kelly, pp. 221ff.

thinking, man dwells in the world in an entirely new way, not now preoccupied with controlling things but—in conformity to the structure of his own being which Heidegger calls *Sorge* (care)—as rather "the shepherd of Being." This is surely an approximation to the Hindu and Zen experience.

The implications of this are genuinely trinitarian in kind. The identity of the true and authentic self with Spirit, for example, means overthrowing inauthentic individual life for genuine life in union with all. This is not entirely unlike the Christian conviction that the coming of the Holy Spirit is the overcoming of the realm of *sarx* and the entrance into the sphere of *pneuma*. Put differently, the Christian scheme of things understands that the Cross of Christ precedes the advent of the Spirit. Redemption is God's negating of inauthentic existence in the crucified humanity of his Son; it is the Spirit who raises mankind to authentic existence in the Resurrection of Christ. Thus St. Paul can note that the Holy Spirit dwells in us as "the Spirit of him who raised Jesus from the dead" (*Rom.* 8:11). Authentic life is life that has its ground in God as Spirit.

But it is the apophaticism of Eastern religion that is most revealing. This can serve as a balance against the spirit of nihilism that has become so pronounced a tendency within Christian thought in the West, by reminding us that the Primordial Silence out of which the Word of God comes to us is not Nothingness as a Void but the Absolute and the All. It is a Source that is not "exhausted" and rendered superfluous by the Word as if the divine utterance were a once-and-for-all occurrence in time rather than Event beyond time. Yet it can be spoken of only by way of the Word that gives it shape. The profoundest implication of this is that it helps us see that the doctrine of the Trinity is not a surreptitious tritheism. It achieves this by reminding us of the *order* that prevails among the persons. The Father alone is unoriginate; the Son at once takes origin from the Father and gives origin to their Spirit; the Spirit gives origin to none but returns all to the Father through the Son. Panikkar articulates this in a phrase that is as apt as it is concise:

> Neither the Son nor the Spirit is *God*, but, precisely, the Son of God and the Spirit of God, equal to the One God (*o theós*) as God (*theós*). (p. 45)

Further, he is quite right in adding "at this point, the inadequacy of the dialectic is clearly shown." But it need not follow from this (as he goes on to suggest) that we cannot speak of the Absolute at all in terms of unity, plurality, equality, etc. Unless we can speak at least dialectically or analogically the sole alternative is silence—but an empty silence that is sterile and devoid of any meaning rather than a silence pregnant with all meaning.

Israel and Islam. What the Christian finds lacking in Eastern religion is the kataphatic side, what Panikkar calls the iconolatrous, meaning God's objectivation of himself in Word and "form," and above all his unveiling of himself as person(s). This dimension is made explicit not only in Christianity, but in the other two major theistic religions as well, namely, Judaism and Islam. Here the ineffability of God in his transcendence (Buddhism), and his universality in his immanence (Hinduism), gain a necessary complement. Only in this way can the relativity of God and man be maintained without collapsing into relativism. Man is freed to be man, to be precisely nondivine; and yet at the same time, in what the Greek Fathers called *theōpoiēsis*, is drawn up into the most intimate of unions with God. This is a hallmark of Christianity far more than of Israel or Islam, and characterizes the Catholic tradition more than it does the Reformational. Part of the reason for this is that in Christianity alone is God confessed as a Trinity of persons and as self-communicating in virtue of this very structure. The God of Israel and Islam, by contrast, is a unipersonal God. The notion of divine personhood is strong in both religious traditions, but from a Christian standpoint relatively impoverished by the lack of a trinitarian doctrine. The Jewish God appears in man's world within finite realities such as the Ark of the Covenant, and under such mediating forms as Yahweh's *Dabar* and *Ruah*, but does not become man. Only a doctrine of distinct persons in God renders the latter possible and intelligible (any suggestion of man becoming God, as in some present-day Christologies "from below," is simply outside the ambit of Jewish credibility). The revelatory communications of God and his actions within history on which Judaism is founded stop short of God's becoming flesh precisely because this demands a divine Son who is not the Father. In Islam, God directs history through the Prophet but with a certain extrinsicism. Paradoxically, history is neither the open and creative project of mankind on the one hand, nor a history that God has assumed as his own, on the other. This is because it is less genuine history rooted in the interplay between divine and human freedom, than a course of events that appears necessary when viewed from Allah's side and merely contingent from man's.

The radical interrelationship of God with all that is—through men—is compromised when God is conceived in unitarian terms.

Clearly, this is a *theological* judgment, and by no means a reflection upon the *religious* convictions of those who stand committed to the traditions of Israel and Islam. Vatican Council II is emphatic on the salvific value of non-Christian religions.[43] It is only to make clear how radical a difference in meaning is conveyed by the trinitarian symbols for those who stand in the tradition they continue to mediate. It is only to suggest that if Christ is, in his dying and rising, the definitive Word of God to man, then there is meaning there not available elsewhere. At the same time, the confession of God as Father, Word, and Spirit must find some touchstone of truth in all genuine religious experience outside Christianity. No matter how difficult to decipher, genuine religious symbols must speak of the sole God of the one human family. As symbols, they are polyvalent; they embody a surplus of meaning within whose depths lies concealed the center towards which all religious symbols converge.

---

[43]See Vatican Council II, *Lumen Gentium*, no. 16; *Gaudium et Spes*, no. 22; *Ad Gentes*, no. 7.

SELECT BIBLIOGRAPHY

Alexander of Hales. *S. Theol.* Critical ed. of B. Klumper. Quaracchi, Italy: Collegium S. Benaventurae, 1924–.

Alfaric, P. *L'Evolution intellectuelle de S. Augustin.* 2 vols. Paris, 1918.

Altizer, T. J. J., et. al. "Discussion: Responses to Paul Lehmann's 'The Tri-Unity of God.'" *Union Seminary Quarterly Review* 21 (1966), pp. 207–18.

Amphilochius of Iconium. *Sententiae et excerpta.* (Migne: *PG* 39 97–118).

Andresen, C. "Zur Entstehung und Geschichte des trinitarischen Person-begriffes." *Zeitschrift für die Neutestaliche Wissenschaft* 52 (1961), pp. 1–39.

Aristotle. *De Anima.* In *The Basic Works of Aristotle,* ed. R. McKeon. New York, 1941.

————. *Politics.* In *The Basic Works of Aristotle,* ed. R. McKeon. New York, 1941.

Athanasius. *De Decretis.* (Migne: *PG* 25 415–76).

————. *Ep. ad Afr.* (Migne: *PG* 26 1029–48).

————. *Expositio fidei.* (Migne: *PG* 25 199–208).

————. *De Incar.* (Migne: *PG* 25 95–198).

————. *Or. contra Arianos.* (Migne: *PG* 26 239–410).

————. *De Synodis.* (Migne: *PG* 26 681–794).

————. *Tomus ad Antiochenos.* (Migne: *PG* 26 794–810).

Augustine. *Confessions.* (Migne: *PL* 32 33–868).

————. *De nat. boni.* (Migne: *PL* 42 551–72).

————. *De Trinitate.* (Migne: *PL* 42 819–1098).

Bailleux, E. "La réciprocité dans la Trinité." *Revue Thomiste* 74 (1974), pp. 356–90.

Balthasar, H. U. von, and Grillmeier, A. *Le Mystère Pascal, Mysterium Salutis.* Vol. 12. Paris, 1972.

Barth, H. *Philosophie der Erscheinung.* 2 vols. Basel, Stuttgart, 1959.

Barth, K. *The Epistle to the Romans.* Tr. E. C. Hoskyns. London, 1933.

————. *The Humanity of God.* Tr. John N. Thomas. Richmond, Va., 1960.

————. *Die kirchliche Dogmatik.* 12 vols. Zurich, 1932–. Eng. tr., *Church Dogmatics,* ed. G. W. Bromiley and T. F. Torrance. 14 vols. Edinburgh, 1936–69.

————. *Church Dogmatics.* Vol. 1: *The Doctrine of the Word of God.* Part One. Tr. G. T. Thomson. Edinburgh, 1936.

————. *Church Dogmatics.* Vol. 2: *The Doctrine of God.* Part Two. Tr. G. W. Bromiley et al. Edinburgh, 1957.

————. *Church Dogmatics.* Vol. 4: *The Doctrine of Reconciliation.* Part One. Tr. G. W. Bromiley. Edinburgh, 1956.

————. *Die protestantische Theologie.* Zollikon-Zurich, 1960. Partial Eng. tr., *Protestant Thought.* New York, 1969.

Basil. *Ep. 38.* (Migne: *PG* 32 325–42).

_____. *Ep. 189.* (Migne: *PG* 32 683–96).

_____. *Ep. 214.* (Migne: *PG* 32 785–90).

_____. *Haer.* (Migne: *PG* 42 407–10).

Basil, Pseudo-. *Adv. Eunomius IV.* (Migne: *PG* 29 497–774).

Bauckham, R. "Moltmann's Eschatology of the Cross." *Scottish Journal of Theology* 30 (1977), pp. 301–11.

Bethune-Baker, J. F. *An Introduction to the Early History of Christian Doctrine.* London, 1929.

Billot, L. *De Deo Uno et Trino.* 4th ed. Rome, 1902.

Bloch, E. *Das Prinzip Hoffnung.* Vol. 2. Frankfurt, 1959.

Boethius. *De Trinitate.* (Migne: *PL* 64 1247–56).

Bonaventure. *Itinerarium mentis in Deum.* Tr. Ewert Cousins. New York, 1978.

Book of Concord: The Confessions of the Evangelical Lutheran Church. Ed. and tr. by T. G. Tappert et al. Philadelphia, 1959.

Bourassa, F. "L'Esprit Saint, 'Communion' de Père et du Fils." *Science et Esprit* 29 (1977), pp. 251–81.

_____. "Personne et conscience en théologie trinitaire." *Gregorianum* 50 (1974), pp. 471–93, 677–720.

_____. "Sur la propriété de l'Esprit Saint." *Science et Esprit* 28 (1976), pp. 243–64; 29 (1977), pp. 23–43.

Bouyer, L. *Le Père Invisible.* Paris, 1976.

Bracken, J. "The Holy Trinity as a Community of Divine Persons." *Heythrop Journal* 15 (1974), pp. 166–82, 257–70.

Branick, V. *An Ontology of Understanding.* St. Louis, Mo., 1974.

Brown, P. *St. Augustine of Hippo.* Berkeley, Calif., 1967.

Brown, R. E. *Jesus: God and Man.* Milwaukee, 1967.

Browning, D. *Psychotherapy and Atonement.* Philadelphia, 1966.

Brugger, W. "Das Mitsein: Eine Erweiterung der scholastischen Kategorienlehre." *Scholastik* 21 (1956), pp. 371–75.

Bultmann, R. "The Problem of 'Natural Theology'." In *Faith and Understanding,* pp. 313–31. New York, 1969.

Burrell, D. *Aquinas—God and Action.* Notre Dame, Ind., 1979.

_____. *Exercises in Religious Understanding.* Notre Dame, Ind., 1974.

Chavalier, I. *Saint Augustin et la pensée grecque.* Fribourg, Switzerland, 1940.

Clarke, W. N. "A New Look at the Immutability of God." In *God Knowable and Unknowable,* ed. R. J. Roth, pp. 43–72. New York, 1973.

Cobb, J. B., Jr. "Christianity and Myth." *The Journal of Bible and Religion,* now appearing as *The Journal of the American Academy of Religion* 33 (1965), pp. 314–20.

_____. *A Christian Natural Theology.* Philadelphia, 1969.

_____. *Christ in a Pluralistic Age.* Philadelphia, 1975.

_____. "A Whiteheadian Christology." In *Process Philosophy and Christian Thought,* ed. D. Brown, R. E. James, and G. Reeves, pp. 382–98. Indianapolis, 1971.

Coffey, D. "The Gift of the Spirit." *Irish Theological Quarterly* 38 (1971), pp. 202–23.

Cousins, E. "A Theology of Interpersonal Relations." *Thought* 45 (1970), pp. 56–82.

_____. "The Trinity and World Religions." *Journal of Ecumenical Studies* 7 (1970), pp. 476–98.

Craddock, F. *The Pre-Existence of Christ in the New Testament.* Nashville, 1968.

Crawford, R. G. "Is the Doctrine of the Trinity, Scriptural?" *Scottish Journal of Theology* 20 (1967), pp. 282–94.

Cullmann, O. *The Christology of the New Testament.* Tr. S. C. Guthrie and C. A. M. Hall. Philadelphia, 1959.

_____. *The Earliest Christian Confessions.* Tr. J. K. S. Reid. London, 1949.

Cunliffe-Jones, H. "Two Questions concerning the Holy Spirit." *Theology* 75 (1972), pp. 283–98.

Cyprian. *De Orat. dominica.* (Migne: *PL* 4 1125–26).

Daniélou, J. *Gospel and Hellenistic Culture.* Ed. and tr. by J. A. Baker. London and Philadelphia, 1973.

Denzinger, H., and Schönmetzer, A., eds. *Enchiridion Symbolorum Definitiorum et Declarationum de Rebus Fidei et Morum.* 33rd ed. Barcelona, 1965.

Didymus the Blind. *De Trinitate.* (Migne: *PG* 39 269–992).

Dobbin, E. "Towards a Theology of the Holy Spirit." *Heythrop Journal* 17 (1976), pp. 5–19, 129–49.

Donnelly, J. "The Inhabitation of the Holy Spirit." *Proceedings of the Catholic Theological Society of America* 4 (1949), pp. 39–77.

Dulles, A. *Models of the Church.* Garden City, New York, 1974.

_____. Review of *Blessed Rage for Order. Theological Studies* 37 (1976), pp. 304–16.

Dunn, J. D. G. "I Corinthians 15:45—Last Adam, Life-giving Spirit." In *Christ and the Spirit in the New Testament,* ed. B. Lindars and B. Smalley, pp. 127–41. Cambridge, 1973.

Dupuis, J. *Jesus Christ and His Spirit.* Bangalore, 1977.

Edwards, D. M. *Christianity and Philosophy.* Edinburgh, 1932.

Eusebius. *Hist. eccl.* (Migne: *PG* 30 45–906).

Evans, E. *Tertullian's Treatise against Praxeas.* London, 1948.

Fabro, C. *God in Exile.* Ed. and tr. by Arthur Gibson. Westminster, Md., 1968.

Fackenheim, E. *The Religious Dimension in Hegel's Thought.* Bloomington, Ind., 1967.

Faricy, R. "The Trinitarian Indwelling." *The Thomist* 35 (1971), pp. 369–404.

Fichte, I. H. *Ueber die Christliche und Antichristliche Spekulation der Gegenwart.* Bonn, 1842.

Flannery, A., ed. *The Documents of Vatican II.* Grand Rapids, Mich., 1975.

Ford, J.M. "Holy Spirit in the New Testament." *Commonweal* 89 (1968), pp. 173–79.

Ford, L. "Process Trinitarianism." *Journal of the American Academy of Religion* 43 (1975), pp. 199–213.

Franks, R. S. *The Doctrine of the Trinity.* London, 1953.

Fuller, R. *The Foundations of New Testament Christology.* New York, 1965.

_____. "On Demythologizing the Trinity." *Anglican Theological Review* 43 (1961), pp. 121–31.

Gadamer, H.-G. *Truth and Method.* Translation ed. by G. Barden and J. Cumming. New York, 1975.

Galot, J. "Valeur de la notion de personne dans l'expression de mystère du Christ." *Gregorianum* 55 (1974), pp. 69–97.

Garrigou-Lagrange, R. *De Deo Trino et Creatore.* Rome, 1951.

Gilkey, L. *Naming the Whirlwind: The Renewal of God Language.* Indianapolis, 1969.

_____. *Reaping the Whirlwind.* New York, 1976.

Gilson, E. "L'être et Dieu." *Revue Thomiste* 62 (1962), pp. 398–416.

Gregg, R. C., and Groh, D. E., eds. *Early Arianism: A View of Salvation.* Philadelphia, 1981.

Gregory of Nazianzus. *Oratio.* (Migne: *PG* 36 133–72).

Gregory of Nyssa. *Orat. catechetica magna.* (Migne: *PG* 45 9–116).

_____. *Quod non sint tres Dei.* (Migne: *PG* 45 115–36).

Griffin, D. "Holy Spirit: Compassion and Reverence for Being." In *Religious Experience and Process Theology,* ed. H. J. Cargas and B. Lee, pp. 107–20. New York, 1976.

_____. "Schubert Ogden's Christology and the Possibilities of Process Philosophy." In *Process Philosophy and Christian Thought,* ed. D. Brown, R. E. James, and G. Reeves, pp. 347–61. Indianapolis, 1971.

Hamilton, K. *The System and the Gospel: A Critique of Paul Tillich.* London, 1963.

Hamilton, P. "Some Proposals for a Modern Christology." In *Christ for Us Today,* ed. N. Pittenger, pp. 154–75. London, 1968.

Hartshorne, C. *The Divine Relativity: A Social Conception of God.* New Haven, 1948.

_____. *The Logic of Perfection and Other Essays in Neo-classical Metaphysics.* La Salle, Ill., 1962.

_____. *A Natural Theology for Our Time.* La Salle, Ill., 1967.

_____. "The Philosophy of Creative Synthesis." *Journal of Philosophy* 55 (1958), pp. 944–53.

_____. *Reality as Social Process: Studies in Metaphysics and Religion.* Glencoe and Boston, 1953.

_____. "Redefining God." *The New Humanist* 7 (1934), pp. 8–15.

Hasker, W. "Tri-Unity." *Journal of Religion* 50 (1970), pp. 1–32.

Hebblethwaite, B. "Perichoresis—Reflections on the Doctrine of the Trinity." *Theology* 80 (1977), pp. 255–61.

Hegel, G. W. F. *Enzyklopädie der philosophischen Wissenschaften.* Ed. J. Hoffmeister. Vol. 5. Leipzig, 1949.

_____. *Hegel's Science of Logic.* Tr. A. V. Miller. New York, 1969.

_____. *Lectures on the Philosophy of Religion.* 3 vols. Tr. E. B. Speirs and J. B. Sanderson. New York, 1962.

_____. *The Phenomenology of Mind.* Tr. J. B. Baillie. Rev. ed. New York, 1931.

————. *Über die Differenz Fichteschen und Schellingschen Systems der Philosophie.* Jena, 1801.

Hibbert, G. "Mystery and Metaphysics in the Trinitarian Theology of St. Thomas." *Irish Theological Quarterly* 31 (1964), pp. 187–213.

Hick, J., ed. *The Myth of God Incarnate.* London, 1977.

Hildebrand, D. von. *Die Metaphysik der Gemeinschaft.* Regensburg, 1954.

Hill, E. "Our Knowledge of the Trinity." *Scottish Journal of Theology* 27 (1974), pp. 1–11.

————. "Karl Rahner's Remarks on the Dogmatic Treatise *De Trinitate* and St. Augustine." *Augustinian Studies* 2 (1971), pp. 67–80.

Hill, W. J. "Does God Know the Future?" *Theological Studies* 36 (1975), pp. 3–18.

————. "Does the World Make a Difference to God?" *The Thomist* 38 (1974), pp. 146–64.

————. "The Eucharist as Eschatological Presence." *Communio* 4 (1977), pp. 305–20.

————. *Knowing the Unknown God.* New York, 1971.

————. "Uncreated Grace: A Critique of Karl Rahner." *The Thomist* 26 (1963), pp. 333–56.

Hodgson, L. *The Doctrine of the Trinity.* New York, 1944.

The Holy Office. *Lamentabile.* Denzinger-Schönmetzer, 3401–66.

Hoye, W. J. *Actualitas Omnium Actuum.* Verlag Anton Hain, 1975.

Hunsinger, G. "The Crucified God and the Political Theology of Violence." *Heythrop Journal* 14 (1973), pp. 266–79, 379–95.

Ignatius of Antioch. *Magn.* (Migne: *PG* 5 661–74).

————. *Trall.* (Migne: *PG* 5 673–86).

————. *Smyrn.* (Migne: *PG* 5 707–18).

Irenaeus. *Adversus haereses.* (Migne: *PG* 7 437–1224).

Jenson, R. *God after God.* Indianapolis and New York, 1969.

————. "Three Identities of One Action." *Scottish Journal of Theology* 28 (1975), pp. 1–15.

John Damascene. *Expositio fidei.* (Migne: *PG* 94 417–36).

Johnston, W. "Zen and Christian Mysticism." *International Philosophical Quarterly* 7 (1976), pp. 441–69.

Justinian. *Liber adv. Origenem.* (Migne: *PG* 86 945–94).

Justin Martyr. *Dialog.* (Migne: *PG* 6 471–800).

Kadowaki, K. "Ways of Knowing: A Buddhist-Thomist Dialogue." *International Philosophical Quarterly* 6 (1966), pp. 574–95.

Kaiser, C. "The Ontological Trinity in the Context of Historical Religions." *Scottish Journal of Theology* 29 (1976), pp. 301–10.

Kasper, W. *Jesus the Christ.* Tr. V. Green. New York, 1976.

Kaufman, G. *God the Problem.* Cambridge, Mass., 1972.

————. *Systematic Theology: A Historicist Perspective.* New York, 1968.

Keefe, D. *Thomism and the Ontological Theology of Paul Tillich.* Leiden, 1971.

Kelly, A. "The Gifts of the Spirit: Aquinas and the Modern Context." *The Thomist* 38 (1974), pp. 193–231.

————. "To Know the Mystery: The Theologian in the Presence of the Revealed God." *The Thomist* 32 (1968), pp. 1–66, 171–200.

————. "Trinity and Process: Relevance of the Basic Christian Confession of God." *Theological Studies* 31 (1970), pp. 393–414.

Kelly, J. N. D. *Early Christian Creeds*. London, 1950.

————. *Early Christian Doctrines*. 5th ed. London, 1977.

Knox, J. *The Humanity and Divinity of Christ*. Cambridge, 1967.

Knudson, A. *The Doctrine of God*. Nashville, Tenn., 1930.

Küng, H. *Menschwerdung Gottes*. Freiburg-im-Br., 1970. Fr. tr., *Incarnation de Dieu*, tr. Elisabeth Galichet and Catherine Haas-Smets. Paris, 1973.

————. *On Being a Christian*. Tr. E. Quinn. Garden City, New York, 1976.

Lampe, G. W. H. *God as Spirit*. Oxford, 1977.

Le Guillou, M.-J. *Le Mystère du Père*. Paris, 1973.

Lehmann, P. "The Tri-Unity of God." *Union Seminary Quarterly Review* 21 (1965), pp. 35–39.

Lloyd, A. C. "On Augustine's Concept of a Person." In *Augustine: A Collection of Critical Essays*, ed. R. A. Markus, pp. 191–205. Garden City, New York, 1972.

Lonergan, B. *De Deo Trino*. 2 vols. Rome, 1964.

————. *De Deo Trino*. Eng. tr., *The Way to Nicea*. Part I. Tr. C. O'Donovan. Philadelphia, 1976.

————. *Insight*. Rev. ed. London and New York, 1958.

————. *Method in Theology*. New York, 1972.

Lowry, C. *The Trinity and Christian Devotion*. New York, 1946.

McCool, G., ed. *A Rahner Reader*. New York, 1975.

McNicholl, A. "Heidegger: Problem and Pre-Grasp." *Irish Theological Quarterly* 44 (1977), pp. 208–31.

————. "On Judging." *The Thomist* 38 (1974), pp. 768–825.

————. "On Judging Existence." *The Thomist* 43 (1979), pp. 507–80.

Macquarrie, J. *Principles of Christian Theology*. New York, 1966.

Maréchal, J. *Le point de départ de la Métaphysique*. Vol. 5: *Le Thomisme devant la Philosophie critique*. Brussels and Paris, 1949.

Markus, R. A. "Trinitarian Theology and the Economy." *Journal of Theological Studies* 9 (1958), pp. 89–102.

Masson, J. "Le Chrétien devant le Yoga et le Zen." *Nouvelle Revue Théologique* 94 (1972), pp. 384–99.

Meland, B. *The Realities of Faith*. New York, 1962.

Metz, J. B. *Christliche Anthropozentrik*. Munich, 1962.

Migne, J. *Patrologiae cursus completus. Series Graeca*. Paris, 1857–.

————. *Patrologiae cursus completus. Series Latina*. Paris, 1844–.

Moltmann, J. *The Church in the Power of the Spirit*. Tr. M. Kohl. New York, 1977.

————. *The Crucified God*. Tr. R. A. Wilson and J. Bowden. New York, 1974.

————. "The 'Crucified God': A Trinitarian Theology of the Cross." *Interpretation* 26 (1972), pp. 278–99.

————. "The Future as a New Paradigm of Transcendence." *Concurrence* 1 (1969), pp. 334–45.

———. *Theology of Hope.* Tr. J. W. Leitch. New York, 1967.

———. "The Trinitarian History of God." *Theology* 78 (1975), pp. 632–46.

———. *The Trinity and the Kingdom.* Tr. Margaret Kohl. San Francisco, 1981.

Montague, G. *The Holy Spirit: Growth of a Biblical Tradition.* New York, 1976.

Moule, C. F. D. *The Origin of Christology.* Cambridge, 1977.

Mühlen, H. *Der heilige Geist als Person.* 2nd ed. Münster, 1966.

———. *Sein und Person nach Johannes Duns Scotus: Beiträg zur Grundlegung einer Metaphysik der Person.* Werl, Westfalen, 1954.

———. *Una Mystica Persona: Eine Person in vielen Personen.* Paderborn, 1964.

Fr. tr., *L'Esprit dans L'Église,* tr. A. Liefooghe, M. Massart, and R. Virrion. 2 vols. Paris, 1969.

———. *Die Veränderlichkeit Gottes als Horizont einer zukünftigen Christologie.* Münster, 1969.

Murray, J. C. *The Problem of God.* New Haven, 1946.

Novatian. *De Trinitate.* (Migne: *PL* 3 885–952). Eng. tr. Herbert Moore. New York, 1919.

Ogden, S. "Bultmann's Project of Demythologization and the Problem of Theology and Philosophy." *Journal of Religion* 37 (1957), pp. 156–73.

———. *The Reality of God.* New York, 1963.

———. "Beyond Supernaturalism." *Religion in Life* 33 (1963–64), pp. 7–18.

Ogletree, T. "A Christological Assessment of Dipolar Theism." In *Process Philosophy and Christian Thought,* ed. D. Brown, R. E. James, and G. Reeves, pp. 331–46. Indianapolis, 1971.

O'Leary, J. S. "The Hermeneutics of Dogmatism." *Irish Theological Quarterly* 47 (1980), pp. 96–118.

O'Meara, J. J., ed. *An Augustine Reader.* Garden City, New York, 1973.

———. *The Young Augustine.* New York, 1954.

Origen. *Contra Celsum.* (Migne: *PG* 11 641–1632).

———. *Comm. in Joann.* (Migne: *PG* 14 21–830).

———. *De Principiis.* (Migne: *PG* 11 115–414).

O'Shea, K. "The Human Activity of the Word." *The Thomist* 22 (1959), pp. 143–232.

Ott, H. *God.* Atlanta, 1974.

Page, J.-G. "L'Appropriation, Jeu de l'Esprit ou Réalisme?" *Laval Theologique Philosophique* 33 (1977), pp. 227–39.

Panikkar, R. *The Trinity and the Religious Experience of Man.* New York, 1973.

Pannenberg, W. *Basic Questions in Theology.* Vol. 2. Tr. George H. Kehm. Philadelphia, 1971.

———. "The Appropriation of the Philosophical Concept of God as a Dogmatic Problem of Early Christian Theology." In *Basic Questions in Theology,* vol. 2, pp. 119–83. Philadelphia, 1971.

———. "The God of Hope." In *Basic Questions in Theology,* vol. 2, pp. 234–49. Philadelphia, 1971.

———. "The Question of God." In *Basic Questions in Theology,* vol. 2, pp. 201–33. Philadelphia, 1971.

———. "Types of Atheism and Their Theological Significance." In *Basic Questions in Theology,* vol. 2, pp. 184–200. Philadelphia, 1971.

_____. "The Doctrine of the Spirit and the Task of a Theology of Nature." *Theology* 75 (1972), pp. 8–21.

_____. "Der Gott der Geschichte: Der Trinitärische Gott und die Wahrheit der Geschichte." *Kerygma und Dogma* 23 (1977), pp. 76–92.

_____. *Jesus: God and Man.* Tr. L. L. Wilkins and D. A. Priebe. Philadelphia, 1968.

_____. "Significance of Christianity in the Philosophy of Hegel." In *The Idea of God and Human Freedom,* tr. R. A. Wilson, pp. 144–77. Philadelphia, 1973.

_____. "Die Subjektivität Gottes und die Trinitätslehre." *Kerygma und Dogma* 23 (1977), pp. 25–40.

_____. *Theology and the Kingdom of God.* Ed. Richard J. Neuhaus. Philadelphia, 1969.

_____. "Appearance as the Arrival of the Future." In *Theology and the Kingdom of God,* pp. 127–43. Philadelphia, 1969.

_____. "Theology and the Kingdom of God." In *Theology and the Kingdom of God,* pp. 51–71. Philadelphia, 1969.

_____. *What Is Man?* Tr. D. A. Priebe. Philadelphia, 1970.

_____. "The Working of the Spirit in the People of God." In *Spirit, Faith, and Church,* ed. W. Pannenberg, A. Dulles, and C. Braaten, pp. 13–31. Philadelphia, 1970.

Pardington, S. P., III. "The Holy Ghost Is Dead—the Holy Spirit Lives." In *Religious Experience and Process Theology,* ed. H. J. Cargas and B. Lee, pp. 121–32. New York, 1976.

Pasquariello, R. "Pannenberg's Philosophical Foundations." *Journal of Religion* 56 (1976), pp. 338–47.

Patfoort, A. "Un projet de 'traite moderne' de la Trinité: Vers une réévaluation de la 'notion' de personne?" *Angelicum* 48 (1971), pp. 93–118.

Pelikan, J. *The Christian Tradition.* Vol. 1: *The Emergence of the Catholic Tradition.* Chicago, 1971.

Pittenger, N. "Trinity and Process." *Theological Studies* 32 (1971), pp. 290–96.

_____. *The Incarnate Lord.* New York, 1959.

Pius X. *Pascendi dominici gregis.* Denzinger-Schönmetzer, 3475–500.

Prestige, G. L. *God in Patristic Thought.* London, 1952.

Rahner, K. *Foundations of Christian Faith.* Tr. W. V. Dych. New York, 1978.

_____. *Geist in Welt.* 2nd ed. by J. B. Metz. Munich, 1957. Eng. tr., *Spirit in the World.* New York, 1968.

_____. *Hörer des Wortes.* Rev. ed. of J. B. Metz. Munich, 1963. Eng. tr., *Hearers of the Word.* New York, 1969.

_____. *Mysterium Salutis: Grundriss Heilsgeschichtlicher Dogmatik.* Ed. Johannes Feiner and Magnus Löhrer. Einsiedeln, 1967. Vol. 2, chapter 5: "Der dreifaltige Gott als transzendenter Urgrund der Heilsgeschichte." Eng. tr., *The Trinity.* New York, 1970.

_____. *Schriften zur Theologie.* Einsiedeln-Zurich-Cologne, 1954. Eng. tr., *Theological Investigations.* 20 vols. to date. Baltimore, 1961–69; New York, 1971–81.

———. "Christology within an Evolutionary View of the World." In *Theological Investigations.* Vol. 5, pp. 157–92. Baltimore, 1966.

———. "The Concept of Mystery in Catholic Theology." In *Theological Investigations.* Vol. 4, pp. 36–73. Baltimore, 1966.

———. "Current Problems in Christology." In *Theological Investigations.* Vol. 1, pp. 149–200. Baltimore, 1965.

———. "Nature and Grace." In *Theological Investigations.* Vol. 4, pp. 165–88. Baltimore, 1966.

———. "On the Theology of the Incarnation." In *Theological Investigations.* Vol. 4, pp. 105–20. Baltimore, 1966.

———. "Science as a 'Confession'." In *Theological Investigations.* Vol. 3, pp. 385–400. Baltimore, 1967.

———. "Some Implications of the Scholastic Concept of Uncreated Grace." In *Theological Investigations.* Vol. 1, pp. 319–46. Baltimore, 1965.

———. "Theology and Anthropology." In *Theological Investigations.* Vol. 9, pp. 28–45. New York, 1972.

———. "Theology of the Symbol." In *Theological Investigations.* Vol. 4, pp. 221–52. Baltimore, 1966.

———. "Theos in the New Testament." In *Theological Investigations.* Vol. 1, pp. 79–148. Baltimore, 1965.

———, ed. *Encyclopedia of Theology: The Concise Sacramentum Mundi,* p. 1770. New York, 1975.

Randall, J. H., Jr. *Hellenistic Ways of Deliverance and the Making of the Christian Synthesis.* New York, 1970.

Ray, W. E., ed. *The Philosophical Approach to God.* Winston-Salem, N. C., 1979.

Reeves, G., and Brown, D. "The Development of Process Theology." In *Process Philosophy and Christian Thought,* ed. D. Brown, R. E. James, and G. Reeves, pp. 21–64. Indianapolis, 1971.

Reichmann, J. "Transcendental Method and the Psychogenesis of Being." *The Thomist* 32 (1968), pp. 449–508.

Richard of St. Victor. *De Trinitate.* (Migne: *PL* 196 887–992). Critical text edited by Jean Ribailler. Paris, 1958.

Richardson, C. *The Doctrine of the Trinity.* Nashville, Tenn., 1958

Richardson, W. J. *Heidegger: Through Phenomenology to Thought.* The Hague, 1963.

Ricoeur, P. "The Hermeneutics of Symbols and Philosophical Reflection," tr. D. Savage. *International Philosophical Quarterly* 2 (1962), pp. 191–218.

Robinson, J. *A New Quest of the Historical Jesus.* London, 1959.

Roy, O. J.-B. du. "Augustine, St." *New Catholic Encyclopedia.* Vol. 1, pp. 1041–58. Washington, D.C., 1967.

———. *L'Intelligence de la foi en la Trinité selon saint Augustin.* Paris, 1966.

Scheler, M. *Der Formalismus in der Ethik und die materiale Wertethik.* 4th ed. Bern, 1954.

Schillebeeckx, E. *Mary, Mother of the Redemption.* Tr. N. D. Smith. New York, 1964.

Schleiermacher, F. *Der christliche Glaube.* 2 vols. Berlin, 1821–22. Eng. tr., *The Christian Faith,* ed. H. R. Mackintosh and J. S. Stewart. Edinburgh, 1928. Harper Torchbook edition. 2 vols. New York, 1963.

———. *On Religion: Speeches to Its Cultured Despisers.* Tr. J. Oman. New York, 1955.

———. *Sämtliche Werke.* 31 vols. 3 parts. Berlin, 1835–64.

———. *Dialektik.* Ed. Ludwig Jones. *Sämtliche Werke,* III/5.

———. "Ueber den Gegensatz zwischen der Sabellianischen und der Athanasianischen Vorstellung von der Trinität." *Sämtliche Werke,* I/2. Eng. tr., "On the Discrepancy between the Sabellian and Athanasian Method of Representing the Doctrine of the Trinity," tr. Moses Stuart. *The Biblical Repository and Quarterly Observer* 5 (1835), pp. 265–353; 6 (1835), pp. 1–116.

Schmaus, M. *Der liber propugnatorius des Thomae Angelicus und die Lehrunterschiede zwischen Thomas von Aquin und Duns Scotus.* Vol. 2: *Die Trinitärischen Lehrunterschiede.* Aschendorff, 1930.

Schmitz, K. "Weiss and Creation." *Review of Metaphysics* 18 (1964), pp. 147–69.

Schoonenberg, P. *The Christ.* Tr. D. Couling. New York, 1971.

———. "Continuïteit en herinterpretatie in de Drieëeheidsleer." *Tijdschrift voor Theologie* 14 (1974), pp. 54–72.

———. "Trinität—der vollendete Bund: Thesen zur Lehre vom dreipersonlichen Gott." *Orientierung* 37 (1973), pp. 115–17. Eng. tr., "Trinity—the Consummated Covenant: Theses on the Doctrine of the Trinitarian God," tr. Robert C. Ware. *Sciences Religieuses/Studies in Religion* 5 (1975–76), pp. 111–16.

Schulz, W. *Der Gott der neuzeitlichen Metaphysik.* 3rd ed. Pfullingen, 1957.

Schweizer, E. *Jesus.* Tr. D. E. Green. Atlanta, 1971.

———. "The Spirit of Power." *Interpretation* 6 (1952), pp. 259–78.

Shea, W. Review of *Blessed Rage for Order. The Thomist* 40 (1976), pp. 665–83.

Smith, J. E. *The Analogy of Experience.* New York, 1973.

Stead, G. C. "Divine Substance in Tertullian." *Journal of Theological Studies* 14 (1963), pp. 46–66.

Stokes, W. "Freedom as Perfection: Whitehead, Thomas and Augustine." *Proceedings of the American Catholic Philosophical Association* 36 (1962), pp. 134–42.

———. "God for Today and Tomorrow." In *Process Philosophy and Christian Thought,* ed. D. Brown, R. E. James, and G. Reeves, pp. 244–63. Indianapolis, 1971.

———. "Is God Really Related to the World?" *Proceedings of the American Catholic Philosophical Association* 39 (1965), pp. 145–50.

———. "A Whiteheadian Reflection on God's Relation to the World." In *Process Theology,* ed. Ewert H. Cousins, pp. 137–52. New York, 1971.

Strauss, D. F. *Die Christliche Glaubenslehre in ihre geschichtlicher Erscheinung und im Kampfe mit der modernen Wissenschaft.* Vol. 1. Tübingen-Stuttgart, 1840–41.

Strawson, P. F. *Individuals*. London, 1959.

Suarez, F. *De Trinitate. Opera Omnia*, ed. D. M. André. Paris, 1856–78. Vol. 1.

Taille, M. de la. "Actuation créée par Acte Incréée." *Recherches de Science Religieuse* 18 (1928), pp. 253–68.

Tallon, A. "Personal Becoming." *The Thomist* 43 (1979), pp. 1–177.

———. "Spirit, Freedom, History." *The Thomist* 38 (1974), pp. 908–36.

Tertullian. *Adv. Praxeam*. (Migne: *PL* 2 153–96).

———. *Adv. Val.* (Migne: *PL* 2 523–96).

TeSelle, E. *Augustine the Theologian*. New York, 1970.

Theilor, W. *Porphyrios und Augustin: Schriften des Königberger gelehrten Gesellschaft, geisteswissenschaftliche Klasse.* X, 1. Halle, 1933.

Theophilus of Antioch. *Ad Autolycum*. (Migne: *PG* 6 1023–168).

Thomas Aquinas. *Sancti Thomae de Aquino opera omnia*. Leonine edition. Rome, 1882–.

———. *Compendium Theologiae*. Leonine ed. T. 42, pp. 75–205.

———. *Summa contra gentiles*. Ed. Leonina manualis. Rome, 1934.

———. *In Ep. ad Romanos*. Vivès ed. Paris, 1871–72. Vol. 20, pp. 377–602.

———. *Expositio super librum De causis*. Vivès ed. Vol. 26, pp. 514–70.

———. *In I Perihermeneias*. Ed. R. Spiazzi. Turin, 1955.

———. *Quaestiones disputatae*. Vol. 1: *De veritate*. Ed. R. Spiazzi. Turin-Rome, 1954.

———. *Scriptum super libros sententiarum*. Ed. P. Mandonnet and M. Moos. 4 vols. Paris, 1929–47.

———. *Summa theologiae*. 60 vols. plus index. Blackfriars edition. London and New York, 1964–76.

———. *Saint Thomas Aquinas Summa Theologiae*. Vol. 24: *The Gifts of the Spirit*. Ed. E. O'Connor. London and New York, 1973.

———. *Saint Thomas Aquinas Summa Theologiae*. Vol. 6: *The Trinity*. Ed. C. Velecky. London, 1965.

Thornton, L. S. *The Incarnate Lord*. London, 1928.

Tillich, P. *Systematic Theology*. 3 vols. Chicago, 1951–63.

Tracy, D. *Blessed Rage for Order*. New York, 1975.

Vander Marck, W. "Faith: What It Is Depends on What It Relates To." *Recherches de Théologie ancienne et médiévale* 43 (January–December, 1976), pp. 123–66.

Vanier, P. *Théologie trinitaire chez Saint Thomas d'Aquin*. Montreal and Paris, 1953.

Wainwright, A. W. *The Trinity in the New Testament*. London, 1926.

Wassmer, T. "The Trinitarian Theology of Augustine and His Debt to Plotinus." *Scottish Journal of Theology* 14 (1961), pp. 248–55.

Webb, C. C. J. *God and Personality*. London, 1918.

Welch, C. *In This Name: The Doctrine of the Trinity in Contemporary Theology*. New York, 1952.

———. "Theology as Risk." In *Frontline Theology*, ed. D. Peerman, pp. 117–25. Richmond, Va., 1967.

Whitehead, A. N. *Process and Reality.* Harper Torchbook edition. New York, 1929.

———. *Religion in the Making.* New York, 1926.

Wiles, M. "Some Reflections on the Origins of the Doctrine of the Trinity." *Journal of Theological Studies* 8 (1957), pp. 92–106.

Wiles, M., and Santer, M., eds. *Documents in Early Christian Thought.* Cambridge, 1975.

Wilhelmsen, D. "The Priority of Judgment over Question: Reflections on Transcendental Thomism." *International Philosophical Quarterly* 14 (1974), pp. 475–93.

Williams, C. *Faith in a Secular Age.* New York, 1966.

Williams, D. D. "How Does God Act?" In *Process and Divinity,* ed. W. L. Reese and E. Freeman, pp. 161–80. La Salle, Ill., 1964.

———. *The Spirit and Forms of Love.* New York, 1968.

INDEX OF NAMES

Newman, John Henry, 41, 250
Niebuhr, Reinhold, 129
Novatian, 37, 40

O'Connor, Edward D., 305n.
Ogden, Schubert, 186, 190, 196–99, 200, 215
Ogletree, Thomas W., 193
O'Leary, J.S., 50n.
O'Meara, John J., 53n., 57n.
Origen, xii, 37–41, 42, 43, 45, 46, 47, 142, 279
O'Shea, Kevin F., 288n.
Ossius, 42
Ott, Heinrich, 122

Pamphilus, 41
Panikkar, Raimundo, 308–13
Pannenberg, Wolfhart, 68, 149, 152, 155–66, 167, 168, 169, 178, 179, 182, 184, 195, 231, 234, 243, 246, 261n., 263n., 268, 285, 298, 299, 300, 302, 307
Pardington, S. Palmer, III, 193, 196n.
Parmenides, 95
Pascal, Blaise, 243
Pasquariello, Ronald D., 158
Paul (St.), 6, 11, 12, 13, 14, 15, 16, 17, 18, 19, 25, 26, 28, 29, 30, 42, 50, 103, 194, 202, 252, 275, 297, 298, 300, 302, 303, 312
Paul of Samosata, 42, 45
Peter (St.), 27
Peter Lombard, 62, 226, 303
Petter, Dominic de, 250
Philo, 11, 32
Photius, 78n.
Pittenger, Norman, 185, 197
Pius X, 130n.
Plato, 55n., 99, 136, 158
Plotinus, 38, 53n.
Polanyi, Michael, 249
Porphyry, 53n.
Praxeas, 34
Prestige, G.L., 36

Rahner, Karl, xi, 55, 56, 61, 62n., 73, 116, 130–45, 146, 147, 149, 172, 179, 180, 214, 215, 219, 220, 222, 223, 224, 234, 247, 249, 250, 254, 255, 258n., 269, 275n., 287, 289, 292, 293, 294, 302
Randall, John Herman, Jr., 55n.
Reeves, Gene, 195n.
Reichmann, James B., 137
Richard of St. Victor, 73n., 78, 79, 225–32, 233, 236
Richardson, Cyril, 3n., 18, 19, 20n., 101–5, 203
Richardson, William J., 274
Ricoeur, Paul, 22

INDEX OF TOPICS

Doctrine of God (A.C. Knudson), 91
Doctrine of the second rank, the Trinity as, 88, 106, 109, 179
Doctrine of the Trinity (C. Richardson), 101
Doctrine of the Word of God (K. Barth), 119
Dogma, dogmatic, xiv, 115n., 123, 226, 229, 250; development, 252
Dogmatism, 108
Doxology, doxological, 162, 253
Dualism, 310
Dyad, dyadic, 186, 188, 189, 192, 203

Eastern religions, 243, 310–13
Ecclesiology, 185
Economic Trinity, Economic Trinitarianism, 17, 30–34, 37, 78, 116, 119, 121, 127, 140, 141, 145, 172, 179, 181, 183, 215, 219, 252, 282; Neo-, 149, 150, 175, 176, 178, 179, 184
Economy of salvation (*oikonomia*), 16, 17, 19, 20, 28, 34, 36, 37, 49, 55, 69, 119, 120, 140, 149, 150, 181, 184, 214, 220, 273, 279, 286
Egolessness, 311
Election, 76, 111, 115
Emanation(s), 38, 39, 55, 75, 77, 230, 263–65, 273, 294; of being and knowing and loving, 262
Emanationism, Greek, 227, 230, 236, 279; Neo-Platonic, 270
Empirical, 63
Empiricism, 244, 246, 247; Anglo-Saxon, 185; of Aquinas, 133
Encyclopedia (G. Hegel), 151
Energeia, 146, 147
Enhypostasis, 120, 129, 181, 293
Enlightenment (*Aufklärung*), xii, 84, 85, 108, 112, 155, 245
Entitative sense of Jesus' sonship, 9
Ephesians (Letter to), 309
Epistemological, epistemology, 59, 120, 121, 131, 168, 176, 249, 284
Equality, 16, 17, 27, 28, 144, 313
Eros, 196
Eschatological (-ly), eschatology, 13, 18, 85, 128, 167–69, 173, 174; futurist, 182, 185; prophet, 297
Eschatological kingdom, 160
Eschaton, 103
Esse, 134, 136; *commune/divinum*, 137
Esse in alio uno, 221
Esse in alio pluribus, 221
Esse in/esse ad, 71, 72n.
Essence (*essentia*), 27, 118–20, 122, 130, 135, 137, 145, 151, 156, 158, 159, 161, 165n.; in God, 213, 214
Essence/existence, 92, 95–99, 124n., 213, 248, 259, 264
Eternal, eternity, 8, 14, 20, 36, 75, 76, 84, 104, 120, 121, 126, 127, 138, 149, 150, 160, 168, 172, 286; divine, 157, 159, 254; generation, 39, 73; ideas, 92n.; life, 175, 216; modes, 147; origin, 49
Eternal objects, 187, 206
Ethical, ethics, 85
Eucharist, 30, 138, 174, 185
Evangelical(s), 83, 113

352   INDEX OF TOPICS

Subsistent centers of operation, 235
Subsistent relationality, subsistent relations, 235, 236, 266, 268, 271, 277
Substance(s), *substantia (-ae)*, 27, 35, 36, 41, 55–57, 60, 69, 71, 113, 114, 117,
    118, 146, 150, 176, 186, 208, 210, 216, 220, 221, 235, 252, 288
Suffering(s), 170–75, 197
Summa contra gentiles (Aquinas), 62, 66
Summa theologiae (Aquinas), 62, 67–69, 77, 111, 209, 282, 296
Superjective nature, 207
Symbol(s), symbolic, symbolism, xi–xiii, 3, 6, 8, 9, 12, 14, 17, 19, 21–23, 25,
    26, 50, 51, 70, 83, 86, 88–92, 95, 97, 98, 100–107, 109, 115, 137, 139, 147,
    149, 150, 153, 154, 163, 174, 176, 178, 181, 193, 196, 197, 203, 205, 206,
    242, 243, 245, 246, 251, 252, 265, 275, 278, 283, 289, 297, 298, 302, 304,
    307, 308, 311; confessional, 182; linguistic, 216; neoclassical, 185; of per-
    son, 283, 296; polyvalent, 314
Symbolic Trinitarianism, 149, 178, 181
Symbolization, symbolizing, 3, 89, 108, 137, 139, 177, 189, 204, 206, 251, 277,
    284, 299, 309
Synoptic(s), 29, 30, 300
Systematic Theology (P. Tillich), 97, 99

Targumim, 23
Teleological (-ly), teleology, 108, 159, 175, 177
Temporal, temporality, 8, 9, 37, 76, 104, 114, 127, 131, 157, 160, 162, 168,
    182, 190, 206, 207, 210, 254, 279, 299; unsurpassability, 124, 126
Terms in knowing and loving, Divine persons as, 295
Testament of Judah (Qumran), 21
Texts, Christian, 67, 84
Theandric, 310
Theism, Whitehead's, 191, 192
Theistic religions, 313
Thematization, thematize (-ed), 134, 137
Theologoumenon, 115
Theology: as philosophic/as revealed, 132n.; as subalternated science, 253;
    notional/mystical, 253; revisional, 247; scholastic, 220; systematic, 247, 250
Theology of Hope (J. Moltmann), 166, 167
Theōpoiēsis, 44, 313
Theos (ho Theos), 15, 20, 143, 252, 269
Theos-anthropos, 101
Thomism, 131
Timaeus (Plato), 11
Time, 37, 39, 44, 86, 89, 121, 126, 140, 150, 153, 157, 159, 160, 167, 168,
    178, 200, 312
Timeless (-ness), 9, 13, 126, 127, 149, 150, 158–60, 204, 206
Tobit (Book of), 4
Tradition(s) (-al), xii, xiii, 12, 22, 32, 54, 61, 66, 67, 69, 89, 98, 132, 142, 159,
    160, 165, 231, 241, 245, 251–53, 266n., 269; Apostolic, 67; Catholic and
    Christian, 208, 209, 284, 287, 313; Eastern and Western, 78, 236; living,
    242; of Israel and Islam, 313; Reformational, 313; transmission of, 157
Transcendence, 5, 20, 31, 34, 63, 64n., 65, 103, 109, 120, 136, 140, 141, 150,
    167, 168, 174, 181n., 191, 208, 210, 235, 248, 313; as absolute, 201; as